THE ETHICS AND ECONOMICS OF THE BASIC INCOME GUARANTEE

Alternative Voices in Contemporary Economics

Series Editor:
Professor Steven Pressman, Monmouth University, USA

The *Alternative Voices in Contemporary Economics* series provides an important platform for new and innovative approaches to economic analysis within the following traditions: Post-Keynesian, Feminist, Institutional, Marxian, Sraffian, Radical, Austrian, and Behavioural. This series offers researchers working in these heterodox traditions the opportunity to address methodological, theoretical or empirical issues. The series editor works closely with authors and editors to ensure the quality of all published works.

Other titles in the series

The Economics of Prevailing Wage Laws
Edited by Hamid Azari-Rad, Peter Philips and Mark J. Prus
ISBN 0 7546 3255 5

Understanding the Entrepreneur
An Institutionalist Perspective
Christos Kalantaridis
ISBN 0 7546 3344 6

Money, Credit and the Role of the State
Essays in Honour of Augusto Graziani
Edited by Richard Arena and Neri Salvadori
ISBN 0 7546 4000 0

Alternative Economic Models of Transition
John Marangos
ISBN 0 7546 3657 7

Welfare, Inequality, and Resource Depletion
A Reassessment of Brazilian Economic Growth
Mariano Torras
ISBN 0 7546 3153 2

The Ethics and Economics of the Basic Income Guarantee

Edited by

KARL WIDERQUIST
Oxford University, UK

MICHAEL ANTHONY LEWIS
Stony Brook University, USA

STEVEN PRESSMAN
Monmouth University, USA

Routledge
Taylor & Francis Group
LONDON AND NEW YORK

First published 2005 by Ashgate Publishing

Published 2016 by Routledge
2 Park Square, Milton Park, Abingdon, Oxon OX14 4RN
711 Third Avenue, New York, NY 10017, USA

Routledge is an imprint of the Taylor & Francis Group, an informa business

British Library Cataloguing in Publication Data
U.S. Basic Income Guarantee Network (Congress) (1st : 2002
: New York, N.Y.)
The ethics and economics of the basic income guarantee. -
(Alternative voices in contemporary economics)
1. Guaranteed annual income - Congresses 2. Income
maintenance programs - Congresses
I. Title II. Widerquist, Karl III. Lewis, Michael Anthony,
1965- IV. Pressman, Steven
362.5'82

Library of Congress Control Number: 2005927755

ISBN 9780754641889 (hbk)

Contents

PART THREE: EVIDENCE

PART FOUR: PROPOSALS

List of Figures

List of Tables

List of Contributors

Randall Bartlett is in the Department of Economics at the University of Guelph, Guelph, Ontario, Canada.

Fred Block teaches sociology at the University of California–Davis. He is a senior research fellow with the Rockridge Institute, a progressive think tank in the San Francisco Bay Area.

Stephen Bouquin is Professor of Sociology at the University of Picardie–Jules Verne and a research fellow at the G. Friedmann Center of the National Center for Scientific Research.

James B. Bryan is Associate Professor and Chair of the Economics Department at Manhattanville College in Purchase, New York. He also serves as senior economist at the Institute of SocioEconomic Studies.

John Cunliffe is in the Department of Politics and International Studies, University of Warwick.

James Davies is in the Department of Economics at the University of Western Ontario, London, Ontario, Canada.

Guido Erreygers is in the Department of Economics, Faculty of Applied Economics, University of Antwerp.

Robert Harris is the former Executive Director of the President's Commission on Income Maintenance, and the former Vice President of the Urban Institute.

Robinson Hollister is Professor of Economics at Swarthmore College, and co-author of *Labor Market Policy and Unemployment Insurance.*

Michael W. Howard is Professor of Philosophy at the University of Maine. He is the author of *Self-management and the Crisis of Socialism* (Rowman and Littlefield, 2000), and the editor of *Socialism* (Humanity Press, 2001).

Michael Hoy is at the Department of Economics at the University of Guelph, Guelph, Ontario, Canada.

Derek Hum is Professor of Economics at the University of Manitoba. He is coauthor of *Experimental Social Programs and Analytic Methods: An Evaluation of the U.S. Income Maintenance Projects* (1984), and (with Wayne Simpson) of *Income Maintenance, Work Effort and the Canadian Mincome Experiment* (1991).

Thierry Laurent is at the Center for Economic Studies (EPEE), University of Evry, France.

Robert A. Levine is Senior Economic Consultant at the Rand Corporation, and is author of *The Poor Ye Need Not Have With You: Lessons From the War on Poverty*.

Michael Anthony Lewis is Associate Professor of Social Welfare at the School of Social Welfare, Stony Brook University. He is the coauthor (with Karl Widerquist) of *Economics for Social Workers*.

Yannick L'Horty is at the Center for Economic Studies (EPEE), University of Evry, France.

Nicoli Nattrass is Professor of Economics at the University of Cape Town. She is the author of *The Moral Economy of AIDS in South Africa* (Cambridge University Press, 2004) and coauthor (with Jeremy Seeking) of *From Race to Class: The Changing Nature of Inequality in South Africa* (Yale University Press, forthcoming).

Alice O'Connor is Associate Professor of History at the University of California–Santa Barbara, and is author of *Poverty Knowledge: Social Science, Social Policy and the Poor in Twentieth Century U.S. History*.

Steven Pressman is Professor of Economics and Finance at Monmouth University. He also serves as Associate Editor of the *Eastern Economic Journal* and North American Editor of the *Review of Political Economy*. He is the author of *Fifty Major Economists* and coeditor of *A New Guide to Post Keynesian Economics*.

Jeremy Seekings is Professor of Political Studies and Sociology at the University of Cape Town. He is the coauthor of *The UDF: A History of the United Democratic Front in South Africa* (Ohio University Press, 2000), and is coauthor (with Nicoli Nattrass) of *From Race to Class: The Changing Nature of Inequality in South Africa* (Yale University Press, forthcoming).

Wayne Simpson is Professor of Economics at the University of Manitoba. He is the author of *Urban Structure and the Labor Market: Analysis of Worker Mobility, Commuting and Underemployment in Cities* (1992) and (with Derek Hum) of *Income Maintenance, Work Effort and the Canadian Mincome Experiment* (1991) and *Maintaining a Competitive Workforce* (1996).

Margaret Somers is Associate Professor of Sociology and History at the University of Michigan. She is the author of *The People and the Law: The Making of Modern Citizenship Rights* (Cornell University Press) and *Studies in Citizenship, Civil Society and the Public Sphere*: *Institutions, Associations, Identities* (Cambridge University Press).

Eduardo Matarazzo Suplicy is a Brazilian senator representing the state of São Paulo (PT/SP), a member and cofounder of the Workers' Party of President Luiz Inácio Lula da Silva. He is also Professor of Economics at the Escola de Administração de Empresas e de Economia de São Paulo of the Getúlio Vargas

Foundation. He is the author of *Da distribuição da renda e dos direitos à cidadania.*

Yannick Vanderborght is Research Associate at the Belgian National Fund for Scientific Research (FNRS) and Hoover Chair at the University of Louvain, Belgium. He is also Newsletter Editor of the Basic Income Earth Network and the coauthor (with Philippe van Parijs) of *L'allocation Universelle* (2005).

Harold Watts is Emeritus Professor of Economics and Public Affairs at Columbia University, and former Director of the Institute for Research on Poverty. He is the coeditor of *The New Jersey Income Maintenance Experiment, Volumes II and III.*

Karl Widerquist holds a Ph.D. in economics from the City University of New York. He is currently working on a Ph.D. in Political Theory at Oxford University, and is the coordinator of the U.S. Basic Income Guarantee Network. He is the coauthor (with Michael A. Lewis) of *Economics for Social Workers.*

Walter Williams is Emeritus Professor of Public Affairs at the University of Washington, and is the author of *Honest Numbers and Democracy: Social Policy Analysis in the White House, Congress, and the Federal Agencies.*

Almaz Zelleke has a Master's degree in political science from Harvard University. She is the author of "Distributive Justice and the Argument for an Unconditional Basic Income" in the *Journal of Socio-Economics* (February 2005).

Foreword

This book is being published just after the Tenth Congress of the Basic Income European Network (BIEN), which symbolically renamed itself the Basic Income Earth Network at that Congress, held as part of the Barcelona Forum in September 2004. The change reflected a remarkable fact: More social scientists and activists in developing countries are realizing that providing people with a minimum income on which to survive is both desirable and affordable.

The realization, and the growing support for a basic income in countries such as Brazil and South Africa, has emerged at a time when many governments of rich countries are insisting that they must cut social spending and that they must reduce "dependency" by shifting to "activation" policies, to "targeting" and to more "conditional" income transfers. "End welfare as we know it!" was President Bill Clinton's cry in 1996. Yes, "welfare rolls" fell, but the US poverty rate remained high; and poverty in the US has risen under President George W. Bush.

Underneath the views of the modern apostles of limiting security for the poor is the age-old mix of fear and the desire to control the "plebs" at the gates of the elite; the outsiders condemned to live in insecurity, twitching as they gaze at the opulence enjoyed by the privileged. It is an ancient set of conflicting sentiments, made worse by the sophistry of modern pseudo-social science, by the claim that providing the poor with a modest income security would induce laziness, drug taking, social irresponsibility, juvenile pregnancies, and so on.

The authors of this book are not scared by this line of attack, nor should they be. It is up to the readers to decide whether or not they agree. There is a broader concern that, as co-chair of BIEN, I addressed in the Tenth Congress. This concerns the place of a basic income in social policy thinking for the twenty-first century. Is it just a "Big Idea" whose time may be coming, or is it to be seen as part of a coherent progressive strategy?

At the Ninth Congress, held at the International Labour Organisation (ILO) in Geneva in September 2002, emphasis was placed on the view that basic income security should be regarded as a human right, as a republican *claim right*, something to which we should hope to move towards.[1] This was subsequently supported by the Declaration of Emerging Human Rights issued at the culmination of the Barcelona Forum, specifically in Article 10, which was endorsed by various human rights bodies.

However, it has been apparent from the outset of modern discussions of basic income that there are two currents at work, one of which represents those who see basic income security as a right and those who wish it to be part of a redistributive strategy as well. Many on the political right can see a basic income as something that would facilitate an efficient market economy, allowing for greater labor market flexibility and making for a society of greater individualism and economic rationality. This is where market liberals, such as Milton Friedman and Sam Brittan, would place their support for a basic income. This camp would extend to the various philosophically minded supporters, mostly libertarians, who focus on the desirability of supporting "Lazy" and his like. This is a solid insightful tradition, valuable for responding to the diverse *paternalists* who dress up their opposition to real freedom that is linked to the idea of unconditional basic income security.[2]

The second current includes many on the political left, who believe basic income must be part of an egalitarian strategy, not to be seen in isolation. There is an implicit tension between the basic income as Big Idea advocates and the "basic income in complex egalitarianism" advocates. The debate has never been fully articulated, and there might be justification for being concerned that the latter has been crowded out by the Big Idea vision. A danger of the Big Idea is that it makes it hard to legitimize basic income and to escape the appearance of a ghetto of researchers and non-mainstream advocates.

This may be changing. Discussion of capital grants, baby bonds and economic democracy may crystallize into a more comprehensive redistributive strategy, with a basic income as a floor or "first pillar" of a rapidly evolving social protection system. Its legitimization may come in the wake of recognizing the desirability of redressing the extraordinary growth of economic insecurity and diverse forms of inequality unleashed by globalization and the spread of individualization.[3]

Part of the appeal of a basic income is that it would help all of us to re-address the place of *work* in our lives. Again, it should not be considered in isolation. It could help to legitimize forms of work that are not *labor*. But to be powerfully helpful in elevating voluntary care and community work to their proper place in our lives, it would need to be accompanied by stronger voice organizations to ensure security for those doing such work.

A basic income would also help more people to take it a little easier, to slow down, to take stock of the frenzy of modern consumerism. In a market society, the pressure to "spend time," to consume more and more, and to rush in a frenzy from office to mall to home, from spending spree to spending spree, is a veritable societal sickness that is in danger of being a form of madness. There are structural reasons for this modern form of "bread and circus" existence. However, anything that could tilt the balance to a slower, more reflective pace and way of life should surely be welcomed. A basic income would help. It would not be a panacea. It could help achieve a redistribution of one of the key assets of our era: quality time.

Most of the following chapters were initially presented at the First Congress on the U.S. Basic Income Guarantee Network, where I gave the opening speech. This book should be read alongside BIEN's *Income Security as a Right*, since the papers are in many respects complementary. This book focuses more on debates in the United States. This is apt, since it is the first major publication of USBIG, a network that has sprung up to promote constructive debate on the feasibility and desirability of a basic income in the United States. It builds on a fascinating set of traditions that spreads across a large part of the American political spectrum, which had a brief flurry of political activity in the 1970s before being eclipsed by the social engineers and paternalists who dominated public policy thinking in the last quarter of the twentieth century.

In spite of the 2004 United States presidential election, that essentially conservative agenda may have, thankfully, run its course, as the evidence pours in to show its limitations. A new agenda for a future of real freedom may be emerging in its wake. I join the authors of this book in devoutly hoping so.

Guy Standing
Director, International Labour Organisation (ILO)

Notes

[1] For the papers emanating from that Congress, see G. Standing (ed.) (2004) *Income Security as a Right*, (London: Anthem Press).

[2] For a critique of that tradition and for a longer defense of basic income, see G. Standing (2002) *Beyond the New Paternalism: Basic Security as Equality*, (London: Verso).

[3] On this, see International Labour Organisation (2004) *Economic Security for a Better World*, (Geneva: ILO).

Acknowledgments

This book is the outcome of a conference that was organized and primarily sponsored by the Stony Brook University School of Social Welfare. The conference was the First Congress of the U.S. Basic Income Guarantee Network, which took place in New York City, March 9–10, 2002.

We would like to thank Dean Frances Brisbane of Stony Brook School of Social Welfare without whose support neither the conference nor the book would have happened. Thanks to Stanley Aronowitz, the Center for Cultural Studies, and the Center for Continuing Education at the Graduate School of the City University of New York for providing space for the conference, logistical support, and a good deal of organizational know-how. The help of Heather Gautney at the center was also invaluable. Thanks also to Steve Shafarman and the Citizen Policies Institute for their support of the conference.

Thanks to everyone who attended and participated in the conference. A special thanks to Robert Harris who not only contributed to the book, but chaired and helped to organize the session on the Negative Income Tax experiments, which has become a chapter in this book. Thanks to Michael Howard who both contributed to the book and gave helpful comments on several other chapters.

Three chapters in this book have appeared in a symposium in the *Review of Social Economy*. Thanks to their editors and reviewers and everyone else who helped put that symposium together.

Finally, we would like to thank all the contributing authors, and especially Donna Reeder, our copy editor, book indexer, and book format consultant.

Michael Anthony Lewis, Steven Pressman, and Karl Widerquist
February 2005

Chapter 1

An Introduction to the Basic Income Guarantee

Michael Anthony Lewis, Steven Pressman, and Karl Widerquist

Basic income guarantee (BIG) proposals have been around in one form or another at least since Thomas Paine proposed his version in *Agrarian Justice* (1796). The idea behind a BIG is rather simple—the lowest income that anyone receives does not have to be zero. As such, BIG is a public policy that unconditionally ensures that the income of every citizen reaches some minimal level. Its guarantee is unconditional in the sense that every citizen receives it without any obligation to work, to have children, to get married, or to perform any socially mandated task.

Over the years, under various names and in various forms, BIG has been endorsed by people as diverse as John Kenneth Galbraith, Milton Friedman, Richard Nixon, Martin Luther King Jr., and Bertrand Russell. Advocates of BIG have presented many arguments to support it, arguing that a small, but universal, floor under everyone's income can eliminate the worst problems of destitution while incorporating better work incentives than traditional redistributive programs based on categorical individual need. Some see it as a way to provide greater economic security in times when jobs are hard to find; others see it as essential to ensuring the freedom of the least advantaged.

The basic income guarantee sparked widespread debate in the United States in the 1960s and 1970s, when, under names such as the "guaranteed income" or the "negative income tax," it was seen as a way to simultaneously streamline and improve the welfare system. Many prominent economists at the time endorsed variants of BIG because they saw it as a "scientific" solution to poverty or as a way to simplify government antipoverty efforts (for example, Hayek 1944; Friedman 1962; Tobin 1966, 1968; Simon 2001). A heavily watered-down version of BIG, proposed by the Nixon administration and called "the Family Assistance Plan," passed the House of Representatives in 1971 and failed by only 10 votes in the Senate. But by 1980, public policy in the United States had turned against BIG, as cutting the welfare system became more popular than improving it. But it remains a logical alternative to the traditional welfare state based on conditions and categorical needs.

Opponents of a BIG have seen it as a costly federal program that encourages individuals to be unproductive members of society. Neoliberal economists and many neoclassical economists have rejected any form of redistribution as contrary to the "tough love" that is necessary to get people to enter the labor force and work hard at keeping their jobs. Giving people a social safety net, so the argument goes, means that there are few incentives to work and almost no incentive to work hard. Other mainstream economists have rejected BIG, believing that its advocates have abandoned "scientific" economic analysis by pursuing a normative policy agenda. For many years, opponents of BIG had been winning both the academic and popular debates. However, more recently, things have started to change. At the academic level, the arguments raised by the critics of BIG have themselves been criticized along a number of lines.

First, one must recognize that "tough love" policies, which give workers greater incentive to work, also give employers less incentive to pay livable wages. An incentive to reject jobs paying less than poverty-level wages may be just what low-income workers need to receive decent pay. "Tough love" policies that make individuals dependent on their employers might thus have too much toughness with not enough love.

Second, many Americans make the value judgment that wages failing to let workers provide adequate food, shelter, and other necessities for themselves and their families are morally objectionable. A value-neutral economist cannot question that value judgment, but should instead limit herself to addressing the following question: If voters and policymakers want to increase the incomes of low-wage workers, what is the most efficient way to do that? One answer to this question is the basic income guarantee (see Bryan in this volume). In addition, the statement "BIG should not be introduced if it causes a decrease in work effort," is a *heavily* value-laden statement that must be rejected by any economist who believes in "value-free" science.

Third, recent philosophical literature provides support for BIG by coming down hard on the attempt to sharply distinguish facts and values. The renowned Harvard philosopher Hilary Putnam (2002) argues that facts and values are frequently intertwined and inter-related in human actions, in language, and in human thought. One implication of Putnam's philosophical case is that arguments regarding the basic income guarantee must be value laden. Supporters of BIG cannot be dismissed because they engage in "policy advocacy" or "normative economics" rather than "hard, scientific economic analysis" any more than opponents of BIG can be dismissed for the same reasons.

Fourth, many scholars recognize that most people do not behave as neoclassical economists assert they must, and that the world is not configured in the simple way that neoclassical economists presuppose. As Robert Frank and others have pointed out, people vote, they donate blood, they engage in acts of heroism, and they refuse to defect in single-play prisoner's dilemma games. Altruistic behavior seems to exist side by side with selfish behavior (Frank 1988), and the possibility is often ignored in economic analysis that is easily capable of incorporating it (Widerquist 2003). Similarly, a good deal of psychological research, stemming from the work of Daniel Kahneman and Amos Tversky, has demonstrated that people frequently act based on habits or heuristics rather than by following the axioms of economic rationality (Plous 1993). The question then becomes an empirical one—which of these forces on human nature is greater in different contexts? Do habits and altruistic behavior tend to trump neoclassical rationality when incomes are guaranteed, or will most people work less hard? There is considerable empirical evidence that government attempts to redistribute income do not adversely affect economic growth or labor efforts, at least given current levels of redistribution and current social mores (see Pressman 2002–2003 and his chapter in this volume). This evidence bodes well for the efficacy of a basic income guarantee.

Fifth, recent work in evolutionary game theory has argued that social interdependencies do matter. Many real world situations take the form of social dilemmas like the famous prisoner's dilemma (see Poundstone 1992) or the ultimatum game (see Thaler 1988). In these situations, short-run individual utility maximization yields outcomes that leave everyone worse off. The best possible results in social dilemmas arise when individuals follow norms of reciprocity and general social rules rather than engaging in selfish behavior. Moreover, evolutionary psychologists have produced substantial evidence that human beings have evolved in such a manner that they have the capacity to learn these norms and rules in order to gain from social interaction (Cosmides and Tooby 1992). Our genetic disposition toward not defecting in social situations implies that individuals may not shirk when given income guarantees. One important reason for this result is that shirking generally leads to punishment. BIG punishes shirkers by forcing them to live off the social minimum, which may be all the punishment we need. BIG can therefore be viewed as a social experiment designed to yield gains from cooperative behavior; but it is an experiment undertaken with the understanding that benefits can be reduced if it turns out that shirking behavior exceeds socially acceptable levels. All this work, from many different perspectives and disciplines, has called into question some of the main objections to a basic income guarantee that have been voiced in the academic debate.

Recent political trends have brought BIG back into the popular debate as well. In 1996, President Bill Clinton signed a welfare reform bill that profoundly altered income maintenance policy in the United States. The main features of this law are a five-year lifetime limit for receipt of income support and an obligation on the part of welfare recipients to work for their welfare benefits. Most politicians, as well as much of the adult population in the United States, believe that this reform legislation was a major success, simply because welfare rolls and welfare expenditures have fallen. But many progressives argue that the number of people on welfare should not be a measure of our success in welfare reform; rather, they contend that the success of welfare policy should be its effect on the number of people living in poverty. By this criterion, welfare reform has been a failure. The poverty rate for 2003 (12.5 percent) was higher than it was 30 years ago and has been climbing since 2000. BIG supporters argue that it is the only comprehensive solution to poverty; it is capable not only of reducing but even eliminating poverty.

Led by a popular movement in Europe during the 1990s, BIG began to make its way back into policy discussions. Several recent books have discussed the idea, most often in a European context (for example, Van Parijs 1992, 1995; Atkinson

1996; Rogers and Cohen 2001; Standing 2002), and BIG has once again surfaced on the public policy radar. There is a grass roots movement for BIG in South Africa (see Nattrass and Seeking in this volume). The Prime Minister of Mozambique has endorsed BIG as a long-term goal of his government. And in Brazil, a bill authorizing the gradual phase-in of basic income beginning in 2005 was recently signed into law. The bill's sponsor, Senator Eduardo Suplicy, is a contributor to this volume.

The U.S. Basic Income Guarantee (USBIG) Network was founded in New York City in December of 1999 to help bring advocates of BIG together. The USBIG Network is committed to generating discussion of BIG among academics, activists, and policymakers. It is not tied to any specific form of BIG such as the negative income tax (which makes up income if private income falls), basic income (which provides an income to everyone regardless of other income), or basic capital (which provides a stake of investment capital or a share of ownership). USBIG held its first conference on March 8th and 9th, 2002 at the Graduate Center of the City University of New York (CUNY). The conference was cosponsored by the CUNY Graduate Center, the Stony Brook University School of Social Welfare and the Citizen Policies Institute. About 100 authors, academics, activists, and students attended the conference; and more than 40 papers were presented, many of which appear in this volume.

This book is divided into four Parts. They cover the history of BIG, philosophical debates over the vision of society it represents, sociological and economic debates concerning its effects, and finally some practical proposals for a BIG in several countries.

The four chapters in Part One trace the history of the BIG proposal from its beginnings in the late eighteenth century to the present with special emphasis on the guaranteed income movement of the 1960s and 1970s in the United States.

In chapter 2, Fred Block and Margaret Somers examine the relationship between the welfare reform passed by the United States Congress in 1996 and Speenhamland, a British town that (in May 1795) decreed the poor were entitled to certain public assistance. As the program spread among English parishes, it generated a great deal of controversy. Critics argued that it provided relief to the able bodied, and thus reduced work effort and increased the local tax rates (to support the poor). Block and Somers revisit the Speenhamland episode. Drawing on four decades of recent scholarship, the authors show that Speenhamland policies could *not* have had the consequences attributed to them. They then seek to explain how the Speenhamland story became part of the accepted wisdom regarding public assistance to the poor and how it contributed to the 1996 welfare reform legislation in the United States. This argument has important consequences of BIG proposals, since it points out that income guarantees have not had negative consequences in the past and so they should not be rejected for this reason.

In chapter 3, economists John Cunliffe and Guido Erreygers focus on the historical antecedents of contemporary basic income proposals. Specifically, they focus on proposals put forth by the nineteenth century American writers Cornelius Blatchly, Thomas Skidmore, and Orestes Brownson. They argue that these writers may have been influenced by the ideas of Thomas Jefferson and Thomas Paine, American revolutionaries whose ideas about economic policy and distribution bear striking similarities to current basic income proposals.

Robert Harris gives an inside account, in chapter 4, of the politics behind the guaranteed income movement of the 1960s and 1970s. The movement grew out of dissatisfaction with the conditional welfare system that had been in place since the New Deal, which was failing to eliminate poverty either for workers or for people unable to work, and which was causing significant poverty traps. Many people on the left and right began to see the guaranteed income as a simpler and more effective system for both the working poor and those on social assistance. Nixon's modified guaranteed income was overwhelmingly passed by the House of Representatives, but failed narrowly in the Senate thanks to opposition from both left and right and to lukewarm support from Nixon himself.

One offshoot of the guaranteed income movement was that five NIT experiments were conducted in the United States and Canada during the 1970s. These experiments divided a group of subjects into two groups. One group was part of a negative income tax plan; the other group was a control group that was subject to the regular income tax. The experiments were designed to measure the impact of NIT on labor force participation and marital dissolution in a rigorous scientific manner. These experiments were not only important for the basic income guarantee, but they were also the first large-scale social experiments and had far-reaching influence on policy research in a number of different areas. Some of the original scholars from the negative tax experiments reunite in chapter 5 to discuss their importance after 30 years. The panel members discuss the political reasons for setting up the experiments and their results. Although the results were largely positive, showing small work-disincentive effects and important effects on health, educational attainment, and well being, some politicians and pundits used the experimental findings to help quash the NIT.

Part Two examines the philosophical debate over BIG. The chapters in this section of the book discuss various justifications for a BIG and compare the case for a BIG to the case for other types of income support plans.

In chapter 6, political theorist Almaz Zelleke examines political rights and BIG. Her concern is that social thinkers on both the right and left tend to agree that income policies should have work or social contribution requirements attached to them. After discussing and criticizing the arguments of thinkers such as Laurence Mead, Mickey Kaus, Anthony Atkinson and others who hold this view, she puts forth an alternative—the market should be regarded as a sphere of citizenship no less important than the polity. That is, the liberty that we grant to United States citizens is tied to the right to partake in the market as much as it is tied to the right to partake in politics. Thus, we should view income that lets people participate in the market as analogous to voting rights that let people take part in the political process. We grant people the right to vote and, likewise, the basic income should be viewed as a right to "vote" in the marketplace.

Philosopher Michael Howard's article (chapter 7) is largely a discussion of the liberal neutrality principle associated with the philosopher John Rawls, and its relevance to the basic income debate. The neutrality principle roughly stipulates that an acceptable theory of justice cannot be biased toward any particular substantive conception of the good life. Howard's thesis, presented with the argumentative and analytic skills philosophers are known for, is that any income policy that requires some contribution to society is biased toward those whose conception of the good life involves such contribution; a basic income isn't biased in this way, rendering it the more just policy.

In chapter 8, Karl Widerquist defends basic income against the "exploitation objection," which asserts that a basic income allows individuals to benefit from social cooperation without contributing to society, thereby exploiting those who do work. He specifically addresses Gijs van Donselaar's version of this objection, and argues this objection has three critical flaws. First, the conclusion that a basic income is exploitive relies on holding the poor responsible for the level of scarcity in the world. Second, van Donselaar treats work rents differently than other rents. Third, van Donselaar's definition of exploitation is unworkable in practice, and the connection between it and a case against basic income is weak.

In chapter 9, Michael Anthony Lewis enters the debate between basic income and the basic stake proposal put forth by Bruce Ackerman and Anne Alstot. This proposal stipulates that a lump sum of $80,000 be provided to each high school graduate at age 18 if the recipient plans to attend college or age 21 if she does not plan to do so. Lewis addresses the question of whether basic income or the stake is better at promoting freedom. He suggests that if one makes assumptions associated with rational choice theory it would seem that the stake is more freedom promoting. However, he goes on to argue that there appear to be pervasive patterns in decision making that might result in people allocating their stakes in ways they might later regret, and that a basic income might be more freedom promoting because it would constrain people's ability to make such decisions.

While Part Two is philosophical in its orientation, Part Three is empirical. The chapters in this section address questions concerning the real world impact of a BIG and its alternatives.

Steven Pressman, in chapter 10, addresses one of the key tradeoffs faced in a BIG plan—the lack of incentives to work hard and make more money that are likely to occur as a result of giving people a sum of money with no strings attached. Generating greater equity with a BIG will therefore also reduce economic efficiency. If these efficiency losses are large enough, reduced efficiency would constitute a good case against BIG. Using an international dataset that stretches back over 20 years (the Luxembourg Income Study), Pressman examines the tradeoff between equity and efficiency empirically. He finds negligible efficiency losses due to government redistribution efforts, and concludes that any efficiency-equity tradeoff is likely to be small (as long as redistribution efforts remain in their current range).

In chapter 11, economist James Bryan focuses on poverty reduction as a central goal of any income policy, but also attends to the effect such policies have on work incentives. Bryan looks at the extent to which the mid-1990s welfare reforms reduced poverty by focusing on trends in poverty before the reforms, from

1993–1995, and trends afterwards, from 1995–1996. He arrives at three conclusions: (1) poverty among families with children declined in the post-reform period but the rate of decrease was slower than during the pre-reform period, (2) among poor single-mother families there were reductions in disposable income, and (3) these reductions in disposable income were only partially offset by cash and in-kind programs such as the earned income tax credit (EITC) and food stamps. Bryan argues that a basic income guarantee could decrease poverty to a larger extent while creating smaller work disincentives than the current package of the Temporary Assistance for Needy Families (TANF), workfare, food stamps, and EITC programs. He attributes this to the high benefit reduction rate in current programs compared to the lower reduction rates that would obtain in basic income plans. From an economic point of view Bryan sees two arguments against the basic income. First, the volume of transfers needed to achieve an acceptable minimum income guarantee may be very high compared to more highly targeted programs. Second, to maintain work incentives for beneficiaries, the benefit reduction rate must be low. This would, in turn, create a small net donor population, thus requiring a high marginal tax rate and generating a larger work disincentive for this group.

In chapter 12, Thierry Laurent and Yannick L'Horty examine the work incentive problems of a basic income guarantee. They argue that most previous studies of the work incentive problem take a static approach. People are thought to balance just the income from working now against the income received now from a guaranteed income plan. However, Laurent and L'Horty note that there are also dynamic considerations. People with jobs today are likely to get promotions and higher pay in the future. So the real choice is a dynamic one, where individuals must balance both the short- and long-term benefits of work against the BIG. The authors then model labor force participation in an intertemporal framework, and use data from French labor market surveys to test their model. Their results show that there are differences between short-run back to work incentives and long-term problems. They also show that there is no obvious link between short- and long-run incentive problems. Finally, their results explain why some workers may have an incentive to accept jobs that do not pay, while others do not.

In chapter 13, Stephen Bouquin presents research results on the effects of tax-credit systems in Europe that use "in-work benefits," which are meant to be combined with the wages of the working poor. He examines the labor market policies of three European countries that have been increasingly relying on in-work benefits, including the United Kingdom (Working Tax Credit, Income Support), France (Tax Credit), and Belgium (several policies). He finds evidence of what he calls the "Speenhamland effect" on wages. That is, in-work benefits can reduce real wages, as employers capture some or all of the benefits (intended for workers) by reducing the wages they pay. Through these effects, expenditures intended to benefit poor workers end up benefiting their employers. The existence of Speenhamland effects raises serious doubt for any policy based on forcing individuals into the paid labor market.

BIG also raises practical questions. How much would a BIG cost? How can it be financed? What is the optimal level of BIG, given tradeoffs between poverty reduction on the one hand, and costs and work disincentives on the other hand? Part Four, the final section of the book, contains chapters that examine the political prospects of BIG and chapters with nuts and bolts proposals for making basic income work in various countries around the world.

In chapter 14, Nicoli Nattrass and Jeremy Seekings discuss the possibility of implementing a BIG in South Africa. South Africa is the only country in the world with a major grassroots movement pushing for BIG, and it has a unique political and economic situation that make BIG politically feasible. The authors argue that BIG has been on the agenda because of the coincidence of four main factors. First, the country already has a system of public welfare that is unusually extensive in its coverage, unusually generous in its benefits and unusually redistributive in its effects. Second, poverty persists due to unemployment and the absence of subsistence agriculture, and there is little prospect of reducing poverty through job creation or land reform in the short- or medium-term. Third, the existence of an extensive system of private welfare, through remittances sent by employed workers to rural kin, means that it is in the interests of the powerful trade union movement to support a BIG. Fourth, the extent of inequality, paradoxically, makes it easier to finance a BIG based on redistribution from the rich to the poor.

In chapter 15, Brazilian Senator Eduardo Suplicy discusses the movement for a BIG in Brazil. Suplicy and others have been pressing for BIG at the federal, state, and municipal level since the late 1980s. The measure was twice approved by the Brazilian Senate but languished until the Workers' Party (of which both Suplicy and President Lula are members) took control of the presidency. Success was finally achieved in January 2004 when President Lula signed a basic income bill into law. The new law gives the executive wide authority to determine the timing of the phase-in, but it authorizes the gradual introduction of a small basic income guarantee within the next eight years.

In chapter 16, political scientist Yannick Vanderborght discusses recent debates over BIG in Belgium and the Netherlands. Reviewing the various arguments both for and against the basic income, he concludes that the supporters of a basic income have an uphill battle. Vanderborght views the main obstacle to the basic income in these two countries as the widely held belief that able-bodied recipients of income assistance should make some social contribution in return for assistance. He concludes with a discussion of the so-called "participation grant," a policy that would provide a universal grant to all citizens or residents as long as they engaged in some socially beneficial pursuit. Such a pursuit does not necessarily mean one has to sell her or his labor. Thus, providing care for children, friends, or relatives, that is not compensated by the market, plus a host of other activities "outside the market" would qualify. Vanderborght argues that such a policy might have a more promising future than the "pure" basic income.

In chapter 17, Derek Hum and Wayne Simpson provide some cost estimates for several possible Canadian BIG programs. Employing two different definitions of poverty, Hum and Simpson estimate that a BIG to eliminate poverty in Canada would cost between $141 billion and $176 billion (or around 15 percent of Canadian GDP). This, they believe, is too costly and would not be politically acceptable in Canada. They also provide estimates of alternative BIG plans that provide income guarantees below the Canadian poverty line. These programs would cost little more than current income transfer programs because they include a negative tax or claw back of the income guarantee. Hum and Simpson find that these programs would do much less to reduce poverty and the income shortfall facing the poor. They conclude by noting that there are numerous possibilities between these two extremes; many of these plans would not be very expensive, yet would be relatively effective in reducing poverty in Canada.

In chapter 18, Randall Bartlett, James Davies and Michael Hoy explore how to set up a negative income tax in the United Kingdom. Their goal was to formulate a set of programs with a guaranteed income and a single flat tax rate that collects the same amount of money as the existing United Kingdom progressive tax system. They then test whether their negative income tax is as progressive as the current United Kingdom tax and transfer system. Their findings are that it would be relatively easy to structure a negative income tax for the United Kingdom that is more equitable than the current system and that does not require high marginal tax rates.

The chapters in this book bring the debate over basic incomes into a contemporary and eclectic context. They provide many different perspectives to the BIG proposal in specific and to antipoverty policy in general. And they show that BIG is a feasible policy alternative.

References

Atkinson, A. (1996) *Public Economics in Action: The Basic Income/Flat Tax Proposal*, (Oxford: Clarendon Press).

Cosmides, L. and Tooby, J. (1992) "Cognitive Adaptations for Social Exchange," in J. Barkow, L. Cosmides and J. Tooby (eds.) *The Adapted Mind: Evolutionary Psychology and the Generation of Culture*, (New York: Oxford University Press), 163–228.

Frank. R. (1988) *Passions within Reason*, (New York: W. W. Norton).

Friedman, M. (1962) *Capitalism and Freedom*, (Chicago: University of Chicago Press).

Friedman, M. and Friedman, R. (1980) *Free to Choose: A Personal Statement*, (New York: Harcourt Brace Jovanovich).

Hayek, F.A. (1944) *The Road to Serfdom*, (Chicago: University of Chicago Press).

Paine, T. (1796) *Agrarian Justice*, (Philadelphia: Printed by R. Folwell, for Benjamin Franklin Bache).

Plous, S. (1993) *The Psychology of Judgment and Decision Making*, (Philadelphia: Temple University Press).

Poundstone, W. (1992) *Prisoner's Dilemma*, (New York: Random House).

Pressman, S. (2002-3) "Fiscal Policy and Work Incentives—An International Comparison," *Journal of Income Distribution*, 11: 51–69.

Putnam, H. (2002) *The Fact Value Dichotomy and Other Essays*, (Cambridge: Harvard University Press).

Rogers, J. and Cohen, J. (eds.) (2001) *What's Wrong With a Free Lunch*?, (Boston: Beacon Press).

Simon, H. (2001) "UBI and the Flat Tax," in J. Rogers and J. Cohen (eds.), *What's Wrong With a Free Lunch*?, (Boston: Beacon Press), 34–38.

Standing, G. (2002) *Beyond the New Paternalism: Basic Security as a Right,* (New York: Verso).

Thaler, R. (1988) "Anomalies: The Ultimatum Game," *Journal of Economic Perspectives*, 2 (4): 195–206.

Tobin, J. (1966) "The Case for an Income Guarantee," *The Public Interest*, 4: 31–41.

——— (1968) "Raising the Incomes of the Poor," in K. Gordon (ed.), *Agenda for the Nation*, (Washington, D.C.: Brookings Institution), 77–116.

Van Parijs, P. (1992) *Arguing for Basic Income: Ethical Foundations for a Radical Reform*, (New York: Verso).

——— (1995) *Real Freedom for All: What (If Anything) Can Justify Capitalism*?, (Oxford: Clarendon Press).

Widerquist, K. (2003) "Public Choice and Altruism," *Eastern Economic Journal*, 29: 317–337.

PART ONE: HISTORY

Chapter 2

In the Shadow of Speenhamland: Social Policy and the Old Poor Law

Fred Block and Margaret Somers[*]

Introduction

"Speenhamland" is not a well-known term. Those who know the reference are most likely to have read about it in Karl Polanyi's classic work, *The Great Transformation.*[1] But even most of those who are familiar with the reference would be astonished to learn that Speenhamland has had a very real impact on social policy debates in England and the United States for two full centuries. In the twentieth century, this impact has generally occurred under the radar of explicit political debate and publicity.

One such incident occurred in the United States during the Nixon administration when Daniel Patrick Moynihan developed his Family Assistance Plan. As Moynihan recalled,

> In mid-April Martin Anderson, of [Arthur] Burns's staff, prepared "A Short History of a 'Family Security System'" in the form of excerpts on the history of the Speenhamland system, the late eighteenth-century British scheme of poor relief taken from Karl Polanyi's *The Great Transformation.*[2]

The gist of Anderson's memo was that in that earlier historical case, the intended floor under the income of poor families actually operated as a ceiling on earned income with the consequence that the poor were further immiserated. Anderson worried that Moynihan's income floor might inadvertently produce the same unintended consequence. Anderson's memo was sufficiently powerful that Nixon asked Moynihan to investigate the accuracy of Polanyi's historical analysis. Moynihan's staff were sent scurrying off to investigate the views of contemporary historians on this question. The Family Assistance Plan was ultimately defeated in the United States Senate but only after Richard Nixon had a conversation about the work of Karl Polanyi.[3]

Canada had a similar episode more recently. In December 2000, newly re-elected Prime Minister Jean Chretien floated, as a trial balloon, the idea of a comprehensive antipoverty program based on a guaranteed annual income for all Canadians. A flurry of press reports followed including an article in the *National Post* that explicitly referred to the Speenhamland enactment of a guaranteed income scheme in 1795. The article insisted that in this earlier episode, employers had paid below-subsistence wages, and some workers chose the collection of benefits over work:

> The first enactment of a guaranteed annual income may have been in 1795 in England, where the Speenhamland system extended subsidies for the infirm to include able-bodied workers.... The system revealed the challenge inherent in designing such a policy; the supplement served as a subsidy that allowed employers to hire workers at below-subsistence wages, and allowed landlords to raise rents. Meanwhile, some workers found themselves better off collecting benefits than working.[4]

In both of these cases, the Speenhamland story in which an income floor was inadvertently transformed into an income ceiling served as a chilling cautionary tale against governmental initiatives to establish a guaranteed annual income.

The same argument has been repeated by progressive thinkers in current debates over the desirability of establishing a universal basic income for all citizens.[5] Analysts who favor using state action to improve the situation of the poor question whether a well-intentioned minimum income would follow the Speenhamland precedent and become a maximum income.[6] They fear that employers would use the increased income received by the poor as an excuse to lower the wages that they pay these employees. The appearance of this argument would be reason enough to revisit the actual history of Speenhamland. But there is a second and more powerful justification for focusing on this historical episode.

Conservative critics of welfare in the United States in the period from 1978 to 1996 formulated their criticisms of the main Federal welfare program—Aid to Families with Dependent Children (AFDC)—in precisely the same terms that English critics of Speenhamland had used in the first decades of the nineteenth century. The parallels in these arguments have been recognized by Albert Hirschman in his analysis of perversity as one of the three "rhetorics of reaction."[7] The core of the perversity thesis is that well-intentioned policies that provide assistance to the poor by means of state intervention will inevitably harm recipients by substituting perverse incentives in place of the market mechanisms that teach the poor to work hard and exercise sexual restraint.

A number of these conservative critics of AFDC were completely self-conscious about the parallels between Speenhamland and AFDC. The same Martin Anderson, who wrote the memo in the Nixon White House, published *Welfare in 1978*, which was one of the first conservative scholarly attacks on AFDC.[8] Anderson quoted Polanyi's account of Speenhamland at length to argue against both income guarantees and programs like AFDC.[9] In 1984, the neoconservative historian Gertrude Himmelfarb published her influential study, *The Idea of Poverty*, in which she carefully recounted the criticisms of the Speenhamland system advanced by Malthus, Burke, de Tocqueville and others.[10] Later on, she published a series of articles and books that explicitly drew the parallels between the dire consequences of the English welfare system in the Speenhamland period and the negative consequences of AFDC.[11] Marvin Olasky, a policy intellectual who George W. Bush credited as the theorist of "compassionate conservatism," published an influential book called *The Tragedy of American Compassion*, whose title encapsulated his restatement of early nineteenth-century critiques of Poor Law assistance.[12]

These self-conscious efforts to mobilize perversity rhetoric against AFDC had an appreciable effect on both elite and public opinion, and contributed to the passage in 1996 of the Personal Responsibility and Work Opportunities Reconciliation Act that ended the long-standing entitlement of poor families to assistance—so much so that it is fair to say that our recent welfare legislation was passed in the shadow of Speenhamland.[13] In fact, in 2002 when the United States Congress debated the reauthorization of the 1996 legislation, the terms of discussion continue to reflect the influence of perversity rhetoric. The debate centered on how many additional hours of work should be mandated for the recipients of relief, and how should the Federal Government promote marriage and sexual restraint among the poor.[14]

It is common for social scientists to complain that public policy is made with insufficient attention to history and social theory. In this article, however, our argument is that for both discussions of guaranteed incomes and welfare policy, a particular and tendentious reading of social history has been given far too much weight by policy makers and policy intellectuals. This is particularly the case because over the past forty years, economic and social historians have produced a large and impressive literature that has reanalyzed the English Poor Law in general and the Speenhamland period in particular.[15] Yet most of this literature is unknown to social scientists, and its findings about the Poor Law have had little impact on social policy debates.[16]

In this chapter, we propose to rethink and retell the story of Speenhamland. This means, fundamentally, showing how the findings of recent studies in social and economic history undermine the Speenhamland stories that have been deployed in social policy debates. But this involves more than simply reporting other scholars' results; we are offering our own analyses of some of the important remaining puzzles in this literature. We are also making a contribution to the history of social theory. While we are critical of Karl Polanyi's history of the Speenhamland episode, we are in fundamental agreement with one of his core theoretical arguments. Polanyi insisted that classical political economy was deeply shaped by the effort to explain the persistence of poverty in the Speenhamland epoch.[17] Specifically, Malthus and Ricardo relied on arguments about biological drives to explain human behavior, and the resulting "naturalism" became an important part of mainstream economics. We hope to build on that insight by unraveling the naturalizing logic that critics of public assistance continue to invoke. Moreover, we will offer our own alternative narrative that both makes sense of recent historical findings and helps to explain the centrality of the Speenhamland story to classical political economy.

The Speenhamland Stories

Speenhamland refers to a town in Berkshire County, England, where the county squires decreed in May 1795 that the poor should be entitled to a specific quantity of assistance depending upon the price of bread and the size of the family. This form of provision is often called aid-in-wages because when the gap between wages and the price of bread widened, the parish used poor relief funds to supplement the wages of workers and their families.[18] As the program spread (although it is a subject of debate as to how widely it was practiced) among England's parishes, it generated controversy. It was perceived by critics that all precedent had been violated by providing relief not just to the infirm, the aged, or the dependent but also to the *able-bodied*. These criticisms were further fueled by the dramatic increase in local poor rates (taxes) and by the findings of a series of parliamentary reports that played a considerable role in shaping public opinion.[19] The most important of these was the Royal Commission Report of 1834 that issued a devastating indictment of Speenhamland and created irresistible pressure for the New Poor Law passed later in the same year. Based on what we now know to be a nonsystematic and ideologically driven method of collecting answers to a survey questionnaire, the published report confirmed what the commission had set out to document in the first place.[20] The main evidence mobilized in the report were hundreds of stories from local parish officials—mostly clergy—confirming the immorality and degradation of the rural poor. The report concluded that Speenhamland and the Old Poor Law more generally were wrong-headed intrusions of state power into self-regulating labor markets. Poor relief created new and perverse incentives that led to increasing pauperization. Exponential increases in childbirth and illegitimacy, declining wages and productivity, assaults on public morality and personal responsibility, and the development of a culture of indolence were only some of the effects attributed to Speenhamland.

The Royal Commission Report was widely distributed, and it influenced a broad range of scholars up through the middle of the next century. In fact, until quite recently, the report was treated as one of the important moments in the rise of the social sciences—one of the first times that a government body relied on systematic collection and analysis of data to address an important social problem. But a number of recent scholars have persuasively shown that the Commissioners did very little data analysis and simply used an elaborate structure of appendixes to give more weight to their "findings."[21] Moreover, there was little in the commission's arguments that was original; their narrative drew heavily on arguments that had been elaborated by Joseph Townsend and T.R. Malthus in the last part of the eighteenth century.

Joseph Townsend's *Dissertation on the Poor Law* appeared in 1786, and it used the fable of dogs and goats on an island in the Pacific to make its case against poor relief.[22] Townsend argued that just as the populations of goats and dogs reached an equilibrium as they each adjusted to the changing food supply, so would the population of the human poor naturally reach equilibrium were it not for the artificial intervention of poor relief:

> Hunger will tame the fiercest animals, it will teach decency and civility, obedience and subjection, to the most perverse. In general it is only hunger which can spur and goad them [the poor] on to labour; yet our laws have said they shall never hunger.[23]

Polanyi's characterization of Townsend's argument is completely apt:

> Hobbes had argued the need for a despot because men were *like* beasts; Townsend insisted that they were *actually* beasts and that, precisely for that reason, only a minimum of government was required.[24]

When the first edition of Malthus's *Essay on the Principle of Population* was published in 1798, there was no mention of Townsend's pamphlet even though Malthus's argument followed along identical lines.[25] Malthus's argument began from two postulates:

> First, That food is necessary to the existence of man.
> Secondly, That the passion between the sexes is necessary and will remain nearly in its present state.[26]

The identification of these two biological drives—hunger and sex—was then the basis for Malthus's central claim that growth of human population will inevitably outstrip the available food supply. Following Townsend, Malthus argued that poor relief interferes with the self-regulating mechanisms that serve as the incentives necessary to drive the poor toward self-disciplined behavior and reproductive prudence. These mechanisms exist in the economy only in its untouched and natural state—the condition of scarcity. So, for example, when poor relief promises child allowances for those parents too poor to make ends meet, young people need no longer delay marriage until they have adequate resources to support a family.[27] Since Malthus strenuously opposed birth control, his goal was for the poor to postpone marriage. Precisely because every additional child promises to produce additional income for the family, the existence of poor relief encourages calculated childbearing as a more expedient means of survival than disciplined productive labor. The consequence is a rise of the birth rate that places an unwanted burden on the rest of society that has to pay the bills.

Malthus also stressed a second line of criticism—that poor relief undermined frugality, personal responsibility, and, above all, work discipline. Once again, the working premise is that the labor market depends on a delicate self-regulating system in which a perfect equilibrium of supply and demand occurs only when it functions in its natural state of scarcity. Remove the scarcity and gone is the spur to labor that only the fear of hunger can provide; no longer will workers be interested in pleasing their employers or in saving for the future. Measures designed to diminish poverty so end up making it worse: "Hope and fear are the springs of industry….It is the part of a good politician to strengthen these: but our laws weaken the one and destroy the other."[28]

For Malthus and those who followed his logic—including the Royal Commissioners—the specific rules for allocating poor relief were not very important; as long as some of the able-bodied poor were eligible for assistance, the negative dynamics were set in motion because people were being protected from the consequences of their own decisions. Hence, supporters of this story tended to assimilate all forms of outdoor relief to the able bodied under the single heading of the allowance system, and as long as per capita per law outlays were high, they were able to make their case that poor relief was making poverty worse.

The Other Story

Leftist critics of unfettered market allocation have had their own version of the Speenhamland story, although their narrative has had a more limited impact on social policy. Marx and Engels drew from the Royal Commission Report, just as they mined other parliamentary documents to piece together the story of early industrialization in England. However, their specific references to Speenhamland are brief. Engels wrote in *The Condition of the English Working Class*:

> As long as the old Poor Law survived it was possible to supplement the low wages of the farm labourers from the rates. This, however, inevitably led to further wage reductions since the farmers naturally wanted as much as possible of the cost of maintaining their workers to be borne by the Poor Law. The burden of the poor rates would, in any case, have increased with the rise in population. The policy of supplementing agricultural wages, of course, greatly aggravated the position.[29]

In *Capital*, Marx wrote,

> At the end of the eighteenth century and during the first decade of the nineteenth, the English farmers and landlords enforced the absolute minimum of wages by paying the agricultural labourers less than the minimum as actual wages and making up the balance in the form of parish relief.[30]

Marx and Engels agreed with the conclusions of the Royal Commission Report, but they rejected its explanatory logic. They agreed that the Poor Law had contributed to the immiseration of the rural poor, but the crucial mechanism was that farmers had pushed wage levels down by shifting costs on to the parish. Since a strapped employer might realistically only be able to pay eight shillings per week to an employee, the parish would add four additional shillings to ensure that the workers' families would have enough bread. But now the employer, having caught on to the dynamic, had a clear incentive to lower his own expenses by paying just seven shillings the next week so that the parish would increase its supplement to five shillings.

It is not difficult to explain why Marx and Engels took this position on the core dynamic of Speenhamland; widespread degradation of the rural poor fit the logic of their broad theory of capitalist development. Both enclosures and the Poor Law were part of the process by which wealth was extracted from the rural poor in order to help finance industrial investment. Moreover, Marx and Engels saw the system of poor relief as nothing more than a feudal remnant.

However, Marx and Engels were able to take this position because they were writing a decade or longer after the militant working-class protests that had been engendered by the 1834 New Poor Law. Had they recognized the centrality of the mobilization against the New Poor Law to the development of the working-class movement in England, they might have seen things differently.[31] They should have considered why industrial workers in the industrial North of England cared so deeply about a mere "feudal remnant." Their failure to address this issue had unfortunate consequences. Given their political and intellectual authority, the view that the Poor Law between 1795 and 1834 played a critical role in immiserating the rural working class gained a credibility that lasted for more than a century. Subsequent historians writing from a perspective critical of capitalism followed their lead. W. Hasbach, a scholar of the German Historical School, published his important study in German in 1894 and in English translation in 1908. He was followed by J.L. and Barbara Hammond, Sidney and Beatrice Webb, Karl Polanyi, and E.J. Hobsbawm and George Rude, all of whom concurred in seeing the Poor Law as a factor in rural impoverishment.[32]

But it is not as though the Royal Commission's narrative completely escaped criticism. It was denounced by the rural and urban poor who mobilized extensively against the 1834 New Poor Law. "Tory radical" opinion allied with the poor in resisting both the dismal implications of Malthus's doctrine and the harshness of the 1834 bill.[33] Even J.R. McCulloch, an important classical economist, called into question the objectivity of the investigation.[34] Criticism continued in the twentieth century in R.H. Tawney's reference to "that brilliant, influential, and wildly unhistorical report."[35] Ironically, the most elaborate criticism was offered by the Webbs in Part II of their Poor Law History. The Webbs note that the Royal Commission,

> was not an inquiry into the prevalence and cause of destitution: for the "poverty of the poor" was at that time deemed to be both explained and justified by the current assumptions underlying the Malthusian "Law of Population" and the economists' "Theory of the Wage Fund."[36]

In other words, the Commissioners neglected all structural sources of poverty because they had already embraced theories that explained poverty by Malthusian and Ricardian mechanisms. But the power of the Webbs' criticism is ultimately vitiated because they accepted the accuracy of the report's central finding—that the allowance system was destructive.

> The active members of the Commission…started with an overwhelming intellectual prepossession, and they made only the very smallest effort to free their investigations and reports from bias—a defect in their work which is not to be excused merely because we are today inclined to believe, as they were themselves complacently assured, that their prepossessions against the Rate in Aid of Wages was substantially right.[37]

All told, the Webbs helped to perpetuate the image of the investigation as a major work of social science when they wrote of the commission's investigation:

> Their voluminous reports, together with the equally voluminous other statements, were printed in full, comprising altogether no fewer than twenty-six folio volumes, containing in the aggregate over thirteen thousand printed pages, all published during 1834–1835, being by far the most extensive sociological survey that had at that date ever been undertaken.[38]

In sum, the Webbs' ambivalent verdict helped the authority of the Royal Commission Report to survive until the revisionist assault began with Mark Blaug's articles in the 1960s.[39]

Polanyi's Contribution

When Karl Polanyi began to explore the Speenhamland episode in the 1930s virtually all of the historical sources available to him affirmed that the Speenhamland episode had degraded the rural poor. Nevertheless, Polanyi was determined to challenge the use that market liberals—especially the Austrians von Mises and Hayek—had made of Speenhamland.[40] They had argued that Speenhamland precisely prefigured the disastrous consequences of state interventionism in the late nineteenth and early twentieth centuries. They claimed that all efforts to use government to improve the life chances of the poor would end up undermining the economy's vitality and would ultimately hurt the people that the policies had been intended to help. As a supporter of the achievements of municipal socialism in Vienna, Polanyi was determined to demonstrate the flaws in the historical parallel that these free market theorists had developed.[41]

Polanyi's strategy was to bring a greater degree of institutional specificity to the historical comparison. Instead of just discussing markets and state action in the abstract, he sought to unpack the Speenhamland episode by looking more closely at the actual workings of institutions. His central argument was that the Speenhamland incident could not be generalized to later cases of state action because it occurred before the working class was capable of mobilizing to defend its own interests. This was exemplified by the existence of the Anti-Combination Laws that prohibited all trade union activity. Polanyi is explicit that had it not been for these laws, Speenhamland aid-in-wages might well have "had the effect of raising wages instead of depressing them as it actually did."[42] But even more fundamental than the legal obstacles to trade union activity was the fact that the complicated payment system that Speenhamland initiated prevented rural workers from understanding their actual social position:

> [Speenhamland] prevented laborers from developing into an economic class and thus deprived them of the only means of staving off the fate to which they were doomed in the economic mill.[43]

In sum, the difference between Speenhamland and Vienna is that, in the former, workers had not organized themselves as a class, so there was no mechanism to block state action from producing perverse consequences.

While Polanyi's analytic strategy was clearly an advance over earlier versions of the Speenhamland story, he, also, was seriously misled by the historical sources. Ironically, Polanyi was warned of the problems in his argument by G.D.H. Cole, the great English labor historian and social theorist. Polanyi had sent Cole the first half of the manuscript of *The Great Transformation* in 1943, and Cole wrote back with extensive criticisms. Cole wrote the following:

> I think that all through this chapter [7] you treat Speenhamland as much more universal than it was, and also make much too light of county differences in wage policy.[44]

However, the criticisms arrived too late since Polanyi had already sent the manuscript to its United States publisher.[45]

Table 2.1 Divergent Speenhamland narratives

Proponents	Cause	Key Mechanism	Outcome
Joseph Townsend T.R. Malthus Royal Commissioners Ludwig von Mises Marvin Olasky	Wide use of bread scale undermines scarcity necessary for market self-regulation, discipline and efficiency.	Poor relief works as perverse incentive to early marriage, increased birth rate, and voluntary unemployment.	Reduced productivity, lower wages, excessive population growth, and increased poverty.
Marx and Engels Hammonds Webbs E.P. Thompson	Wide use of bread scale facilitates unilateral wage reductions by employers.	Farmers shift costs on to the parish to save on their wage bills.	Reduced productivity and lower wages.
Karl Polanyi	Wide use of bread scale and Anti-Combination Acts facilitate unilateral wage reductions by employers.	Farmers shift costs on to the parish at a time when rural workers cannot act collectively.	Reduced productivity and lower wages.
Our synthesis of recent historical scholarship. Mark Blaug, J.P. Huzel, K.D.M. Snell	Bread scale not widely used. Rural impoverishment caused by massive shift of industries to North and deindustrialization in the South; unemployment, enclosures, and decline of crafts.	Economic contraction after 1815, intensified by England's return to gold at the pre-War parity, increases agricultural unemployment and rural poverty.	Poor relief significantly buffers rural poor against unemployment and loss of other income sources; provides food and clothing.

Divergent Narratives

As Table 2.1 shows, these various efforts to make sense of Speenhamland shared similar conclusions about its ultimate impact on the rural poor. Leftist critics of capitalism saw a very different dynamic at work than that identified by free market theorists, and Polanyi, in particular, added another layer of institutional causality. The body of historical scholarship that has developed over the past forty years, however, makes it difficult to hold on to any of these narratives.

Complexities and Causal Gaps

Speenhamland has to be understood in the context of England's long and unique Poor Law history.[46] Although initial practices date to the late thirteenth century, the famous 1597 and 1601 Elizabethan Tudor statutes were the most important of the English Poor Law legislation. The law established an obligation at the local level to assist those who were impoverished as a consequence of illness, infirmity, family breakdown, or temporary unemployment. There was much variation in actual Poor Law practices as parishes experimented with a variety of different policies designed to protect the poor while maintaining work incentives.[47] There was also considerable variation over time within parishes; efforts to find the right policy mix at the local level sometimes produced alternating periods of generosity and stinginess.[48]

Some degree of controversy over the Poor Laws existed from their inception, but it was in the last years of the eighteenth century that debate intensified with calls for the complete abolition of all "outdoor"—outside the workhouse—relief. Much of the blame for this shift in attitudes is generally placed on the rapidly rising cost of maintaining parish relief in this period. Per capita poor relief outlays are estimated to have more than doubled between 1749 and 1801.[49]

Considerable uncertainty about these rising expenditures remains to this day because of the sheer empirical difficulty of understanding a highly decentralized system of social welfare in which critical decisions were made by local parish officials. We have data on the total poor law outlays of fifteen thousand parishes in England for selected years from 1802 to 1834, but we do not know precisely how the expenditures were divided among assistance to the vulnerable populations—the elderly, the sick, orphans and unwed mothers; support for local poorhouses; and various forms of outdoor relief, including assistance to the able-bodied poor. In some parishes, detailed registries of all outlays have survived, but it is often difficult for historians to reconstruct the particular rules under which a specific individual was given six shillings each week. Even after two centuries, historians have closely analyzed the surviving records of a relatively small number of parishes.[50] There were some periodic parliamentary surveys that sought to find out about local relief policies, but generally responses were received from only a small fraction of all parishes. It is difficult to know if the responses are representative.[51]

Table 2.2 Forms of relief by modern names

Minimum guaranteed income. This is the Speenhamland bread scale that provides specific amounts of aid in support of wages depending on the price of bread and the size of the family.

Seasonal unemployment insurance. During the winter months when agricultural work was scarce, some parishes provided unemployed farm workers and their families with a weekly stipend that varied depending upon family size.

Public works. Some parishes put the unemployed to work building roads or performing other types of work. Sometimes the supervision was done by public authorities and sometimes by private contractors.

Employer subsidies. Some parishes used poor relief funds to reimburse farmers and other employers who hired the unemployed. This was often called the "roundsman" system because the unemployed workers would make the rounds of local employers.

Workfare. Some parishes allocated a certain proportion of the unemployed to each local employer with the idea that they would provide employment instead of paying taxes for poor relief. This is often referred to as the labor rate system.

Child allowances. Many agricultural parishes provided a supplement to the income of male agricultural workers who had more than two or three children who were not yet of working age.

Workhouse. Well before 1834, a minority of parishes required that the unemployed seeking relief enter a residential facility that imposed work requirements. Some of these facilities were publicly administered, and some were run by private contractors.

Out-of-parish relief. Individuals were entitled to assistance in the parish in which they had been born or gained settlement. Sometimes, however, individuals would experience hardship while away from the home parish and request assistance. The implied threat was that if they did not receive help, they would return home and the parish would be obliged to assist them.

It is clear, however, that the sharp rise in poor law expenditures was largely a regional phenomenon—focusing on Southeastern England, both the wheat growing areas and the pastoral areas where both rural and cottage industries were in decline.[52] In the older cities, it is believed that poor relief for the able bodied was rare, except for periods of acute unemployment or abrupt increases in the price of bread.[53] In the North, the combination of sheep and cattle pasturage, a tradition of small-owner cottage industry, and rapidly growing urban industry meant that per capita poor relief outlays were far lower than in the South.[54] These regional differences were magnified by the greater seasonality in the demand for labor that was characteristic of the wheat-producing areas, especially as alternative income sources began to dry up.[55]

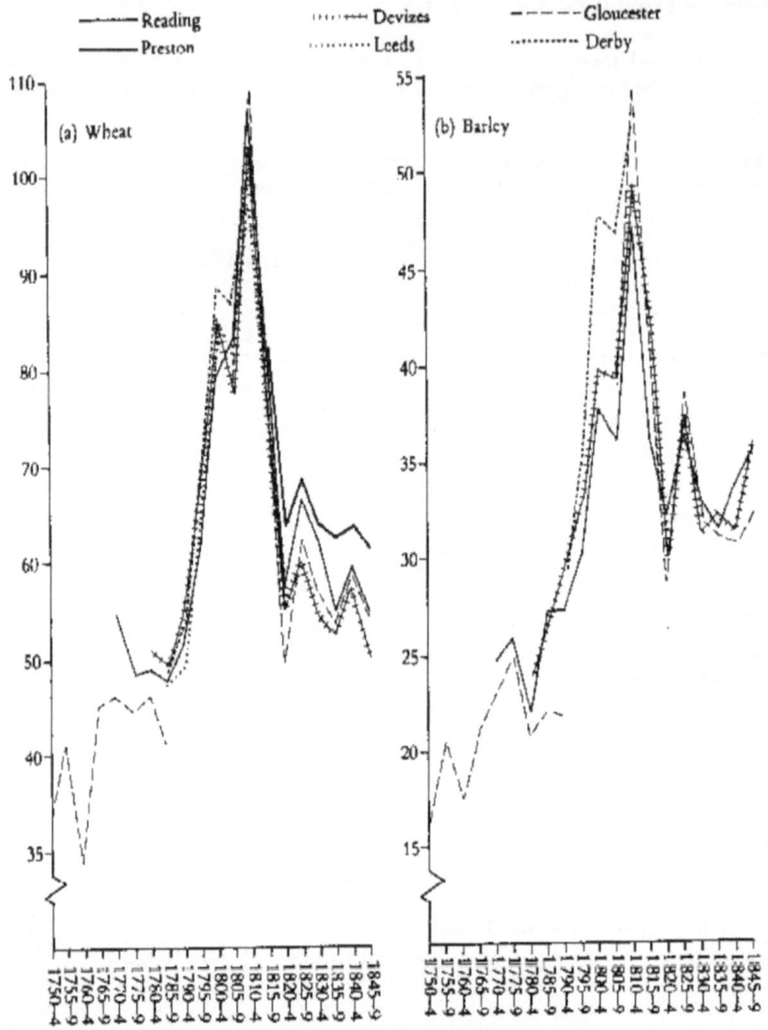

Fig. 3.2. Regional grain prices, 1750–1849
(quinquennial averages, shillings per Winchester quarter)

Sources: *Reading Mercury*; *Salisbury and Winchester Journal*; *Gloucester Journal*; *Preston Chronicle*; *Leeds Intelligencer*; *Derby Mercury*.

Figure 2.1 Trends in grain prices

Source: Richard Perren, "Markets and Marketing," in *Agrarian History*, vol. 6., edited by G.E. Mingay (Cambridge: Cambridge University Press), 190–274. Reprinted with permission from Cambridge University Press, 231.

But if we focus on the Southeastern parts of England, there is a second dimension of empirical complexity. During the Speenhamland period—1795 to 1834—parishes experimented with a broad array of different ways of distributing relief that would have quite varying consequences. In fact, the range of measures closely resembles the repertoire of relief policies that are still debated two hundred years later. And because of the decentralization of administration, we lack definitive information on how widely each of these particular practices was employed. These policies are listed by their modern names when available (see Table 2.2).

One of the recurrent problems in the literature is that analysts group a number of these distinct policies under one heading and proceed as though all the methods can be expected to have the same consequences. For example, "the allowance system" and "aid-in-wages" are often used to cover the first six different policies. As we will see, these disaggregation problems contribute to the difficulties in developing a clear understanding of Speenhamland.

STATISTICAL APPENDIX

Table I.1. *Annual average prices of grain per Imperial quarter in England and Wales 1771–1850*

Year	—	—	Wheat		Barley		Oats		Rye		Beans		Peas	
			s.	*d.*	*s.*	*d.*	*s.*	*d.*	*s.*	*d.*	*s.*	*d.*	*s.*	*d.*
1771	—	—	48	7	26	5	17	2	35	4	29	4		
1772	—	—	52	3	26	1	16	8	37	9	30	11		
1773	—	—	52	7	29	2	17	8	34	4	34	—		
1774	—	—	54	3	29	4	18	4	35	4	32	1		
1775	—	—	49	10	26	9	17	—	33	10	29	6		
1776	—	—	39	4	20	9	15	5	27	8	27	3		
1777	—	—	46	11	21	1	16	1	28	10	29	4		
1778	—	—	43	3	23	4	15	7	29	2	28	6		
1779	—	—	34	8	20	1	14	5	24	—	24	11		
1780	—	—	36	9	17	6	13	2	22	10	22	10		
1781	—	—	46	—	17	8	14	1	27	8	23	8		
1782	—	—	49	3	23	2	15	7	29	8	26	9		
1783	—	—	54	3	31	3	20	5	36	9	35	11		
1784	—	—	50	4	28	8	18	10	33	2	33	2		
1785	—	—	43	1	24	9	17	8	28	10	31	7		
1786	—	—	40	—	25	1	18	6	28	—	34	2		
1787	—	—	42	5	23	4	17	2	28	6	32	9		
1788	—	—	46	4	22	8	16	1	28	6	28	—		
1789	—	—	52	9	23	6	16	6	30	9	38	—		
1790	—	—	54	9	26	3	19	5	35	—	31	11		
1791	—	—	48	7	26	10	18	1	32	7	31	5	33	2
1792	—	—	43	—	—	—	16	9	29	10	31	7	32	4
1793	—	—	49	3	31	1	20	6	36	2	37	6	39	11
1794	—	—	52	3	31	9	21	3	37	5	39	3	48	5
1795	—	—	75	2	37	5	24	5						
1796	—	—	78	7	35	4	21	10						
1797	—	—	53	9	27	2	16	3						
1798	—	—	51	10	29	—	19	5						
1799	—	—	69	—	36	2	27	6						
1800	—	—	113	10	59	10	39	4						
1801	—	—	119	6	68	6	37	—						
1802	—	—	69	10	33	4	20	4						
1803	—	—	58	10	25	4	21	6						
1804	—	—	62	3	31	—	24	3						
1805	—	—	89	9	44	6	28	4						
1806	—	—	79	1	38	8	27	7						
1807	—	—	75	4	39	4	28	4						
1808	—	—	81	4	—	—	33	4						
1809	—	—	97	4	47	—	31	5						
1810	—	—	106	5	48	1	28	7	59	3	54	4	56	11
1811	—	—	95	3	42	3	27	7	48	4	49	4	53	11

STATISTICAL APPENDIX

Table I.1. (*cont.*)

Year	—	—	Wheat		Barley		Oats		Rye		Beans		Peas	
			s.	*d.*	*s.*	*d.*	*s.*	*d.*	*s.*	*d.*	*s.*	*d.*	*s.*	*d.*
1812	—	—	126	6	66	9	44	6	78	7	74	7	76	10
1813	—	—	109	9	58	6	38	6	71	11	76	4	81	11
1814	—	—	74	4	37	4	25	8	44	8	46	2	51	10
1815	—	—	65	7	30	3	23	7	38	1	36	2	39	4
1816	—	—	78	6	33	11	27	2	45	1	39	4	39	10
1817	—	—	96	11	49	4	32	5	58	3	51	7	53	4
1818	—	—	86	3	53	10	32	5	55	4	63	7	61	9
1819	—	—	74	6	45	9	28	2	49	6	54	1	56	1
1820	—	—	67	10	33	10	24	2	42	—	43	3	45	10
1821	—	—	56	1	26	—	19	6	32	—	30	11	32	8
1822	—	—	44	7	21	10	18	1	20	10	24	5	26	4
1823	—	—	53	4	31	6	22	11	31	10	33	1	34	11
1824	—	—	63	11	36	4	24	10	41	5	40	—	40	7
1825	—	—	68	6	40	—	25	8	42	3	42	9	45	4
1826	—	—	58	8	34	4	26	8	41	1	44	3	47	7
1827	—	—	58	6	37	7	28	2	40	2	49	—	49	—
1828	—	—	60	5	32	10	22	6	34	2	38	4	40	6
1829	—	—	66	3	32	6	22	9	34	10	36	8	36	8
1830	—	—	64	3	32	7	24	5	35	10	36	1	39	2
1831	—	—	66	4	38	—	25	4	40	—	39	10	41	11
1832	—	—	58	8	33	1	20	5	34	7	35	4	37	—
1833	—	—	52	11	27	6	18	5	32	11	33	2	36	5
1834	—	—	46	2	29	—	20	11	32	9	35	3	39	4
1835	—	—	39	4	29	11	22	—	30	4	36	11	36	6
1836	—	—	48	6	32	10	23	1	33	4	39	1	38	4
1837	—	—	55	10	30	4	23	1	34	9	38	7	37	4
1838	—	—	64	7	31	5	22	5	35	1	36	8	37	2
1839	—	—	70	8	39	6	25	11	42	—	41	3	41	2
1840	—	—	66	4	36	5	25	8	37	—	43	5	42	5
1841	—	—	64	4	32	10	22	5	36	9	39	10	40	4
1842	—	—	57	3	27	6	19	3	33	—	32	5	32	11
1843	—	—	45	5	29	6	18	4	30	7	29	2	31	1
1844	—	—	51	3	33	8	20	7	33	11	34	5	33	5
1845	—	—	50	10	31	3	22	6	32	6	38	11	38	8
1846	—	—	54	8	32	8	23	8	35	0				
1847	—	—	69	9	44	2	28	8	49	0				
1848	—	—	50	6	31	6	20	6	30	5				
1849	—	—	44	3	27	9	17	6	25	8				
1850	—	—	40	3	23	5	16	5	23	3				

Sources: 1771–1842: BPP 1843, LIII; 1843–50: BPP 1878–9, LXV, p. 429 (wheat, barley, oats and rye), House of Lords Sessional Papers, XX, p. 391 (1843–5 beans and peas).

Figure 2.2 Grain prices

Source: G.E. Mingay, ed., *Agrarian History*, vol. 6 (Cambridge: Cambridge University Press), 974–975. Reprinted with permission from Cambridge University Press.

A third empirical complexity results from the rapid change in prices that occurs across the Speenhamland period. The first half of the period coincides with the Napoleonic Wars that produced an extremely sharp increase in price levels, particularly for wheat—the dietary staple of both the rural and urban working classes. From 1813 on, as the war winds down, there is a sharp fall in price levels; this continues beyond 1834 (see Figures 2.1 and 2.2). These dramatic shifts in price levels generated enormous debates among contemporaries, and to this day, economic historians are still debating the appropriate measures of price changes in this period.[56]

A final empirical complexity may well be the most serious and the most telling. As only parish officers could be counted on to give the kinds of answers that commissioners or parliamentary investigators were seeking, it is extremely rare that an actual recipient of poor relief would ever be questioned. Hence, the testimony of recipients is not available to counter or compare against the extensive reports from local elites, most of whom readily complied with the commissioners in making broad generalizations about the behavior, motivation, and mental states of the recipient population. Only now are we beginning to break these long silences as historians mine letters, wills and petitions from the rural poor to create a more holistic view of the system of poor relief.[57]

Causal Gaps

Both the narrative constructed by Malthus and the Royal Commissioners and the alternative narrative constructed by critics of the market have gaps in their causal logics. In the market liberal story, the work disincentive effects of poor law assistance are simply assumed and treated as invariant. But let us imagine a parish in which poor law assistance primarily took the form of seasonal unemployment insurance. This was often the case in the 1820s when seasonal unemployment had become the dominant cause of poverty.[58] When jobs were available on local farms, able-bodied workers would not be eligible for assistance, but as demand for labor diminished in the winter months, those who had been employed would become eligible for unemployment benefits. As long as the administration of the poor law blocked those with real work opportunities from receiving these unemployment benefits, it is difficult to see any work disincentive effects. Moreover, it would have been rational for local farmers to provide this seasonal unemployment insurance or much of their labor force would be tempted to move elsewhere.[59]

Indeed, there is reason to believe that many parishes were administered in exactly this way. Given the small size of most rural parishes, parish officials knew well the condition of the local labor market, including whether or where vacancies or layoffs were occurring. Moreover, parish officials were not shy about denying assistance when they suspected that an individual was simply shirking.[60] This makes it implausible that large numbers of people were able to cheat routinely and work only when they felt like it. If large increases in poor law outlays were primarily caused by the growth of seasonal unemployment insurance, there is no reason to believe there were significant work disincentive effects.

A second causal gap is shared by both stories—a failure to focus specifically on the type of relief that sought to create employment for the unemployed. Public works projects, the employer subsidies and workfare jobs were all efforts to deal with a growing problem of rural unemployment, and they all faced the classical dilemma involved in "make work" projects. When public agencies create employment specifically with the goal of making recipients work in exchange for relief, supervisors usually find it difficult to elicit high levels of work effort because recipients know that they are not working in a real job.[61] On the one side, the threat of being fired does not have the same credibility as in an ordinary employment relation. On the other, there is no particular reward for hard work since there are no prospects for promotion or greater employment security. These difficulties can be somewhat mitigated if recipients can be persuaded that success in this activity will lead to some form of real employment. But when the unemployment problem is structural and intractable, *make work* efforts are likely to be accompanied by declining morale among recipients.

Many of the specific complaints in the historical record about the corrosive effects of the Poor Law actually center on "roundsmen" or others who were engaged in these kind of *make work* activities. The Royal Commission Report quotes Mr. Hennant of Thorney Abbey, Cambridge, who describes his experience with employees hired under the labor rate system:

> If I complain of the little work done, or its being ill done, the reply is, (interlarded with the grossest blackguardism,) "Oh, we don't care a _______; if you don't like it as it is, you may do your work yourself; for, if you discharge us, you must keep us, or have others of the same sort in our stead."[62]

A similar sentiment toward such workers follows from Mr. Stephen Cadby of Westbury, Wiltshire:

> The greatest evil, in my opinion, is the spirit of laziness and insubordination that it creates; if you remonstrate with these men, they abuse or injure, certain, however their conduct, they shall receive their money.[63]

There may be truth to these complaints, but the obvious problem is with structural unemployment that deprived so many of both meaningful work and social dignity. Moreover, there is little reason to credit fears that the attitudes of the unemployed subverted the work discipline of those who were regularly employed. It is much more logical to assume that the sight of the roundsmen would serve to reinforce the regular employees' fear of unemployment. While they might very well sympathize with the plight of the roundsmen, they would not be eager to share that fate. There is little reason to believe that poor productivity on the part of "make work" laborers would subvert the productivity of those who were still gainfully employed.[64]

A third gap in causal logic can be found in the assumption that employers would deliberately lower wages to take advantage of the parish's guaranteed wage supplement. There are several serious problems with this argument. First, we know that farmers competed with each other to attract the most skilled and energetic employees, and there was considerable employment turnover in this period.[65] Hence, even though trade unions were outlawed in this period, there were still limits on what employers could do.[66] Unilateral reductions in wage levels—even if they were balanced by poor relief supplements—seem like a perfect way to signal that a particular employer was seeking only lower quality workers. Moreover, even if all the farmers in a given parish managed to agree on a collective strategy to lower wages, they would still have to worry that the better workers would defect to higher paying farms in nearby parishes. This was a real threat because agricultural workers were often in walking distance of employment opportunities in neighboring parishes so that they could change employers.

To be sure, employers were able to impose unilateral wage cuts in periods of sharp economic downturn, but this was because employers experienced a general and simultaneous reduction in their need for workers and rising unemployment deprived workers of any bargaining power. But in the absence of this kind of generalized downturn, there were significant obstacles to unilateral wage reductions.

Arguments that assume unilateral wage reductions mistakenly assume that the characteristics of one particular type of parish were general across the countryside. The conventional image of eighteenth-century Southern England is a homogeneous arable countryside dominated by the manorial landholdings of wealthy semi-aristocratic commercial gentry. Their farming parishes were termed "close" (today, the more easily accommodated "closed" is acceptable) because residential in-migration was restricted and controlled by a very small number of wealthy landholders who governed simultaneously as local magistrates, supervisors of the poor law officials and employers of agricultural laborers. As a means of reducing the present and future population that would be entitled to poor law relief, this local property-owning elite sometimes made a practice of demolishing cottages that had earlier housed agricultural workers. This had the added benefit of allowing them to shift the burden of poor relief onto those living in neighboring parishes.[67] For their workforce, they relied instead on nonresident workers who commuted from neighboring "open" parishes—so-called because in the absence of dominating landlords, they were open to anyone who could gain settlement there.

The combination of economic and legal power exercised by these parish oligarchs caused *great* hardship for those subjected to this regime. But the existence of closed parishes hardly sustains the Speenhamland story. For one thing, even though employers in closed parishes were able to shift their poor law costs unto others, they also had to worry that lowering of wage levels might mean that vacancies went unfilled. More important, we know now that closed parishes represented a relatively small percentage of all rural parishes and an even smaller percentage of rural population. Among recent analysts, Banks is highly skeptical of the open/closed distinction, while Song—who considers the distinction important—finds that in Oxford in 1831, 25 percent of parishes conform to the full definition of closed with low population density, minimal poor relief outlays and domination by a few large landholders.[68]

Furthermore, most open parishes had a substantial number of "middling sorts"—small farmers, craftsmen, shopkeepers and rural artisans—some of whom rotated from being recipients to being those who paid some of the taxes out of which poor relief was financed.[69] In their capacity both as ratepayers and as potential recipients of poor relief in bad years, it is unlikely that these middling sorts would see any reason to join with larger agricultural employers in a strategy to keep wage levels low by shifting costs on to the parish.

The final gap in causal logic has been the focus in much of this literature on adult male agricultural wages when the reality of rural life was that family income had been for generations pieced together from multiple different sources, including the earnings of wives and children and money made my men outside of their primary work.[70] In fact, when we look at the data on trends of male agricultural wages, the most striking thing is that they move far less dramatically than shifts in the price index. It was possible for farmers to resist more rapid adjustment of wages to price levels precisely because neither employers nor laborers assumed that working-class families could survive on the male workers' wages alone.

This problem of focusing on male wages suggests that when the famous debate between "optimists" and "pessimists" over the impact of the Industrial Revolution on working-class standards of living shifted to the countryside, it often became a dialogue of the deaf.[71] At the beginning of our period—around 1790—most rural laboring families pieced together their household incomes from agricultural wage labor, including that of women and children; from periodic work in rural industries; from their own production on small plots or the parish commons; and from multiple miscellaneous sources of income such as gleaning, fishing, hunting and casual jobs. By the end of our period, structural changes in the economy including enclosures and the decline of rural industries in Southeastern England had undermined some of these important streams of rural working-class income.[72] Hence, as we shall see, even if wages did not follow the trajectory outlined in the standard Speenhamland stories, the standard of living of many rural people suffered significantly in this period.

Reconstructing the Reality of Speenhamland

The empirical complexities and causal gaps are enough to make us suspicious about both of the Speenhamland stories, but a close examination of the historical evidence is even more devastating. First, the very Speenhamland system that allegedly produced significant work disincentive effects turns out to have been far less common than earlier believed. When properly defined as strictly limited to a bread scale that provided different levels of support depending on family size, it becomes apparent that Speenhamland could not have produced the effects that have been attributed to it. Second, there is strong evidence against the decline in rural productivity that both stories have claimed to have been one of the effects of Speenhamland. Finally, when we look more closely at what happened to the rural standard of living across the period from 1790 to 1834, it is very difficult to resist the conclusion that rising poor law outlays were a response to the loss of established forms of family income rather than a cause.

The Limited Pervasiveness and Episodic Nature of the Bread Scale

"Speenhamland" is itself a contested term. Some have used it to cover the full range of relief policies in which able-bodied individuals and their families received assistance, while others have used it more narrowly to refer to the specific use of a bread scale in allocating assistance. Precisely because of the need to differentiate items number 1 and 2 from our list in Table 2.2 from the various forms of employment creation, we will define Speenhamland strictly as the use of a bread scale to determine assistance by the size of the family and the cost of wheat.[73] While the Royal Commission Report takes pains to condemn all forms of assistance to the able bodied, its initial focus is on the allowance system, and it differentiates between parishes that occasionally provide allowances and others where such assistance has been made routine:

> In others it is considered that a certain weekly sum, or more frequently the value of a certain quantity of flour or bread, is to be received by each member of a family. The latter practice has sometimes been matured into a system, forming the law of a whole district, sanctioned and enforced by the magistrates, and promulgated in the form of local statutes, under the name of *Scales*.[74]

This is immediately followed by the printing of a number of representative examples of such scales, including one particularly impressive table from a parish in Essex that provides precise allowances for more than twenty different wheat prices ranging from one to seven shillings per peck. Much of the report's subsequent fury is then directed against this "allowance system."

Yet few of the indictments of Speenhamland hold up against the evidence. The claim that the use of the bread scale starting in 1795 was unprecedented is simply wrong. Wage-price indexing for the able bodied goes back to the 1349–1351 Ordinance and Statute of Labourers and was most elaborately spelled out in the famous 1563 Tudor Statute of Artificers (5 Eliz c 4).[75] Moreover, bread scales were used in years of high wheat prices at other times in the second half of the eighteenth century.[76]

Another misperception is the belief in Speenhamland as a continuous forty year policy with territorial and temporal uniformity. Mark Blaug first called this into question with pathbreaking research that challenged the geographical uniformity of its application.[77] Blaug showed that the use of the bread scale was not geographically universal even in wheat-growing areas. Neuman in a sample of sixteen parishes in Berkshire County itself found none that used the Speenhamland scale in the whole period up to 1834.[78] Poynter, Baugh, Huzel, Lees and King also stress the limited use of the bread scale.[79] Baugh suggests that it was much more common for parishes to respond to years of very high grain prices by using poor relief funds to purchase grain that was then redistributed to households. In others, the farmers sold wheat to their employees at below-market prices or, as had happened in earlier famine years, extra charitable efforts by the rich provided some of the poor with food.[80]

Even so, it is useful to think of the bread scales in certain parishes in 1795 and subsequent famine years as the first Speenhamland episode. In 1795, from 1802 to 1803, and again in 1812, a confluence of factors created the kind of calamity that forced many parishes to take action. In each case, two bad harvests in a row coincided with wartime limitations on agricultural imports from the Continent. The dramatic and severe upward spike in the price of wheat that followed placed this dietary staple well beyond the reach of most agricultural, rural-industrial, and even urban working people. Moreover, as the poor shifted their demand to coarser but cheaper grains, their prices spiraled upwards as well. The consequence was severe distress and the outbreak of food riots in which protesters seized grain from middlemen and bakers.[81] In 1795, these riots occurred against the backdrop of revolutionary events on the other side of the English Channel, so that local elites had strong incentives to respond to the threat of famine and revolutionary disorder. The claims of Speenhamland's critics notwithstanding, the use of the bread scale as a response to famine was a very logical method to these immediate crises without permanently altering wage rates or long-term relief patterns. (It is consistent with Sen's argument that famines are rooted not in absolute shortage but in problems of entitlement to food.[82]) As soon as the price spike passed, most households would no longer be eligible for assistance because the standard wage would purchase a sufficient amount of bread.

There are two striking features of this initial Speenhamland episode. First, there is very little difference in the trend of poor law outlays between those parishes that adopted the bread scale and those that used other means to distribute food to the hungry. Baugh analyzed data from more than seven hundred parishes in Essex, Kent and Sussex and showed that poor relief outlays very closely tracked the fluctuations in the price of wheat (see Figure 2.3).[83] Sokoll extensively analyzed Ardleigh, a parish in Essex that did not adopt the bread scale in this early period, and he shows that its outlays also rose and fell in parallel with the other agricultural parishes in Essex that Baugh examined.[84] Second, as Sokoll emphasizes these patterns undermine one of the core claims of the Royal Commission Report—that allowances have a kind of addictive and self-expanding effect.[85] The Commissioners claimed,

> Profuse allowances excite the most extravagant expectations on the parts of the claimants, who conceive that an inexhaustible fund is devoted to their use, and that they are wronged to the extent of whatever falls short of their claims.[86]

But in this episode, whether parishes used the formal mechanism of the bread scale or other methods of distributing relief, what is so striking is that outlays fell virtually immediately as the price of wheat fell.

The second discrete Speenhamland episode occurred in the years after the end of the Napoleonic Wars and was not related to famine conditions.[87] With the end of the war, there was a period of severe economic contraction marked by a dramatic decline in wheat prices (see Figures 2.1 and 2.2). There was some downward adjustment of wage rates in this period, but this adjustment was much smaller than

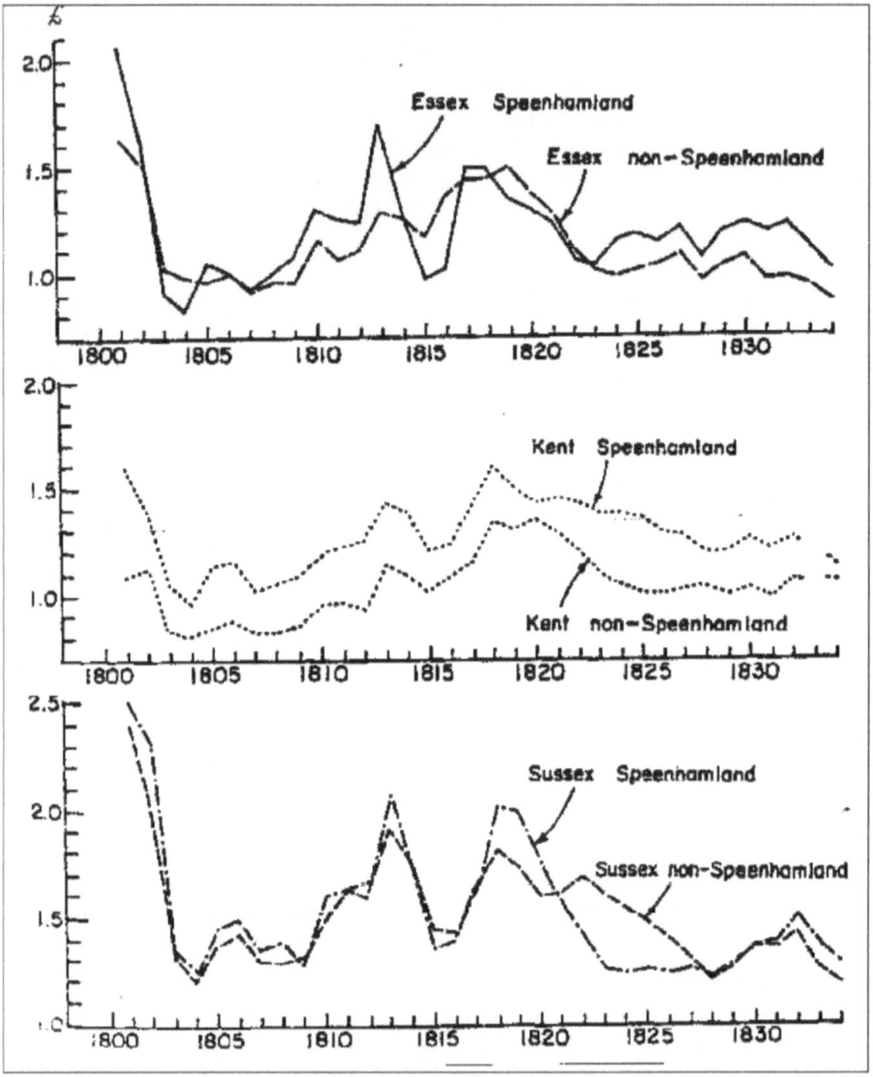

Figure 2.3 Per capita poor relief expenditures in Speenhamland and non Speenhamland counties (agricultural parishes only)

Source: Thomas Sokoll, *Household and Family among the Poor* (Bochum: Universitatsverlag Dr. N. Brockmeyer, 1993), 65.

the sharp fall in prices. As a consequence, some farms simply went out of business and other agricultural employers sharply reduced their employment levels both during the growing season and particularly during the winter months. Assisted by the introduction of threshing machines—the proximate trigger of the famous 1830 Captain Swing riots—that further reduced the demand for labor in the critical months after the harvest, all these processes significantly increased rural unemployment and distress and accounted for the sharp rise in poor relief outlays after 1813.[88]

There is strong consensus in the recent literature that the post-1813 renewal of Speenhamland measures was catalyzed by a shift from inflation to structural transformation in employment opportunities, leading primarily to radically new seasonal unemployment.[89] The period was also marked by the decline of women's farm labor income and an accelerated decline of rural crafts that had provided employment for women.[90]

But while the bread scale returned, its meaning nonetheless shifted in an important way. In the earlier period, employed farm workers would receive an income supplement, contingent on family size and the wheat price, to help them get through the period of high food prices. In the later period, the bread scale was used primarily to determine the amount of relief that seasonally unemployed farm workers were entitled to, given the size of their families.[91] The importance of this seasonal dimension of poor relief is amply supported by data showing that poor relief outlays were often two or three times higher in the winter months than in the spring or summer.[92] As Boyer has argued extensively, there were strong reasons for parish authorities to provide relief in the winter for unemployed farm workers. Employers were constantly worried about the threat of out-migration, which would mean labor shortages during the summer months and severe shortages at harvest time.[93] Without such relief, levels of out-migration whether to the North or to urban areas would have been much higher.

This second phase of Speenhamland is exemplified by events in Ardleigh—the Essex parish that has been closely studied by Sokoll. The parish had no earlier history of the use of the bread scale, but a formal bread scale was instituted in September of 1823 followed in 1831 by another Speenhamland statute.[94] This late adoption of the bread scale by parish officials is especially notable because it occurs after decades in which Speenhamland had been denounced for its horrible consequences. This suggests that there was widespread skepticism at the time with the anti-Speenhamland rhetoric and that local officials were undeterred by the rhetoric because they were simply trying to find the best practical way to deal with the crisis presented by high levels of unemployment.

Trends in Productivity and Wages

The standard Speenhamland stories insist that rural productivity collapsed in the face of the corrosive impact of the Poor Law. The available data provide no support for this claim. Total wheat production increased substantially between 1790 and 1834; Fairlie's estimate shows that wheat production fluctuated sharply between 1791 and 1811 and then more than doubled by 1834.[95] This increase was facilitated by an expansion in acreage; Holderness estimates that acreage increased from about 2.45 million acres in 1801 to 3.4 million in 1836—an increase of almost 39 percent.[96] But it wasn't only increased acreage; Holderness suggests that yields per acre might have risen by 33 percent between 1790 and 1830;[97] Overton suggests that the increase was 15 percent between 1801 and 1831.[98]

The official decennial census of population did not begin until 1801. Even then, the early censuses did not ask about employment, so estimates of the size of the agricultural labor force between 1801 and 1831 in the Southeastern counties are little more than guesswork. Nonetheless, the labor force seems to have grown substantially more slowly than either wheat output or acreage. Wrigley estimates that for the whole country, the number of adult males employed in agriculture increased from 910,000 in 1811 to 981,000 in 1831—growth of only about 8 percent.[99] Since the wheat-growing counties were home to a large portion of English farm workers, it is unlikely that labor force growth in these counties was substantially faster than national growth. Given the doubling of wheat output between 1811 and 1834, there can be little doubt that output per worker rose in this period. Overton suggests quite substantial increases in labor productivity in agriculture across the whole period from 1800 to 1850.[100] Moreover, even Clark who has been most outspoken in criticizing the idea of a productivity-increasing "agricultural revolution" in the first three decades of the nineteenth century acknowledges that labor productivity was either constant or increasing slightly in this period.[101]

Since the available data on productivity in the wheat-growing regions are sketchy at best, a number of analysts have supported the Speenhamland thesis by arguing that agricultural wages fell sharply in this period and that it is reasonable to see wages as a reliable proxy for productivity. Influential historians writing in the first half of the century such as Hammond and Hammond, Webb and Webb, and Mantoux have insisted that wage levels fell dramatically during the Speenhamland period.[102] However, most of the available data series that we have that trace rural wages in this period reveal the same basic pattern. Rural weekly wages for men rise from 1790 through to the end of the Napoleonic Wars, there is then a sharp decline during the agricultural depression, followed by a recovery and a slightly rising trend from the early 1820s through to 1834. The first systematic series on agricultural wages was developed by Bowley at the end of the nineteenth century; it rises from 53 in 1790 to 105 in 1812, then falls to 72 in 1824 before rising to 79 in 1834 (see Figure 2.4).[103] Eccleston found a similar pattern in five Midland counties, and Richardson reports a parallel pattern in wages on a large farm in Essex.[104] More recently, Clark has developed a series for weekly winter wages in the Southeastern counties based on various surviving estate records, including those used by Richardson, and he finds the same basic pattern (see Figure 2.5).[105] The respected historian K.D.M. Snell calculated trends in annual wages for farm servants in a number of Southern counties from a unique data set drawn from settlement examinations. For most counties or groups of counties, Snell's findings move in the same pattern as weekly wages cited elsewhere in the literature, but in some counties he did find that wages fall steadily from the 1820s onward.[106]

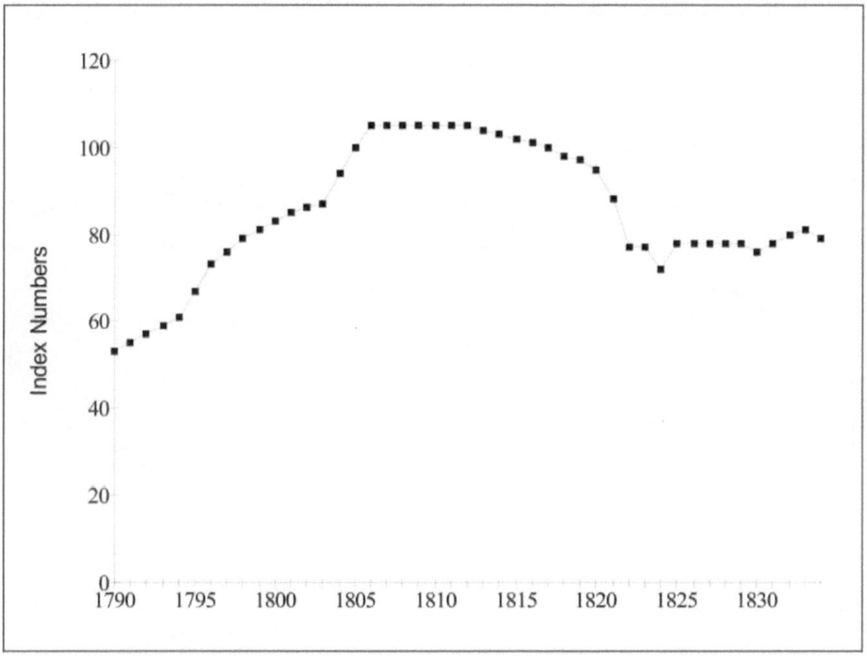

Figure 2.4 Agricultural wages 1790–1834

Source: This is Bowley's series taken from B.R. Mitchell and Phyllis Deane, *Abstract of British Historical Statistics* (Cambridge: Cambridge University Press, 1962), 348–349.

Note: The series is for all of England, but his reported data for specific counties in the Southeast follow the same general pattern.

Interpreting these patterns of nominal wages has been extremely difficult because of the dramatic price changes that occur across this period. There is no question that in the famine years, such as 1795, 1802–03 and 1812, the price-spike in grains led to dramatic, albeit temporary, declines in the real wage. Nevertheless, the view advanced by Prothero that wage levels during the Napoleon War doubled while prices actually tripled is no longer accepted.[107] When one brackets the famine years, real agricultural wages clearly rose between 1790 and 1815. Second, since the post-Napoleonic period was one of steadily falling price levels, the small recovery in nominal wages between 1824 and 1834 reported by Bowley understates the gain in real wages in this period.

In the end, we come to the conclusion that the question that preoccupied so many analysts—were agricultural real wages higher or lower in 1834 than they were in 1795—is the wrong question. There are three different reasons. First, the

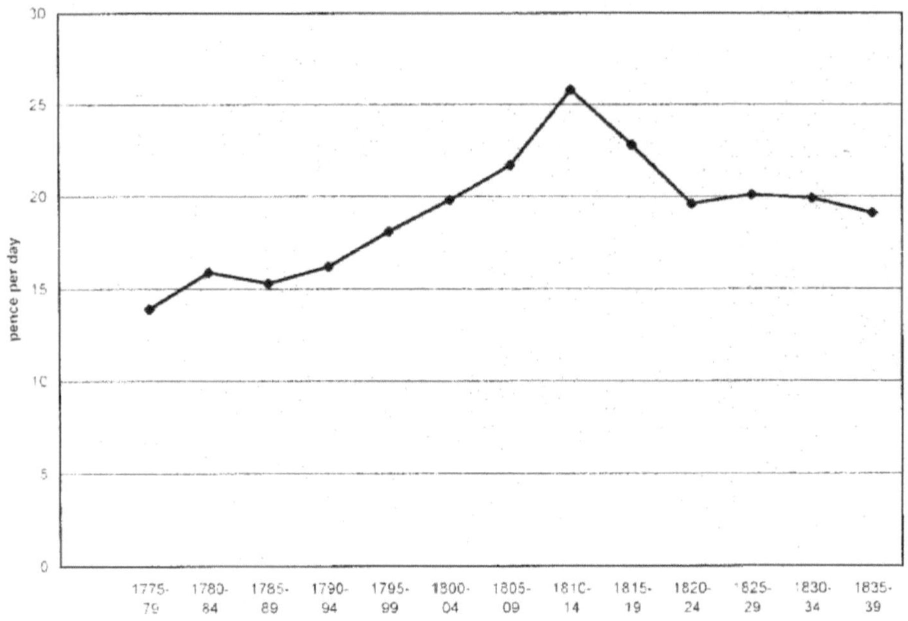

Figure 2.5 Winter wages of Southeastern farm workers

Source: The chart was created from a table in an unpublished version of Greg Clark, "Farm Wages and Living Standards in the Industrial Revolution: England, 1670–1850" (University of California, Davis), 17.

Note: The series is based on between seven and twelve separate wage observations per year.

reality was that real wages—with the critical exceptions of the famine years—first rose, then fell, then rose. Second, when rural workers are compared to the inhabitants of urban England who had greatly expanded access to a wide variety of manufactured goods between 1790 and 1834, there can be no doubt that their relative standard of living declined sharply during this period of industrial transformation. Finally, translating weekly wages into a standard of living depends critically on the number of weeks of employment available per year, and we know that seasonal unemployment rose dramatically in the countryside after the Napoleonic Wars.[108]

Instead of focusing on the wrong question, then, it is the Royal Commissioners' claim that Speenhamland policies damaged rural productivity that must be scrutinized. The argument is already undermined by evidence that the bread scale was not pervasive or continuous. It is further weakened by both the data on agricultural output and the trends in weekly wages that provide no support for a claimed collapse of rural productivity.

Household Income and the Poor Law

It is precisely because of the variety and variability of the income sources on which families relied that it is extremely difficult to identify any clear trends in average family income across this period. The best estimates that we have come from surviving family budget data that have been compiled by Horrell and Humphries.[109] They indicate that for the low-wage agricultural sector—that tends to overlap with the Southeastern counties—there was a small upward trend in real household income between 1790 and 1834. But this average figure conceals much variation, and poor relief outlays represented a rising component of family income, rising from a negligible level in the early period to eight percent of family income for the 1821–1840 period. In this context, poor relief can best be understood as a mechanism to sustain family income in a context in which it had become increasingly difficult for the rural poor—through no fault of their own—to piece together an adequate income.

The increasing importance of poor relief can be seen as compensating for three broad trends. First, rural craft industries suffered a dramatic decline in the southeastern counties in the period after 1790.[110] Some of this decline had been going on for centuries, but the pace of decline was clearly accelerated by the rapid rise of industrial production in the northern part of the country.[111] This meant that opportunities for family members, especially women, to supplement income with labor on rural craft production simply disappeared in many places. Second, enclosures and consolidations of holdings meant that many rural laboring families lost the capacity to earn additional income by keeping farm animals or maintaining a vegetable garden. In fact, during the Speenhamland period, a major alternative to the poor law that was widely debated was to provide laboring families with allotments—small pieces of land—that would make self-provisioning a real alternative to poor relief in hard times.[112] But while the idea was widely discussed, it was only implemented in a few localities. Third, particularly after 1813, the demand for farm labor diminishes, so that there are reduced earning opportunities for wives and children while men experienced longer periods of unemployment in the winter and early spring months.[113] Reay, for example, finds that in one Kent Parish, 60 percent of farm laborers and small farmers required poor relief during the winter months in the 1830s.[114]

In short, the family budget data provide a different angle of vision that further undermines the conventional Speenhamland stories. Instead of bread scales undermining work effort, we get a picture of a rural population facing broad structural forces that undermine their capacities for self-support. In this context it is difficult to see increasing poor relief as anything but a partial remedy to problems outside the control of the rural poor.

A Revisionist Narrative

The strength of the evidence against the standard Speenhamland stories raises the obvious question of why the past forty years of historical scholarship have not yet had any significant impact on social policy discussions. There are undoubtedly multiple reasons but two are especially compelling. The first is that the Malthusian foundation on which the perversity thesis rests followed the logic of Newtonian physics. Just as Newton explained the causal logic behind the fall of an apple not by the simple appearance of things but by explicating the real, albeit hidden, law of gravity, so Malthus explained the perverse consequences of poor relief not by citing data but by invoking a hidden and constant causal logic. By insisting that there was a deeper truth than that of empirical "appearances," Malthus effectively insulated his argument from empirical disconfirmation.[115] This is the reason the perversity thesis has been so effortlessly recycled to analyze poverty populations who live under radically different conditions than those of the Speenhamland epoch. The second is that since the revisionist work has been produced by a theoretically diverse group of scholars, the findings have not been organized into a coherent alternative account. As of yet, a counter-perversity thesis approach to Speenhamland lacks a compelling narrative structure.

It seems useful, therefore, to suggest an alternative narrative that would place these new historical findings into a framework that social policy analysts might find compelling. This alternative narrative centers on the problems of legitimating the new science of political economy that emerged out of the fundamental contributions of Malthus and Ricardo. Malthus and Ricardo famously disagreed on some key theoretical and policy issues, and later thinkers, such as Marx and Keynes, explicitly embraced one while denigrating the other.[116] But there was also much agreement between the two figures, and ultimately it was Malthus' critique of the Poor Law that helped divert attention from the negative consequences of Ricardo's first great policy success—the decision at the end of the Napoleonic Wars to restore the pound's parity to its prewar level. In short, the construction of the Speenhamland story was intimately connected to Britain's embrace of the gold standard.

The Return to Gold

As described earlier, the second Speenhamland episode resulted from the severe agricultural downturn at the end of the Napoleonic Wars that led to significant increases in Poor Law outlays. But the most important fact is that the agricultural downturn was not just a brief postwar interlude; rather it became a long-term reality continuing through and beyond the passage of the New Poor Law in 1834.[117] But the rural distress was itself closely linked to policy decisions, especially England's decision to restore the prewar value of the pound in relation to gold. What happened in this period is remarkably similar to the decision by England to restore the prewar relationship between the pound and gold after World War I. Keynes had famously denounced this policy as deeply misguided and insisted that it would produce a period of intense deflationary pressure.[118] Less recognized is that Keynes's prescience derived from his knowledge of economic history and the history of economic theory. He realized that English statesmen in the post–World War I era were simply repeating the mistake that had been made—at the urging of David Ricardo—a century earlier.[119] Ricardo argued forcefully for restoring the pound to its prewar parity from his first publication in 1810 of a pamphlet called "The High Price of Bullion."[120] He insisted that the wartime inflation was a direct consequence of the suspension of gold convertibility and that the only way to return prices to their proper level was to restore the prewar parity. His views and those of other bullionists were endorsed by the Parliamentary Bullion Committee in its 1810 Report. By 1816, Ricardo had retired from business, and he reasserted his advocacy of a return to gold with a pamphlet titled "A Proposal for an Economical and Secure Currency." With the publication of Ricardo's *Principles* in 1817 and his entrance to Parliament in 1819, his influence on public policy became greater and was central to the government's decision to restore gold to its prewar parity in 1819.[121]

This restoration, however, occurred against the backdrop of a severe rural crisis that had begun right at the end of the Napoleonic Wars. The fall in wheat prices in 1813 and 1814 produced a massive collapse of rural banks that had failed to hold on to any reserves. Between 1814 and 1816, 240 rural banks stopped payments leading to a destruction of wealth and a disappearance of credit.[122] The result was a dramatic increase in unemployment as both farmers and other employers were forced to cut back both investment and the size of their labor force. But as the deflation took hold, there was an ironic consequence—the value of the pound started to rise so that the goal of restoring the prewar parity appeared substantially closer. The response of the authorities in 1816 and 1817, therefore, was to prepare for the resumption of gold payments at the old parity, and in May of 1819, Parliament passed legislation to restore gold payments within two years.[123] While there is intense controversy over the specific policies that the government and Bank followed in restoring gold, there is widespread consensus that the sustained effort to return to the prewar parity had a profoundly deflationary impact. On the one side, the government was precluded from pursuing the kind of countercyclical policies that could have revived the rural economy. On the other, the sustained tight money policies greatly restricted the availability of the credit that farmers desperately needed.

Moreover, the deflationary pressures did not end with the success of restoration; the gold standard simply made the pressures on the rural economy permanent. Wheat prices continued to fall until 1829, and after that, prices were stabilized at a very low level. The failure of rural banks was also continuous across the whole period from 1815 to 1830.[124] This context of falling prices and limited credit forced farmers to reduce labor costs and that, in turn, produced chronic rural unemployment and increased use of poor relief. The ongoing pressure of low wheat prices forced the more successful farmers to put increasing resources into labor-saving technology such as the threshing machine. Since hand threshing of wheat could represent as much as one-quarter of the whole year's quantity of farm work, mechanization had a huge impact on the rural demand for labor in the winter months.[125] Triggered by these high rates of unemployment, the machine smashing in the Captain Swing riots of 1830 exploded.[126] This outbreak of rural disorder played a key role in undermining elite support for the Old Poor Law.[127]

Absent Ricardo's eloquent pleas for a restoration of the prewar parity, policy makers might well have chosen a less deflationary set of policies. Had the rural economy not suffered the additional shock of the deflationary pressures of gold, the wheat-growing areas might have experienced a recovery and an earlier rebound of wheat prices. Without the ideological commitment to laissez-faire policies, moreover, the government might have embraced policies that helped to cushion the economy in periods of contracting demand, including provisions for a steady flow of credit to farmers.[128] Under any set of policies, there would ultimately have been a problem of a rural labor surplus that could only be solved by more rapid rates of out-migration. But the Ricardian policies dramatically intensified the problem—so that this massive readjustment had to be handled over twenty years rather than forty. As Polanyi eloquently argues, government policies can help protect ordinary people simply by slowing the rate of change, but the Ricardian policies did exactly the opposite; they vastly accelerated the problem of rural surplus population.[129]

Malthus, Parliament, and the Road to the New Poor Law

The New Poor Law of 1834 officially placed the blame for the rural distress not on macroeconomic policies but on the Speenhamland system that had allegedly demoralized and degraded the rural poor. But the Royal Commissioner's "solution" did not emerge automatically out of the reality of rural distress. The solution had to be politically and rhetorically constructed, and this construction depended, in turn, on two prior conditions—dramatic changes both in elite opinion and in the political system. In short, the path from Malthus's *Essay* to the Royal Commission Report was hardly simple.

Ironically, the influence of Malthus's call for abolition of the Poor Law probably reached its high point in the period between 1815 and 1818—even before the return to gold. Repeated editions of the *Essay*, along with reprints of Townsend's pamphlet, were extraordinarily influential in shaping elite views. Poynter suggests the following:

> it was in these years that fundamental disapproval of a legal provision for the poor (and especially for the able-bodied) became sufficiently widespread to be regarded as orthodox, while defence of the Poor Law became, if not quite heretical, at least old-fashioned.[130]

The influence was reflected in a series of Parliamentary Reports, culminating with reports in 1817 and 1819 that endorsed the call for abolition of the Poor Laws.[131]

Yet this intellectual influence did not translate into legislation in this period because there was no consensus within the Parliament on the right course of action. In addition to the usual conflicts among factions, some in Parliament were reluctant to abolish the Poor Laws out of the same fear of revolution that had produced the original Speenhamland policy in 1795. Rural unrest was acute in this period, and the unreformed Parliament had good reason to fear that abolition might generate broad protests that would bring together rural laborers, urban workers and middle-class radicals.[132]

After 1820, the political strength of the abolitionist position seems to have weakened, but the parliamentary impasse continued. While there were initiatives at the local level to "reform" poor relief to limit outlays, there were still wide disagreements about what to do about rural distress.[133] The situation was complicated by further economic downturns between 1819 and 1822 and again in 1825 to 1826. The continuing economic strains generated intense criticisms of the return to gold and calls for aggressive government action to revive the economy. An explicitly anti-Ricardian political economy emerged in this period that drew some of its key inspiration from Malthus's rejection of the view that supply creates its own demand.[134] These underconsumptionist thinkers directly challenged the government's laissez-faire policies and argued for cheaper money, an expansion of rural credit and programs of public works to increase employment and demand. But these arguments had little impact on government policies.

The Captain Swing riots in 1830 gave new urgency to Poor Law debates. Yet the parliamentary stalemate was not broken until the Whigs came to power and passed the Reform Act of 1832 that expanded the suffrage and gave the middle class effective representation.[135] When the Reform Act was still pending, the Whig government appointed the Royal Commission to investigate the Poor Laws. While all of the Commissioners had been deeply influenced by Malthus's arguments, they rejected his abolitionist policy solution. Their critical rhetorical move was to adopt the language of reform and to argue that "reformed parishes"—those that replaced outdoor relief with workhouses for the poor—had effectively eliminated all of the negative consequences of Speenhamland. In short, by narrowing Malthus's critique of the Poor Law to focus on the "allowance system" and by proposing concrete reforms rather than abolition, the Royal Commission was able to generate a strong parliamentary consensus that led to passage of the New Poor Law.[136]

What the Royal Commissioners succeeded in doing was to mobilize and modify Malthus's arguments to rescue political economy from its responsibility for the plight of the rural poor. By effectively blaming the victims for the macroeconomic policy mistakes that had intensified rural poverty, they turned a potential disaster into a policy triumph. In doing this, they made an enormous contribution to the legitimization of political economy. The severity of the agricultural downturn might well have undermined the whole belief in laissez-faire and self-regulating markets. Classical political economy was in its infancy in this period, and its ultimate maturation and worldwide influence were hardly a foregone conclusion.[137] While it is difficult to think through such a radical counterfactual, an alternative and more pragmatic strand of economic thinking might have become institutionalized in the place of the Ricardo tradition. Instead, the ultimate policy triumph of the New Poor Law diverted attention from the new science's first major policy failure and solidified the electorate's faith in market self-regulation.

In sum, the Speenhamland myth was created in the years of agricultural downturn to divert blame for a deep agricultural crisis away from government policy and toward the rural poor who were the major victims of the economic downturn. Since the decision taken by the government on Ricardo's advice to restore the prewar parity of the pound intensified the rural depression, the mythology worked to cover up the first major policy failure of the new science of political economy. The importance of this myth becomes apparent in thinking about the diffusion of economic liberalism during the course of the nineteenth century. England's ability to persuade other countries to adopt free trade, the gold standard and the belief in market self-regulation depended on its ability to present itself as a great economic success story.[138] Were other societies aware that the price that England had paid for economic liberalism was severe economic hardship in the countryside in the 1820s, 1830s and 1840s, both the English model and its policy ideas would have been considerably tarnished. By shifting the blame for the problems on to Speenhamland and all its pernicious evils, the economic liberals successfully reframed the agricultural downturn into a problem of individual morality and an enduring parable of the dangers of government "interference" with the market.

Conclusion

The major lesson that we learn from this study is a renewed appreciation for the persuasive power of the metaphors of nature, natural laws and the "science" of political economy to influence how history is experienced and why certain explanations for distress triumph over others. The critical point is that the Malthusian morality tale about the disastrous consequences of poor relief was produced before any evidence had been gathered and too early for the Speenhamland decision to have produced its alleged consequences. In Malthus's 1798 *Essay on Population*, all the elements of the story line are already in place. Poor relief, by ending the scarcity that is endemic to nature in its untouched state, destroys both the incentive to work in order to eat as well as those to control childbirth and thus leads to a precipitous decline in productivity and a rapid growth of the pauper populations. The only way to return the poor to their natural state of self-discipline in both work and procreation is to abolish the system of poor relief and return to the natural state of scarcity and the human discipline it teaches.

In subsequent years, as political economy gained the privileged status of a recognized science, this story was repeated so frequently by political economists, the clergy and various parliamentary commissions that it gained the quality of truth. By the time the Royal Commission was created, a newly reformed Parliament included a significant number of factory owners determined to create an available, cheap and "free" labor force; the thesis was elevated to an absolute Scientific Truth based entirely on the laws of nature. Despite volumes of literature devoted to the subject, it took the next 130 years before there was a serious scholarly effort to show the shallowness and distortions of that document. But even after years of detailed scholarly work had effectively debunked the Speenhamland legend, contemporary social welfare theorists were successful in mobilizing precisely the same story line to discredit current welfare institutions. Charles Murray's influential 1984 book, *Losing Ground*, simply updated the old story to argue that an excessively generous welfare system in the United States had undermined both the work ethic and sexual restraint among the poor.[139] Moreover, the work of Murray and like-minded scholars played a critical role in creating the climate for the 1996 Personal Responsibility and Work Opportunity Reconciliation Act that eliminated the entitlement of poor children to government assistance.

Our review of the historical evidence suggests two conclusions. First, the perversity story lacks empirical support. The experience of the Speenhamland period is that poor relief did not hurt the poor; it helped to protect them from structural changes in the economy that had made it far more difficult for people to earn a living. Second, the doubts that have hung over guaranteed income proposals since Speenhamland lack historical foundation. While it is theoretically possible that a floor under incomes would be transformed into a ceiling, this certainly did not happen during the Speenhamland period, and there is little evidence that it has ever happened. In fact, there are good reasons this theoretical possibility is rarely likely to occur in practice. In contrast to Speenhamland, most contemporary income guarantee proposals, including variants on the negative income tax, do not require that recipients work. Hence, when employees are faced with an employer who is progressively lowering wages to take advantage of the income guarantee program, they are likely to quit and look for alternative employment since they know that they will be protected by the income guarantee from economic hardship during their period of unemployment. Moreover, under most circumstances, employers avoid unilateral reductions in wages precisely out of the fear that they would drive away existing employees and make it harder to fill vacancies. It seems only logical that if an income guarantee were in place, employers would become even more cautious about imposing wage cuts.

Welfare and income maintenance policies need to be debated free of the mythologies that were created two hundred years ago. Above all, we need to move beyond the naturalized Malthusian accounts that see the behavior of the poor as always determined by their biological drives. Discarding the naturalizing blinders and examining the actual situation of the rural poor during the Speenhamland period, we are forced to recognize the central role of larger economic processes such as the severe agricultural deflation and the shift of industry to the North in explaining mounting rural poverty. Relief payments actually provided some protection against these structural pressures. The contemporary lesson is obvious; it is time to reject the ideological claim that the best way to fight poverty is by imposing increasingly stringent conditions on ever shrinking transfer payments to poor households.

Notes

* The ordering of names indicates equal responsibility. Valuable research assistance has been provided by Jane Rafferty, Michael Flota, Rene Poitevin, Dan Schinnerer and Dan Samson. Colleagues at the University of California, Davis—Greg Clark, Norma Landau and Peter Lindert—have been very generous in providing data, references and feedback on earlier formulations of these arguments. Karl Widerquist provided references on the recent Canadian case. Frances Fox Piven provided valuable feedback on earlier drafts. An earlier version was presented to the U.S. Basic Income Group in New York City in November 2000 and to the First Congress of the U.S. Basic Income Guarantee Network in March 2002. Block received support for this research from the Institute for Labor and Employment at the University of California. Somers would like to thank the Institute for Research on Women and Gender, University of Michigan; the Agrarian Studies Program, Yale University; and the George and Eliza Howard Foundation, Brown University for their generous support in making this research possible. An earlier version of this chapter was published in *Politics & Society*, 31: no. 2 (June 2003).

1 Polanyi (2001) chs. 6–7.
2 Moynihan (1973) 179.
3 Ibid., 179–180.
4 Chwialkowska (2000).
5 Recent writings in favor of the basic income idea include Van Parijs (1992), Block and Manza (1997), and some of the pieces included in Cohen and Rogers (2001).
6 Bluestone and Ghilarducci (1996), Howell (1997), Lement (1997).
7 Hirschman (1991). See also Reekie (1998), Persky (1997).
8 Anderson (1978).
9 Ibid., 92–98.
10 Himmelfarb (1984).
11 Himmelfarb (1994, 1995).
12 Olasky (1992).
13 Weaver (2000).
14 Greenberg (2002).
15 Key works include Blaug (1963, 1964), Baugh (1975), Marshall (1985), Snell (1985), Huzel (1989), Boyer (1990), Sokoll (1993), Lees (1998), King (2000).
16 To be sure, this literature does not speak with one voice, and many important issues of historical interpretation continue to be debated.
17 Polanyi (2001) ch. 10, Procacci (1991).
18 Polanyi (2001) ch. 7, Webb and Webb (1927) 168–189.
19 Among the most important reports were Parliamentary Papers (1817, 1819 and 1824). The Royal Commission Report was published as His Majesty's Commissioners (1834).
20 Blaug (1963, 1964), Marshall (1985), Finer (1972), Cowherd (1977) chs. ix–x, Henriques (1979) ch. 2.
21 In addition to the citations in the previous note, see Brundage (1978), Boyer (1990) 60–65.
22 Townsend (1971).
23 Cited in Polanyi (2001) 118.
24 Ibid., 119.
25 Malthus (1985). In the second edition, published in 1803, Malthus did acknowledge Townsend's pamphlet; Malthus (1992).
26 Malthus (1985) 70.

[27] In this period, couples, on average, married in their late twenties. See Wrigley and Schofield (1997).

[28] Townsend (1971) 17.

[29] Engels (1958).

[30] Marx (1930) 662.

[31] Rose (1970), Edsall (1970), Knott (1986), Driver (1993) ch. 7.

[32] Hasbach (1920), Hammond and Hammond (1966), Polanyi (2001), Hobsbawm and Rude (1968). Also relevant is the work of the important English institutional historian who emphasized the negative consequences of Speenhamland, see Cunningham (1922) 718–723. The book was originally published in the 1880s.

[33] See the references in note 32 and Hill (1929), Driver (1956), Ward (1962).

[34] McCulloch (1938) 290.

[35] Cited in Webb and Webb (1963) 84.

[36] Ibid., 83.

[37] Ibid., 86–88.

[38] Ibid., 54.

[39] Blaug (1963, 1964).

[40] Polanyi (2001) 298–299. On Polanyi in Vienna, see Polanyi-Levitt and Mendell (1987) and Congdon (1990) 78–84.

[41] For more on Polanyi's analysis of Speenhamland, see Block (2003).

[42] Polanyi (2001) 85.

[43] Ibid., 103.

[44] Cole (1943).

[45] Polanyi did try to respond to some of Cole's criticisms in the additional note on "Poor Law and the Organization of Labor" that he appended to the 1945 edition of the book. But while Polanyi added some qualifications to his argument, he did not change its main thrust.

[46] Solar (1995), Lindert (1998).

[47] Marshall (1926), Webb and Webb (1927).

[48] Thomson (1991).

[49] Lindert (1998) 114.

[50] Sokoll (1993), King (2000), Huzel (1989).

[51] Williams (1981).

[52] To be sure, in those years in which wheat prices were unusually high, poor law outlays would rise across the whole country since parishes had to adjust the income of dependent populations. On declining rural industry, see Kreidte, Medick and Schlumbohm (1981).

[53] On London, see Sharpe (1997), Steinberg (1999). On the role of trade unions and secret societies in providing assistance, see Leeson (1980).

[54] Somers (1993), King (2000).

[55] Berg (1994), Valenze (1995), Hudson (1989).

[56] Feinstein (1998), Clark (2001).

[57] Snell (1985), Taylor (1989), Hitchcock, King and Sharpe (1997), Valenze (1995).

[58] Boyer (1990) 86–93.

[59] Ibid.

[60] Sharpe (1997) 99–103.

[61] Webb and Webb (1927) 221–240, provides the classic account of the failure of numerous efforts to make profits from the labor of those who were in need of relief.

[62] His Majesty's Royal Commissioners (1834) 223.

[63] Ibid.

64 On the other hand, high rates of unemployment certainly played a role in radicalizing employed farm workers, such as those who participated in the Captain Swing rebellion in 1830. One of the main targets of the rebels was the threshing machines that increased seasonal unemployment. See Hobsbawm and Rude (1968), Charlesworth (1983) ch. 6, Reay (1990) , Wells (2000).

65 Kussmaul (1981), Snell (1985).

66 Rule (1979), Rule and Wells (1988), Dobson (1980).

67 Holderness (1972), Mills (1980). See also the discussion on 601 in Somers (1993).

68 Banks (1988), Song (1998).

69 Boyer (1990), Sokoll (1993).

70 Kumar (1988), Horrell and Humphries (1995), Reay (1996) 89–117, Berg (1994), Valenze (1995).

71 On the standard of living debate, see Taylor (1975).

72 Snell (1985) ch. 1; Reay (1996).

73 Our definition of Speenhamland also excludes child allowances. The justification is simply practical—to make the story more manageable. Child allowances represented only a small proportion of poor law outlays and played little role in arguments about work disincentives. Moreover, this article will not address the issue of child allowances as a possible encouragement to excess fertility.

74 His Majesty's Royal Commissioners (1834) 21.

75 Tawney and Power (1924) 338–350, Tawney (1938), Lipson (1943), Somers (1993, 1994).

76 Henriques (1979), Neuman (1982).

77 Blaug (1963, 1964).

78 Neuman (1982) 160.

79 Poynter (1969) 79–85, Huzel (1989), Baugh (1975), Lees (1998), King (2000).

80 Baugh (1975) 59.

81 The best account of these famine years is Wells (1988); see also Tilly (1995) 228–232.

82 Sen (1982).

83 Baugh (1975).

84 Sokoll (1993) 138.

85 Ibid., 142.

86 His Majesty's Royal Commissioners (1834) 49.

87 Napoleon abdicated for the first time in early April 1814, and then returned from Elba for three more months of war in 1815. Hence, in annual series, 1813 generally marks the peak of the wartime boom since it was the last full year of war.

88 On the threshing machine, see Fox (1978). On Swing, see Hobsbawm and Rude (1968). On the rise in unemployment, see Gash (1935), Snell (1985), Boyer (1990).

89 Note, for example, that Snell (1985) and Boyer (1990) agree on this point.

90 Berg (1994), Valenze (1995), Snell (1985).

91 With this change in meaning, there was also a change in generosity. The post-1813 scales, even holding the price of wheat constant, were considerably less generous than those used in famine years. But the famine payments established a floor for full-time employed workers, while the post-1813 payments were going to households of unemployed workers. For a somewhat misleading comparison of the scales, see Hammond and Hammond (1966) 181–182.

92 Emmison (1933), Snell (1985), Boyer (1990), Reay (1996).

93 Boyer (1990) 31–43.

94 Sokoll (1993) 140.

95 These estimates are cited on 1054–1055 in John (1989).
96 Holderness (1989).
97 Ibid., 140.
98 Overton (1989). Eric Jones (1974) estimated that yields per acre rose 16 percent between 1815–1819 and 1832–1836.
99 Wrigley (1986).
100 Overton (1996).
101 Clark (1991, 1999).
102 Hammond and Hammond (1966) ch. 7, Webb and Webb (1927) 422–423, Mantoux (1962) 431–439.
103 Bowley's figures are cited in Mitchell and Deane (1962) 348–349.
104 Eccleston (1986), Richardson (1991).
105 Clark (2001).
106 Snell (1985) 412–417.
107 Prothero (1912) 313–315.
108 Snell (1985), Boyer (1990).
109 Horrell and Humphries (1995).
110 Snell (1985), Allen (1992) 246–248, Boyer (1990) 38–42.
111 Hudson (1986, 1989, 1992), Kriedte, Medick and Schlumbohm (1981).
112 Barnett (1967).
113 Drawing on settlement hearings, Snell (1985) argues that there was a significant decline in women's employment opportunities in the wheat-growing regions from the 1790s onward. However, Horrell and Humphries (1995) use family budget data to show women and children providing an increasing share of family income in the later period.
114 Reay (1996) 129; see also Emmison (1933).
115 Malthus's distrust of appearances is indicated by the following passage: If I saw a glass of wine repeatedly presented to a man, and he took no notice of it, I should be apt to think that he was blind or uncivil. A juster philosophy might teach me rather to think that my eyes deceived me and that the offer was not really what I conceived it to be. (Malthus (1985) 70).
116 Marx was bitterly critical of Malthus, but he generally treated Ricardo with respect as an intellectually honest defender of the interests of the bourgeoisie. For Marx's writings on Malthus, see Meek (1954). Keynes reversed this ordering and praised Malthus' underconsumptionist views while criticizing Ricardo's confidence that markets would reach equilibrium. See his essay in Keynes (1951 [1933]).
117 Gash (1935), Fussell and Compton (1939), Snell (1985) ch. 1.
118 Keynes (1932 [1925]).
119 In an essay first published in 1923, Keynes was explicit about the parallel when speaking of his contemporaries who favored an immediate return to the prewar parity: "This view is in accordance with that expressed by Ricardo in analogous circumstances a hundred years ago." Keynes (1932 [1925]) 194. Polanyi also recognized the parallels between the two postwar periods in a short unpublished piece titled "1820 vs. 1920" that is in the Karl Polanyi Archive, but he chose not to emphasize this parallel in *The Great Transformation.*
120 Redman (1997) 276.
121 Viner (1965), Fetter (1965), Gordon (1976), Hilton (1977).
122 McCulloch (1938 [1845]) 175, Fussell and Compton (1939).
123 Viner (1965 [1937]) 172.
124 Fussell and Compton (1939) 186–189.
125 Gash (1935).

126 Hobsbawm and Rude (1968), Tilly (1995) 315–321.
127 Dunkley (1982), Mandler (1987).
128 Hilton (1977) 69–97, Gordon (1976) 71–79.
129 Polanyi (2001) 39.
130 Poynter (1969) 224.
131 For the consolidation of laissez-faire ideas in this period, see Mandler (1990), Waterman (1991). See, also, Poynter (1969), Brundage (1978).
132 Poynter (1969) ch. 6.
133 Poynter (1969) ch. 8, Hilton (1977) 98–169.
134 See Link (1959), Hilton (1977) 77–79. Malthus supported public works projects in this period, Hollander (1997) 624.
135 Poynter (1969) ch. 9, Brundage (1978), Dunkley (1982).
136 The actual impact of the New Poor Law is still intensely debated. For recent discussions, see Driver (1993), King (2000).
137 For the precariousness of Ricardian orthodoxy in this period, see Checkland (1949). On the intensity of the anti-Ricardo backlash after the 1825 crash, see Gordon (1979) ch. 4.
138 Semmel (1970), Kindleberger (1975).
139 Murray (1984).

References

Allen, R.C. (1992) *Enclosure and the Yeoman,* (Oxford: Clarendon).

Anderson, M. (1978) *Welfare: The Political Economy of Welfare Reform in the United States,* (Stanford: Hoover Institution Press).

Banks, S. (1988) "Nineteenth-Century Scandal or Twentieth Century Model? A New Look at 'Open' and 'Close' Parishes," *Economic History Review*, XLI (1): 51–73.

Barnett, D.C. (1967) "Allotments and the Problem of Rural Poverty, 1740–1840," in *Land, Labour and Population in the Industrial Revolution*, E.L. Jones and G.E. Mingay (eds.), (London: Edward Arnold).

Baugh, D.A. (1975) "The Cost of Poor Relief in South-East England 1790–1834," *Economic History Review*, XXVII (1): 50–68.

Berg, M. (1994) *The Age of Manufacturers 1700–1820: Industry, Innovation and Work in Britain*, 2nd ed., (London: Routledge).

Blaug, M. (1963) "The Myth of the Old Poor Law and the Making of the New," *Journal of Economic History*, XXIII (2): 151–245.

——— (1964) "The Poor Law Report Reexamined," *Journal of Economic History*, XXIV: 229–245.

Block, F. (2003) "Karl Polanyi and the Writing of The Great Transformation," *Theory and Society,* 32: 275–306.

Block, F. and Manza, J. (1997) "Could We End Poverty in a Postindustrial Society? The Case for a Progressive Negative Income Tax," *Politics & Society*, 25: 473–511.

Bluestone, B. and Ghilarducci, T. (1996) "Rewarding Work," *The American Prospect*, 7: 40–46.

Boyer, G.R. (1990) *An Economic History of the Poor Law 1750–1850,* (Cambridge: Cambridge University Press).

Brundage, A. (1978) *The Making of the New Poor Law: The Politics of Inquiry, Enactment, and Implementation, 1832–1839,* (New Brunswick, N.J.: Rutgers University Press).

Charlesworth, A., ed. (1983) *An Atlas of Rural Protest in Britain 1548–1900,* (Philadelphia: University of Pennsylvania Press).

Checkland, S.G. (1949) "The Propagation of Ricardian Economics in England," *Economica*, New Series, 16 (61): 40–52.

Chwialkowska, L. (2000) "Subsidies Paid in Loaves of Bread in England in 1700s," *National Post* (Canada), 12 December: A6.

Clark, G. (1991) "Labour Productivity in English Agriculture, 1300–1860," in *Land, Labour and Livestock: Historical Studies in European Agricultural Productivity*, B.M.S. Campbell and M. Overton (eds.), (Manchester: Manchester University Press).

——— (1999) "Too Much Revolution: Agriculture and the Industrial Revolution, 1700–1860," in *The British Industrial Revolution: An Economic Assessment*, 2nd ed., J. Mokyr (ed.), (Boulder: Westview).

——— (2001) "Farm Wages and Living Standards in the Industrial Revolution: England, 1670–1869," *Economic History Review*, LIV (3): 477–505.

Clement, A. (1997) "Revenue Minimum: Les Lecons de Speenhamland," *Lien Social et Politique*, 42: 49–60.

Cohen, J. and Rogers, J. (2001) *What's Wrong with a Free Lunch?*, (Boston: Beacon Press).

Cole, G.D.H. (1943) "Notes on *The Great Transformation*," 5 November, in the Karl Polanyi Archive, Concordia University, Montreal.

Congdon, L. (1990) "The Sovereignty of Society: Polanyi in Vienna," in *The Life and Work of Karl Polanyi*, K. Polanyi-Levitt (ed.), (Montreal: Black Rose).

Cowherd, R.G. (1977) *Political Economists and the English Poor Laws,* (Athens: Ohio University Press).

Cunningham, W. (1922) *The Industrial Revolution*, (Cambridge: Cambridge University Press).

Dobson, C.R. (1980) *Masters and Journeymen: A Pre-history of Industrial Relations, 1717–1800,* (London: Croom Helm).

Driver, C. (1956) *Tory Radical: The Life of Richard Oastler,* (Oxford: Oxford University Press).

Driver, F. (1993) *Power and Pauperism: The Workhouse System, 1834–1884,* (Cambridge: Cambridge University Press).

Dunkley, P. (1982) *The Crisis of the Old Poor Law in England: An Interpretative Essay*, (New York: Garland).

Eccleston, B. (1986) "Malthus, Wages and the Labour Market in England 1790–1830," in *Malthus and His Time*, M. Turner (ed.), (New York: St. Martin's).

Edsall, N.C. (1970) *The Anti-Poor Law Movement, 1834–1844,* (Manchester: Manchester University Press).

Emmison, F.G. (1933) "The Relief of the Poor at Eaton Socon, 1706–1834," *Publication of the Bedfordshire Historical Record Society*, 15: 3–98.

Engels, F. (1958 [1845]) *The Condition of the Working Class in England*, tr. by W.O. Henderson and W.H. Chaloner, (Stanford: Stanford University Press).

Feinstein, C. (1998) "Pessimism Perpetuated: Real Wages and the Standard of Living in Britain during the Industrial Revolution," *Journal of Economic History*, 58 (3): 625–658.

Fetter, F.W. (1965) *Development of British Monetary Orthodoxy 1791–1875,* (Cambridge: Harvard University Press).

Finer, S.E. (1972) "The Transmission of Benthamite Ideas 1820–1850," in *Studies in the Growth of Nineteenth-Century Government*, G. Sutherland (ed.), (London: Routledge & Kegan Paul).

Fox, N.E. (1978) "The Spread of the Threshing Machine in Central Southern England," *Agricultural History Review*, 26 (1): 26–28.

Fussell, G.E. and Compton, M. (1939) "Agricultural Adjustments after the Napoleonic Wars," *Economic History*, III (14): 184–204.

Gash, N. (1935) "Rural Unemployment, 1815–1834," *Economic History Review*, VI (1): 90–93.

Gordon, B. (1976) *Political Economy in Parliament 1819–1823,* (London: Macmillan).

Greenberg, M. (2002) "Bush's Blunder," *The American Prospect*, Special Supplement on Reforming Welfare Reform, Summer: A2–A5.

Hammond, J.L. and Hammond, B. (1966 [1911]) *The Village Labourer,* (London: Longmans, Green).

Hasbach, W. (1920) *A History of the English Agricultural Labourer*, tr. by R. Kenyon, (London: P.S. King & Son).

Henriques, U.R.Q. (1979) *Before the Welfare State: Social Administration in Early Industrial Britain,* (London: Longmans).

Hill, R.L. (1929) *Toryism and the People, 1832–1846,* (London: Constable & Co.).

Hilton, B. (1977) *Corn, Cash, Commerce: The Economic Policies of the Tory Governments 1815–1830,* (Oxford: Oxford University Press).

Himmelfarb, G. (1984) *The Idea of Poverty: England in the Early Industrial Age,* (New York: Knopf).

——— (1994) "A De-moralized Society," *The Public Interest*, 117: 57–80.

——— (1995) *The De-moralization of Society: From Victorian Virtues to Modern Values,* (New York: Knopf).

Hirschman, A.O. (1991) *The Rhetoric of Reaction: Perversity, Futility and Jeopardy*, (Cambridge, Mass.: Harvard University Press).

Hitchcock, T., King, P. and Sharpe, P., (eds.) (1997) *Chronicling Poverty: The Voices and Strategies of the English Poor, 1640–1840,* (Houndsmill: Macmillan).

Hobsbawm, E.J. and Rude, G. (1968) *Captain Swing*, (New York: Pantheon).

Holderness, B.A. (1972) "'Open' and 'Close' Parishes in England in the Eighteenth and Nineteenth Centuries," *Agricultural History Review*, 20: 125–139.

——— (1989) "Prices, Productivity and Output," in *Agrarian History of England and Wales*, vol. 6, G.E. Mingay (ed.), (Cambridge: Cambridge University Press).

Hollander, S. (1997) *The Economics of Thomas Robert Malthus,* (Toronto: University of Toronto Press).

Horrell, S. and Humphries, J. (1995) "Women's Labour Force Participation and the Transition to the Male-Breadwinner Family, 1790–1865," *Economic History Review*, XLVII (1): 89–117.

Howell, D. (1997) "Block and Manza on the Negative Income Tax," *Politics & Society*, 24: 533–539.

Hudson, P. (1986) *The Genesis of Industrial Capital: A Study of the West Riding Wool Textile Industry, c. 1750–1850*, (Cambridge: Cambridge University Press).

———, ed. (1989) *Regions and Industries: A Perspective on the Industrial Revolution in Britain,* (Cambridge: Cambridge University Press).

——— (1992) *The Industrial Revolution,* (London: Edward Arnold).

Huzel, J. (1989) "The Labourer and the Poor Law," in *The Agrarian History of England and Wales*, vol. 6, G.E. Mingay (ed.), (Cambridge: Cambridge University Press).

John, A.H. (1989) "Statistical Appendix," in *The Agrarian History of England and Wales*, vol. 6, G.E. Mingay (ed.), (Cambridge: Cambridge University Press).

Jones, E.L. (1974) "The Agricultural Labor Market in England, 1793–1872," in *Agriculture and the Industrial Revolution*, E.L. Jones (ed.), (Oxford: Basil Blackwell).

Keynes, J.M. (1932 [1925]) "The Economic Consequences of Mr. Churchill," in *Essays in Persuasion*, by J. M. Keynes, (New York: Harcourt Brace).

——— (1951 [1933]) "Robert Malthus: The First of the Cambridge Economists," in *Essays in Biography*, by J.M. Keynes, (London: Rupert Hart-Davis).

Kindleberger, C.P. (1975) "The Rise of Free Trade in Western Europe, 1820–1875," *Journal of Economic History*, 35 (1): 20–55.

King, S. (2000) *Poverty and Welfare in England 1700–1850: A Regional Perspective,* (Manchester: Manchester University Press).

Knott, J. (1986) *Popular Opposition to the 1834 Poor Law,* (London: Croom Helm).

Kreidte, P., Medick, H. and Schlumbohm, J. (1981) *Industrialization before Industrialization,* (Cambridge: Cambridge University Press).

Kumar, K. (1988) "Employment and Unemployment: The English Experience," in *On Work: Historical, Comparative, and Theoretical Approaches*, R.E. Pahl (ed.), (London: Blackwell).

Kussmaul, A.S. (1981) *Servants in Husbandry in Early Modern England,* (Cambridge: Cambridge University Press).

Lees, L.H. (1998) *The Solidarities of Strangers: The English Poor Laws and the People, 1700–1948,* (Cambridge: Cambridge University Press).

Leeson, R.A. (1980) *Travelling Brothers: The Six Centuries' Road from Craft Fellowship to Trade Unionism,* (London: Granada).

Lindert, P. (1998) "Poor Relief Before the Welfare State: Britain Versus the Continent, 1780–1880," *European Review of Economic History*, 2: 101–140.

Link, R.G. (1959) *English Economic Fluctuations 1815–1848,* (New York: Columbia University Press).

Lipson, E.E. (1943) *The Economic History of England*, vol. 3, (London: A. and C. Black).

Malthus, T.R. (1985 [1798]) *An Essay on the Principle of Population,* (London: Penguin).

——— (1992 [1803]) *An Essay on the Principle of Population*, 2nd ed., (Cambridge: Cambridge University Press).

Mandler, P. (1987) "The Making of the New Poor Law Redivivus," *Past and Present*, 117: 131–57.

——— (1990) "Tories and Paupers: Christian Political Economy and the Making of the New Poor Law," *The Historical Journal*, 33 (1): 81–103.

Mantoux, P. (1962 [1928]) *The Industrial Revolution in the Eighteenth Century,* (New York: Harper & Row).

Marshall, D. (1926) *The English Poor Law in the Eighteenth Century,* (London: Routledge).

Marshall, J.D. (1985) *The Old Poor Law, 1795–1834*, 2nd ed. (London: Macmillan).

Marx, K. (1930) *Capital*, vol. 2, tr. by E. and C. Paul, (New York: E. P. Dutton).

McCulloch, J.R. (1938 [1845]) *The Literature of Political Economy,* (London: London School of Economics).

Meek, R., ed. (1954) *Marx and Engels on Malthus,* (New York: International Publisher).

Mills, D.R. (1980) *Lord and Peasant in Nineteenth-Century Britain,* (London: Croom Helm).

Mitchell, B.R. and Deane, P. (1962) *Abstract of British Historical Statistics,* (Cambridge: Cambridge University Press).

Moynihan, D.P. (1973) *The Politics of a Guaranteed Income: The Nixon Administration and the Family Assistance Plan,* (New York: Vintage).

Murray, C. (1984) *Losing Ground: American Social Policy, 1950–1980,* (New York: Basic Books).

Neuman, M. (1982) *The Speenhamland County: Poverty and the Poor Laws in Berkshire, 1782–1834,* (New York: Garland).

Olasky, M. (1992) *The Tragedy of American Compassion,* (Wheaton, Ill.: Crossway Books).
Overton, M. (1989) "Agricultural Revolution? England 1540–1850," in *New Directions in Economic and Social History*, A. Digby and C. Feinstein (eds.), (Houndsmill: Macmillan).
——— (1996) "Re-establishing the English Agricultural Revolution," *Agricultural History Review*, 44 (1): 1–20.
Parliamentary Papers (1817) *Report from the Select Committee on the Poor Laws.*
——— (1819) *Report from the Committee on the Poor Laws.*
——— (1824) *Report from the Select Committee on Labourers Wages.*
Persky, J. (1997) "Classical Family Values: Ending the Poor Law as They Knew Them," *Journal of Economic Perspectives*, 11 (1): 178-189.
Polanyi, K. (2001 [1944]) *The Great Transformation,* (Boston: Beacon).
——— "1820 vs. 1920," undated manuscript, Karl Polanyi Archive, Montreal.
Polanyi-Levitt, K. and Mendell, M. (1987) "Karl Polanyi: His Life and Times," *Studies in Political Economy*, 22: 7–39.
Poynter, J.R. (1969) *Society and Pauperism: English Ideas in Poor Relief, 1795–1834,* (London: Routledge & Kegan Paul).
Procacci, G. (1991) "Social Economy and the Government of Poverty," in *The Foucault Effect: Studies in Governmentality*, G. Burchell, C. Gordon and P. Miller (eds.), (Chicago: University of Chicago Press).
Prothero, R. (1912) *English Farming Past and Present,* (London: Longmans, Green and Co.).
Reay, B. (1990) *The Last Rising of the Agricultural Labourers: Rural Life and Protest in Nineteenth-Century England,* (Oxford: Clarendon).
——— (1996) *Microhistories: Demography, Society and Culture in Rural England, 1800–1930*, (Cambridge: Cambridge University Press).
Redman, D.A. (1997) *The Rise of Political Economy as a Science: Methodology and the Classical Economists,* (Cambridge: MIT Press).
Reekie, G. (1998) *Measuring Immorality: Social Inquiry and the Problem of Legitimacy,* (Cambridge: Cambridge University Press).
Richardson, T.L. (1991) "Agricultural Labourers' Wages and the Cost of Living in Essex, 1790–1840: A Contribution to the Standard of Living Debate," in *Land, Labour and Agriculture, 1700-1920: Essays for Gordon Mingay*, B.A. Holderness and M. Turner (eds.), (London: Hambledon).
Rose, M.E. (1970) "The Anti-Poor Law Agitation," in *Popular Movements c. 1830–1850*, J.T. Ward (ed.), (London: Macmillan).
Rule, J. (1979) *The Experience of Labour,* (London: Croom Helm).
Rule, J. and Wells, R. (1988) *Crime, Protest, and Popular Politics in Southern England, 1750–1850: The Formative Years*, (London: Longman).
Semmel, B. (1970) *The Rise of Free Trade Imperialism,* (Cambridge: Cambridge University Press).
Sen, A. (1982) *Poverty and Famines: An Essay on Entitlement and Deprivation,* (Oxford: Clarendon).
Sharpe, P. (1997) "'The Bowels of Compation': A Labouring Family and the Law, c. 1790–1834," in *Chronicling Poverty: The Voices and Strategies of the English Poor, 1640–1840*, T. Hitchcock, P. King and P. Sharpe (eds.), (Houndsmill: Macmillan).
Snell, K.D.M. (1985) *Annals of the Labouring Poor: Social Change and Agrarian England,* (Cambridge: Cambridge University Press).
Sokoll, T. (1993) *Household and Family among the Poor,* (Bochum: Universitatsverlag Dr. N. Brockmeyer).

Solar, P.M. (1995) "Poor Relief and English Economic Development before the Industrial Revolution," *Economic History Review*, XLVIII (I): 1–22.

Somers, M. (1993) "Citizenship and the Place of the Public Sphere: Law, Community, and Political Culture in the Transition to Democracy," *American Sociological Review*, 58 (5): 587–620.

——— (1994) "Rights, Relationality and Membership: Rethinking the Making and Meaning of Citizenship," *Law and Social Inquiry*, 19 (1): 1301–1350.

Song, B.K. (1998) "Landed Interest, Local Government, and the Labour Market in England, 1750–1850," *Economic History Review*, LI (3): 465–488.

Steinberg, M.W. (1999) *Fighting Words: Working-Class Formation, Collective Action, and Discourse in Early Nineteenth Century England,* (Ithaca, N.Y.: Cornell University Press).

Tawney, R.H. (1972 [1938]) "The Assessment of Wages in England by the Justices of the Peace," in *Wage Regulation in Pre-industrial England*, W.E. Minchinton (ed.), (New York: Barnes and Noble).

Tawney, R.H. and Power, E., (eds.) (1924) *Tudor Economic Documents*, vol. 1, (London: Longmans).

Taylor, A.J., ed. (1975) *The Standard of Living in Britain in the Industrial Revolution,* (London: Methuen).

Taylor, J.S. (1989) *Poverty, Migration, and Settlement in the Industrial Revolution: Sojourners' Narratives,* (Palo Alto, Calif.: Society for the Promotion of Science and Scholarship).

Thomson, D. (1991) "The Welfare of the Elderly in the Past: A Family or Community Responsibility," in *Life, Death and the Elderly: Historical Perspectives*, M. Pelling and R.M. Smith (eds.), (London: Routledge).

Tilly, C. (1995) *Popular Contention in Great Britain 1758–1834,* (Cambridge, Mass.: Harvard University Press).

Townsend, J. (1971 [1786]) *A Dissertation on the Poor Laws,* (Berkeley: University of California Press).

Valenze, D. (1995) *The First Industrial Woman,* (New York: Oxford University Press).

Van Parijs, P., ed. (1992) *Arguing for Basic Income: Ethical Foundations for a Radical Reform,* (London: Verso).

Viner, J. (1965 [1937]) *Studies in the Theory of International Trade,* (New York: Augustus Kelley).

Ward, J.T. (1962) *The Factory Movement 1830–1855,* (New York: St. Martin's).

Waterman, A.M.C. (1991) *Revolution, Economics and Religion: Christian Political Economy, 1798–1833,* (Cambridge: Cambridge University Press).

Weaver, R.K. (2000) *Ending Welfare as We Know It*, (Washington, D.C.: Brookings Institution).

Webb, S. and B. (1927) *English Local Government: English Poor Law History. Part 1: The Old Poor Law,* (London: Longmans, Green).

——— (1963 [1929]) *English Local Government: English Poor Law History. Part II: The Last Hundred Years,* (Hamden, Conn.: Archon Books).

Wells, R.A.E. (1988) *Wretched Faces: Famine in Wartime England, 1793–1801,* (Gloucester, U.K.: Sutton).

——— (2000) "The Moral Economy of the English Countryside," in *Moral Economy and Popular Protest: Crowds, Conflict and Authority*, A. Randall and A. Charlesworth (eds.), (Houndsmill: Macmillan).

Williams, K. (1981) *From Pauperism to Poverty,* (London: Routledge & Kegan Paul).

Wrigley, E.A. (1986) "Men on the Land and Men in the Countryside: Employment in Agriculture in Early-Nineteenth Century England," in *The World We Have Gained: Histories of Population and Social Structure*, L. Bonfield, R.M. Smith and K. Wrightson (eds.), (London: Basil Blackwell).

Wrigley, E.A. and Roger Schofield, (1997) *English Population History from Family Reconstitution, 1580–1837,* (Cambridge: Cambridge University Press).

Chapter 3

Inheritance and Equal Shares: Early American Views

John Cunliffe and Guido Erreygers*

Introduction

The idea that each young adult is entitled to an equal capital endowment funded mainly from inheritance taxation is an important part of current liberal-egalitarian debate. For instance, Ackerman and Alstott (1999) have advocated the principle of "stakeholding," through which each United States citizen has the right to a share in the wealth accumulated by preceding generations. Similarly, Nissan and Le Grand (2000) have proposed that each 18-year-old in Britain should receive a capital grant from the state, funded from reformed inheritance taxes. Such proposals endorse the fundamental economic framework of a capitalist society, while addressing especially those inequalities in opportunity generated and maintained by intergenerational mechanisms of resource transfer.[1] In some versions, the endowment consists of an unconditional cash lump sum; in others, the payment is conditional on a range of actual or potential productive uses; and in still others, it would be granted as a set of credits for approved purposes.[2]

In this chapter, we trace some of the less familiar intellectual antecedents of these contemporary proposals. Our motivation for writing the chapter is, however, not exclusively historical; as Terence Ball has put it, unless we suffer from "present-minded conceits," all of us might learn something useful by considering debates from different historical contexts.[3] Reflecting on these antecedents should warn us against any easy assumption that the proposals are merely a product of current intellectual concerns.[4] Indeed, the recurrent historical demand for equal initial stakes indicates that the issue of intergenerational transfers is enduring and endemic in liberal egalitarian thought.

The three specific cases we examine come from American writers of the first half of the nineteenth century. The first and least developed case was presented by Cornelius Blatchly in 1817; the second and more comprehensive case was presented by Thomas Skidmore in 1829; and the third and perhaps most intriguing case was presented by Orestes Brownson in 1840. In common with many social critics at the time, each of these writers argued that America's unique prospect was already being betrayed: the ideal society was one in which all citizens (or at least all white males) were independent property owners, but in reality a permanently propertyless class was emerging. The distinctive and radical response of all three writers called for the provision of an equal capital endowment to each young adult, irrespective of gender and race. Although the endowments would be in the form of an unconditional cash lump sum, the presumption was that these would be used productively with their level being sufficient to make self-employment a realistic alternative to wage labor. For these writers, equal opportunities required equal starts. But the existing inheritance regime perpetuated and accentuated a strongly unequal division of individual wealth, which violated equal starts and jeopardized equal opportunities. Accordingly, they called for a drastic reform or even abolition of private inheritance, suggesting alternative mechanisms to disperse the value of the property of the deceased so as to secure equal starts and thus to promote genuine equal opportunity.

Although there is no easily identifiable transmission of intellectual influence, we begin by considering a common and possibly shared background to the three writers, provided especially by the views of Jefferson and Paine. Both argued, albeit with important caveats, that each individual had an equal birthright in land, or at least its equivalent, which should take priority over any inherited property arrangements. We then turn to Blatchly and his endorsement of that argument together with his justification of an equal division of inherited property among all maturing individuals in each generation. Next we deal with the much more radical proposal by Skidmore for both achieving and maintaining equal division of property among all adults. After that we turn to Orestes Brownson, and his fascinating claim to have synthesized French Saint-Simonianism and the American spirit of equal opportunity. In the final section, we assess the intellectual provenance and coherence of this set of contributions.

Inheritance and the Revolutionary Legacy

Broadly speaking, the revolutionary generation in America could choose between two strategies on the inheritance of private property. The first, and most radical, was to repudiate it totally, in the name of a republican equality of opportunity, along with hereditary political power. The second, and more reformist, was to distinguish sharply between the inheritance of private property and the inheritance of political power, accepting the one while rejecting the other. The reformist strategy eventually prevailed, and paved the way for statutory reform which "removed devices of compulsory inequality, but stopped short of requiring equality."[5] As a result, virtually all states abolished the legal devices of primogeniture and entail. This elimination was rather formal and symbolic, however, given that actual practices in the transmission of real property rarely used those devices, which were indeed absent in many of the former colonies.

Significantly, however, the logic even of the reformist strategy could easily generate the radical conclusion of the total abolition of individual inheritance. In the dominant jurisprudential tradition, individual inheritance was far from being regarded as a natural right to be supported and not infringed by positive state law.

On the contrary, the natural law position at least in Blackstone's authoritative view, was that on the death of the possessor his estate reverted to common property. Insofar as individual inheritance was permitted, it was only as a matter of positive law, justified by considerations of convenience and utility. For the reformists, those considerations took precedence over the natural law position. But in conceding the conventional nature of individual inheritance, they opened the way for the radicals to assert the priority of the natural law position. For them, the natural right to property could be realized across generations only if property reverted to the state on the death of its possessors. The right of inheritance might be convenient and useful for its beneficiaries but not for those permanently excluded from property.

In a familiar set of contrasts, Jefferson implemented the reformist strategy in practice, but came very close to endorsing the radical position in his theoretical pronouncements on intergenerational issues as they related to real or landed property. On the one hand, he was instrumental in securing the revision of the laws of inheritance in Virginia, in order to replace any provision for entails and primogeniture by equal distribution between all children of the decedent.[6] On the other, in his more philosophical reflections whether from the 1780s or some twenty-five years later, Jefferson adopted the natural law position. The earth had been given as "a common stock" to mankind "to labor & live on."[7] Each generation had an equal right to a free usufruct over it unconstrained by past property dispositions.[8] That right trumped established practices of the individual transmission of property. Those practices were based on mere legal fictions whereas the reality was that "The will and the power of man expire with his life, by nature's law."[9] The portion of land "occupied by an individual ceases to be his when himself ceases to be, and reverts to society."[10] Insofar as individual transmission was permitted, it was not as a "natural right, but by a law of…society."[11] Such laws could be justified, if at all, only as an "artificial continuance, for the encouragement of industry."[12]

In the American context, Jefferson viewed the seemingly endless supply of "free" land as mitigating any tension between the utilitarian defense of individual inheritance and the concern with a fair distribution consistent with an equal birthright across generations. Under those fortunate conditions, redistribution would be superfluous because that birthright could be realized directly through widespread private ownership, with no one being excluded permanently from his own portion. In the European setting, by contrast, Jefferson argued that the dominance of the established landed monopoly could be justified neither by considerations of efficiency nor equity. Jefferson conceded that the situation in those "old" countries, which combined "uncultivated lands and unemployed poor," was such an extension of "the laws of property…as to violate natural right."[13] Despite that, he considered that this acknowledged violation should be remedied not by sweeping redistribution, but through the abolition of primogeniture as well as sharply progressive estate taxes. These measures might go some way toward realizing dispersed ownership. In any event, nevertheless, the permanently excluded were entitled to a surrogate for their equal birthright by the state taking action to secure employment. Or, failing that, the unemployed landless were at liberty to use any uncultivated land, even if others privately owned it, subject to a modest rent.

Like Jefferson, Paine was committed to the principle of generational sovereignty and hence to the potentially radical conclusion of the total abolition of individual inheritance, but in practice he endorsed the reformist strategy of challenging only the perceived excesses of that regime.[14] He presented his views on the issue in two works from the 1790s: the second part of the *Rights of Man* (1792) and especially *Agrarian Justice* (1797). In the first, Paine proposed a series of measures to relieve the poverty attributed to an excessive and unfairly distributed tax burden in Britain. These measures were intended principally to support education for the young and pensions for the old; they were to be funded by steeply progressive inheritance taxation which would effectively result in the end of primogeniture and the dispersal of large estates. Insofar as Paine presented any sustained justification for them, it rested on a distinction between the undoubted legitimacy of "property acquired by industry" and the more dubious character of large fortunes acquired by bequest.[15]

In *Agrarian Justice*, Paine presented considerably more radical welfare proposals including the provision of a universal cash endowment for each young adult, together with a sustained philosophical justification for them. This justification was based on two distinct principles. The first was that each proprietor of cultivated land owed "to the community a *ground-rent*"[16] the proceeds of which should be disbursed equally to all dispossessed persons. So a system of compensation between appropriators and non-appropriators, mediated by the state, reflected Paine's contention that "the earth, in its natural uncultivated state was, and ever would have continued to be, *the common property of the human race*."[17] As such, each person had a claim right to an (uncultivated) share equal to that of any other person. But, any improved value resulting from cultivation by previous or current owners was legitimately subject to private property rights including inheritance: "While, therefore, I advocate the right…of all those who have been thrown out of their natural inheritance by the introduction of the system of landed property, I equally defend the right of the possessor to that part which is his."[18] The second principle assimilated personal to landed property by maintaining that "it is as impossible for an individual to acquire personal property without the aid of society, as it is for him to make land originally."[19] Only returning a part of it could discharge the obligation of property owners to the society that had made the accumulation possible.

In his financial calculations, Paine initially affirmed that the fund proposed in his welfare plan would be derived from ground-rent based on the original value of unimproved land, estimated at one tenth of the total market value of improved land. But, for administrative convenience, and to avoid "deranging any present possessors,"[20] this revenue was to be collected only by inheritance taxes. A 10 percent tax would apply to all personal property left as a bequest, and in addition, an extra 10 percent would apply when there were no direct heirs. The funds would be disbursed in three ways: by a capital sum to each person at age 21; by an annual payment to all those aged 50 or over; and through an annual payment to "the lame and blind" under the age of 50.[21]

Paine's objective was to ensure that "the condition of every person born into the world, after a state of civilization commences, ought not to be worse than if he had been born before that period."[22] Those dispossessed of "their natural inheritance" by the system of landed property were entitled to "indemnification"[23] or "compensation."[24] This endowment would ensure that everyone would be "an inheritor of something to begin with."[25]

To sum up, for both Jefferson and Paine there was nothing wrong with individual inheritance, as long as all received their legitimate share. Ideally this share should take the form of land, but failing that, one would have to resort to a surrogate such as cash endowments or employment opportunities. Provided that entitlements to an equal natural birthright were respected, the conventional practices of individual inheritance were considered legitimate. This moderate egalitarian view was continued by one of America's first political economists, Daniel Raymond. In principle he supported a system of an equal division of inherited wealth among all the members of each new generation, but for practical reasons he settled for the substantially diluted version of equal division among family members only.[26] In this chapter, however, we focus on the more radical interpretations of the Jefferson–Paine legacy, demanding the complete abolition of individual inheritance and a strictly egalitarian redistribution of property.

Blatchly

Cornelius Camden Blatchly was born on January 1, 1773 in Mendham, New Jersey. As a physician graduating from the New York College of Physicians and Surgeons, he practiced among New York's poor.[27] His first important publication dates from 1817: it was an essay entitled *Some Causes of Popular Poverty*, appended to Thomas Branagan's *Pleasures of Contemplation*.[28] Around 1820 he founded the New York Society for Promoting Communities, which two years later published his *An Essay on Common Wealths*, containing a large number of excerpts from Robert Owen's *A New View of Society*.[29] Later in the 1820s he supported the working men's political movement in New York.[30] Blatchly died on December 5, 1831.[31]

It seems that the origins of Blatchly's ideas lie, to a great extent, in the religious domain. In his writings he referred frequently to the Bible, which might be explained by his background as a radical and even dissident Quaker.[32] But at the same time he was extremely critical of existing religious institutions, as shown by his affirmation that "All national religions…have been, and naturally must be tyrannies."[33] Clearly, his thinking was also influenced by the natural rights approach of Jefferson and Paine. Blatchly sent a copy of *An Essay on Common Wealths* to Jefferson, and in his reply Jefferson expressed his sympathy for Blatchly and his Society.[34] Whether the writings of Robert Owen had any effect on Blatchly is difficult to say. We do know that when Owen visited New York in

November 1824, he was a guest at a meeting of Blatchly's Society, and Blatchly proudly showed him Jefferson's letter.[35]

In *Some Causes of Popular Poverty* Blatchly concentrated on five causes of poverty and oppression that, in his opinion, had "attracted too little attention," viz. interests, rents, duties, inheritances and churches established by laws of men.[36] All of these violated what he claimed to be the three legitimate titles to property. Using the Bible as his ultimate source, he identified the first title as God's gift to man of *dominion* over the world. He hastened to add that "man" had to be understood as "a term including all men and women," and that the title was given to him "not in his *individual*, but in his *aggregate* capacity."[37] God's creation, therefore, was meant "for *general* use and benefit, and not for *individual* aggrandizement and oppression of the multitude."[38] Rights to particular items of property could be obtained only on the basis of the second title, *occupancy*, or on that of the third, *improvement*, by which Blatchly referred to the "improvement, use, and multiplication of the productions of the earth, seas, and air, by industry, art, and ingenuity."[39] Claims to income or goods that had no connection with the public good, occupancy or improvement, were deemed unjust.

The main message that Blatchly tried to convey with his essay was that interests, rents, duties, tithes, etc., all being unjust rights to property, had devastating effects for a large part of the population. After having mentioned "a few of the evils, afflictions, and deaths attributable to interests, duties, and unequal inheritances," he concluded pessimistically: "The miseries are more than I am able to depicture."[40] For its denouncement of the oppression and exploitation of the laboring population, Blatchly's essay might rightly be considered as "the first significant contribution to modern socialist theory in the United States."[41] For our purposes, however, the essay is interesting because it contains the germs of a proposal for an alternative property regime guaranteeing a basic capital to all.

Blatchly formulated the proposal when discussing inheritance. First he emphasized the dual origin of (private) property: "If property is considered in respect to its origin, it is social and individual: being the result and fruits of social protection, policy and assistance, or of individual care, wisdom, and industry."[42] Without the aid of society, individuals would not be able to acquire and preserve much property. For Blatchly this had profound consequences when people died. As long as individuals lived, they had full property rights. As soon as they died, however, their previous property rights simply disappeared with them. On this issue Blatchly shared the views of Jefferson and Paine:

> How can a man who is dead, be said to will? All his mental and corporal powers, have ceased as to this world. He has no property; he has no power; he can have no will; for he has no existence in this world; and consequently, he has in this world no property.[43]

But then, of course, the question arose: to whom should the rights to the property of the deceased be transferred? Given the dual origin of property, Blatchly's initial response was that the property belongs to society:

> To whom can it more naturally and rationally revert than to its most immediate source, to the society, the community, the nation whence his property was derived? It is the commonwealth's.[44]

Although the precise form of this community of property remained unclear, it turns out that Blatchly was thinking more along the lines of an individual right to an equal share than along the lines of common property. This is revealed in particular by his insistence that all young men and women had "a right to their averaged share, which is due from the society."[45]

According to Blatchly, a mechanism had to be devised in order to ensure that the principle "to every man and woman an equal portion" held through time for each individual in every generation.[46] Blatchly's solution was remarkably simple: in every year the property of the deceased had to be divided equally among the men and women reaching adulthood. The property of the deceased should be distributed not by the absurd legal fiction of wills, all too often "unjust and oppressive," but in equal shares determined by natural rights: "Every child in a nation has perhaps a *natural* right to an equal proportion of all the property of every deceasing member of the national family…."[47] To illustrate the principle, Blatchly gave the following example:

> Suppose we were a nation of seven millions of inhabitants, and that each person, (if the whole property in the union was equally divided,) would be entitled to a dividend worth 3000 dollars; and suppose (of the men and women who are adult, and hold property,) one seventieth of the population, or 100,000, die annually, these would leave a property of three hundred millions of dollars and more. As about 100,000 young people might annually arrive to the legal state of inheriting, each of these [w]ould be justly entitled, (according to this statement,) to about three thousand dollars, as their inheritance.[48]

Unlike Jefferson and Paine, who in practice advocated only limited infringements upon the existing inheritance regulations, Blatchly therefore proposed a much more radical reform.

In *An Essay on Common Wealths*—a curious pamphlet emanating from the New York Society for Promoting Communities but usually attributed to Blatchly—he reaffirmed his opposition to "usury, rents, and interest", which allowed some "to feed like drones on the labours of the industrious."[49] More significantly, Blatchly now presented a full-blown critique of all exclusive property rights. He argued that the only solution to the problem of pauperism lay in the creation of "the purest kind of communities."[50] In these, inclusive rights "to all real and personal property" would replace all exclusive rights:

> If men lived in pure and perfect communities, where all things were as they should be, man's social rights would not *destroy*, as they now do, the *natural rights* he possessed in his wild and unassociated state; but would *increase*, *exalt* and *perfect all* his *natural* into *social* rights. And, as men claimed a right in their *natural* and *unassociated* state to *every thing around them*; so they should claim, in a pure community, a right to *all around them*.[51]

At the request of the Society, Blatchly sent the pamphlet to Jefferson.[52] Although Jefferson wrote that its "views of equal rights of man" merited his entire approbation, he reacted cautiously to the proposals of Blatchly and his society:

> That, on the principle of a communion of property, small societies may exist in habits of virtue, order industry and peace, and consequently in a state of as much happiness as heaven has been pleased to deal out to imperfect humanity, I can readily concieve, and indeed have seen it's proofs in various small societies which have been constituted on that principle. But I do not feel authorised to conclude from these that an extended society, like that of the US, or of an individual state, could be governed happily on the same principle.[53]

Skidmore

Thomas Skidmore was born on August 13, 1790 in Newtown, Connecticut. At the age of thirteen he became a teacher, being employed at different schools in Connecticut, New Jersey, Virginia and North Carolina. In June 1819 he settled in New York City, where he worked as a machinist. He continued to live there until his early death on August 7, 1832 as a victim of the cholera epidemic.[54]

Skidmore has deserved a place in history for at least two reasons: his involvement in the Working Men's Party of New York, and the publication of his main work, *The Rights of Man to Property!*, in 1829. The party only existed in New York for a short period of time, as did the other labor parties that flourished during the Jacksonian period.[55] The New York party had a turbulent history.[56] It was founded in 1829, and Skidmore was its first leader. He managed to get his ideas translated into the party's radical program, summarized by the motto adopted in the first issues of the weekly paper *The Working Man's Advocate*, which served as a kind of organ of the party: "All children are entitled to equal education; all adults, to equal property; and all mankind to equal privileges." Almost immediately the party obtained a success: in the elections for the State Assembly held in November 1829, it won one of the eleven seats.[57] In December 1829, however, the members decided to renounce Skidmore's "Agrarian" program, and Robert Dale Owen took control of the party. With the support of Frances Wright and George H. Evans, he shifted the focus to a program of equal and publicly funded education. Skidmore abandoned the party and formed the Original Workingmen's Party, with little or no success. But the party that he left did not do much better: soon after Skidmore's departure another split occurred. By 1831 all labor parties in New York had ceased to exist.

Thomas Skidmore's only major book, *The Rights of Man to Property!*, was published at the end of 1829 and can certainly be seen as an attempt to give a solid foundation to the party's "agrarian" program.[58] In contrast to Blatchly, Skidmore drew explicitly on the work of Jefferson and Paine.[59] On the title page of his book, Skidmore modified a famous passage of Jefferson's Declaration of Independence, substituting "I" for "we" and "property" for "the pursuit of happiness":

"I hold these truths to be self-evident; that all men are created equal; that they are endowed by their Creator, with certain inalienable rights; and that among these are life, liberty and *property*." – Altered from Mr. Jefferson's Declaration of American Independence.[60]

Skidmore thought it was "self-evident" and "indisputable" that every man (and woman) had a "*natural* right to an equal portion of property."[61] But given that the existing property rights in society were distributed extremely unequally, a mechanism had to be found to set the situation straight. The way to proceed was indicated by the book's long and significant subtitle, which aptly summarized Skidmore's ideas on property: *Being a Proposition to Make it Equal among the Adults of the Present Generation: and to Provide for its Equal Transmission to Every Individual of Each Succeeding Generation, on Arriving at the Age of Maturity*. The first part of his plan was to re-establish equality immediately, in a draconian attempt to restore the original equality of property rights. After that, in order to prevent inequality from reappearing in the future, the rights of bequest and inheritance had to be drastically reduced. Hence the second part of his plan consisted of the abolition of the system of individual inheritance and its replacement by an equal share mechanism, strongly reminiscent of Blatchly.

The novelty of Skidmore's theoretical position lay in the proposition to equalize property in the present generation. This feature above all has led to the book being described as probably "the single most comprehensive statement of...pre-Marxian American radicalism."[62] In his brief and controversial role within the New York Working Men's Party, moreover, Skidmore turned this theory into "a political challenge" and "radical crusade."[63] From the start, however, people like Robert Dale Owen condemned it and expressed the opinion that it hampered the cause of the New York laborers.[64] Skidmore's lack of success after quitting the party seems to suggest that his ideas were not widely supported, but this view has been challenged.[65]

The essence of Skidmore's revolutionary program was laid down in an ambitious 20 article plan.[66] It consisted on the one hand of the proposal for a "General Division of Property," aimed at the equalization of property amongst all existing adults, and on the other of a scheme for an "Annual Dividend," meant to preserve equality over time. In principle the General Division of Property was a simple operation, but Skidmore was well aware that it would involve complicated legal issues, certainly if the plan were adopted only by New York State. Schematically, he proposed the following procedure:

1. Assembly of a new State Convention.
2. Adoption of a new State Constitution, decreeing the abolition of all debts, and claiming all the property of its citizens.
3. Organization of a Census of the population.
4. Organization of a General Inventory of all real and personal property held by the citizens of the State.

5. Assignment, in the Credit-Book of the State, of an equal amount of credit to each adult citizen, corresponding to the share or dividend of each in the total amount of wealth.
6. Organization of a General Sales, in which all property is publicly auctioned to the highest bidder, with the understanding that "All persons having such credit, on the books before mentioned, are authorised and required, to bid for an amount of property, falling short not more than ten per cent. of the sum placed to their credit, and not exceeding it more than ten per cent."[67]
7. Calculation, after the close of the General Sales, of the new dividend of each adult person, which will be called each person's Patrimony.
8. Institution of a system of Annual Dividends, in which the property left by those who have died in a given year, is divided equally among all the new adults of that year; the dividend may be taken up in cash or in credit.

In addition Skidmore gave detailed explanations on how to deal with property of foreigners, indivisible items, state property, etc. Without going into details, we note that the General Division was sufficiently complex to require a "universal suspension of all business, except in so much as is necessary for subsistence, until the whole can be accomplished."[68] Although at first sight it seemed to be "a matter of great difficulty," Skidmore was confident that "on examination, it will be found to be of very easy execution."[69]

Leaving aside all of the issues raised by this specific procedure, the more interesting issue is why Skidmore considered it so important to establish an equal division of property within the present generation, instead of restricting it to future ones as suggested by his predecessors. Skidmore explicitly rejected that gradualist strategy on two grounds. The first of these was based on the familiar problem that inheritance limitations could and certainly would be evaded by *inter vivos* transfers:

> For, as property which is not money, may yet be converted into money; so *will* it be; and if a man, with the present erroneous views of his right to property, is not permitted, in his lifetime, to make a will, which will be valid after his death; he may yet, although against the law of the land, and no doubt, would, (I speak generally,) secretly and clandestinely *give it away* to his favorites, children or others, in his lifetime.[70]

Unless that evasion could be countered, the attempt to equalize inherited wealth would be defeated: The present unequal transmission between individuals would continue in a clandestine form, together with a reduction in any pool available for equal redistribution. Gifts *inter vivos* were "only a will by anticipation,"[71] and permitting them "would open a door, through which posterity might be defrauded out of their rights of property."[72] So, in order to equalize inherited property, severe restrictions on transfers *inter vivos* were necessary. But this modified gradualist strategy presented the prospect of future rectification only, and offered no consolation for the present generation. It could not meet Skidmore's second and decisive objection, which was simply that the dispossessed had already waited long enough to reclaim their rights. Given that time horizon, a general division was needed at present and not in some future: better late than never, but even better now rather than later. It was only "THE LIVING who give the present holders of property the possession of it; *it is we ourselves*, (for in us and us alone, rests the title,) who have done it."[73] The present holders were not legally rightful owners through any inherited title but only because of an "unjust and undeserved gift"[74] conferred by the living. Now was the time to reclaim the gift, and to restore property in equal shares to its morally rightful owners.[75]

Once an equal division had been achieved, the remaining problem was to ensure its equal transmission to every individual in all succeeding generations. Skidmore's objections to individual wills combined familiar jurisprudential arguments about the distribution of the pool of inherited wealth with utilitarian concerns over its magnitude. The jurisprudential arguments against wills were threefold: that they contravened "the rights of the succeeding generation"; that they were merely a legal fiction; and that they prolonged a maldistribution of property originating in force and fraud.[76] The utilitarian claim that the existing convention of individual transmission was a crucial incentive to the conservation of property through time was also contested. Insofar as the claim was supposed to apply to the link between parents and their own children, Skidmore was especially dubious. If parents were so concerned to secure the future of their offspring, then why were transfers made typically *causa mortis* when those offspring were likely to be already mature? That concern would be expressed more usefully by transfers *inter vivos* when the offspring were young adults starting out on their own lives.[77] Skidmore's conclusion was that like himself most people wanted property for their own sake rather than with the intention of bestowing benefit to specific future individuals. Of course, future generations might benefit from this property, but that was an unintended consequence. He therefore rejected the suspicion that the combination of an initially equal division with a prohibition on gifts *inter vivos* and *causa mortis* would induce idleness and reduce the size of the pool of inherited wealth.[78]

Brownson

Orestes A. Brownson was born on September 16, 1803 in Stockbridge, Vermont. He was a prolific writer, well-known for his versatile religious opinions.[79] For most of his life he was heavily involved in the labor movement and a supporter of the Democratic Party. In 1840 he published two articles in his own journal, the *Boston Quarterly Review*, which sparked a controversy that may have played a role in the presidential election of that year. The July issue carried his "The Laboring Classes" and the October issue a much longer article with the same title, which later became known as "Brownson's Defence of the Article on the Laboring Classes."[80] The most controversial points appeared to be his views on priesthood and on property.[81] Perhaps because of all the commotion they stirred, the articles have not been included in his collected works, edited in 20 volumes by his son Henry. Brownson died on April 17, 1876.

The intellectual sources of his views on property are many and diverse. In his autobiographical book *The Convert* he mentioned the early influence of the "communism" of Robert Owen, the "individualism" of William Godwin, and the medium between the two, Frances Wright, with whom he collaborated for some time. In the 1829–1830 period he became involved in the labor movement of New York. For a while he was an independent preacher, but under the influence of William Ellery Channing he became a Unitarian minister in 1832. He learned French and German, and began to study French and German philosophy and theology. The works of Benjamin Constant, Victor Cousin, and Heinrich Heine seem to have made a lasting impression upon him. But perhaps his main source of inspiration in that period were the writings of the Saint-Simonians.[82] It is unclear whether he ever read the works of Saint-Simon, Bazard or Enfantin,[83] but he certainly had good sources on Saint-Simonian thought. In 1840, for instance, he wrote a lengthy review of the American translation of Michel Chevalier's *Lettres sur l'Amérique du Nord*,[84] including a summary account of the Saint-Simonian movement in France.[85] He was also a *personal friend* of Dr. Charles Poyen de Saint-Sauveur, once an active member of the Saint-Simonian sect.[86] Although sympathetic to the Saint-Simonians, Brownson distrusted their technocratic vision:

> For ourselves, though we have found much in the doctrines of the Saint-Simonians to approve, and in their enthusiasm to admire, we are far from relishing their scheme for the organization of society. They go on the grounds that the mass of the people must be led, and that all the concerns of human life should be entrusted to a few chiefs, or leaders. If these leaders could be gods, perhaps this would not be amiss; but all experience proves that individuals can rarely possess power over their brethren, without abusing it. The possession of power almost always corrupts…[87]

Instead he maintained that "industry is best encouraged by not being taken under the especial care of authority, but by being left free."[88]

This preference for a more liberal organization of society also characterizes his proposal with respect to inheritance. He agreed with the Saint-Simonians that the individuated inheritance of property should be abolished, yet he firmly rejected their idea of a centrally planned distribution of the means of production according to individual capacities. In the first article on the *laboring classes*, however, he mentioned only the first aspect. The abolition proposal was presented briefly at the very end, as a logical consequence of the destruction of all forms of privilege:

> There are many of these. We cannot specify them all; we will select only one, the greatest of them all, the privilege which some have of being born rich while others are born poor. It will be seen at once that we allude to the hereditary descent of property, an anomaly in our American system, which must be removed, or the system itself will be destroyed…as we have abolished heredity monarchy and hereditary nobility, we must complete the work by

abolishing hereditary property.[89]

At that stage, no further arguments in favor of the abolition proposal were developed by Brownson, apart from the statement that a man's

> power over his property must cease with his life, and his property must then become the property of the state, to be disposed of by some equitable law for the use of the generation which takes his place.[90]

Although Brownson stressed that he launched the proposal "for its free and full discussion,"[91] and not "as a measure for the immediate action of the community,"[92] the Whigs eagerly seized the opportunity to present Brownson's proposal as an example of the dangerous tendencies in the Democratic camp.[93] Despite these attacks and the pleas of some of his friends to reconsider his views on inheritance, he did not back off but instead published a long defense of his views in the second article on the laboring classes. A new argument underpinning the inheritance abolition proposal was the need to have laborers equipped with property:

> The doctrine we have long labored to maintain is, that the work of this country is to emancipate labor, by raising up the laborer from a mere workman, without capital, to be a proprietor, and a workman on his own farm, or in his own shop.[94]

What was at stake, therefore, was not simply the eradication of a privilege, but the "complete emancipation of labor by raising up each individual laborer to be an independent worker."[95] Such a policy would be widely supported, Brownson believed, since Americans preferred equality to privilege, at least in principle. In particular the idea that all should have equal chances in society would have unanimous support. "But equal chances imply equal starting points,"[96] Brownson observed, and so the system of hereditary property had to be changed drastically:

> if society, as far as it depends on her, – as Americans, to say the least, very generally believe, – is bound to furnish equal chances to all her members, hereditary property must unquestionably be abolished; unless, what will amount to the same thing, a plan be devised and carried into operation, by which the portion inherited by each shall be absolutely equal.[97]

The solution advocated by Brownson in fact combined the abolition of inheritance with the provision of equal shares. He claimed that his proposition was "virtually the same with Jefferson's," and in conformity with the views of "a very respectable string of authorities."[98]

Brownson arrived at his solution on the basis of an analysis of the origins and nature of property rights. More specifically, he emphasized the following negative arguments:

1. The denial of common property: "The very essence of property is individual, peculiar, exclusive."[99]
2. The denial of a natural right to bequeath property: "a man's natural right to property expires at his death."[100]

3. The denial of a natural right to inherit property from parents or close relatives: "the child stands in relation to the property of the father, precisely as stands any other individual, having equal and only equal claims to the inheritance."[101]

Arguments 1 and 2 implied that the rights to the property left by the deceased could not be of the common property type, but had to be rights held in severalty. Argument 3 implied that every child had an equal claim to inheritance. Brownson concluded that the property left by the deceased had to be divided equally among all the new adults: "one man can rightfully appropriate to himself no more than, in an equal division of the whole among all the members of the new generation, would be his share."[102] This would be "his share of the general inheritance," "which serves him for an outfit, as a capital with which to commence operations."[103] Women as well as men would receive a share.

At this point a slight ambiguity in Brownson's reasoning must be pointed out. He seems to suggest that the property of the deceased in a given period, say a year, must be divided equally among those that have arrived at the age of maturity in that same period. Perhaps out of fear that the individual portions might vary too much from year to year, he proposed to calculate each new adult's portion as his share in the total capital of the nation:

> In order to get at the proportion due to each, a general valuation as now of all the property of the commonwealth will need to be made. The general valuation of all the property in the commonwealth once fixed, the simple rule of division will determine how much is the portion of the new occupant. Then a valuation of that vacated will determine how much of it must be allotted to one individual.[104]

Brownson was well aware that his solution diverged from the Saint-Simonian one, in the sense that he replaced the Saint-Simonian division of the means of production according to capacities by a strictly equal one. This is clear from the following statement, which echoes only half of their famous slogan: "All we ask is, that men should, so far as society is concerned, be dealt by as equals, and after that, in all that depends on themselves, be treated according to their works."[105]

An Assessment

Our three authors each carried familiar doctrines of an equal birthright in land to the radical conclusion that all individuals were entitled to an equal share of all inherited assets in the form of an unconditional capital endowment. Although they might have presumed that the endowment would be used productively, none of them actually prescribed any legal restrictions on its authorized uses. An equal share was simply a natural right, and only in very exceptional cases, such as insanity,[106] could infringements upon this right be tolerated. What individuals made of the opportunities provided by the endowment was their choice and hence their responsibility. The assumption was that the level of the one-off cash payment would be sufficient to provide an effective opportunity for self-employment. It would not sustain a lifetime of idleness but with frugal consumption it might allow a period of voluntary unemployment, or even an interlude of riotous excess. Many found such radical conclusions alarming, and it was no coincidence that both Skidmore and Brownson sparked heated controversies when they first presented their ideas. Although many respectable radicals supported the idea of an equal birthright in land, they did so only on the proviso that it could be realized without threatening existing holdings, by the free distribution of public lands.[107] Similarly, the commitment to equal opportunities in general or to equal initial endowments in particular might have been acceptable in those circles, but not if they were to be financed from 100 percent inheritance taxation, regarded as threatening the very institution of private property. None of them wanted to be associated with Skidmore's ideas.[108]

Whether there are any traces of mutual influence between the three authors is difficult to establish. When they originally formulated their ideas, none of them referred explicitly to the others' proposals. In the case of Blatchly this would have been materially impossible, because in 1817, when he first published his proposal, the other two had not yet written on property. The case of Skidmore is not as clear. At least one commentator has argued that: "From the similarity of his ideas with those of Blatchly it seems very likely that he read Blatchly's essays."[109] If that is true, it remains puzzling why he did not refer to Blatchly's writings, and even more so because Skidmore was possibly personally acquainted with Blatchly. Both lived in New York City during the 1820s, and both were on the Working Men's Party ticket in the 1829 election for the New York State Assembly.[110] We have not been able to find out whether Blatchly was on Skidmore's side in the battles which raged in the party.[111] As far as Brownson is concerned, he was a voracious reader; and it is certainly not excluded that he was familiar with both Skidmore's and Blatchly's ideas. In fact, we believe it is highly probable that he would have known Skidmore's agrarian views. At the time when the members of the New York Working Men's Party were debating Skidmore's ideas, Brownson was closely affiliated with Robert Dale Owen, one of Skidmore's most ardent critics. Precisely in the period in which the debate reached a peak on the pages of *The Free Enquirer*, the journal edited by Robert Dale Owen and Fanny Wright, Brownson was an "agent," i.e., correspondent, for this publication, representing the area of Auburn, New York.[112]

It might of course be that ten years later, when he was writing his articles on the laboring classes, he had forgotten all about the ideas that had been circulating in New York. Shortly after those articles, however, Brownson presented an assessment of various responses to the present social condition. Amongst these he included several forms of socialism, with Skidmore being used as the American exponent of the agrarian variant. Brownson distanced himself from Skidmore's project "of introducing a better state of society by an equal division of property."[113] Although acknowledging that his own scheme had been labeled agrarian, Brownson emphasized that this was inappropriate because it called for the equal division of inherited property alone. As such, it recognized the following:

> the right to property is sacred, and the Legislature has no right to disturb it. The Legislature has discretionary power only over that portion of property which becomes vacant through default of ownership, whether by the death or abandonment of the proprietor.[114]

Although our three authors were committed to equal relative shares within each successive generation, none of them seemed particularly preoccupied by the intractable issue of the absolute size of those shares between generations. As they saw the matter, the size of shares through time was of secondary importance to an equal distribution by the annual sharing of bequests among maturing adults. They did realize that random short-term fluctuation in mortality, bequests, etc. might cause unwanted variations in the amount of the annual share, a tendency which could, however, be neutralized by an appropriate averaging procedure.[115] They were apparently much less worried by the variability of the annual share due to long-term demographic and economic tendencies. Obviously, the annual share remains constant only if the amount of bequests and the number of maturing adults change in the same proportion, which need not be the case. An additional problem would arise if it were required that the annual share be equal to the "fair share" of property, by which is meant the average amount of property per adult. The sustainability of the system is then by no means guaranteed, and depends upon both demographic and economic factors. It can be shown that the "bequest rate," i.e., the ratio of bequests to wealth, has to be equal to or higher than the "maturing adult rate," i.e., the ratio of maturing adults to the adult population. Skidmore and Brownson knew very well that *inter vivos* gifts might curtail bequests and hence undermine the system, and therefore they favored stringent measures to close at least that loophole.[116] But the rest were rather naively confident that the system was sustainable and that it would deliver roughly equal absolute shares across generations.

Notes

* The chapter was started when John Cunliffe was Visiting Professor at the Department of Economics, Faculty of Applied Economics, University of Antwerp, in January 2001; he thanks the University of Antwerp for its kind hospitality. We are grateful to Andrew Reeve, Tom Schatteman, Kristine Smets, Hillel Steiner, Robert van der Veen, Gijs van Donselaar, Philippe Van Parijs, Walter Van Trier and participants at the *HES 2001 Conference* (Wake Forest University, Winston–Salem (NC), June 30–July 2, 2001), the lunch seminar of the Department of Economics of the University of Antwerp (November 13, 2001), and the U.S. Basic Income Guarantee Network Conference (City University of New York, March 8–9, 2002) for their remarks and suggestions on various aspects of the chapter.

1 Wright (2000) 154. He provides an excellent analysis of the various contending schemes.

2 White (2001) 11, footnote 15, indicates the range of current proposals.

3 Ball (2000) 62–63.

4 These issues are explored by Levy (1983).

5 Katz (1977) 28.
6 Katz (1976) 470–473.
7 Jefferson to James Madison, October 28, 1795 (Jefferson 1999: 107).
8 Jefferson to James Madison, September 6, 1789 (Jefferson 1999: 593), Sloan (1993: 281–315) provides a detailed account of these philosophical reflections, and points out that this famous letter was made available to the public only in 1829, after Jefferson's death.
9 Jefferson to J.W. Eppes, June 24, 1813 (Jefferson 1999: 599).
10 Jefferson to James Madison, September 6, 1789 (Jefferson 1999: 593).
11 Ibid., 593.
12 Jefferson to J.W. Eppes, June 24, 1813 (Jefferson 1999: 599).
13 Jefferson to James Madison, October 28, 1795 (Jefferson 1999: 107).
14 Ball (2000: 73–74) suggests that Paine's view might be more extreme than Jefferson's. Both claimed that past generations had no power over the present one; but whereas Paine argued that the present generation had no obligation to the future, Jefferson's in usufruct or in trust proviso imposed such an obligation.
15 Paine (2000) 243.
16 Paine (2000) 325.
17 Ibid., 327.
18 Ibid., 326.
19 Ibid., 334.
20 Ibid., 328.
21 Ibid., 330–331.
22 Ibid., 324–325.
23 Ibid., 326.
24 Ibid., 327.
25 Ibid., 333.
26 Raymond (1823) vol. II, 14–15. For England, however, he seemed to prefer the more radical solution (Ibid., 82). For more details on Raymond's work, cf. Harris (1966) 20–33.
27 Harris (1966) 12.
28 The full title is *Some Causes of Popular Poverty, Derived from the Enriching Nature of Interests, Rents, Duties, Inheritances, and Church Establishments, Investigated in their Principles and Consequences, and Agreement with Scripture*. The name of the author is spelled as C.C. Blatchley.
29 Bestor (1970) 97–98.
30 Harris (1966) 12.
31 Hinshaw (1936), vol. III: 37.
32 Wilentz (1986) 158–161.
33 Blatchly (1817) 210.
34 Blatchly to Jefferson, October 6, 1822; Jefferson to Blatchly, October 21, 1822 in *The Thomas Jefferson Papers at the Library of Congress*, Series 1, General Correspondence, 1651–1827: 418–421, 445.
35 Bestor (1970) 99, 104; see also Lynd (1982) 86. The episode is not mentioned in Harrison (1969), the standard work on Owen.
36 Blatchly (1817) 195.
37 Ibid., 199.
38 Ibid., 199.
39 Ibid., 200.
40 Ibid., 210.

41 Harris (1966) 10.
42 Blatchly (1817) 205.
43 Ibid., 205.
44 Ibid., 206.
45 Ibid., 206.
46 Ibid., 206.
47 Ibid., 206.
48 Ibid., 206.
49 Blatchly (1822) 24.
50 Ibid., 5.
51 Ibid., 25.
52 Blatchly to Jefferson, October 6, 1822, in *The Thomas Jefferson Papers at the Library of Congress*, Series 1, General Correspondence, 1651–1827: 418.
53 Jefferson to Blatchly, October 21, 1822; ibid., 445.
54 Gilbert (1834), Harris (1966) 92–96, Hugins (1960) 82–83 and passim.
55 Pessen (1956).
56 See Carlton (1907) and Sumner [1918] for a general overview.
57 See Harris (1966) 94, Pessen (1963) 209, and Carlton (1907) 404. Skidmore obtained almost as many votes as Ebenezer Ford, who was elected for the Working Men's Party.
58 See Conkin (1980) 222–258 for an excellent account of American agrarianism. Pessen (1967) 148–149 claims that it is "reasonably certain" that Skidmore was influenced by the English agrarians Thomas Spence, William Ogilvie and Thomas Paine.
59 Skidmore (1829) 30–77. Note that in 1822 Skidmore wrote a long letter to Jefferson, to which Jefferson replied, but in it Skidmore dealt only with the plans of a revolutionary telescope he wanted to construct; see: Skidmore to Jefferson, August 18, 1822; Jefferson to Skidmore, August 29, 1822; in *The Thomas Jefferson Papers at the Library of Congress*, Series 1, General Correspondence, 1651–1827: 328–338, 344–345.
60 Skidmore (1829) title page, 58–63. This is, in fact, a return to the original Lockean formulation; cf. Katz (1976) 488.
61 Ibid., 127.
62 Lynd (1982) 88.
63 Conkin (1980) 225.
64 Owen (1829, 1830).
65 Pessen (1967) 147.
66 Skidmore (1829) 137–144.
67 Ibid., 139.
68 Ibid., 285.
69 Ibid., 284.
70 Ibid., 334.
71 Ibid., 102.
72 Ibid., 267.
73 Ibid., 284.
74 Ibid., 284.

75 Skidmore emphasized this point in an acerbic exchange of letters between Alexander Ming and himself with Owen published in *The Free Enquirer*. Skidmore and Ming maintained that the argument advanced in *The Rights of Man to Property!* did not simply call for the equal distribution of all inherited property in the form of a capital endowment. More significantly, it also demanded "a rational and equal division of property in the first instance" (Thomas Skidmore and Alexander Ming to Robert Dale Owen, *The Free Enquirer*, Second series, 2: 101 (January 23, 1830)). Otherwise, the adults of the present generation would remain dispossessed of their rightful property (Thomas Skidmore and Alexander Ming to Robert Dale Owen, *The Free Enquirer*, Second series, 2: 150 (March 6, 1830)). In similar vein, Skidmore admitted the significance of education for youngsters, but emphasized that this alone did nothing for the welfare of the adults themselves (Pessen 1967: 184).

76 Skidmore (1829) 256.

77 Ibid., 223.

78 Ibid., 230.

79 He was nicknamed "Weathercock" Brownson (Doudna 1978: v); see also Lasch (1991) 184–194.

80 Both articles were reprinted that same year; we will quote from the 1978 Doudna edition of these reprints.

81 Lasch (1995) 64–66, 69–70; Gilhooley (1972) 33–63.

82 See Brownson (1857) 90–99.

83 In 1840 he called Enfantin systematically "L'Enfantin."

84 Michel Chevalier, *Society, Manners, and Politics in the United States: Being a Series of Letters on North America*, Boston, Weeks Jordan and Co, 1839.

85 Brownson (1840a).

86 Brownson (1857) 92.

87 Brownson (1840a) 222.

88 Ibid., 223.

89 Brownson (1840b) 24.

90 Ibid., 24.

91 Ibid., 24.

92 Ibid., 3; this is in fact a quotation from the "Prefatory Note" added to the 1840 reprint of the article.

93 See Schlesinger (1966) 100–111.

94 Brownson (1840c) 59. It might be that he refers to his article "Equality" published in *The Gospel Advocate* of September 5, 1829 (7: 282–283), recently reprinted in Brownson (2000) 372–375.

95 Brownson (1840c) 60.

96 Ibid., 60.

97 Ibid., 61.

98 Ibid., 70.

99 Ibid., 66.

100 Ibid., 70.

101 Ibid., 72.

102 Ibid., 75.

103 Ibid., 78.

104 Ibid., 77.

105 Ibid., 79.

106 Skidmore (1829) 140–141.

107 Scott (1977) 60–70 discusses their ideas and their influence on public policy culminating in the Homestead Act of 1862.
108 Wilentz (1986) 211–216.
109 Harris (1966) 93.
110 Owen (1829). Ten of the eleven candidates on the ticket received over 6,000 votes; Blatchly received only 4,787 votes; see Sumner [1918] 240.
111 According to Wilentz (1986) 199, Blatchly was perceived as a supporter of Owen rather than Skidmore. In view of Blatchly's adoption of a communitarian stance, it seems quite plausible that he distanced himself from Skidmore.
112 He was first mentioned as an agent in the issue of November 7, 1829; his name disappeared from the issue of May 8, 1830 onwards. See also Brownson (1857) 62–63.
113 Brownson (1842) 487.
114 Ibid., 487.
115 Skidmore (1829) 259–60, Brownson (1840c) 77.
116 Skidmore (1829) 267–268, 346–348, Brownson (1840c) 81–82. Brownson thought it was possible to distinguish between genuine *inter vivos* gifts done for "charitable or benevolent purposes" and *causa mortis* gifts "made with a view to a man's death, and for the purpose of exercising indirectly a sort of dominion after his death." Only the last ones should be prohibited.

References

Ackerman, B. and Alstott, A. (1999) *The Stakeholder Society,* (New Haven and London: Yale University Press).

Ball, T. (2000) "The Earth Belongs to the Living: Thomas Jefferson and the Problem of Intergenerational Relations," *Environmental Politics*, 9: 61–77.

Bestor, A. (1971) *Backwoods Utopias: The Sectarian Origins and the Owenite Phase of Communitarian Socialism in America: 1663–1829,* (Philadelphia: University of Pennsylvania Press).

Blatchly, C. (1817) "Some Causes of Popular Poverty, Derived From the Enriching Nature of Interests, Rents, Duties, Inheritances, and Church Establishments, Investigated in Their Principles and Consequences, and Agreement With the Scripture," in *The Pleasures of Contemplation*, T. Branagan (ed.), (Philadelphia: Eastwick and Stacy), 195–220.

——— (1822) *An Essay on Common Wealths,* (New York: New York Society for Promoting Communities).

Brownson, O. (1840a) "Chevalier's Letters," *Boston Quarterly Review*, 3: 209–24.

——— (1840b) *The Laboring Classes,* (Delmar, N.Y.: Scholar's Facsimiles and Reprints).

——— (1840c) *Brownson's Defence of the Article on the Laboring Classes,* (Delmar, N.Y.: Scholar's Facsimiles and Reprints).

——— (1842) "Brook Farm", *The United States Democratic Review*, 11: 481–496.

——— (1857) *The Works of Orestes A. Brownson,* (Detroit: T. Nourse).

——— (2000) *The Early Works of Orestes A. Brownson, Vol. I: The Univeralst Years*, P. Carey (ed.), (Wisconsin: Marquette University Press).

Carlton, F. (1907) "The Workingmen's Party of New York City: 1829–1831," *Political Science Quarterly*, 22: 401–415.

Conkin, K. (1980) *Prophets of Prosperity: America's First Political Economists,* (Bloomington: Indiana University Press).

Doudna, M. (1978) "Introduction," in *The Laboring Classes (1840) with Brownson's*

Defence of the Article on the Laboring Classes, O. Brownson (Delmar, N.Y.: Scholar's Facsimiles and Reprints), v-xx.

Gilbert, A. (1834) "Sketch of the Life of Thomas Skidmore," *The Free Enquirer*, Third Series, 1: 179–180, 186–187, and 199–200.

Gilhooley, L. (1972) *Contradiction and Dilemma: Orestes Brownson and the American Idea,* (New York: Fordham University Press).

Harris, D. (1966) *Socialist Origins in the United States: American Forerunners of Marx, 1817–1832,* (Assen: Van Gorcum and Company).

Harrison, J. (1969) *Robert Owen and the Owenites in Britain and America: The Quest for a New Moral World,* (London: Routledge and Kegan Paul).

Hinshaw, W. (1936) *Encyclopedia of American Quaker Genealogy,* (Michigan: Edwards Bros.).

Hugins, W. (1960) *Jacksonian Democracy and the Working Class: A Study of the New York Workingmen's Movement, 1829–1837,* (Stanford: Stanford University Press).

Jefferson, T. (1999) *Political Writings,* J. Appleby and T. Ball (eds.), (Cambridge: Cambridge University Press).

——— *The Thomas Jefferson Papers at the Library of Congress.* http://memory.loc .gov/ammem/mtjhtml/mtjhome.html.

Katz, S. (1976) "Thomas Jefferson and the Right to Property in Revolutionary America," *Journal of Law and Economics*, 19: 467–488.

——— (1977) "Republicanism and the Law of Inheritance in the American Revolutionary Era," *Michigan Law Review*, 76: 1–29.

Lasch, C. (1991) *The True and Only Heaven: Progress and its Critics,* (New York and London: W.W. Norton and Company).

——— (1995) *The Revolt of the Elites and the Betrayal of Democracy,* (New York and London: W.W. Norton and Company).

Levy, M. (1983) "Liberal Equality and Inherited Wealth," *Political Theory*, 11: 545–564.

Lynd, S. (1982) *Intellectual Origins of American Liberalism,* (Cambridge and London: Harvard University Press).

Matthews, R. (1984) *The Radical Politics of Thomas Jefferson: A Revisionist View,* (Lawrence: University of Kansas Press).

Nissan, D. and Le Grand, J. (2000) *A Capital Idea: Start-up Grants for Young People,* (London: Fabian Society).

Owen, R. (1829) "The Election," *The Free Enquirer*, Second series, 2: 24.

——— (1830) "Movement of the People," *The Free Enquirer*, Second series, 2: 161–164.

Paine, T. (2000) *Political Writings,* B. Kuklick (ed.), (Cambridge: Cambridge University Press).

Pessen, E. (1956) "The Workingmen's Movement of the Jacksonian Era," *Mississippi Valley Historical Review*, 43: 428–443.

——— (1963) "The Working Men's Party Revisited," *Labor History*, 4: 203–226.

——— (1967) *Most Uncommon Jacksonians: The Radical Leaders of the Early Labor Movement,* (Albany: State of New York University Press).

Raymond, D. (1823) *The Elements of Political Economy, In Two Parts,* (Baltimore: F. Lucas Jun. and E.J. Coale).

Schlesinger, A. (1966) *A Pilgrim's Progress: Orestes A. Brownson,* (Boston and Toronto: Little, Brown and Company).

Scott, W. (1977) *In Pursuit of Happiness: American Conceptions of Property from the Seventeenth to the Twentieth Century,* (Bloomington and London: Indiana University Press).

Skidmore, T. (1829) *The Rights of Man to Property! Being a Proposition to Make it Equal*

Among the Adults of the Present Generation: and to Provide for its Equal Transmission to Every Individual of Each Succeeding Generation, on Arriving at the Age of Maturity, (New York: Burt Franklin).

Sloan, H. (1993) "The Earth Belongs in Usufruct to the Living" in *Jeffersonian Legacies*, P. Onuf (ed.), (Charlottesville: University Press of Virginia).

Sumner, H. (1966) [1918] "Citizenship (1827–1833)" in *History of Labour in the United States*, J. Commons et al. (eds.), (New York: Augustus M. Kelly).

White, S. (2001) "Rediscovering Republican Political Economy," *Citizen's Income Newsletter*, 1: 3–12.

Wilentz, S. (1986) *Chants Democratic: New York City and the Rise of the American Working Class, 1788–1850,* (New York and Oxford: Oxford University Press).

Wright, E. (2000) "Reducing Income and Wealth Inequalities: Real Utopian Proposals," *Contemporary Sociology*, 29: 143–156.

Chapter 4

The Guaranteed Income Movement of the 1960s and 1970s

Robert Harris

Introduction and Overview

The late 1960s and early 1970s saw great activity in the development of American social policy. Long-standing programs were modified and expanded, and much new legislation was passed. A civil rights revolution took place, and providing equal access to the American Dream for all was given a prominent place on the political agenda. In addition, a war on poverty was declared and the goal of eradicating rather than ameliorating poverty was established. Areas of sizable program expansion of particular interest to the poor included cash transfer programs, education, housing, and health financing programs. But by the end of the Carter administration the mood had changed and "reform" came to be associated with cutting rather than improving the welfare system. Under the names "guaranteed income" and "negative income tax" (NIT) the prospects for a basic income guarantee rose and fell with the movement to make the welfare system more effective.

At the time the war on poverty was declared in 1964, 36 million people were counted as poor by federal statisticians. In 1976, after federal outlays for income security and other social welfare programs had grown rapidly for 12 years, the number counted as poor remained at about 26 million. By 2002, the number in poverty rose to 30 million. Despite massive increases in direct income transfers, poverty remains. The reason for this seeming paradox is that most growth in outlays was not in programs carefully targeted on the poor or having impacts on their incomes. Most new money has been added to social insurance programs—primarily Social Security. While some of any such increase in benefits goes to poor people, it is a small fraction. Other programs funded under the banner of war on poverty—training, health care, education, and other services—proved to have little or no short-run impact on people's incomes or employability even though they have proven useful in achieving other objectives and may still prove to have significant longer run benefits.

Controversial as all of the social welfare expansions were, particularly many of the antipoverty programs, none were more controversial and conflict laden than the attempt to enact structural reform in the welfare system during the late 1960s and early 1970s. At the start of the 1960s, a large number of program proposals for improving the existing set of income transfer programs circulated widely, within government and outside. By the end of the Johnson years in power, most such proposals had been discarded as excessively costly in relation to the benefits they would yield, or had been enacted. The welfare system, extensively criticized, had not been reformed; and the tasks of choosing a plan and transmitting it to Congress were left to an incoming Republican president, Richard Nixon.

Many specific program plans for welfare reform were discussed during the Democratic years, most falling within one of two well-defined strategies:

- Provide direct government income support to all low-income Americans, and build other initiatives on that base of support (the guaranteed income approach).
- Provide income support to those who are unemployable, or whom society has deemed not required to work, and let everyone else earn their incomes, either in the private sector or government jobs (the more traditional conditional approach).

Each strategy can accommodate numerous reform plans, and the apparent simplicity with which the strategies can be stated disappears quickly as specific operational plans are enumerated.

Within each strategy there were liberal and conservative plans, and liberals and conservatives were found among proponents of each strategy. This makes for complex politics, which is sometimes difficult to follow. The reform debate within the last Johnson administration took place largely among liberals, and involved different views of the proper strategy to follow. Conservatives involved in the public debate over reform also split over which strategy was to be preferred, but generally preferred less generous plans within either strategy. President Nixon in his early proposals chose modest plans consistent with the universal strategy.

The legislative struggle that took place in the early 1970s also revolved, in large part, around choice of strategy. The House opted for the universal income support strategy, at a moderately low level. The Senate opted for the categorical strategy, at an abysmally low level. The president could possibly have resolved the issue one way or another, but chose not to intervene in the last days. That struggle ended in stalemate, with traditional family welfare programs unchanged, but with two new federal programs added—one consistent with each of the strategies. The Supplemental Security Income (SSI) program, adopted in 1972, federalized and liberalized welfare for the aged, blind and disabled. The Food Stamp program, made universal in 1974, is a low-level universal income supplement plan, with eligibility determined by low income.

This chapter reviews the debate in Washington over the major proposals that were put forward during the decade of the 1960s, with special attention to comprehensive reform proposals using guaranteed income. Section 1 begins by briefly tracing the development of the programs in need of reform. This is necessary because the system was developed over a long period, following a strategy laid out in the 1930s. Section 2 outlines the criticisms of the income security system of the 1930s that developed during the debates, and the split that developed among "liberals." The congressional struggle over a specific reform plan is outlined in Section 3, leading up to the death of President Nixon's Family Assistance Plan in 1972.

1. Development of the United States Welfare System

A major federal role in income security appeared fairly recently in our history. Other than some early provisions for veterans, and providing opportunities to participate in economic development of the frontier, the federal government left the task of providing income security to states until the Great Depression of the 1930s. The states continued to follow their colonial practices, largely modeled on earlier English practice. Persons viewed as employable were generally not generously treated.

Easy access to free or cheap land provided access to a living for many for much of our early history. As this outlet for "employables" closed, rapid urbanization, emigration, mobility, and rootlessness caused breakdowns in earlier support systems—family responsibility, church charity and private charity, and ultimately local assistance systems. As America became increasingly urbanized and industrialized, tales of urban squalor, poverty, malnutrition, and the like increasingly dominated the social reform literature. Pictures of unhealthy children and large families crowded into small apartments were widely circulated.

To deal with these problems of an industrializing society with a rapidly growing population that had neither land, capital, nor skills, a patchwork set of state and private programs developed. These included programs of unemployment compensation, mothers' pensions, aid to the blind, aid to the aged, and workman's compensation programs, and elaborately organized private charitable organizations. For the poor population not eligible for assistance under the public programs, work in the private sector was the sole or main source of income available. If earnings were inadequate, families might do without, and many did.

This system could not deal with problems of severe economic crisis and prolonged mass unemployment. In such conditions it would break down, and prove inadequate for maintenance of a stable society. The Great Depression led to such a breakdown in the system, and forced a search for something better. Long-term mass unemployment on what seemed to be an unprecedented scale appeared, and federal action to provide relief became necessary. State and municipal systems of relief and private charity were financially unable to deal with such widespread distress.

The New Deal

The history briefly noted above is known today only to students of the subject. First-hand experience with the fairly widespread deprivation that existed until well into the twentieth century, fortunately, has been denied to most living Americans.

The severity of the Great Depression forced the federal government to create programs that would function even under very serious conditions. Many programs were adopted during that crisis, and a national strategy for income security was developed that achieved wide political acceptability. At least until the 1980s, it was generally and enthusiastically embraced by most liberals, and accepted as a necessary evil by most conservatives.

The overall structure put forth was based on a model of how a modern society must function to provide economic security to all of its members. The model required that the economy should be made to function so well that anyone who is capable of work would be able to find a job at a high enough wage to adequately support himself and his dependents. The government could do this by stimulating private employment, statutorily mandating a minimum wage, and financing public works and other public employment if needed. It was assumed that such employment would insure adequate income.

With this vision of the desired society, a program strategy such as the one we adopted made sense then, and would now if the institutions functioned as envisioned.

- Long-term income assistance would only be provided to those outside of the labor force for socially acceptable reasons. It would, to the extent possible, be related to past earnings. Social insurance is to be the key antipoverty program.
- The involuntarily unemployed would receive similar earnings-related benefits for a defined period, while they sought their next job.
- For those in the dependent categories, but without insurance coverage, income-tested assistance would be provided.
- Able-bodied non-aged individuals who are not the sole custodians of young children are expected to fully earn their way during their working years: The government is to ensure that they have that opportunity. While working they are to accumulate credit for various insurance through their earnings history.
- Welfare programs available to employables—including the later Aid to Families with Dependent Children (AFDC) and local general assistance programs—have always been intended as short-term or emergency aid.

The system has changed a great deal since the Great Depression, but—notwithstanding the exception of harsher treatment of single mothers after the introduction of Temporary Aid to Needy Families (TANF) in 1996—it still reflects the same underlying strategy and assumptions that emerged from a long and continuous historical evolution of economies and ideas. Elements of the system have been traced back to medieval times, when guilds performed some social insurance functions and the church provided assistance to the helpless.

Refinement of the System up to the 1960s

Those aspects of the 1930s strategy calling for creation of plentiful jobs have never been adopted as a permanent and regular part of national policy, although debate and political conflict have been continuous. Thus, the model has never been fully implemented. Development of a comprehensive income security policy lagged in the 1940s and 1950s, in part due to a stalemate between liberals and conservatives and in part due to pressing external events.

These years saw continual political battle between liberals and conservatives over its completion. The tendency was for "liberals" to support the overall strategy outlined. That is, they tend to favor the following: a) large-scale public works and public employment to create plentiful jobs at all times, on the grounds that such activity is needed to achieve a full system of economic security, b) steadily higher minimum wage rates to ensure that workers' incomes are adequate, c) improved social insurance programs, and d) generous welfare benefits for those not in the labor force. "Conservatives" tended to accept the income security programs as enacted, but to oppose other actions except during serious recessions. They argued that minimum wage increases eliminate jobs, and that government efforts to keep tight labor markets during periods of relative prosperity are inflationary, breed economic inefficiency and prove counterproductive in the end.

During the immediate post-war period, political concern was more narrowly focused on avoiding a serious post-war recession and fostering economic growth. During the 1950s the view was fairly widely held that the poor would benefit more from economic growth than from redistributive policies, and little was directly done for the employable population. It was commonly assumed that low unemployment, a rising average income, and general economic growth would eliminate poverty.

Even during this period of retrenchment and consolidation older programs were modified somewhat and extended, largely improving economic security for "deserving" people outside the labor force. Numerous incremental changes in the New Deal programs took place, and some new ones were added to the original set. Four reforms in this period are notable:

1. The Employment Act of 1946 created a Council of Economic Advisors and a Congressional Joint Economic Committee. These political mechanisms ensure that the need for economic policies to stimulate employment and growth are highly visible and considered publicly. No specific policies are required, however, and attempts to pass a Full Employment Act failed.
2. Those mechanisms and others have been used to develop and implement fiscal and monetary policies to regulate the economy. Tools used have included public works projects, public employment, and tax cuts. Each recession leads to unique solutions—some successful, some not. Such policies have, occasionally, been held responsible for creating both inflation and recession.

3. Programs enacted in the 1930s were expanded, extended, and liberalized, but within their basic framework. Disability Insurance was added to basic Old Age and Survivors Insurance in 1956, Aid to the Permanently and Totally Disabled was added to public assistance in 1950. Minimum wage rates were periodically raised.
4. Narrow provisions were enacted during the 1950s to allow medical vendor payments to pay for some health care of public assistance recipients.

By 1960, however, complete implementation of the vision of a comprehensive system had not been achieved. Regular programs to stimulate and generate adequate employment opportunities were not in place, nor had provisions been made to finance health care needs. Serious consideration of the entire income security system awaited the 1960s.

2. Resurgence of Social Policy Development and Reconsideration of Strategy

The 1960s ushered in a new period of activity based in part on the long deferred plans of liberals and the coming to power of an activist Democratic administration. A set of new social welfare programs was adopted in the first half of the 1960s, many inspired by the earlier vision. Starting with the Area Redevelopment Act of 1961 and the Manpower Development and Training Act of 1962, we adopted programs to stimulate employment and otherwise improve the well-being of individuals at a rapid pace. Among the major ones are the following:

- The addition of Aid to Families with Dependent Children–Unemployed Parent (AFDC-UP) to the basic AFDC program in 1961, a first departure from the principle of not providing routine federal welfare assistance to unemployed employables.
- A Food Stamp program, initiated as a pilot project by executive order in 1961, was enacted in 1964. This program was originally available at local option and remained small until federal benefit and eligibility standards were imposed in 1971 and all counties were required to adopt it in 1974.
- The Social Security amendments of 1962 and 1965, which created broad, federally funded social services programs and medical care programs for welfare recipients and retirees under Social Security, respectively.
- The Economic Opportunity Act of 1964, implementing the war on poverty declared by President Johnson, created the Office of Economic Opportunity (OEO).
- A sizeable permanent income tax cut in 1964, stimulating the economy and generating higher levels of employment.
- The Elementary and Secondary Education Act of 1965, to improve educational opportunities of disadvantaged children.

As this legislative activity took place and programs were implemented, some of the analysts, planners, and political officials who were pushing for these reforms began to have doubts about the New Deal strategy. They had few doubts about the objectives being pursued—opportunity, equality, ending poverty, or providing jobs. They did, however, begin to question whether the entire structure of the New Deal vision, even if fully implemented, could achieve the intended objectives.

Basic criticisms of both the vision and programs emerged by the middle 1960s that provided the inspiration for the guaranteed income movement. The conflict among liberals over the workability of the structure envisaged in the New Deal model complicated the traditional liberal–conservative clashes over whether to do anything by creating additional clashes over which liberal strategy to pursue. The origins of the clash were in the war on poverty, which caused review of both the model and the programs of the 1930s. The doubts first emerged in criticisms of the welfare system, then moved on to other programs, and quickly were expressed about the self-help strategy implicit in the war on poverty itself. This led some, who can be referred to for convenience as the "poverty analysts," to seek a new strategy.

Programmatic Criticisms

Early in the review of programs, the public assistance system was found wanting. Among the revealed sins were the following:

- Many recipients of welfare remained poor despite the aid they received.
- Benefits provided to equally poor people varied widely, depending on geographic location, age, sex, family composition, and other criteria unrelated to need.
- The structure of the system provided financial disincentives for socially acceptable behavior. Recipients had little financial incentive to work. And poor families could gain financially by splitting.
- The programs were extremely complex and key elements were left to local or caseworker discretion. Their administration was inevitably rife with errors and seeming inequities.

When looking beyond the assistance programs to the social insurance part of the system, things seemed not much better.

- Social insurance programs troubled the poverty analysts. Many Social Security beneficiaries remained poor despite expensive redistributive elements that had been added to the system over the years. Unemployment Insurance (UI) benefits and coverage varied widely by state, with many benefits being very low. And the bulk of benefits did not help the poor.
- Upon careful scrutiny, however, it did not seem likely that social insurance programs could serve as very efficient or effective vehicles for significantly aiding those who remained poor. Because benefits were tied to past earnings records, they could not be easily made to help those who had never had decent earnings.

Finally, relying on labor markets to help employables was scrutinized. Here, the results were not promising.

- Many of the poor were excluded from eligibility for both social assistance and social insurance programs, despite having incomes lower than some "eligibles." The ineligible working poor, in particular, were discovered.
- Early experience with manpower training and other service programs designed to change the characteristics of the poor were very disappointing. They did not seem capable of increasing potential earnings—at least in the short run.
- Jobs were not in plentiful supply for the unskilled, and had not been for quite some time.

The poverty analysts reached a conclusion very early: The war on poverty was doomed to fail without directly increasing the incomes of the poor. Choosing a programmatic means of achieving this obvious goal led to a split among liberals

Table 4.1 Unemployment rate; number of persons and families in poverty, 1960–1975

	Unemployment Rate (percent)			Poverty Count (millions)	
Year	**All Workers 20 and Over**	**Males 20 and Over**	**Females 20 and Over**	**Persons**	**Families**
1960	5.5	4.7	5.1	39.9	8.2
1961	6.7	5.7	6.3	39.6	8.4
1962	5.5	4.6	5.4	38.6	8.1
1963	5.7	4.5	5.4	36.4	7.6
1964	5.2	3.9	5.2	36.1	7.2
1965	4.5	3.2	4.5	33.2	6.7
1966	3.8	2.5	3.8	28.5	5.8
1967	3.8	2.3	4.2	27.8	5.7
1968	3.6	2.2	3.8	25.4	5.0
1969	3.5	2.1	3.7	24.1	5.0
1970	4.9	3.5	4.8	25.4	5.3
1971	5.9	4.4	5.7	25.6	5.3
1972	5.6	4.0	5.4	24.5	5.1
1973	4.9	3.2	4.8	23.0	4.8
1974	5.6	3.8	5.5	23.4	4.9
1975	8.5	6.7	8.0	25.9	5.5

Source: Unemployment data, *Economic Report of the President*, 1977, p. 221. Poverty data, U.S. Bureau of the Census, *Characteristics of the Population Below the Poverty Level*, 1974, Series P-60, No. 102, p. 13; and *Money Income and Poverty Status of Families and Persons in the United States: 1975 and 1974 Revisions*, Series P-60, No. 103.

because it involved reconsideration of a long-accepted strategy. By starting to review programs using the criterion of poverty *elimination*, a more stringent test of performance was being applied than before.

This test was a new element in program review. Once poverty was defined statistically in 1960 and officially measured by the government, analysts and politicians made a discovery: There are lots of poor people, even when jobs are relatively plentiful. Table 4.1 presents the problem as analysts saw it in its simplest form. In 1969, when unemployment was at its lowest since World War II, there were still 24 million people counted as poor. Many of the poor already worked, or were members of employable groups ineligible for assistance. Others received assistance, but still were poor.

Because such low unemployment rates were still associated with tens of millions of people living in poverty, analysts came to regard the full employment vision as insufficient, even if attractive and worth achieving. Many concluded that the principles of the program were based upon a wish rather than reality. They concluded on the basis both of simplistic analyses, such as that presented in Table 4.1, and improved econometric projections, that the tightest attainable labor markets, coupled with further "perfection" of the traditional programs, would not eliminate poverty. There would still be workers with low earnings relative to need; there would still be some unemployed persons.

They concluded that to achieve the objective while relying exclusively on earnings for workers required very large commitments to high-wage public employment for millions and the possibility of inflation. A cheaper way was needed. Despite the great accomplishments of the New Deal programs, they concluded that programs based on that strategy could not completely provide economic security to all Americans except at unbearable cost, both in budgetary terms and in terms of societal and economic disruption.

The New Strategy of the Poverty Analysts

The first overall antipoverty plan was presented to the White House in 1964 by Sargent Shriver (director of OEO 1964–1969). It stressed three programs: a large-scale public employment plan, community action, and a negative income tax. In each succeeding year a new plan was presented. The plans varied from year to year, but each included a negative income tax plan. The NIT would provide a basic guaranteed income, to be reduced by only 50 percent of earnings. This was designed to maintain work incentives for new recipients of cash aid, and to strengthen work incentives for recipients of AFDC, which along with other public assistance programs would be completely displaced by the negative income tax after a phase-in period.

Detailed memoranda were provided each year outlining many reasons for this proposal, and presenting different ways of phasing in such a plan. Several elements of the analysts' reasoning are crucial to understanding their recurring insistence of the need for this program.

- Data on the characteristics of the poor indicated that the only way to increase their incomes quickly and with certainty was to provide a system of direct income supplements to all of the poor.
- The fact that employables were ineligible for public assistance created inequities. It was possible for an AFDC family without a worker to have a higher income than a family headed by a low-earner.
- Improving welfare benefits within the categorical framework of the program would exacerbate this inequity. A universal rather than a categorical program was needed to eliminate the inequity and to raise the incomes of employables and the working poor.
- A NIT with a poverty-level guarantee would completely displace the existing state-run public assistance programs. This was desired because of the great variation and excessive complexity of the state programs, and because the programs were amenable to coercive administration.
- The assumptions behind AFDC were being questioned. By program design, some people were deemed "unemployable," and earnings reduced grants on a dollar-for-dollar basis. This disincentive conflicted with some basic facts: a) many of the women receiving aid were capable of work, and many did; b) many mothers of young children not on welfare worked; c) sentiment with respect to their employability was shifting, reflected in the 1962 amendments providing rehabilitative services.
- The NIT provided strong work incentives. This was viewed as necessary for two reasons: Employables were to be eligible. To solve the age-old dilemma of providing aid to the able-bodied without encouraging malingering required that they be given a strong self-interest in working.
- Finally, advocates at the OEO noted that the NIT program would be smaller and less necessary if full employment were maintained, and if the service programs worked. They argued that if the NIT were adopted, the cost of failure to deliver jobs would be borne by the government rather than the poor.

These reports took a fundamentally different position than most traditional liberals had. It called for a shift from the traditional policy that the "helpless" should be deemed out of the labor market and provided for adequately by society. It argued instead that society should provide a floor for everyone, and that everyone should be expected to help themselves to higher levels through work. Basically, they argued for keeping most of the old programs, although each might be modified, and for adding a new program of basic income support for all.

Congress, in 1967, partially adopted this general stance, at least with respect to recipients of AFDC; albeit in a limited way. It provided for work incentives to AFDC recipients and mandated that employable recipients be referred to training and jobs—the WIN program.

Defense of the Traditional Strategy

On the other side, supporters of the existing system argued strongly that their system had never been completed, and that the basis for a fair test was lacking. They argued that government had shirked its responsibility to make the strategy work by not ensuring that jobs at adequate wages were abundant. They felt that if the federal government would undertake this task, the system could be made to operate as envisioned in the 1930s, and would eliminate poverty as well. Traditionalists at the Department of Heath, Education, and Welfare (HEW), at the Department of Labor, and in the AFL-CIO—many of whom had lived through the New Deal and helped nurture its programs over the years—tended to adopt this view. They argued that we should not discard their strategy until it had been fully implemented, and they had little regard for the economists' *projections* that it would not work.

Legislative proposals emanating from these circles tended to emphasize incremental changes in the income programs of the 1930s:

- Mandate minimum benefits in state public assistance and UI programs.
- Mandate AFDC-UP in all states.
- Increase Social Security benefits.
- Expand and improve manpower training programs.
- Considerably raise minimum wages.
- Actively pursue policies to maintain very tight labor markets.

Some argued for the government to become the employer of last resort and to guarantee employment. Some also advocated children's allowances, whereby the government would provide payments to all families based on the number of children to tailor family income to family size. In effect, they also argued for keeping all of the old programs, but perfecting them and adding the missing element: plentiful jobs. They opposed, in principle, treating employables on the same basis as "unemployables."

Bert Seidman, Director of the AFL-CIO Department of Social Security in the 1970s, summarized this view.

> Any genuine welfare reform must, first and foremost, emphasize the child's welfare. It should rely primarily on nonwelfare programs to develop and assure suitable jobs at decent wages supplemented by improved social insurance, health security, and other programs aimed at eliminating poverty. This will require a multifaceted approach.... (W)elfare, or whatever it is called, could become a residual program providing a decent level of living to people who can't work at all or ought not to be required to work... (*American Federationist*, AFL-CIO, February 1973).

Debate over the OEO Proposal

The OEO proposal was debated within the administration from 1965 until President Johnson left office in 1969. OEO submitted such a recommendation to the White House each year as part of the budget and legislative cycle. Formal considerations took place within a series of annual White House Task Forces on Income Maintenance. In 1965 such a task force, chaired by Otto Eckstein of the Council of Economic Advisors, did considerable staff work on the NIT idea and explored a number of variants. It viewed the creation of such a program favorably and dubbed it the Minimum Income Allowance. Later task forces considered many similar plans. While generally favorably disposed towards such plans, the task forces were cautious, viewing them as politically difficult. Typically, recommendations were made to incrementally improve existing programs while continuing to study NIT. The 1966 Task Force recommended creation of a presidential commission to conduct such a review.

The President's Commission on Income Maintenance was appointed in 1968, chaired by Ben Heineman. The commission reported late in 1969, during the Nixon Administration. In its report, it proposed adoption of a universal negative income tax to replace the existing welfare system and improvements in other programs. It essentially accepted the line of reasoning developed at OEO, and called for adopting the new income security strategy outlined above. Its report was overshadowed somewhat by the fact that President Nixon had already announced support for a more limited version of the negative income tax.

3. Development and Fate of the Family Assistance Plan (FAP)

President Nixon took office in 1969, having pledged to reform the welfare system. His staff's consideration of options drew upon the extensive body of analytic work that had been undertaken in the previous several years. The starting point was a pre-election Nixon task force report prepared under the supervision of Richard Nathan of the Brookings Institution. The Task Force report presented a set of recommendations that fit the traditional liberal pattern. It would have, among other things, provided for continuation of the existing set of categorical programs, federally mandated a minimum benefit level, and increased the federal share in program cost. The working poor continued to be excluded.

The Nathan plan was the beginning point for a debate that split the Nixon Administration and continued for almost a year. This debate split Republicans much as the debate over the NIT had earlier split liberals in the Democratic administration. The first casualty was the Nathan plan itself, which was knocked out of consideration early when it was noted that although the plan would provide more income to the lowest income welfare recipients, it would thereby create new inequities because it did nothing for those not categorically eligible for aid. Department of Health, Education, and Welfare (HEW) planners came forward with an alternative proposal that would have both increased the incomes of the lowest welfare recipients and moderated the inequities by making male-headed families eligible for income supplements. They proposed substituting a negative income tax for families with children for the AFDC program. In addition, minimum benefits would have been mandated for public assistance recipients who were aged, blind, or disabled.

The HEW plan was seized upon by Daniel Patrick Moynihan, a former Democratic official (and future Democratic senator) turned Domestic Affairs Advisor to President Nixon. He viewed it as a plan providing an opportunity to eliminate inequities in the current system, increase the incomes of the poorest, and start thorough reform of the system. It ran into stiff opposition from administration conservatives, however, led by Arthur Burns, Counselor to the President. The argument hinged, as had earlier debates, on whether to aid employables at all, and how to define that group. Burns strongly opposed extending welfare aid to the latter group, and instead argued that welfare be restricted to the strictly helpless. In his view, anyone employable should be required to work—including existing welfare parents. His plan would have encouraged states to move up to a nationally determined minimum welfare standard for the traditionally eligible groups, and expanded training and day care centers to put welfare mothers to work. He thus not only opposed supplementing incomes of the working poor and employables generally, but also wished to cut back on eligibility for existing aid. In the end, the HEW plan was adopted by the president, and in August 1969 he proposed his version of the NIT (the Family Assistance Plan) in a television address.

The Backdoor Guaranteed Income

While the income debate was underway, the politics of hunger was independently moving towards legislation. In the late 1960s a campaign had been mounted to end recently discovered hunger in America, largely led by congressional liberals, and supported by the poor and their representatives. In May of 1969, President Nixon proposed to Congress an expanded Food Stamp program, to head off independent congressional consideration of a similar plan put forward by Senator McGovern, which might have left the administration in the position of favoring hunger. A nationwide Food Stamp program emerged from that political battle that entitled all low-income people to receive subsidized food stamps. The Food Stamp program, in effect, is a universal (in-kind) negative income tax with benefits in coupons redeemable only for food instead of money. It provides an income guarantee (in stamps), which is reduced by 30 percent of earnings. The Food Stamp program was enacted in 1969, and after liberalization in the 1970s provided a modest guaranteed income to all Americans.

This program, if coupled with FAP, would have provided a guaranteed income to all Americans. When proposed by President Nixon in 1969, the two plans would have provided benefits of about $2,400 for a family of four with no other income. Those benefits would have been reduced by 65 percent of earnings under both programs combined, a higher "tax rate" than NIT advocates preferred. And the childless would not have received cash aid, but food stamps alone. This was not quite the program proposed by NIT advocates of the previous administration, but structurally it reflected the break with past traditions they felt necessary.

Congressional Consideration of the Family Assistance Plan

FAP was proposed in late 1969, and strongly supported by the administration. In 1970 the House passed the bill, with some changes. It did not fare so well in the Senate, however. The Senate Finance Committee held hearings, and conservative Republicans led an attack on the bill. They identified serious imperfections in planning and program design and used them to attack the plan. The plan was also attacked by many traditional liberals, and by organized welfare recipients and their representatives. The traditional liberals viewed it as not generous enough and repressive in that it implicitly required AFDC recipients to be viewed as potential workers, as well as incorporating a work requirement for others. Organized welfare recipients coming from relatively generous states would not have been helped by the plan, and feared ultimate losses because they were conceptually thrown into the same category as employables.

In 1971 the administration put forward a similar plan correcting some of the technical flaws used earlier to reject it. The House made significant structural changes, but, again, passed a bill similar to that proposed. The main difference was that it became FAP-OFF, with employables segregated into the Opportunities for Families program, to be run by the Department of Labor, aimed at providing them with training and employment. These families were, however, still eligible for the same benefits in the absence of employment, and the working poor received supplementation. The Finance Committee this time not only failed to approve the House bill, but substituted its own plan for FAP. The "Guaranteed Job Opportunity for Families" plan put forward by Senator Long (one of the fiercest opponents of the NIT in Congress at the time) contained a mix of elements designed to infuriate both traditional liberals and the poverty analysts. He had taken some of their ideas and given them a perverse twist. He would have created a Government Work Administration to provide jobs for those who could work, but pay only $1.50 per hour for up to 32 hours of work per week, providing total income of $2,400 per year—the same amount as FAP plus food stamps. It also provided wage supplements for persons employed in the private sector and a work bonus that in effect rebated Social Security taxes to low-income workers. AFDC would have continued to provide support, but only to mothers of preschool children. The plan garnered no praise except from extreme conservatives.

Senator Ribicoff, who supported reform efforts, developed a more generous version of FAP, and tried to use this as a basis for compromise. By being more generous he hoped to win liberal support. By following the White House reform structure he expected administration support. The Ribicoff plan was offered as an amendment to the Finance Committee bill. By then, however, President Nixon had lost interest and would not agree to support the Ribicoff compromise. By a vote of 52–34 the amendment was rejected and Senator Long's version was passed.

Despite its lack of support, it was embedded in a generally popular bill raising Social Security benefits.

The House and Senate had passed irreconcilable amendments to AFDC, and in conference both were dropped, so that AFDC remained unchanged by the 1972 Social Security Act Amendments.

The rest of the welfare system, however, has been extensively changed by the decade of activity. The 1972 Social Security Amendments incorporated a radical change in the adult public assistance programs. Federally assisted but state-run programs of Old Age Assistance, Aid to the Blind, and Aid to the Permanently and Totally Disabled were replaced by SSI—a federally operated income support program structured as a negative income tax. This liberalization passed both houses without opposition. While AFDC has changed little, the addition of a universal Food Stamp program has ironed out some of the inequities inherent in the categorical cash aid system. Many of the problems identified in 1964 remained, but many were alleviated.

4. What killed the Family Assistance Plan?

FAP ultimately failed in the Senate by a 52–34 vote. If the White House had been able to swing 10 votes, a version of the negative income tax would have been in place by 1972, albeit a flawed one. Whether such a vote swing was possible must remain conjectural. Some have used the failure of FAP to argue that global policy changes are impossible, that only incremental policy changes are possible. In that case, the cause of the basic income guarantee (which involves a fundamental change in the model of the welfare system) is permanently doomed. Fortunately, FAP is not a good test case for that hypothesis.

It was clear at the time of final consideration of the plan in Congress that the White House was not actively working to try to swing those votes, and it most certainly could have changed some of them: Presidents have a great deal to offer in the political trading that accompanies most major pieces of legislation, and they can usually swing a large number of votes for their legislative priorities. Moreover, we now know that although the proposal came from Nixon himself, the president did not want it to pass and that the White House may have worked actively against passage. H.R. Haldeman, Nixon's chief of staff, published his diaries in 1994 and notes the following on July 13, 1970:

> About Family Assistance Plan, wants to be sure it's killed by Democrats and that we make a big play for it, but don't let it pass, can't afford it.

And killed by Democrats it was, with a number of liberals refusing to support even the Ribicoff proposal which, while following the structure of the administration's plan, was more generous.

Conclusions

In the aftermath of the partial failure of a decade-long reform effort, many new proposals were studied and put forward. Through the 1970s many of these proposals contained elements of a negative income tax, including the Earned Income Tax Credit, which is a conditional negative income tax tied to participation in the low-wage labor market. But, beginning in the 1980s the political climate changed. The dark ages arrived with President Reagan and we started going backwards, cutting back on eligibility both for AFDC and Food Stamps, and the like. Conservatives who had grudgingly accepted the welfare system gained the political strength to cut programs and to toughen the conditions. The effort to move toward greater universality was forgotten by both sides. Under Clinton, we retrenched even further in some respects, abolishing important features of the AFDC program, handing more discretion over the program to states—and giving governors lots of money saved through the new restrictions on the program—and, in the process, making many of the poor worse off while removing a level of protection from the next recession for many others. It is unsurprising that poverty has gradually increased since efforts to improve the welfare system were abandoned in the late 1970s.

The opportunity to change the theory behind the welfare state from the conditional model of the New Deal to the comprehensive model of the guaranteed income was lost. However, Food Stamps, the EITC, and the more recent move toward refundable tax credits are direct outgrowths of the guaranteed income movement of the 1960s and 1970s. The flaws in the assumptions behind the conditional welfare system are as apparent now as when they were discovered in the early 1960s. The move toward universal income support remains a ready alternative if and when the government recognizes that something has to be done about 30 million people who live in poverty.

References

This reference list is brief, but it contains some of the most important publications on the guaranteed income in the period. Remarkably little was available at the time. The field blossomed toward the end of the period, and much more is available today. However, these few publications were instrumental in the movement that nearly succeeded in creating a negative income tax and that eventually lead to the creation of Food Stamps, the Earned Income Tax Credit, and refundable tax credits. Brief annotations follow some of these reference entries. A more complete and up-to-date bibliography can be found at the BIG website: http://www.widerquist.com/usbig/index.html. The reference list is divided into four parts: Books, Articles, Government Documents, and Other.

Books

Burke, V.J. and Burke, V. (1974) *Nixon's Good Deed: Welfare Reform*, (New York: Columbia University Press).

Coll, B.D.V. (1969) *Perspectives in Public Welfare*, (Washington, D.C.: U.S. Department of Health, Education and Welfare).

Friedman, M. (1962) *Capitalism and Freedom*, (Chicago: University of Chicago Press).

Green, C. (1967) *Negative Taxes and the Poverty Problem*, (Washington, D.C.: Brookings Institution).

Lampman, R.J. (1971) *Ends and Means of Reducing Income Poverty*, (Chicago: Markham).

Marmor, T.R. (1971) *Poverty Policy: A Compendium of Cash Transfer Proposals*, (Chicago: Aldine-Atherton).

Moynihan, D.P. (1973) *The Politics of a Guaranteed Income: The Nixon Administration and the Family Assistance Plan*, (New York: Random House).

Rhys-Williams, J. (1943) *Something to Look Forward to: A Suggestion for a New Social Contract*, (London: MacDonald).

Theobald, R. (ed.) (1966) *The Guaranteed Income: Next Step in Socioeconomic Evolution?* (New York: Doubleday Anchor Books).

Wogaman, P. (1968) *Guaranteed Annual Income: The Moral Issues* (New York: Abingdon Press).

Articles

Orshansky, M. (1969) "How Poverty Is Measured," *Monthly Labor Review*, 92: 37–41.

Tobin, J. (1965) "On the Economic Status of the Negro," *Daedalus*, 94 (4): 878–898.

——— (1966) "The Case for an Income Guarantee," *The Public Interest*, 4: 31–41.

——— (1967) "It Can Be Done," *The New Republic*, 3 : 14–18.

Tobin, J., Pechman, J.A., and Mieszkowski, P.M. (1967) "Is a Negative Income Tax Practical?" *The Yale Law Journal*, 77 (1): 1–27.

Government Documents

Advisory Council on Public Welfare (1966) *Having the Power, We Have the Duty: Report* (Washington, D.C.: U.S. Department of Health, Education and Welfare).

Beveridge, W. (1942) *Social Insurance and Allied Services: Report by Sir William Beveridge*, (London: Macmillan).

Commission on Technology, Automation, and Economic Growth (1966) *Technology and the American Economy, Report*, (Washington, D.C.: U.S. Government Printing Office).

Committee on Economic Security (1935) *Report*, (Unpublished report from a cabinet-level committee appointed by President Franklin Roosevelt in 1934 that laid the groundwork for the Social Security Act of 1935).

Lampman, R. J. (1959) *The Low Income Population and Economic Growth*, Joint Economic Committee, Study Paper No. 12 (Washington, D.C.: 86th Congress, 1st Session).

President's Commission on Income Maintenance Programs (1969) *Poverty Amid Plenty, Report*, (Washington, D.C.: U.S. Government Printing Office).

——— (1970) *Background Papers*, (Washington, D.C.: U.S. Government Printing Office).

Shriver, S. (1965) "Memorandum to the President, National Anti-Poverty Plan," October 20, with covering memo to Charles L. Schultze, Director, Bureau of the Budget (Unpublished).

U.S. Congress, Joint Economic Committee, Subcommittee on Fiscal Policy (1974) *Income Security for Americans: Recommendations of the Public Welfare Study*, (Washington, D.C.: U.S. Government Printing Office).

U.S. Department of Health, Education and Welfare (1966) *Income and Benefit Programs*, (Washington, D.C.: U.S. Department of Health, Education and Welfare).

Other

Ad Hoc Committee on the Triple Revolution (1964) Open letter and manifesto submitted to the president by this self-appointed group, which included Robert Theobold, Bayard Rustin, and Gunnar Myrdal—among others (Unpublished).

CBS-TV (1968) Hunger in America, (Documentary).

Fisher, G.M. (1993) "From Hunter to Orshansky: An Overview of (Unofficial) Poverty Lines in the United States from 1904 to 1965," Census Bureau, Poverty Measurement Working Papers. (Paper presented at the Fifteenth Annual Research Conference of the Association for Public Policy Analysis and Management in Washington, D.C.)

Chapter 5

A Retrospective on the Negative Income Tax Experiments: Looking Back at the Most Innovate Field Studies in Social Policy

Robert A. Levine, Harold Watts, Robinson Hollister, Walter Williams, Alice O'Connor, and Karl Widerquist

Introduction, Karl Widerquist

The United States government conducted four negative income tax (NIT) experiments between 1968 and 1980. NIT is a form of basic income guarantee (BIG) that was popular in the 1960s and 1970s. It differs from basic income in that it gives money only to those with low incomes. However, both are basic income guarantees in the sense that they guarantee everyone a minimum income. Although the differences between the two policies are important, they have enough similarities so that what was learned from the NIT experiments can help us understand the consequences of either BIG plan.

The experiments began under the direction of the Office of Economic Opportunity (OEO) near the end of the Johnson administration and continued within the Department of Health Education and Welfare (HEW) after the Nixon administration abolished OEO. Their main goal was to determine the labor supply response to an income guarantee. That is, how much will work effort decline if a negative income tax is introduced? But as the experiments went on, many more questions were examined. The first experiments were conducted in New Jersey and Pennsylvania between 1968 and 1972, on a largely urban population of two-parent families. Two more experiments were soon added—one in Gary, Indiana to examine the effects of an NIT on single parents, and one in North Carolina and Iowa to examine its effects on rural populations. Finally the Seattle–Denver Income Maintenance Experiment (SIME–DIME) was added with a much larger experimental population.

These experiments were the first large scale social science experiment ever conducted, and they have become a model for social experiments. They employed the method (common in the natural sciences) of dividing subjects into a control group and an experimental group through random assignment. The experimental group was given a negative income tax and the control group was not. Researchers collected income information and conducted interviews with both groups to determine how those receiving the NIT behaved compared to those not receiving it. The experiments eventually included thousands of subjects and collected data on variables such as time spent working (for all members of the family), school attendance, health, and marital status.

The experiment's results were widely discussed in policy circles and in the popular media at two times. In 1970, Nixon's modified version of the NIT, the Family Assistance Plan, was being debated in Congress. To help its policy cause, the administration pressed experimenters to release their findings long before they were ready to do so. While preliminary results showed very moderate reductions in labor supply due to work-incentive effects, Congressional opponents criticized the findings as premature.

The results were again discussed in the late 1970s during hearings for Jimmy Carter's Program for Better Jobs and Income. The finding that the work disincentive was not so large that it made the program unaffordable was overshadowed by two other findings. Although the experimenters expected to find some negative work incentive effects, and were pleased with how small they turned out to be, many newspapers reported the results as if the very existence of such effects was a crushing blow to the idea. Also, a controversial finding that the negative income tax increased the divorce rate caused a furor against the policy both in Congress and the media.

In the following years, hundreds of articles in books and scholarly journals debated the results of the NIT experiments. For a critical review and extensive bibliography, see Widerquist (2005).

In February 2002, the First Congress of the U.S. Basic Income Guarantee Network brought together four of the original experimenters and one historian to discuss the meaning of the experiments today. The session moderator was Robert Harris, former executive director of the President's Commission on Income Maintenance, and former vice president of the Urban Institute. The speakers were Robert Levine, senior economic consultant of the Rand Corporation and author of *The Poor Ye Need Not Have With You: Lessons From the War on Poverty*; Robinson Hollister, professor of economics at Swarthmore College and coauthor of *Labor Market Policy and Unemployment Insurance*; Harold Watts, emeritus professor of economics and public affairs at Columbia University, former director of the Institute for Research on Poverty, and coeditor of *The New Jersey Income Maintenance Experiment*, Volumes II and III; Walter Williams, emeritus professor of public affairs at the University of Washington, author of *Honest Numbers and Democracy: Social Policy Analysis in the White House, Congress, and the Federal Agencies*; and Alice O'Connor, associate professor of history at the University of California–Santa Barbara, author of *Poverty Knowledge: Social Science, Social Policy and the Poor in Twentieth Century U.S. History*. What follows is taken from their remarks.

The Political Background of the Experiments, Robert Levine

In the nineteenth century, economists were engaged in a great controversy over whether something called "value" was determined by supply or demand. Around the turn of the century some brilliant mind said "Why don't we substitute 'and' for 'or,' and make it 'supply and demand'?" The discussion today about jobs guarantees or income guarantees reminds me of that. The first formal proposal for a negative income tax (NIT) by the United States government was made in the five-year antipoverty plan of 1965. NIT was very quickly thought to be in conflict with a job guarantee. But the question of full employment or basic income guarantee strikes me as a non-argument. That was the way some of us thought of it then, and I still think that was the right way to think of it. But the negative income tax experiment came out of that debate.

Part of the political context is well known, at least in our esoteric circles. Alice O'Connor quoted me in her book as saying that when we brought the idea of a NIT to the high command of the Office of Economic Opportunity (OEO), the director of congressional relations said "that won't be an experiment in negative income tax, that will be an experiment on how to kill a program on the Hill." Sargent Shriver, to his credit, dismissed that, even though he was a politician to his fingertips. He said, "No, this is important, this is interesting, and we will go ahead with it." That was the political birth of the experiments that we're still discussing more than 30 years later.

Some of the political background to the NIT in OEO has not been commonly known. Because the money for the experiment was to be taken from the Community Action Demonstration Program (which had existed from the beginning of OEO in 1965), there was a substantial sum of tens of millions of dollars available. Some of the more controversial demonstration programs were in Chicago and Mississippi and a lot of the money was used to fund programs that were considered not just intellectually, but politically, radical; and they caused OEO much trouble at the time. Basically the accusation was made that the government was funding political power.

Then, we came in; we were the reactionary economists who wanted to do something else. Before I became assistant director of OEO, I was in charge of the division of research and planning. Robinson Hollister succeeded me, Walter Williams succeeded Rob. The only reason Harold Watts wasn't in the sequence is that he went back to Wisconsin before we could catch him. We wanted to try *science* to find out something very specific. My colleagues will describe the specifics, but we believed that the basic political obstacle to anything like a negative income tax was the widespread belief that it would kill work incentives. We set out not to prove that it would not, but to find out whether it would. That was the very narrow, scientific focus of the experiment.

We set control groups to get information on that particular topic, not to prove anything to support an agenda. Community action people attacked from the left and congressional people attacked from the right. Those attacking from the left believed in "the culture of poverty" and didn't think income had much to do with why people were poor. Those on the right didn't know why we wanted to get this information since the program was impossible anyhow. With Shriver's aid, we got through these obstacles.

After Nixon's election in 1968, it was generally felt within OEO that he was going to kill the poverty program when he took over from Johnson. He didn't; he appointed a new head of the program named Don Rumsfeld who brought in an assistant named Dick Cheney. Rumsfeld systematically invited OEO folks to talk to him in his congressional office. My impression was that he attempted to preserve the program by shifting it in a Republican direction—experimentation rather than action. This put a focus on the NIT experiment.

The Makeup of the Experiments, Harold Watts

I understand that Sargent Shriver said "We've got this institute up in Wisconsin and they aren't good for anything else, so why don't we have them experiment?". We took that as a serious recommendation. We took very seriously the question of whether a set of programs would produce a generation of layabouts. That was the hypothesis that needed to be examined. If you're worried about the layabout possibility, you really want to start out with people who are working. And so the first experiment did not look at the welfare population but at the working poor.

A negative income tax can be looked at as having two parts—a lump-sum grant (G) and a reduced wage (Y-tY). From the standpoint of static economic theory, both of those things should reduce the tendency to work. The lump sum grant should produce more leisure and more non-wage work. The reduced price of leisure, which comes from the reduced wage, should also produce more leisure: "Time off is cheaper, let's buy some more of that." There was no question of the direction of the effect of NIT on hours worked, and there was no lack of confirmation of that in the experiments. But the question was quantitative: How much would NIT reduce work time? The same theory that says that people would definitely be inclined to work less also says that they are made better off, because the NIT expands the alternatives available to them. This was confirmed because almost no one refused to take part in the program. That part of economic theory works fine.

But do we need an experiment to answer these questions? There are different people at various levels of unearned income and different levels of net wage running around loose in the streets. Why don't we just see what they do? The experimental problem with using these people is that nothing is imposed from the outside; there is no exogenous change. The experiment tried to make the change in income and net wage rate exogenous, so that the behavior of recipients would be representative of a national program.

The size of the work response was important, because if work effort declined sufficiently it would largely vitiate the strategy of using the NIT as a means of increasing family income. If recipients used their entire NIT to buy more leisure, it succeeds in making them better off, but it wouldn't be a good antipoverty program.

I want to emphasize a couple of ways the experiment tended to maximize the size of the work-effort response. First, we applied no additional treatments that would tend to prod them into the labor market. We had to check what they earned to determine how much to pay them, but we weren't critical if they didn't work. Second, it was a short-term experiment. In our case, essentially leisure was on sale for a three-year period. When laundry soap is on sale, what do you do? You buy a lot of it. You might expect people in the experiment to act the same way. Not everyone will; someone who has a good job (it may not pay much, but it's stable) may not want to mess around with that by working less. That kind of rigidity could be built into their job. But by and large the poor families we were looking at didn't tend to have terribly steady jobs. There were a few with stable janitor jobs at Princeton, but for the most part, that wasn't the case, and there was a disincentive. People did work less, but percentage-wise it tended to be in the single digits for men in particular. Some of the work response came from taking more time to look for work. Some of it came from cutting down hours, say from 65 to 60 hours a week, which doesn't seem like a tragedy. I don't remember finding anyone (on an anecdotal basis), who as soon as they got the grant, left the labor market and sat on the porch and whittled for three years.

That's what we found and those are the tools we used to find it. The whole flavor of the OEO at that point was something rather new to the government: a willingness to look at evidence, to do some examination, to check some facts out. That hadn't always been there, and in that sense, this idea of doing some experimentation fell on fertile ground.

The Findings of the Experiments, Robinson Hollister

My part of this discussion covers three points. First, I review the results of the experiments with respect to the labor supply, which was the central issue driving the design of all these experiments. Second, I talk about the non-labor supply outcomes that have largely been ignored and that covered a territory that was ahead of its time in many ways. These bear heavily on what other benefits come from having a basic income guarantee. Third, I map the findings of the experiments to what we have found since then.

Labor supply results showed about a 13 percent reduction of work effort for the family as a whole starting from an initial work effort of 35 hours per week for the entire family. One-third of the response came from the primary earner, one-third from the secondary earner, and one-third from the tertiary earner in the family. In most cases, the primary earner worked more hours than the secondary and tertiary earners, and therefore, when measured in percentage terms, there were relatively small responses from the primary earner. Percentage term responses were much bigger from the female spouses in the family and from the third workers in the families. The biggest response overall came in reduction in the female labor supply and that mostly took the form of slower reentry to the labor market after absence. This labor supply response added about 25 percent to the static costs of a national program with a guarantee level approximately at the poverty line. You could look at these results as either half empty or half full. You could say that 25 percent is too much or not too much.

The most common non-labor supply result mentioned was an erroneous finding by some sociologists (from an initial analysis of the Seattle–Denver Income Maintenance Experiments) that the marriage-dissolution rate for black families in the experimental groups was 57 percent greater than the control group, and 53 percent greater for white families. When these results came out in congressional hearings, Senator Moynihan, who had been a backer of Nixon's Family Assistance Plan, and who had written a very controversial report about instability in the black family, recanted his support for the guaranteed income. Those particular findings greatly contributed to killing the Carter administration's guaranteed income scheme. In the 1980s, Glen Cain carefully reanalyzed the data from the Seattle–Denver experiment. The results were technically quite complicated, but there was basically no family dissolution effect. Some of the results were suspect from the beginning, because the effect seemed to occur in the sector of people with the lowest guarantee rate, the lowest incentive to strike out on their own—those who had the least to gain from breaking up showed the largest amount of marital breakup. Cain's study appeared in the *American Journal of Sociology* in 1990, with a rebuttal by the authors of the original findings, but subsequent studies (and those from the other NIT experiments) also found no effects on marital stability.

The rural experiment in North Carolina and Iowa collected data on educational attainment. In North Carolina there were significant positive influences in grades 2–8 in attendance rates and teacher rating, and on test scores. The literature on education shows that it is nearly impossible to raise test scores through direct intervention. Yet, BIG had large positive effects on the test scores of children in the worst-off families in the rural South. The New Jersey experiment didn't collect data on test scores, but there was a very significant effect on school continuation; that is, BIG was an effective anti-dropout program. Again, if you look at programs that are trying to reduce dropouts directly, it's a pretty dismal scene. In Gary, there were positive test score effects for males in grades 4–6. In Seattle–Denver, there was a positive effect on adults going on in continuing education.

Some of the experiments collected data on low birth weight, nutrition, and other quality-of-life variables. Low birth weight is associated with very serious deficits later on in life, and programs that try to reduce the incidence of low birth weight have been largely ineffective; but the Gary experiment found that NIT reduced low birth rates in the most at-risk categories. The rural experiment showed significant effects in various categories of nutritional adequacy. Homeownership showed significant effects in New Jersey, in the rural experiment, and in the first year of the Gary experiment.

It is important to map these results into more recent experience, both experimental and non-experimental. Later experiments such as the Minnesota work-welfare reform (MFIP), SSP in Canada, and New Hope in Milwaukee tended to be work related with strong financial incentives. People who wanted to get benefits had to work a minimum of hours and, as you would expect, these experimental programs elicited greater work effort. But across all the experiments, secondary earners used some of the benefits to buy more time in the home. Non-experimental studies using income tax returns also found effects similar to the NIT. Two-parent families receiving an Earned Income Tax Credit (EITC) used some of the extra income to increase time at home; this was especially true for secondary earners. The order of magnitude of the labor supply elasticity is essentially the same in more recent experiments. The Minnesota experiment found positive effects for marital stability and reduced domestic abuse. The Canadian experiment found an increase in marital stability in New Brunswick and a decrease in marital stability in British Columbia. The New Hope experiment found some long-term effects on the educational performance of males (in the experimental group) in elementary school.

The Use and Misuse of Experimental Information, Walter Williams

I'm greatly concerned about the growing misuse of policy information in the current political environment. Elliot Richardson (1980: 105), a distinguished secretary of several United States government departments wrote, "in a sense, all of the abuses of Watergate have been abuses of information: its theft, distortion, misuse, fabrication, misrepresentation, concealment and suppression." Today's efforts are not new, but these activities, with the exception of theft, are much worse today than in earlier times. And the growing abuses of information undermine informed consent by the people and ultimately American democracy itself.

I will argue that the negative income tax experiment set a standard in seeking reliable information, which should be current practice, and that the Office of Economic Opportunity (OEO) policy analysis staff of which I was a member exemplified sound analytic practices. This did not come about because the analysts involved had greater personal integrity than current practitioners, but because the political environment facilitated such efforts. It is the deterioration of political institutions that is the problem, not the skills and standards of today's policy analysts and researchers.

The policy analysts at OEO were not public relations types but academically oriented social scientists. They understood that their one comparative advantage was to go after hard evidence on the negative income tax. It is true that the OEO analytic staff hoped that families receiving negative income tax payments would not significantly reduce their work efforts. However, and this is critical, they sought a carefully designed state-of-the-art field experiment to provide a rigorous assessment of the extent to which negative income tax payment recipients changed the labor supply response. And the social scientists at the University of Wisconsin at Madison who were administering the study were even more concerned about meeting the highest research standards.

The OEO analytic unit had a basic commitment to increasing the supply of sound, relevant social policy information and undertook an extensive research program to develop it. For example, the analytic unit set up and fully funded the

University of Wisconsin's Institute for Research on Poverty, and supported in its initial stage a critically important longitudinal study at the University of Michigan following 5,000 American families and that has continued for 35 years. OEO launched the first major, rigorous social policy evaluations and large-scale field experiments. As to the latter, the New Jersey negative income tax experiment was funded largely because the OEO analytic office, in summer of 1965, sold agency director Sargent Shriver on a negative income tax plan, and he recommended it to the president in that year's agency submission to the budget bureau. Then in October 1965, the office sent the budget office a more detailed, more accurate estimate for the cost of a negative income tax aimed at ending poverty by 1976—the 200th anniversary of the Declaration of Independence.

The United States has experienced a radical change in the political environment since the 1965–1968 period. During that period, the OEO analytic staff could engage in sound analyses of the pros and cons of policy options to support agency decision-making. The commitment to good information at OEO certainly did not run throughout the government. But, between then and now, the changes that have come about have been negative. Although emphasis on sound data remains essential for reasoned policymaking, I have found over the years that there is more and more distortion of information and policy analyses. Over time, the willful use of deceptive statistics and misleading analyses has increased materially, with the current administration using distorted evidence as its main weapon in misleading the public about its major policies.

Our political system has been deteriorating because people in senior positions, including the highest officials in the White House and Congress, have been propagandizing citizens who often do not perceive the nature and extent of the subterfuge. Take President George W. Bush's 2001 tax bill, where the top one percent of the income distribution got thirty percent of the tax cuts and the bottom forty percent got only about fifteen percent. Yet, the Bush administration was able to pass the tax legislation by engaging in an extended propaganda campaign claiming falsely that those at the bottom benefited the most.

The overriding problem is that the public is fed distorted information and false assertions based on it; yet, the politicians lack either the political will or the institutional capacity to restore integrity to national politics. As I observed in *Reaganism and the Death of Representative Democracy*, "The extent to which deceptive propaganda has been employed in [President George W.] Bush's first three years to sell major policy proposals makes the Bush administration radically different from any earlier presidency" (Williams 2003: 259). Ultimately, the issue is whether the public receives sound policy information and interpretation—prior to the making of major public decisions—for there to be informed consent. If not, democracy withers. Policy analysts are accused of aggrandizing the importance of valid information so let me turn finally to an impeccable source, James Madison, the father of the Constitution: "The people who mean to be their own Governors must arm themselves with the power knowledge gives" (Hunt 1910: 103). In sum, American democracy requires the informed consent of the people on major policy choices; and such informed consent can come only when the needed relevant policy information is available to citizens in time for them to consider the policy at issue and assent to it.

Political Ramifications of the Experiments, Alice O'Connor

The period we're talking about seems like ancient history; not only is there now less integrity in the inquiries behind policy changes, but also antipoverty is now easily dismissed as a serious policy objective. Sometimes when I tell my students that Lyndon B. Johnson made speeches about ending poverty in America, they laugh. That to me is extraordinarily sad commentary.

The NIT experiments were not just fundamentally scientific undertakings, but fundamentally political undertakings as well. Within a broader political context, we need to understand them as experiments whose design, implementation, and ultimately whose meaning, were all shaped by the volatile and rapidly changing politics of social provision, social welfare, and social citizenship. We can also see the experiments as a form of political advocacy—they sought to establish the legitimacy of the NIT in the absence of widespread political awareness or support.

As a scientific undertaking, the experiments were highly successful, but as a political undertaking the experiments had the opposite effect. They were used to undermine the NIT/BIG concept. More importantly, they show us some of the fundamental weaknesses of framing the BIG idea narrowly, as a highly targeted antipoverty measure as opposed to a more universal citizenship right, framing it as policy with labor-market effects as opposed to an intervention that actively tries to reshape labor markets. I also want to discuss what the experiments tell us about the limitations of a style of policy making that looks to these experiments as a source of policy innovation.

The politics at the time affected the experiments. The guaranteed income was talked about in the late 1960s as an idea whose time had come, but there was no significant mobilization in terms of any grassroots or major constituency groups like labor behind the idea. Instead, guaranteed income came to the fore with extremely diverse advocates. There was a group of free market economists who saw it as an antidote to the burgeoning welfare state. Some in the civil rights movement and the growing welfare rights movement talked about the NIT as a response to the problems of structural unemployment in the labor market (as well as to racism in the labor market and gender bias in the labor market), and activists attached it to an expanded notion of citizenship rights. Most important of all in terms of getting these experiments going were the Keynesian economists within the Johnson administration, specifically within OEO, who came to embrace the negative income tax as a key to eliminating poverty by 1976 as laid out in the five-year plan developed by OEO analysts. This group saw the income guarantee as a supplement to the overriding full employment growth strategy embraced in the war on poverty.

The experimenters were determined not to advocate something that would violate the basic principles of a market economy. That is to say, they didn't insist that

BIG was a response to market failure so much as to the incapacity of certain segments of people in the labor market to earn adequate wages. The experiments, therefore, were concerned with proving NIT's efficacy as a tool for raising incomes above the poverty line, and to prove the hunch (that had been based on some econometric studies) that the NIT could eliminate poverty without a massive work disincentive and within the boundaries of liberal social policies at the time. Those who held this view saw the NIT as emphasizing growth over redistribution. They were reluctant to regulate labor markets explicitly, and considered the antipoverty measures not to be about changing the dynamics of inequality, but about expanding opportunities to be part of the economic system. As a result, the experiments were highly targeted. They focused on the poorest people (up to 150 percent of the poverty line), not a broad segment of the population. They were not concerned with some of the broader labor market effects such as how a basic income guarantee affects the choice and power of workers to go elsewhere, and did not attempt to look at the impact on racial or gender segmentation of the labor market. These problems were not acknowledged within the framework of these experiments. This leads me to say that the experiments were narrowly focused on individual behavior and predicting it, not on the structural impact of the NIT.

Another kind of politics that shaped the experiments was the politics of social provision for poor people. From the standpoint of the economists who designed the experiments, one of the appeals of income guarantees was that they were efficient and would cut through some of the inefficiencies of the Aid to Families with Dependent Children ("welfare") program, and especially would be fairer to the working poor because they wouldn't be targeted to women with children. This led to a political decision in the New Jersey experiment to focus on two-parent, male-breadwinner families, assuming that welfare mothers (and their potential work falloff) wouldn't be a major political issue at the time. (This despite the fact that in 1967 Congress passed the WIN "work incentives" legislation that tried to put more welfare recipients to work.) Similarly, the assumption was that the potential work falloff among wives in two-parent families would not become a political issue. In fact, however, Nixon later played very heavily on the two-parent/single-parent divide in promoting his family assistance plan and in his more dedicated efforts to break up the political coalition behind the Great Society. By pitching his plan as a matter of fairness for the forgotten two-parent families who were ineligible for welfare, he drew a sharp, artificial distinction between the popular, stereotypically white, two-parent working poor/working-class family, on the one hand, and the "welfare poor" on the other hand, who were increasingly imagined in the public mind as predominantly black, drug using, etc.—none of which was true.

These divisive, racial politics quickly came to determine the political meaning of these experiments. They became political fodder in the Nixon-era wars over welfare reform. At first, it actually looked like this was going to be a moment of congruence between research and political priorities: Nixon's Family Assistance Plan (FAP), after all, was a version of the NIT with a work requirement attached. Before the results were in, they were able, under extreme pressure from White House advisor Daniel P. Moynihan, to put together a report that was used in testimony in favor of FAP, saying there were no work disincentive effects whatsoever.

The moment of congruence quickly passed, however. The use of the experiments in favor of FAP drew public and political attention to the experiments. And Senator Williams from New Jersey, an opponent of FAP, used this as an occasion to sic the General Accounting Office on the experiment, claiming that the families were double-dipping and should be prosecuted for welfare fraud. He tried to get Congress to invade the office of the experiments and look into the files of the experimental families. David Kershaw, who was running the experiments, essentially camped out to prevent congressional investigators from ruining the confidentiality agreement with the families. Thus, after looking like there was some congruence between social science and politics, as the war on welfare turned into a war on dependency, the findings of these experiments were actually used to undermine the very idea of an income guarantee. As others on the panel have indicated, the initial rosy scenario from the experiments changed once the longer-range results were in: there was, after all, some measurable work disincentive from the guaranteed income, albeit relatively modest and partly due to reduced hours among secondary as well as primary household earners. There were also the subsequently challenged findings linking the NIT to family breakup. By the late 1970s, when the Carter administration attempted to revive a version of the NIT, even some of its former advocates turned against it. Moynihan, in a very public and I can't help but think, strategically timed manner, said to Congress, "I am shocked to look at these findings and say we scientists were wrong." Meanwhile, the right wing mobilized, in the form of Charles Murray and others, to use these findings to say that these experiments proved that an income guarantee was impossible.

A final political dimension to the NIT experiments is that they were considered highly innovative, not just because they were testing this "idea whose time had come," but also because they represented a new approach to policy making. It was thought that an experimental design would give definitive proof that an idea can work. I think it led to consequences that were unanticipated. The experiments ushered in a time of increasing rigor, increasing emphasis on experimental design in program planning and evaluation, but they also helped raise the bar especially for innovative antipoverty policies, which now had to prove their value before passage. Antipoverty and welfare policy has been subjected to a scrutiny that is not applied to other areas of social policy, certainly not to military policy even though the military costs far more.

To conclude, looking at the NIT experiments as a political undertaking shows us how politics can confound efforts to inform policy with scientific knowledge. Even as social scientists were sorting through and debating the meaning of the experimental findings, political opponents were using those findings to tell a simple story of lazy poor people and family decline. I would point to the importance of using the experimental findings to tell a different story, and the importance of working harder to change this prevailing narrative with a more complex alternative. And yet, those of us who know better have let the simpler narrative rule the day. This also points to the limitations of narrow antipoverty justifications for an income guarantee. The experiments, like the welfare reform debate that followed and distorted their meaning, turn on the individual behavior of poor people; and when we frame this as a behavioral issue, we rarely get the outcome that progressives want. Finally, I think the experiments point to the political limitations of a style of policy making that doesn't pay enough attention to the need to articulate research with the needs of social movements at the same time.

Note

* Special thanks to Robert Harris who moderated the session on which this chapter is based and gave extensive comments on the written version.

References

Hunt, G. (ed.) (1910) *The Writings of James Madison*, vol. 9, (New York: G.P. Putnam's Sons).

Richardson, E. (1980) *The Creative Balance,* (New York: Holt, Rinehart & Winston).

Widerquist, K. (2005) "A Failure to Communicate: What (If Anything) Can We Learn From the Negative Income Tax Experiments," *Journal of Socio-Economics*, 34: 49-81.

Williams, W. (2003) *Reaganism and the Death of Representative Democracy,* (Washington, D.C.: Georgetown University Press).

PART TWO: DEBATE

Chapter 6

Basic Income in the United States: Redefining Citizenship in the Liberal State

Almaz Zelleke

Introduction

In the United States, the debate over welfare reform has been dominated by those who believe welfare should be conditional on work. This domination holds both at the level of policy, with the passage of the 1996 Personal Responsibility and Work Opportunity Reconciliation Act (PRWORA), and at the level of theory, with almost all welfare analysts, liberal and conservative, united on the importance of the integration of poor adults into the workforce as a condition not only of liberation from poverty but also as a prerequisite to full and equal citizenship. This argument holds sway in the United States not only because of its relatively full employment economy, but also because of its founding image as the land of opportunity where no barriers stand in the way of those who would work hard to achieve social, political, and economic liberty. Even among analysts of the American left who believe that this image is mythical for many Americans, for reasons of race, education, or socioeconomic background, it is hard to find any who advance an alternative conception of citizenship and independence that does not include paid employment as an essential element.

The re-emerging United States debate over basic income—a guaranteed minimum income distributed to each citizen as a right—stands alongside the debate over welfare reform, intersecting with it at certain points, especially over the question of conditionality on work requirements. Basic income has a broader scope than the welfare system, targeting many citizens not currently defined as welfare eligible or poor, but—like the welfare system—its greatest effect, should it be enacted, would be on the poor. And as in the debates over welfare reform, the question of work requirements for recipients of basic income is a central one.

In one sense, the debate over work requirements for basic income in the United States might seem to be settled. The Earned Income Tax Credit (EITC) approximates a modest conditional basic income for families with children—no more than $4,204 for families with at least two children, with up to another $1,000 per child under the Child Tax Credit.[1] All in all, the federal benefit comes to less than

$2,000 on a per person basis in the most generous case, with some additional EITC benefits available in a few states. The EITC aims to reward the work effort of low-income workers, to boost their wages without economically distorting wage subsidies, and to make even low-income work more attractive than welfare benefits. The EITC is a favored policy of American welfare theorists who argue that employment must be the foundation of a multi-pronged attack on the problem of poverty, even if low-wage jobs cannot by themselves lift the poor out of poverty. David Ellwood (1988), whose slogan is "making work pay," is the exemplar of this approach, but he is not alone. And though it is not characterized as a basic income, the EITC is a conditional cash grant that modestly achieves *some* of a basic income's goals.

If this is the case, should basic income advocates concede the matter, drop the push for unconditionality, and settle instead for a conditional basic income—in effect, an expanded EITC with some administrative modifications to increase take-up, and with funding at a higher level? Perhaps, but it is premature to concede the conditionality issue just yet. What basic income advocates have yet to do is present a positive account of a non-work-centered notion of liberal citizenship that surpasses the work-centered notion currently dominant in the United States. And while it is the debate in the United States that has the most to gain from this effort, it has implications for western Europe as well, where the more advanced debate over basic income is increasingly dominated by those who advocate a basic income conditional on a social contribution or participation requirement, in effect a weak work requirement that, while more liberal than a strict work requirement in intention, suffers from the same inegalitarian effects of selectivity.

In this chapter, I examine arguments for work-conditioned welfare and basic income. I focus on arguments for work requirements that extend beyond the terms of the traditional welfare debate, where work requirements can be seen as the price the poor pay for benefits redistributed from the middle class and the wealthy, because the scope of an unconditional basic income extends beyond the poor and must be justified in a manner that goes beyond alleviating poverty. Therefore, I review and critique arguments about work and participation requirements which advance a definition of citizenship. A review of arguments for conditionality and the theories of citizenship they posit shows what advocates of unconditionality have yet to do in making the case for basic income. Arguments from distributive justice, the kind that dominate the basic income debate (e.g., Van Parijs 1995), go only so far in making the case for an unconditional basic income; and a compelling and persuasive account of the kind of society and citizenship to which it leads is necessary for the justification to be complete. To address this omission, I offer as a liberal alternative a radically pluralist notion of citizenship with a kind of universal economic suffrage, made possible by an unconditional basic income, at its core. This proposal may not sway those who do not share the inclination toward a liberal, indeed a libertarian, foundation for society and social policy, but the analogy I posit between the political and economic spheres should, at the least, challenge supporters of work requirements to address the inequities in their own conceptions of citizenship that underlie and justify their calls for work requirements.

In what follows, I argue that the most common citizenship-based justifications for work requirements—the paternalistic and civic republican arguments—are flawed because of their selectivity, and that the only defensible citizenship-based justification for work requirements is the socialist model, which applies universally to all. Therefore, the choice for basic income advocates is not between conditionality and universality, but between the two starkly different forms of universality embodied in the socialist and liberal alternatives.

Citizenship and Work Requirements

The citizenship-based arguments for work-conditioned welfare and basic income fall into three categories that can be summarized as follows. The paternalistic argument sees work as the solution to the "pathology" of poverty—a deficit that inheres in the character of the poor themselves, the social and economic climate in which they are mired, or the structure of the welfare system (e.g., Mead 1986, 1992; Wilson 1987, and Murray 1984, respectively). Whatever the locus of the "pathology," advocates of this view regard paid work as the means for the poor to achieve the "independence" that welfare "dependency" precludes and that is necessary for full citizenship in contemporary society. The civic republican argument also sees paid work as the path to full integration into society, but its advocates emphasize the ideal of reciprocity as the basis for conditioning income benefits on paid work. In their view, full citizenship requires not independence, but participation in a web of mutual dependence. Some may require supplemental assistance, but beneficiaries are seen to be doing their part toward contributing to society's (paid) work (e.g., Gutmann and Thompson 1996, Kaus 1992, and White 1997). Finally, the socialist model posits citizenship based on each taking part in society's paid, public work as well as having access to whatever benefits they need. In this model, both benefits and obligations are universal and not, as in the first two models, distributed according to economic class or status (e.g., Gorz 1992, 1986, 1994b, 1989). I examine each of these arguments for work-conditioned benefits in turn.

The Paternalistic Argument for Work Requirements

The paternalistic view of welfare and entitlements for the poor dominates the debates about welfare in the United States and is embodied in current American welfare policy. It is characterized by its belief in the power of paid work to address what it views as the "pathology" of poverty. Its different strains vary as to whether they locate that "pathology" in the character of the poor; their environment; or in the system of benefits, incentives, and disincentives of the pre-PRWORA welfare system; but they share an emphasis on paid work as the way to address it.

In the United States, Lawrence Mead is the strongest advocate for conditioning welfare benefits on work, and one of those who advances an explicitly work-centered notion of citizenship. Mead argues that the entitlement theory of citizenship—the one he claims was embedded in the pre-PRWORA welfare system—is harmful to the poor and to the greater society. Without the discipline imposed by social obligations, he says, the poor cannot exercise the self-government that is the foundation of freedom (1986: 88–89). The social obligation that concerns Mead most is the obligation to work, at least in return for monetary benefits like welfare payments. Mead focuses his attention on work for three reasons. First, he believes steady work to be the best reliable means of escaping dependence on the government for subsistence, if not for escaping poverty itself (1992: 60). Second, he argues that sufficient work is available for the unskilled unemployed, who are able to reject undesirable low-wage jobs when benefits are not contingent on their acceptance (1986: 70–76, 1992: 12). Third, he believes that there is a national interest in enforcing low-wage work (1986: 153–154).

Mead refers to work as a means to "integration" of the poor, and he means it in both a racial and a social sense. Mead suggests that the poor, especially poor blacks, have different values from the mainstream of American society. Enforced work requirements achieve physical integration by bringing poor blacks into contact with the working (white) majority, and cultural integration by enforcing dominant values (1986: 254–256). Mead's views on work requirements are filtered by his understanding of the ends of democratic government. While we privilege freedom in our political culture, he says, true freedom requires an underlying order and the government's willingness to be authoritative rather than permissive where necessary; social policy is one means of achieving this order (1986: 6–7). Mead argues that a consensus around a "new paternalism" has emerged, and the American government no longer shies away from imposing paternalistic programs on welfare recipients, teenage mothers, drug abusers, the homeless, and other social "outsiders," nor from the need to inculcate among its citizens the values that used to be fostered by the family (1997, 1998, 1992: 181–184).

While Mead's policy recommendations target poor and disadvantaged members of society, his political theory has a broader focus and purpose. His vision of democratic society as a unified, homogeneous, and disciplined citizenry working toward a common set of goals chosen, or at least ratified by, the majority puts him firmly in the conservative tradition of paternalism. His commitment to the integration of the mostly minority poor into mainstream society is bounded by his unwillingness to address the structural explanations for contemporary poverty in America, including racism, gender inequality, or the organization of the economy, or indeed to contemplate a genuinely pluralist vision of American society. What he advocates is a paternalistic integration, rather than an egalitarian one, with equal respect earned only by those who prove themselves through hard work and obedience to dominant norms.

The paternalistic argument depends in large part on the idea of economic "independence." Mead endorses continued economic "dependence" on government benefits for those who work but are still poor, calling into question the value of the independence ostensibly conferred by paid employment (1992: 60). Furthermore, economic independence can be achieved through one's own efforts, the efforts of a spouse or partner, or the efforts of a forebear or other benefactor. Because this independence can derive from gifts or inheritance, it bears no necessary relation to the character of the individual. In the case of marriage, this "independence" relies on the *dependence* of one spouse or partner on the other, shifting the locus of independence from the individual to the household, and the object of dependence from the community to an individual partner.

Nancy Fraser and Linda Gordon, in their article "A Genealogy of 'Dependency'" (1997), trace the shifting connotations of the term from its description of the normal state of most of the pre-industrial population, through the revolutionary valorization of independence and its adoption by wage earners to distinguish themselves from dependent slaves, paupers, and women despite their own economic dependence on employers, to the rise of its current pejorative sense as an individual pathology rather than a structural social condition. Fraser and Gordon argue that:

> unreflective uses of this keyword serve to enshrine certain interpretations of social life as authoritative and to delegitimate or obscure others, generally to the advantage of dominant groups in society and to the disadvantage of subordinate ones (1997: 123).

This is clearly the case in the arguments of paternalists like Mead who, forced to acknowledge that even full-time work cannot guarantee a level of economic independence sufficient to obviate supplementation from the state, claims that some residual dependency on welfare benefits is allowed for those who play by society's rules by working for below-subsistence wages. But how can we endorse economic independence as an essential quality of citizenship if it remains out of the reach, not only of those who choose not to work or are unable to work, but of some who work full-time? Work requirements for the poor do not lead to a genuine independence, but only to a form of ideologized independence that obscures their structural subordination in the contemporary economy.

Furthermore paternalism, by valorizing the ideologized independence of the wage earner, gives insufficient consideration not only to alternative lifestyles that fall outside of society's dominant norms, but to important ways of life that fall within them. It is not only the poor single parent, deemed deviant from the norm by the lack of a partner, who suffers in comparison to the "independent" wage earner, but also the married parent who withdraws from paid employment to care for children and depends economically on her or his spouse. The caregiving spouse's "independence" is even more tenuous than the wage earner's, and is dependent on both the wage earner's employer and the wage earner's affections (see Moller Okin 1989: 134–169). The paternalist model fails to address adequately either of these important dependencies or to reconcile them to the ideal of independence it seeks to advance.

The Civic Republican Argument for Work Requirements

The civic republican argument for work requirements is more egalitarian than the paternalistic argument, and less overtly class based. Its advocates also value adherence to shared norms, especially to the ideal of reciprocity. But they recognize the limits of work-based "independence" and characterize the ideal social condition instead as one of mutual dependence.

Two advocates of this view, Amy Gutmann and Dennis Thompson, reject the paternalistic rhetoric of dependency and advocate selective work requirements for welfare beneficiaries on the basis of the ideal of reciprocity (1996). They argue that income supports are made possible by those who participate in productive economic activity, and therefore that it is wrong for beneficiaries to refuse to participate in the "scheme of fair social cooperation" that makes such supports possible (1996: 279–280). Societies which provide income supports "cannot be neutral between ways of life that contribute to economic productivity and those that do not" (1996: 280). But reciprocity requires also that society provide some of the conditions necessary to make work a possibility for the poor. "Fair workfare," as Gutmann and Thompson term it, requires government action similar to that advocated by David Ellwood: "making work pay" through an expanded EITC, a system of enforcement and government guarantee of child support, and full employment policies (1996: 294).

> The obligations of welfare should be mutual: citizens who need income support are obligated to work, but only if their fellow citizens fulfill their obligation to enact public policies that provide adequate employment and child support (1996: 276).

Like Mead, Gutmann and Thompson believe work to be one of the foundations of citizenship, a "necessary condition to social dignity" (1996: 293), although they are ambiguous about whether that work must be paid employment outside the home.[2] They argue that those who are wealthy enough to choose not to work may be judged lacking.

> If they choose to exempt themselves from a scheme of social cooperation, they may rightly be denied the equal respect of citizens who are motivated to support social cooperation (1996: 280).

They argue that such a view of work might lead to steeper inheritance taxes being imposed on the wealthy, but these taxes are not part of their program of fair workfare. Thus, while the wealthy may be denied respect, the poor may be forced to work, as long as the conditions of fair workfare have been met.

Both the paternalistic and civic republican arguments for work-conditioned welfare benefits attempt to justify selective work requirements in return for welfare benefits in order to support and advance dominant social norms, while conceding that these norms are not universally adhered to, nor can they be universally enforced. By focusing on poverty, its advocates are able to endorse work as a solution to the problem of poverty without affecting the lifestyle choices of more affluent citizens or the underlying inequalities of a system that allows some to choose work or leisure and others to have no choice.

The civic republican argument for selective work requirements is more attractive than the paternalistic argument because the ideal of reciprocity seems to treat all citizens as worthy of respect and care, and it avoids the illusion of an ideologized independence in favor of recognizing our mutual dependence across society. But reciprocity is too general a principle to specify particular obligations like paid employment in return for welfare benefits. It falls victim to two criticisms in particular. First, those who do unpaid work in the home or in the community certainly participate in the scheme of social cooperation and contribute to society's prosperity, whether the contributors are part of a household with a paid worker or not. And second, all members of society receive benefits from that membership; it is unclear why work requirements should be restricted to recipients of one particular kind of benefit only.

The first objection can be answered by the substitution of participation requirements for work requirements. Advocates of participation requirements want to recognize the contributions to society made by some of those who choose not to work. Thus, they endorse the notion of enforcing, or at least promoting, reciprocity for society's benefits, but wish to expand the range of activities that count towards a social contribution beyond paid employment.

Anthony Atkinson, a British economist, proposes abandoning welfare programs in favor of a *participation income*, a basic income conditional on a "social contribution" broadly defined to include caregiving, studying, volunteer work, and looking for work; working in paid or self-employment; or being excused due to illness, disability, or reaching retirement age (1995b, 1998, 1995a: 302–303). Atkinson views the participation income as a compromise between basic income and means-tested benefits because he believes that an unconditional basic income is politically unfeasible. He sees the conditionality of the participation income as much less objectionable than welfare means testing because the definition of participation is so broad that most would qualify, and the positive connotation of qualifying for benefits would encourage all to seek them, as is not currently the case for Britain's welfare programs, which do not reach all who qualify (1996: 94, 1998: 146).

Advocates of participation requirements succeed in resolving one objection to the civic republican model by expanding the definition of social contribution to include forms of socially useful activities other than paid employment. But they fail to resolve the second objection, the problem of selectivity. All members of contemporary society with earned or unearned (e.g., interest) income receive monetary benefits in the form of tax credits and exemptions for certain kinds of income or expenses. If the recipients of welfare must work to reciprocate for their monetary benefits, why not the recipients of other tax system benefits, like the mortgage interest deduction, which can benefit those with only interest income, or Social Security spousal benefits, which benefit households where only one spouse works, or those who send their children to public schools? Individuals who are able to claim such benefits without having earned income might give them up before submitting to a work or participation requirement, but the fact remains that society engages in many forms of economic distribution that benefit classes of individuals without submitting each to a work or participation test. If reciprocity is the guiding principle, why should the work test be reserved for only one class of beneficiaries?

The Socialist Argument for Work Requirements

The socialist model answers that work in the public sphere is a *universal* obligation of all citizens, and income supports a *universal* right. One version of this argument can be found in the work of André Gorz in the 1980s and 1990s.[3]

Gorz argues that the increasing mechanization of many forms of production, the consequent substitution of capital for labor in the manufacturing sector, and the growth of the service sector would lead to two potential divisions taking hold in society. The first is the division of society into those who work and those who do not (or who do not work outside the home) but are supported by welfare payments financed by those who work. The second is the division between those who have "good" jobs that are productive, stimulating, and located in the public sphere; and those who have "bad" jobs—jobs that provide personal services for those who can afford them and who no longer have the time to perform them themselves, such as child care and housecleaning, and that are located primarily in the private sphere (1992, 1986, 1994b: 44–52, 1989: 153–157). Gorz terms these divisions the "South Africanization" of the economy, referring to the old apartheid economy's division of society into a small group of well-paid workers and professionals, and a large group of poorly paid servants and low-skilled workers (1989: 156). Gorz also notes that the extension of equal opportunity to women intensifies this division, allowing a minority of women to participate in the professional economy while domestic work is further shifted to low-paid service workers (1986: 7).

Here Gorz differs markedly from most American welfare theorists, who argue that any kind of employment carries dignity and admits the individual into the sphere of independent citizenship. Gorz rejects this idea unequivocally, arguing that only productive work in society, as opposed to reproductive work, which traditionally has taken place in the private sphere, engenders "independence"—that is, liberation from personal dependence (1992: 181–182, 1989: 13–15, 206, 1994b: 34–35, 48–50; see also 1994a, 1985). To decrease unemployment without increasing the number of service workers and to insure a livable wage for all members of society, Gorz proposes job sharing through a reduction in working hours, together with a citizen's income to supplement the reduction in earned income.

Gorz (1994b) holds that a program of job sharing and a citizen's income is economically feasible. But he also believes it is the only welfare reform program consistent with the full dignity and citizenship of all members of society. With paternalists and civic republicans, he argues that "public citizenship" entails an obligation to contribute to society in addition to a right to benefit from its fruits (1992: 179–180, 1989: 205). But he sees the private sphere, in which individuals take care of themselves and their loved ones, as falling outside the sphere of work. As a result, Gorz opposes the increasing "outsourcing" of caregiving, entertainment, education of young children, and other formerly private activities, and does not consider jobs in these areas to be consistent with public, or social citizenship (1986: 9–11; see also 1994b: 169). Gorz is concerned not only with reshaping the welfare state, but with using its reform as a foundation for reshaping the structure of social and economic life to advance individual freedom and as an ideal of social citizenship. In contrast to those in the paternalistic and civic republican traditions, Gorz, as a socialist, is prepared to enforce public work requirements on *all* citizens.

Gorz makes a persuasive case for liberating many low-skilled and unpaid service and domestic workers from what are often socially isolating positions without much chance of advancement, and for giving each citizen the opportunity to feel the kind of pride that only earning a paycheck can bring. But like the paternalistic and civic republican advocates of work requirements, he imposes on all citizens a uniform view of what activities are valued and rewarding, rather than letting individuals choose for themselves. Universal work requirements are fair in the sense of being egalitarian, but this is not a liberal solution.

Those who argue for participation requirements, like Atkinson, paint a more attractive picture of recognition for currently unpaid social contributions without requiring the state to get involved in job creation and allocation, and without wading into the morass of trying to compensate caregiving and other voluntary activities directly. Universal participation requirements redeem the inegalitarian civic republicanism of reciprocity advocates by infusing it with an ethic of egalitarianism and respect for the various contributions of a diverse citizenry. Both on economic and personal grounds, the flexibility of a broader definition of social contribution is more attractive, especially in the American context, than a socialist economy with mandated job sharing. Nevertheless, both the socialist model of universal work requirements and the egalitarian model of universal participation requirements are defensible positions to hold, and each articulates a theory of citizenship that has merit. Should advocates of basic income then concede the issue of unconditionality and advocate a basic income conditioned on universal participation requirements?

The Liberal Alternative of Radical Pluralism

Supporters of an unconditional basic income should not give in just yet. There is an alternative to the socialist and civic republican (however egalitarian) ideals that is inherent in American political and economic culture, but it requires reframing the debate over conditionality and overcoming leftist distaste for the institution of the market.

The first step is to break the hold of poverty and welfare analysts on the debate on conditionality, despite the fact that no American who advocates for basic income can do so without keeping the poor in mind. The motivating impulse behind the work of basic income advocates is in large part the elimination of the poverty that persists in the richest societies in the world. As Philippe Van Parijs notes, the institution of basic income can be seen as the culmination of the welfare state, necessitated by the recognition of the limits of all previous safety net structures (1992a: 465–466). But an *unconditional* basic income is not an incremental change in welfare policy; it is a revolutionary change in our understanding of democratic citizenship.

> The introduction of a basic income is not just a feasible structural improvement in the functioning of the welfare state; it is a profound reform that belongs in the same league as the abolition of slavery or the introduction of universal suffrage (Van Parijs 1992b: 7).

If the "real libertarian" entitlement argument that Van Parijs advances is correct, surfers are no less deserving of a basic income than double-shift parents, since we are under no moral obligation to use what is legitimately ours in any socially approved manner. But the *radical pluralism* implied by this view requires additional justification if it is to survive the critique of those who claim that work or participation requirements are an essential element of citizenship. Assuming a basic income could be instituted in the United States, why not make it conditional on work or participation requirements?

American society offers two institutions as examples of radical pluralism to which we can appeal for a more liberal vision of what an unconditional basic income could accomplish: the market economy and the democratic polity. As many basic income advocates have noted, basic income, or its close cousin the negative income tax, is the favored form of welfare benefit of many economists of varying political stripes, including Milton Friedman and James Tobin in the United States, among others. Many economists prefer basic income to categorical grants, wage supplements, or large-scale governmental job creation because basic income interferes less with the efficient functioning of the market than these other alternatives, even with the higher marginal tax rates necessary to finance it. Even Friedrich Hayek, the most passionate defender of laissez-faire economics, wrote positively about redistributive measures that do not interfere with the market's allocative function (1979: 54–56).

But market considerations do more than merely give a green light to basic income as an acceptable form of welfare. The free-market economy derives its legitimacy not only from the high standard of living it enables, but from the liberty it provides those who participate in it to pursue their own preferences, subject to the constraints of their own resources and what they can trade for with others. The free market leads to better outcomes—that is, outcomes more closely matched to individual preferences—than other economic systems. This is true on condition that each begins with something to trade. It is no accident that philosophical analyses of property rights, distributive justice, and exploitation begin with scenarios of natural resources divided equally among the population. The equal division of resources, which one is then free to trade according to one's preferences, makes intuitive sense. The trouble begins when unforeseen events alter preferences when resources have already been allocated, or when offspring come along and find themselves constrained by a previous generation's choices. How do we recreate the initial egalitarian distribution to preserve the legitimacy of the market once we leave the ideal state?

There is no way to do so completely, at least without fatally disrupting the workings of the market and severely limiting the scope of individual freedom, but basic income can be seen as a partial solution. It need not (re)create a completely egalitarian distribution to have significantly egalitarian—and democratic—effects, providing each individual with renewable resources to save, consume, or invest as he or she sees fit. Basic income maintains for each an inalienable right to participate in the economy, much as the democratic system maintains our inalienable right to participate in politics. We make no claim that all citizens have *equal* political power in a democracy; representative democracy in fact ensures that some—those we elect—have more power than the rest of us. But the right to vote, together with periodic elections, means that however foolishly we "spend" our votes in one election, we still get to vote in the next election, which is never too far off. The market is no less important a sphere of citizenship than the polity, and the ground rules should be similarly egalitarian. No less; and perhaps no more.

I characterize this approach as radical pluralism, because it has no place for any constraints on what recipients may do with their basic income, just as there are virtually no constraints on what one may do with earned income; nor does it have any place for restraints on qualification, just as there are virtually no qualifications required for citizens to vote. It should go without saying that a market-based approach to justifying basic income cannot be conditional on work, since only market pricing and individual preferences for more income than basic income provides should determine who works and who does not, and because economic autonomy requires a more even balance of power between employers and employees than would be fostered by enforced work. Under this approach, basic income provides some compensation for the unpaid caregiving and voluntary activities envisioned in the participation requirement advocated by Atkinson and others, but it also requires us to endorse the rights of fellow citizens to behave badly, squandering their basic income on lottery tickets and liquor, or surfboards and tickets to Malibu. Most importantly, an unconditional basic income allows each citizen to have a role in shaping social mores as well as to pursue individual goals, helping to determine what we view as the "normal" balance of paid work, unpaid caregiving, and leisure, and the appropriate division of labor between the sexes. In this way, an unconditional basic income is not a prioritization of the individual good over the common good, but an alternative approach to achieving the common good that values the contributions and life choices of all individuals, including the poor and those who do not conform to dominant mores.

Conclusion

What I have presented here is only the framework of the case for a radically pluralistic notion of citizenship, to counter the paternalistic, civic republican, and socialist notions that currently dominate the basic income debate. What paternalism, civic republicanism, and socialism share is a willingness to impose constraints on the liberty of individuals in order to achieve patterned outcomes. This conflicts with the libertarian ethos, which so clearly underlies the American economic and political spheres (and to a degree its social sphere as well). To be sure, libertarian capitalism is a mixed blessing, responsible for so much of the inequality and insecurity the welfare state is designed to mitigate, but responsible also for the surplus that makes a generous welfare state, or basic income, a possibility. But pairing a libertarian economic sphere with a paternalistic social sphere seems like the worst of both worlds. Liberal supporters of basic income must offer an attractive alternative vision of a pluralistic society in which all citizens have a guaranteed and unalienable minimum of economic, as well as political, autonomy to make an unconditional basic income a political possibility in the United States.

Notes

[1] The EITC is available to low-income workers without children, but at such a low level—a maximum of $382 for incomes up to $11,230 ($12,230 for married couples)—as to be considered trivial.

[2] They say both that poor parents with young children should be required to work outside the home, and elsewhere that "having a job" includes working in the home in a household where others work outside the home (Gutmann and Thompson 1996): 297–98, 293.

[3] Gorz occupies a distinct position in the debate on basic income and work requirements, as he argued vehemently *against* an unconditional basic income for many years, but now argues in favor of it. His long-held position advocated both a universal obligation to work and a basic income; that is, he supported both compelling employment outside the home and, to a certain extent, decoupling income and employment.

References

Atkinson, A.B. (1995a) *Incomes and the Welfare State: Essays on Britain and Europe*, (Cambridge: Cambridge University Press).

——— (1995b) *Public Economics in Action: The Basic Income/Flat Tax Proposal*, (Oxford: Clarendon Press).

——— (1996) "James Meade's Vision: Full Employment and Social Justice," *National Institute Economic Review*, 157: 93–94.

——— (1998) *Poverty in Europe*, (Oxford: Blackwell).

Ellwood, D. (1988) *Poor Support: Poverty in the American Family*, (New York: Basic Books).

Fraser, N. and Gordon, L. (1997) "A Genealogy of 'Dependency': Tracing a Keyword of the U.S. Welfare State," in *Justice Interruptus: Critical Reflections on the "Postsocialist" Condition*, N. Fraser, (New York: Routledge).

Gorz, A. (1985) "Allocation universelle: version de droite et version de gauche," *La Revue Nouvelle*, 81: 419–428.

——— (1986) "Reshaping the Welfare State: The Conservative Approach and its Socialist Alternative," *Praxis International*, 6 (1): 5–12.

——— (1989) *Critique of Economic Reason*, trans. G. Handyside and C. Turner (London: Verso).

——— (1992) "On the Difference between Society and Community, and Why Basic Income Cannot by Itself Confer Full Membership of Either," in *Arguing for Basic*

Income: Ethical Foundations for a Radical Reform, P. Van Parijs (ed.), (London: Verso).

——— (1994a) "Revenu minimum et citoyenneté: droit au travail vs. droit au revenu," *Futuribles*, 184: 49–60.

——— (1994b) *Capitalism, Socialism, Ecology*, (London: Verso).

Gutmann, A. and Thompson, D. (1996) *Democracy and Disagreement*, (Cambridge: Harvard University Press).

Hayek, F. (1979) *The Political Order of a Free People*, vol. 3 of *Law, Legislation and Liberty*, (Chicago: University of Chicago Press).

Kaus, M. (1992) *The End of Equality*, (New York: Basic Books).

Mead, L. (1986) *Beyond Entitlement: The Social Obligations of Citizenship*, (New York: Free Press).

——— (1992) *The New Politics of Poverty: The Nonworking Poor in America*, (New York: Basic Books).

——— (1997) "The Rise of Paternalism," in *The New Paternalism: Supervisory Approaches to Poverty*, L. Mead (ed.), (Washington, D.C.: Brookings Institution).

——— (1998) "Telling the Poor What to Do," *The Public Interest*, 132: 97–112.

Moller Okin, S. (1989) *Justice, Gender, and the Family*, (New York: Basic Books).

Murray, C. (1984) *Losing Ground: American Social Policy, 1950–1980*, (New York: Basic Books).

Van Parijs, P. (1992a) "Basic Income Capitalism," *Ethics*, 102 (3): 465–484.

——— (1992b) "Competing Justifications of Basic Income," in *Arguing for Basic Income: Ethical Foundations for a Radical Reform*, P. Van Parijs (ed.), (London: Verso).

——— (1995) *Real Freedom for All: What (If Anything) Can Justify Capitalism?*, (Oxford: Oxford University Press).

White, S. (1997) "Liberal Equality, Exploitation, and the Case for an Unconditional Basic Income," *Political Studies*, 45: 312–26.

Wilson, W. J. (1987) *The Truly Disadvantaged: The Inner City, the Underclass, and Public Policy*, (Chicago: University of Chicago Press).

Chapter 7

Basic Income, Liberal Neutrality, Socialism, and Work

Michael W. Howard*

Introduction

The proposal for an unconditional basic income (BI) can be expected to draw opposition from the political right. Those who find no fault with the inequalities of contemporary capitalism or who think poverty is due to personal failings of the poor are not apt to be receptive to unconditional income grants or to the taxes required to support it. Although it is important to address such opposition and consider possibilities for conservative support for BI, in this chapter I concentrate on opposition from the political left, including egalitarian liberals, Marxists and socialists. Some recent liberal proposals for BI are framed with reference to changing labor market conditions, accepting as given the trend toward more flexible labor markets and declining full-time employment, and BI is partly defended as both facilitating and compensating for this trend. Liberal critics often object to BI on the grounds that it violates reciprocity and is biased toward those who choose voluntarily to opt out of work, and thus violates the principle of liberal neutrality toward conceptions of the good life. In Part 1 of this chapter I argue that liberal neutrality favors BI. Marxist critics of BI are less likely to accept liberal neutrality, but I argue in Part 2 that the argument for BI in Part 1 applies with equal force to Marxist objections that BI is unfairly exploitative of workers. Marxists are also less likely to accept current labor market trends—seeing socialism as affording more opportunity for guaranteeing everyone a right to decent work, and suspecting BI of making the unfair inequalities of capitalism a little more palatable while diverting attention from a more equitable socialist alternative. I argue that BI is not incompatible with socialism or Marxism, and should not be opposed to, but rather combined with, strategies for full employment.

1. Basic Income and Liberal Neutrality

Since the first part of this chapter is framed in terms of "liberal neutrality", I should first clarify what I mean by this and explain why it should be taken seriously. I'm using the term, as does Rawls, to refer to a theory of justice that is not biased toward a particular substantive conception of the good life. Immediately one might wonder whether such a theory of justice is even possible or, if it is, whether it would be so empty as to have nothing interesting to say about justice.[1]

I think both horns of this dilemma can be avoided if we understand the "neutrality" aimed for not to be absolute, but relative to the substantive and conflicting conceptions of the good that otherwise divide a political community. It is the standpoint one moves to, in the face of irreconcilable normative convictions, in order to achieve justice. Rawls himself conceives of it as an extension of the principle of religious toleration. European societies came to the realization that no reasonable universal agreement could be expected among the warring religious factions, and they agreed to disagree. Moreover, this mutual toleration came to be a core liberal principle in each of the main religious traditions, so that these traditions themselves supported, by an overlapping consensus, the principle of religious toleration. So too, comprehensive metaphysical and moral doctrines, about which reasonable people disagree, should not be among the premises of the theory of justice; rather we should assume neutrality toward such doctrines, or in other words, a principle of respect for differences (Rawls 1993; Larmore 1987).

That said, the theory of justice is not devoid of moral commitments—such as the priority of justice, certain notions of what constitutes a person, the primary goods, and other ideas that people can agree upon despite their conflicting ideals of the good life. Nor is the theory of justice a mere *modus vivendi*. The neutrality of the theory is not a mere truce among warring parties; rather, it is the result of incorporating into conflicting traditions a principle of toleration as central to those traditions themselves.

What this means of course is that in any contemporary society—perhaps any society at all—there will be people and groups who will not consent to justice. The theory won't speak for them or to them. I have in mind not merely hardened criminals, but, more to the point, people whose conceptions of the good life preclude respect and toleration of other reasonable conceptions. No theory of justice can be expected to persuade everyone.

Neutrality, Work and Leisure

In Rawls's original formulation of the theory of justice, the primary goods that are the focus of distribution—those goods that one wants, whatever else one wants—included basic liberties, opportunity, wealth, income, power and authority, and the bases of self-respect (Rawls 1971). Absent from the list was leisure, until it was pointed out that this absence biased the theory toward "the Lazy," those with a preference for leisure (Musgrave 1974; Rawls 1988).

To see why this is the case, consider the following. If we leave leisure off the list, and then assume further that the parties to the original position would choose the Difference Principle (DP) for the distribution of wealth, income, power and authority, the Lazy will be favored over those with a preference for higher income available through work (following Van Parijs (1995: 92)), let's call them "the Crazy" to avoid a bias in our discussion). DP stipulates that distribution should maximize the minimum for the least advantaged group. Now suppose over time there is an increment in total wealth and income. Those who live only on the socially guaranteed minimum—including the Lazy—will get the maximum sustainable share of this increase. The Crazy can protest that the Lazy, unlike those dependent on this minimum who are unable to work or find employment, or to meet basic needs from their wages, are favored on account of their conception of the good life, which involves a lot of leisure and low consumption.

To avoid this bias, Rawls added leisure to the list of primary goods, defined as "twenty-four hours less a standard working day. Those who are unwilling to work would have a standard working day of extra leisure, and this extra leisure itself would be stipulated as equivalent to the index of primary goods of the least advantaged" (Rawls 1988: 257). This entails that there is no right to income or wealth that is not conditional on the willingness to work or the inability to work.

Van Parijs has argued that Rawls, in the way he has addressed the original bias in favor of the Lazy, "swings all the way and introduces the opposite bias" in favor of the Crazy (Van Parijs 1995: 90).

Let's go back to the hypothetical increment in total wealth and income, and this time further stipulate that the increase is due to some external good such as plentiful rainfall or discovery of oil, rather than greater expenditure of labor. What happens to the least advantaged group—in particular those who don't work at all—in the distribution of this increment? Their income will increase to the level of the least paid full-time worker, but workers on the whole will enjoy a higher proportion of the windfall, even though it resulted not from their labor but from natural good fortune. Is this not a bias toward those with a preference for paid work? The point made here with respect to a natural windfall can be generalized to all wealth and income that results not from labor but from external assets such as land. And there is, Van Parijs holds, "a nonarbitrary and generally positive legitimate level of basic income that is determined by the per capita value of society's external assets" (Van Parijs 1995: 99).

> (This level) must be entirely financed by those who appropriate these assets. If Lazy gives up the whole of his plot of land, he is entitled to an unconditional grant at a level that corresponds to the value of that plot. Crazy, on the other hand, can be viewed as receiving this same grant, but as owing twice its amount because of appropriating both Lazy's share of land and her own. (Van Parijs 1995: 99)

There is a technical problem of how to assess the value of external assets, which I set aside (Van Parijs 1995: 99). The key point is that although *some* wealth and income is due to labor, some is due to the appropriation of external assets, which (from the standpoint of justice) is common; thus those who appropriate unearned wealth owe compensation to those who don't, and such compensation can take the form of unconditional basic income. (It could also be given to all in kind, as free education, free health care, a one-time lump sum grant, etc.) This income will typically fall between Rawls's bias toward the Crazy and his earlier pro-Lazy bias.

Van Parijs's position has numerous precedents, notably Tom Paine's proposal for a universal grant based on the rent of land, and Henry George's single tax, again focused on land and rent. Van Parijs proposes to widen the basis of the social dividend from land to include capital, and socially inherited technology. But he claims once one adjusts for incentive effects (which, for a Rawlsian warrant inequalities when they are to the advantage of the least advantaged), the amount of basic income per capita that would be generated would be so small as not to be worth the trouble. (I think this conclusion may be too pessimistic, but won't argue the point here.)[2]

Van Parijs's principal innovation is to widen the basis for basic income further to include *jobs* as assets:

> The crucial fact to notice is that, owing to the way in which our economies are organized, the most significant category of assets consists in jobs people are endowed with. Jobs are packages of tasks and benefits. Of course, for jobs to count as assets, they must be in scarce supply...As long as jobs are scarce, those who hold them appropriate a rent which can be legitimately taxed away, so as substantially to boost the legitimate level of basic income. (Van Parijs 1995: 90)

If jobs are treated as assets, the highest sustainable level of basic income could be very substantial in an affluent society.

But does justice require "real freedom for all"—entailing the maximum feasible BI? Returning to Rawls, recall that he conceives of justice as a set of principles arrived at through agreement among members of a society who share in the benefits and *burdens* and who conceive of society as an ongoing *cooperative* arrangement. Does liberal neutrality really rule out as perfectionist the expectation that all able-bodied people be willing to work in exchange for their share of the benefits? Rather isn't it central to the very idea of justice as a fair agreement that there be a bias toward the Crazies? And isn't it to be expected that *reciprocity* be affirmed by moral traditions that form the overlapping consensus?

Interestingly, Van Parijs is willing to concede this point, not by loosening his strict interpretation of neutrality, but by appeal to the conditions for social solidarity. With Rawls, he accepts as a requirement of a theory of justice that it possess "stability"—that once justice is in place it should be reasonable to expect a just society to sustain and reproduce itself, with the necessary level of citizen allegiance and solidarity (Rawls 1971: 496–504). So he is willing to entertain the superiority of a "participation income"—guaranteed basic income that is *conditional* on some form of public service—over an unconditional BI:

> But it must be clear that the argument is neither about economic viability (a compulsory public service of sizeable length would *reduce* the economic potential for financing a substantial basic income), nor about ethical justification ...but about the sociological conditions for widespread allegiance to solidaristic justice." (Van Parijs 1995: 297n73)

In other words, the ethical justification still aims for neutrality between those who desire to contribute to society and those whose idea of the good life involves no such contribution, but in practice "the sociological conditions for widespread allegiance" would dictate reciprocity. It then remains to be shown sociologically that social solidarity really depends upon a generalized work ethic.[3]

If one wants to argue more deeply that the core assumptions of the theory of justice should incorporate a bias toward the Crazy, one is in effect saying that Malibu surfers—the paradigmatic Lazies—lack moral standing in the community with respect to their conception of a good life, in the same way that murderers and rapists as such lack moral standing. The latter are beyond the pale in any moral tradition worthy of consideration. But is it so obvious that surfers are?[4]

Liberal neutrality does not and cannot require neutrality toward any conception of the "good" that includes violating the bodily integrity or liberty of others. The question is whether the Lazy, whom one might also be tempted to call parasites, are in some analogous way injuring or stealing from others (Torisky 1993).

The plausibility of this idea that noncontribution is harmful may stem from the illusion that all of the wealth that results from labor is due only to that labor. (Even Marx, who holds that all exchange value is the result of labor, acknowledges that not all wealth is due to labor, since nature also contributes, sometimes lavishly and sometimes without any admixture of labor.) The illusion is compounded when labor is the principal source of wealth, but is combined with other assets that, in exchange, will yield to the worker (or whoever appropriates the product) more than the value of the labor expended (at equilibrium).

But once we grant that external assets partially constitute and contribute to one's capacity for wealth creation, the wealth that flows from labor employing these assets is only partly the fruits of labor; it is also partly the consequence of *others*, or of society enabling the worker to produce. Van Parijs effectively blocks the idea that the Lazy are merely parasites by arguing that their basic income is essentially not a handout but compensation for their letting go of their per capita share of social wealth.[5]

> *Crazy* would be the "invader" [in the broad sense of unfair taking from society] if she took the whole of (what looks like) her product instead of contributing to an endowment given to all in order to enable them as much as possible to pursue realization of their noninvasive (this time in the narrower sense of invasive) conception of good life.[6]

Eugene Torisky tries to make the case that the Lazy have an "invasive" conception of the good life, not in the narrower sense but in a broader sense of "unfair taking," that presupposes that everyone who receives support from society should give something in return. He thinks this idea of reciprocity is evenhanded: "What liberal justice denies the Crazies of society, the benefits of mutual cooperation without contributing to it, is precisely what it denies the Lazies" (Torisky 1993: 296). However, real libertarians might make an equally compelling claim to evenhandedness: Liberal justice denies equally to Lazies and Crazies any *additional* benefits (beyond BI) without some contribution. And the real libertarian will ask, what is the basis for denying the BI to *everyone*, if not a perfectionist work ethic?

Torisky tries to argue that the Lazies are injured alike with the Crazies without a reciprocity condition:

> *unconditional* basic income…goes too far, by exempting its recipients from the minimal cost of membership in society and thereby depriving them of the dignity and status of a member. (Torisky 1993: 296)

But the recipients are free to participate—more free with a BI than without one. It is unclear how forced participation is more empowering and respectful than the mere freedom to participate. And it might be said that BI, along with the affirmation of basic liberties and equality of opportunity, adequately affirms the dignity and status of each member.

As a final remark, anyone unpersuaded of the *justness* of BI with respect to liberal neutrality, either because of reasons favoring Rawls's position or because of a rejection of liberal neutrality as a premise, may still be moved to support BI on pragmatic grounds.

Even if one were to favor a *participation income* in principle, it raises questions of how to define participation, who will monitor it, and what the cost of such monitoring will be, including the price paid in the dignity of the recipients (Barry 1996). Does raising children count? Political action? Writing poetry? Only good poetry? (Suppose James Joyce had written *Ulysses* while receiving a BI. Would he have been considered a free rider? Probably worse by those who initially judged his book obscene. On the other hand, it is seldom questioned whether a person making and selling landmines is contributing, because his product has a market). Assuming that most people want to contribute to society, is it not better to endure a few real slackers in order to liberate the rest to contribute creatively and without surveillance than to try to catch the slackers, burden bureaucrats with arbitrary judgments, and exclude many genuine and needy contributors? The current means-tested system errs in the opposite direction, always failing to catch all the needy in the safety net. Should we not err on the side of generosity from the standpoint of a theory of justice that favors the least advantaged?

2. Why Marxists and Socialists Should Favor Basic Income

So much for the arguments within liberalism. But should Marxists and socialists also support BI? One might think the answer an obvious yes for anyone in a tradition in which the ultimate principle of distribution in the "higher phase of communism" is to each "according to need."[7] However, in his classic formulation, Marx considered such a principle irrelevant for the "lower phase of communism," more commonly called socialism, that might conceivably replace capitalism, because in the latter there would still be substantial material scarcity, a division of mental and manual labor inherited from capitalism, and work that is mostly done out of necessity rather than as a form of self-realization. More appropriate for socialism is distribution "according to work" (Marx 1977b). This amounts to a conditional reciprocity principle and, if the fruits of social labor are to be shared equitably, would seem to entail a right to work, but not an unconditional right to income.

These conceptions of socialist rights and distribution can be grounded in Marx's theory of alienation (Marx 1977c). For Marx, to be a human being is to be fundamentally a social being, interdependent with others of the species. This interdependence can be conscious and positive, as in the love relations of a family, or the idealized bonds of citizens in the ancient Greek polis, or it can be unconscious, externalized, estranged, as in the universal system of needs embodied in the market economy. In the latter, it is typical for one to come to regard others as mere means for the satisfaction of one's own individual needs. Basic income might be thought to further this sort of egoistic false consciousness, insofar as it is proclaimed to rest on a right to individual "real freedom"—freedom to opt out of the system of reciprocal exchange by taking one's basic income and refusing to work. Although real libertarianism shares with Marx an egalitarian critique of the inequality of wealth, income, and power in capitalist society, it aims to establish greater equality without challenging alienation from the species.[8]

Alienation from the species, according to Marx's theory, is grounded in the alienation of labor. The worker alienates the product of labor when it is appropriated by the capitalist who has purchased the worker's labor power. The product, in the typical cycle of capitalist production, has the value added by the worker to the raw material; but the worker is paid only for the value of the labor power, not the value of the labor expended. The difference between these values is the source of capitalist profit and accumulation. Capital grows ever larger—and with this, the domination of the worker increases—as capital growth reduces other possibilities for access to the means of labor or the means of life. The worker is *forced* to labor to the degree that there is no alternative to starvation except working for wages. In the *Communist Manifesto*, Marx and Engels sum up the goal of the communist workers' movement as the abolition of private property or capital (Marx and Engels 1977: 232). The point could be interpreted as putting an end to all "unearned income," i.e., all income other than wages, such as that from interest, dividends, rent, and inheritance. This aversion to unearned income could be extended in a socialist society to unconditional basic income, insofar as it too is unearned. As Jon Elster has put it (1986: 719), basic income goes

> against a widely accepted notion of justice…it is unfair for able-bodied people to live off the labor of others. Most workers would, correctly in my opinion, see the proposal as a recipe for exploitation of the industrious by the lazy.

David Schweickart (2000) goes further:

> we do not have a moral right to a BI. We do have a moral *obligation* to work. When we consume, we take from society. Justice requires that we give something back in return.

The overcoming of alienation, the first step of which is the abolition of private property, is more positively a democratization of the means of production. This involves, first, bringing the market economy under conscious collective control. This has often been understood to mean the replacement of the market economy by central planning, but it can also include more modest strategic planning and democratization of investment decisions, with space left for a market economy in goods and services. Second, democratization of the means of production includes the overcoming of the tyranny of the workplace through worker self-management. Alienation and domination give way to self-determination and self-realization through work. If everyone is to be so emancipated, there must be a right to employment for everyone who is able to work.

Let me first note that accepting the right (and obligation) to work does not entail rejecting BI. Pragmatic defenses of BI as a more effective way of eliminating the poverty trap than means-tested and work-linked alternatives are compatible with a view that there is no fundamental moral right to BI, and that there is in principle an obligation to *work* or at least to give back in some way.[9] Proponents of *participation income*—a guaranteed income conditional on some form of social participation including not only paid work but also child care, elder care, volunteer activity, etc.—explicitly recognize this obligation, or at least its political salience, and make the BI at least loosely contingent on giving back (Atkinson 1996). And one argument for BI is that it enables people to work by pricing themselves into a job, i.e., "making jobs paying less than a living wage viable" (Barry 1996: 243). That is, with a guaranteed income, individuals could augment their income through wages that otherwise would be insufficient for subsistence.[10]

The objection that BI is exploitative has been answered sufficiently in Part 1 of this chapter. I only add here that, to render this consistent with Marxism, we only need to think about *unearned income* in a different way. Traditionally, following the language of the *Manifesto*, private property, and with it unearned income, is to be "abolished," and following the model of the *Critique of the Gotha Program*, replaced with income proportional to labor. But an alternative is to socialize the property and share the unearned income equitably. John Roemer (1994) has proposed one way to do this, issuing citizens shares of socialized capital from which they would draw dividends, i.e., a basic income.[11] It is worth noting further that the *abolition* involved in the first path is only apparent—masking the unearned income tied to the control of land, capital, inherited technology, and jobs as assets (now controlled by collectives of workers rather than capitalists) in the form of payment proportional to labor. But those labor payments include unearned as well as earned income.

The most controversial part of unearned income is that deriving from employment rents on "jobs as assets." Without a tax on employment rents (described in Part I), the basic income yielded from other sources is likely to fall short of subsistence, and then many of the benefits associated with BI (such as the freedom to refuse work) diminish. Thus any substantial BI will probably require among its funding sources a tax on wages. Just how much would this be, and would full-time workers feel exploited in comparison with their situation under conditional welfare schemes? Would BI therefore promote conflict between workers and unemployed BI recipients? Charles Clark (2003: 150–152) has shown that a basic income system for the United States, based on 1999 figures, that would give everyone under 18 years old $3,500; every adult between 18 and 65 years old $8,667; and everyone over 65 years old $7,990 would cost a little under $2 trillion. (Bear in mind that, because everyone receives the BI, the net effect on one's income after taxes and transfers will be *much smaller* than the price tag suggests for the middle income taxpayers.) The BI could be funded by a flat tax on all incomes at a rate of 35.8 percent.[12] (Clark refers to a flat tax, not because it is superior to a progressive income tax, but because it is easier to model.) With BI, the average household income of the lowest 60 percent would increase by several thousand dollars. Taxpayers in the top 40 percent would lose. But those in the fourth quintile would not lose by much, having on average $1,092 less than they would have without BI. And these might be persuaded that the price was worth it for the increased freedom and numerous social benefits that would come with BI, not least the elimination of poverty. The big losers would be those in the top quintile, whose income would be on average $20,034 less with BI.[13] The tax burden could be shifted further off the fourth quintile and onto the fifth with a more progressive tax rate than that in Clark's analysis. But even without that, it should be clear that most workers would gain, not lose, from BI, in comparison with the status quo. So there is an economic basis for workers making common cause with those who would opt out of the waged labor market (and the latter would at various times include many of these workers). The universal character of the grant facilitates this: Everyone gets it; we are all in the same boat. The truly divisive form of welfare reform is not BI but workfare, establishing a discipline that is socially required but economically unnecessary, and dividing society into payers and receivers, typically along race and gender lines (Fraser 1989).

The objection that species interdependence, alienated by the market, will be further alienated by basic income is misplaced. Anyone who seeks more than the minimum will still need to work for it, and it will be immediately apparent that such work involves one in a web of connections with the rest of the species. Moreover, the failure to acknowledge unearned income by folding it all into wages would, itself, mask two equally important sorts of interdependence. First, wage workers often depend on others for the relatively high wages they enjoy, and this dependence is masked by too tight an allocation of income in proportion to work. For example, particularly in the United States in the 1950s and 1960s, the male wage earner implicitly was being paid for his own reproduction through the labor of a wife who was not remunerated, and who was economically dependent on the male in an invidious way.[14] A basic income enabling homemakers to stay out of the wage labor market and to be less economically dependent upon a male wage earner is one way to acknowledge this unpaid labor and to call attention to a kind of interdependence that has been masked, without turning housework into wage labor (the household wage idea). Important here, also, is the dependence of the money economy and its agents on informal, household, and other economies that cannot easily survive transformation into commodity form. Becoming aware of this sort of interdependence is also a step beyond alienation. I'm a market socialist. But the only way the *socialist* in market socialism can be sustained against the alienating forces of the market is if the sphere of the market is clearly limited. The market should not dominate the household, the media, education, health care, or politics (Walzer 1983). The second sort of interdependence is that between ourselves and nature, or more generally, the sources of unearned wealth and income. A BI tied to these is one way of socially acknowledging our shared dependence on natural resources, historical inheritances, etc.

Most importantly, this objection overlooks the core aspect of alienation, which is the *coercion* to work. One is alienated from one's labor because one is forced to sell it to another and then to labor under the other's domination; under such conditions one feels estranged from one's labor and from the whole web of species interdependence with which it connects one. BI at a sustainable level is a step beyond alienation because it gives more workers the option to say no, and thus will exert some pressure on employers—whether capitalists or collectives of workers—to make the conditions of work more palatable. As work becomes more humane, the worker works more freely, and thus can become interdependent in a nonalienated way.

Closely related to the objection that BI masks our interdependence as a species, there is the criticism that it rests on an individualistic conception of freedom that is incompatible with socialist democracy or with a movement to socialist democracy. BI, it could be argued, promotes the idea that each person has a right to opt out of social participation; *real freedom* includes the right not to work or participate. Socialist freedom, on the other hand, is at least partly a freedom of groups—collectives of workers, communities, or whole societies—to determine their joint destiny collectively through democratic processes. Anyone excluded from such processes, by choice or by lack of available positions for participation, is deprived of an important freedom, analogous to being deprived of voting rights. Further, it might be added, the full overcoming of alienation involves self-realization through work.

The importance of self-realization through work can be understood in two different ways. First, it can be grounded in a philosophical ideal of human perfection. If this is what is meant, then it runs afoul of liberal neutrality. Some Marxists might say so much the worse for liberal neutrality, but in a pluralistic society the burden of proof will fall on them to show why everyone should embrace and be bound to this ideal. A less controversial understanding of the importance of work rests on empirical evidence that work is an important source of independence, achievement, advancement, family security, and self-esteem (Karst 1997: 534, quoted in Harvey 2003; Solow 1998; Howard 1984b). But work is not the only source of these important values; even if it is one of the most important and if by work we mean paid employment, such strong linkage as there might be is in part due to the absence of other sources of independence, affirmation of one's worth, and opportunities for meaningful activity such as BI might afford.

This brings us to the question of what "work" should mean, and how it should be related to income and leisure in a socialist society. As Schweickart (2000) puts it,

> a genuine socialist alternative to capitalism should "abolish welfare as we know it," and undertake the difficult task redesigning our institutions so that every citizen can make a meaningful, productive contribution to the well-being of his or her fellow citizens. Not "real freedom for all," but rather, "real work for all"– "real work" that allows us to develop our individual abilities and to contribute meaningfully to our collective being.

A genuine socialist alternative should begin by acknowledging the ambivalent moral significance of work. On the one hand, it is one of the key ways we contribute to society, integrate ourselves into it, find our identity, exercise our capacities for creativity, etc. On the other hand, it is necessary; and one way or another, human beings are constrained to labor in order to survive. The reality of work is that it shares in both of these aspects, some kinds of work more closely approximating the first, other kinds the second. The best summation I know of was made by Marx (1977a: 496–497):

> The actual wealth of society, and the possibility of constantly expanding its reproduction process, therefore, do not depend upon the duration of surplus labor, but upon its productivity and the more or less copious conditions of production under which it is performed. In fact, the realm of freedom actually begins only where labor which is determined by necessity and mundane considerations ceases; thus in the very nature of things it lies beyond the sphere of actual material production. Just as the savage must wrestle with Nature to satisfy his wants, to maintain and reproduce life, so must civilized man, and he must do so in all social formations and under all possible modes of production. With his development this realm of physical necessity expands as a result of his wants; but, at the same time, the forces of production which satisfy these wants also increase. Freedom in this field can only consist in socialized man, the associated producers, rationally regulating their interchange with Nature, bringing it under their common control, instead of being ruled by it as by the blind forces of Nature; and achieving this with the least expenditure of energy and under conditions most favorable to, and worthy of, their human nature. But it nonetheless still remains a realm of necessity. Beyond it begins that development of human energy which is an end in itself, the true realm of freedom, which, however, can blossom forth only with this realm of necessity as its basis. The shortening of the working-day is its basic prerequisite.

Economic Democracy (workplace democracy and democratic allocation of investment funds) addresses the rational regulation of our interchange with Nature "under conditions most favorable to, and worthy of" our human nature. Basic income is a step toward the realm of freedom, constrained in its extent by the realm of necessity as its basis. Real work for all *and* real freedom for all, these should be the long term goals of socialism.

Fortunately, these two goals are complementary. As Van Parijs (2001: 19) argues, in comparison with employer subsidies that keep up the pressure on workers to seek employment,

> UBI [universal basic income] makes it easier to take a break between two jobs, reduce working time, make room for more training, take up self-employment, or join a cooperative. And with UBI, workers will only take a job if they find it suitably attractive, while employer subsidies make unattractive, low-productivity jobs more economically viable. If the motive in combating unemployment is not some sort of work fetishism—an obsession with keeping everyone busy—but rather a concern to give every person the possibility of taking up gainful employment in which she can find recognition and accomplishment, then the UBI is to be preferred.

There are different ways we might redesign our institutions so that everyone will have work, and I don't mean to suggest that employer subsidies are the only alternative to BI. But we must be careful not to be so tied to paid employment that we propose, even under socialism, something akin to employer subsidies—subsidies to cooperatives might have the same effect vis-à-vis an unemployed worker—and in the process perpetuate "work fetishism." Of even greater practical importance, should we oppose a reform that is feasible under capitalism, and could be continued and expanded under socialism, and thereby indirectly strengthen the movement for employer subsidies as the default option in the effort to reduce unemployment?

There remains one further objection that makes reference both to the medium-term goal of democratic socialism and to the path toward this goal. If the goal is an egalitarian, democratic socialism of the sort described earlier, then—the ways Van Parijs describes of how BI can support employment strategies notwithstanding—there is a legitimate worry that BI amounts to a resignation to, and way of compensating the losers for, a two-tiered economy consisting of a core of full-time, high-waged and highly skilled workers on the one hand, and a marginalized class of part-time, temporary, less-skilled and more lowly paid workers on the other. Andre Gorz (1992) calls this "basic income apartheid." By dividing the working class, progress toward a more egalitarian society, in which the work is shared and everyone has an equal opportunity to participate, is thwarted. A right to work, on the other hand, is partly constitutive of the goal of equal participation, and can guide social policies on the path from here to there. If capitalism is incompatible with full employment, socialism may be necessary to bring about real work for everyone; once people realize that, support for socialism can be expected to grow (Schweickart 2002: 135–138).

The response to this criticism is not, as some BI advocates have done, to inveigh against work and a right to work, but rather to combine BI with labor market policies that ensure everyone a right to a decent job.[15] These can include government funded work-creation schemes as well as statutory shortening of the work week. While it is important to acknowledge other forms of work besides paid employment and to facilitate them, it is important that these be choices for the unemployed, not poor alternatives to paid employment. So long as paid work remains a major source of self-expression, social advancement, and income—which we can expect in any capitalist or socialist society at the current level of technology—many who are excluded for lack of available jobs will be marginalized socially and financially.[16] This is not to say that labor market policy cannot include space for significant part-time and temporary work. But it is important that people taking such work do so because it enables them to undertake other meaningful activity such as care work and civic participation, or because they prefer the leisure, not because better paying and more fulfilling jobs are not available.

If we then avoid basic income apartheid by pairing BI with a guarantee of a right to work, we confront another problem. Philip Harvey has argued that a right to work would accomplish many of the aims of BI, if combined with adequate conditional programs for those unable to work. Such a right to work policy would eliminate poverty and reduce attendant social problems such as crime and drug abuse. Since the recipients would pay taxes, what they create could be sold, government expenditures in unemployment compensation and other areas could be reduced, and the right to work could be implemented, Harvey claims, "without imposing additional fiscal burdens." So would the additional cost of BI on top of such a program be worth it? Harvey recognizes the additional appeal of BI for its administrative simplicity (including letting go of the invidious distinction between the deserving and the undeserving poor), the compensation it provides for nonmarket forms of work, and the support it gives to personal development and freedom, but thinks the high cost of BI weakens its attractiveness (Harvey 2003). But the enormous cost and tax burden, we should remember, is partly illusory, since for many people their additional taxes will be exactly balanced by their BI. While communicating this poses considerable challenges for political discourse and strategy, it should not be an obstacle to including BI among the medium- as well as the long-term goals of socialists.

Notes

* An earlier version of this chapter appears as "Liberal and Marxist Arguments for Basic Income," in *Promoting Income Security as a Right in Europe and N. America,* Guy Standing, ed. (Geneva: International Labor Organization, Forthcoming). I am grateful to David Schweickart for presenting a series of objections to basic income that inspired Part 2 of this chapter; these objections are explicitly addressed in Part 1 of the book chapter. For helpful comments on earlier drafts of this chapter, I thank Steve Pressman and two anonymous reviewers, participants in the USBIG conference, New York City, March 2002; the BIEN Congress, Geneva, Switzerland, September 2002; the Radical Philosophy Association Conference, Providence, Rhode Island, November 2002; and the University of Maine Philosophy Department Colloquium, February 2002.

1 For an argument that such neutrality leaves the theory indeterminate with respect to some central questions of distributive justice, see Howard (1984a).

2 See Van Parijs (1990): 106. At the high end, Robert Schutz optimistically estimates that

each adult could receive $30,000 of unearned income (Schutz 1996): 14–15. Schutz does not explore possible disincentives to work or misallocations of labor that might diminish over time the total available for distribution, other than to point out that people work for many reasons besides money and that automation can replace the more expensive and undesirable jobs.

3 Objections to a participation income, as attractive as it might seem in principle, are of a more pragmatic character: See below.

4 I'm not sure which traditions they speak for, but there are many distinguished thinkers who have endorsed a right to unconditional income, including Bertrand Russell (1935), Paul LaFargue (1986), and Nobel economists James Tobin (Tobin et al. 1967; Tobin 1998), Herbert Simon (2001), and James Meade (1989). Thus it seems hazardous to maintain that anyone who thinks this way adheres to a conception of the good life that is beyond the pale of liberalism.

5 This is not an argument for the capitalist's contribution. On the contrary, often the contribution of capital involves *no* contribution of the capitalist. From the standpoint of justice all such assets are collective property. Even when these assets are institutionalized in the form of private property, cooperative property, or state property, we must not lose sight of the requirement of justice to equalize the opportunities associated with control over such assets.

6 Philippe Van Parijs, correspondence quoted in Torisky (1993): 296.

7 See van der Veen and Van Parijs (1986) for an argument for BI as a step toward this "communist" principle of justice.

8 I owe this objection and many of the other objections addressed in this section to David Schweickart's comments (Schweickart 2000) on my book (Howard 2000). In this book I defended a form of worker-managed market socialism, together with a basic income.

9 Barry (1996) makes a pragmatic case for basic income.

10 The jobs people price themselves into at the lower end of the job market will be part-time, temporary, and more lowly paid. On the one hand, some see this as a desirable situation both for employers who seek more flexible labor markets and for those employees who seek a more flexible work schedule to accommodate family and other priorities. On the other hand, critics see BI as here facilitating the erosion of good jobs—jobs that are well paying, permanent, and full time, and the entrenchment of two-tiered labor markets. However, BI is compatible with a policy of promoting full employment of the more robust sort, aiming at full-time regular employment for all who seek it. The worker's right to refuse undesirable forms of employment, which BI strengthens more the higher its level, should lead many employers to offer more *good* jobs in order to attract workers. The issues raised here underscore that BI needs to be part of a package of measures that includes labor market policy.

11 Roemer estimates the annual dividend on non-financial, non-farm corporate and non-corporate wealth per adult in the 1980s to be about $1,200, if these assets were to be nationalized and distributed equally (1994: 133–43). A real world example of a citizen's dividend is the Alaska Permanent Fund, which grants to every resident of Alaska an unconditional income based on investments from the Alaskan oil revenues. The dividend in 2002 was $1,540.76 per resident. Current information on the Alaska Permanent Fund can be found at the following website: http://www.apfc.org.

12 For a higher estimate, based on Clark's data, see Harvey (2003).

13 For the bottom quintile, the average household income would increase by $9,613; for the second, by $7,250; and for the third, by $4,262 (Clark 2003: 150–52). For an analysis of who would benefit from a more modest, tax-neutral BI for the United Kingdom, see Atkinson (1996).

[14] This is not to imply that these wages were determined by the needs of workers' families, rather than the bargaining power of the workers. The decline in such bargaining power has forced both members of two-adult households into the labor market.

[15] One such critic of the right to work is Standing (2002), cited in Harvey (2003).

[16] For these and other important points in support of a right to work, see Harvey (2003).

References

Atkinson, A.B. (1996) "The Case for a Participation Income," *The Political Quarterly*, 67 (1): 67–70.

Barry, B. (1996) "Survey Article: Real Freedom and Basic Income," *Journal of Political Philosophy,* 4 (3): 242–276.

Clark, C.M.A. (2003) "Promoting Economic Equity: The Basic Income Approach," in *Institutional Analysis and Economic Policy,* M.R. Tool and P.D. Bush (eds.), (Boston & Dordrecht: Kluwer Academic Publishers): 133–156.

Elster, J. (1986) "Comment on Van der Veen and Van Parijs," *Theory and Society*, 15 (5): 709–721.

Fraser, N. (1989) *Unruly Practices: Power, Discourse, and Gender in Contemporary Social Theory,* (Minneapolis: University of Minnesota Press).

Gorz, A. (1992) "On the Difference Between Society and Community and Why Basic Income Cannot by Itself Confer Full Membership," in *Arguing for Basic Income*, P. Van Parijs (ed.), (London: Verso).

Harvey, P. (2003) "The Right to Work and Basic Income Guarantees: A Comparative Assessment," US Basic Income Guarantee Discussion Paper (February). http://www .usbig.net/.

Howard, M.W. (1984a) "A Contradiction in the Egalitarian Theory of Justice," *Philosophy Research Archives*, 10: 35–55.

______ (1984b) "Worker Control, Self-Respect, and Self-Esteem," *Philosophy Research Archives*, 10: 455–472.

______ (2000) *Self-management and the Crisis of Socialism: The Rose in the Fist of the Present,* (Lanham, Md.: Rowman and Littlefield).

Karst, K.L. (1997) "The Coming Crisis of Work in Constitutional Perspective," *Cornell Law Review*, 82: 523–71.

LaFargue, P. (1986) "The Right to Be Lazy," in *Essential Works of Socialism*, 3rd ed., I. Howe (ed.), (New Haven: Yale University Press).

Larmore, C. (1987) *Patterns of Moral Complexity,* (Cambridge: Cambridge University Press).

Marx, K. (1977a) *Capital*, in *Karl Marx: Selected Writings,* D. McLellan (ed.), (Oxford: Oxford University Press): 415–528.

______ (1977b) *Critique of the Gotha Program*, in *Karl Marx: Selected Writings,* D. McLellan (ed.), (Oxford: Oxford University Press): 564–570.

______ (1977c) *Economic and Philosophic Manuscripts*, in *Karl Marx: Selected Writings,* D. McLellan (ed.), (Oxford: Oxford University Press): 75–112.

Marx, K., and Engels, F. (1977) *The Communist Manifesto*, in *Karl Marx: Selected Writings,* D. McLellan (ed.), (Oxford: Oxford University Press): 221–247.

Meade, J.E. (1989) *Agathotopia: The Economics of Partnership,* (Aberdeen: Aberdeen University Press).

Musgrave, R. (1988) "Maximin, Uncertainty, and the Leisure Trade-off," *Quarterly Journal of Economics*, 88: 625–632.

Rawls, J. (1971) *A Theory of Justice,* (Cambridge, Mass.: Harvard University Press).
______ (1988) "The Priority of Right and Ideas of the Good," *Philosophy and Public Affairs,* 17: 251–276; also published as ch. 5 of *Political Liberalism.*
______ (1993) *Political Liberalism,* (New York: Columbia University Press).
Roemer, J. (1994) *A Future for Socialism,* (Cambridge, Mass.: Harvard University Press).
Russell, B. (1935) *In Praise of Idleness,* (New York: W.W. Norton & Company).
Simon, H.A. (2001) "UBI and the Flat Tax," in *What's Wrong With a Free Lunch?*, P. Van Parijs et al. (Boston: Beacon Press): 34–38.
Schutz, R. (1996) *The $30,000 Solution,* (Santa Barbara, Calif.: Fithian Press).
Schweickart, D. (1993) *Against Capitalism,* (Cambridge: Cambridge University Press).
______ (2000) "Comment," Symposium on Michael W. Howard's *Self-management and the Crisis of Socialism: The Rose in the Fist of the Present*, Radical Philosophy Association Fourth National Conference, Loyola University, Chicago, unpublished.
______ (2002) *After Capitalism,* (Lanham, Md.: Rowman and Littlefield).
Solow, R. (1998) *Work and Welfare,* (Princeton: Princeton University Press).
Standing, G. (2002) *Beyond the New Paternalism: Basic Security as Equality,* (London: Verso).
Tobin, J. (1998) "James Tobin, the Demogrant and the Future of U.S. Social Policy," (interview) *Basic Income* 29 (Spring). http://www.etes.ucl.ac.be/bien/bien.htm.
Tobin, J., Pechman, J.A., and Mieszkowski, P.M. (1967) "Is a Negative Income Tax Practical?," *Yale Law Journal*, 77: 1–27.
Torisky, E.V. Jr. (1993) "Van Parijs, Rawls, and Unconditional Basic Income," *Analysis*, 53 (4): 289–297.
van der Veen, R.J., and Van Parijs, P. (1986) "A Capitalist Road to Communism," *Theory and Society*, 15 (5): 635–655.
Van Parijs, P. (1995), *Real Freedom for All: What (If Anything) Can Justify Capitalism?,* (Oxford: Clarendon Press).
______ (2001) "A Basic Income for All," in *What's Wrong With a Free Lunch?,* P. Van Parijs et al. (Boston: Beacon Press).
Walzer, M. (1983) *Spheres of Justice: A Defense of Pluralism and Equality,* (New York: Basic Books).

Chapter 8

Does She Exploit or Doesn't She?

Karl Widerquist

Introduction

Several authors have voiced the "exploitation objection" to the unconditional basic income guarantee, arguing that all those who wish to share in the social product have an obligation to contribute to it (Gauthier 1986; White 1997, 1999, 2000, 2003; Phelps 2001). Some of these authors aim their criticism directly at Van Parijs's (1995) case for unconditional basic income; others argue more broadly against all unconditional transfers, against Rawls's (1971) difference principle, or against Dworkin's (1981b) resource auction.[1] Williams (1999) argues against basic income on resource-egalitarian grounds. These authors present a distinct challenge to the basic income guarantee from those arguing against all transfers because they come from a pro-redistributional perspective, but argue only against the unconditionality of transfers in the form of the basic income guarantee. Gijs Van Donselaar (1997) is an important representative of this exploitation objection because his criticism is thorough and specific.

Van Donselaar (1997) derives the following definition of exploitation or parasitism from Gauthier's (1986) principle of not taking advantage: A exploits B if A is better off and B worse off than either of them would have been if the other did not exist or if the two had nothing to do with each other. He uses this "Donselaarian exploitation" and a closely related principle called the "abuse of rights" to argue that Van Parijs's (1991, 1992, 1995) use of a Dworkin-style resource auction (Dworkin 1981a, 1981b) as a basis for an unconditional basic income allows exploitation. He concludes that redistribution of property should be conditional on the responsibility to work, for all those who are able (i.e., that there should be no basic income guarantee).

Part 1 of this chapter explains Van Donselaar's argument in which he concludes that, although people may believe that other principles override this concern, "a principled choice for or against parasitism cannot be avoided" (p. 13).[2] Part 2 argues that Van Donselaar's conclusion, that a basic income is exploitive, relies on holding recipients responsible for the level of scarcity in the world. Part 3 argues that Van Donselaar's conclusions come from treating work rents inconsistently with other rents. Part 4 argues that a principled choice for or against parasitism cannot be made, because parasitism cannot be clearly identified or eliminated. In a large number of plausible cases, the existence or nonexistence of exploitation is unknowable; importantly, it is not certain that work makes a person innocent of exploitation or that living off basic income makes a person guilty. Therefore there is no necessary connection between Van Donselaar's principles and the responsibility to work.

1. Donselaarian Exploitation and Abuse of Rights

Van Donselaar (p. 3) offers the following definition of exploitation or parasitism: In virtue of a property rights relationship, A exploits B if A is better off and B worse off than either of them would have been if the other did not exist or if they had nothing to do with each other.[3] Although this definition is derived from Gauthier (1986), let's call it "Donselaarian exploitation" because he seems to be the first to define it this specific way and the first to employ it to such an extent.

Van Donselaar defines the "abuse of rights" as receiving an income from an asset above one's independent interest in it. An "independent interest" is an interest in an asset *other* than the desire to resell it. He uses an example to illustrate this point (pp. 1–5). A farmer diverts the stream running through his property solely to get his neighbor to pay him to return the stream to its natural flow. According to Van Donselaar this transaction would have been acceptable if the farmer had some private reason to divert the stream such as to create a pond or irrigate his field, but if he does it solely to get his neighbor to pay him to stop, he abuses his water rights. The abuse of rights condemns Dworkin's (1981a, 1981b) clamshell auction, because it allows the equality of resources even for those who have no use for those resources. But also, Van Donselaar is well aware that it also condemns private property, as we know it. As he puts it, "there can be no fixed rights to property," if the abuse of rights is to be avoided. People have the right to work with assets (or to compensation if they are for any reason unable to work with the assets that they want to work with) but they do not have a right to income from assets they have no desire to work with.

Abuse of rights comes in two forms: *usurpation* and *usury*. Usurpation is the sale of an asset (or a right) in which one has no independent interest (p. 143). Usury is the sale of an asset in which one has an independent interest for more than the amount of the independent interest (p. 144). In economic terms, the sale price of an asset or a right must be strictly limited to the seller's reservation price—just enough to make her indifferent to the trade. Any gain from it is said to be usurious.

Using the concepts of exploitation and abuse of rights, Van Donselaar demonstrates that one example Van Parijs (1995) uses to support basic income is both exploitive and abusive. Van Parijs uses the story of Crazy and Lazy to illustrate how one person could trade her right to resources for the product of another person's labor without exploiting him. In this example, Crazy and Lazy[4] are the only two inhabitants on an island, and both have equal claim to its land. Lazy prefers to work as little as he needs for subsistence, using less than half of the land. Crazy prefers to work as much as possible and wants to use all of the available land to produce enough crops to live in luxury. The two strike a deal, in which

Crazy farms all of the land and gives Lazy enough crops so that he can subsist without working at all. Van Parijs judges this transaction to be exploitation free in terms of several different definitions of exploitation, but he does not consider Donselaarian exploitation. It is not necessary here to consider other definitions of exploitation, except to note that the primary reason Van Parijs judges the outcome to be exploitation free is because Lazy and Crazy are both better off than they would be if each owned half the land and without exchange.

Van Donselaar finds this trade to be exploitative relative to how well off each would be if the other did not exist. Crazy would be (materially) better off alone, because she could work the entire island without sharing anything with Lazy. Lazy, however, would be worse off alone, because he would have to work to produce his own subsistence. This is Donselaarian exploitation: Lazy is better off and Crazy is worse off than either of them would have been had the other not existed. This is also Donselaarian abuse of rights: Lazy sells land that he has no independent interest in. According to Van Donselaar, Lazy has no legitimate claim to ask for compensation for land he has no desire to work with. Thus, he should work with the land he wants and leave the rest to Crazy. From this he concludes that there should be a social obligation to work, and if assets are to be distributed in a Dworkinian auction, the proceeds from that auction should go only to those who demonstrate a willingness to work with those assets.

Van Donselaar views property as something that only has value in the production process. People equally deserve access to property they want to work with but they deserve no access to property simply to resell it. He, therefore, advocates distributing property according to an individual's interest in working with it, which he calls the X-distribution or the Q-distribution in the multiperson case (chapter 4). This policy amounts to seizing all economic rents (unearned income), distributing them to all people in proportion to how much they work. This distribution is meant to be against a background, in which, if possible, all people have equal access to jobs, and if not possible, people are compensated for the lack of access to jobs. Compensation is paid if and only if an individual demonstrates a willingness to work (chapter 5). It is only the willingness to work that matters, and therefore, the disabled are entitled to a share of rents even if it technically makes them parasites. Only those who can, but refuse to, work are denied a share of rents in Van Donselaar's system.

2. The Level of Scarcity

This section demonstrates that it is not Van Donselaar's definition of exploitation, but his point of comparison that allows him to draw different conclusions on the exploitive nature of basic income in the Crazy–Lazy example. Without using this point of comparison, Van Donselaar would be unable to get the result that Lazy exploits Crazy; but using this point of comparison, he is forced to condemn mutually beneficial trades that do not involve the abuse of rights.

Van Donselaar's definition of exploitation allows the suspected victim to compare her situation either with how well off she would have been if the other did not exist or with how well off she would have been if the two had nothing to do with each other. He does not attempt to determine how these points of comparison differ, and in his analysis he employs only the comparison of "if the other did not exist." He seems to assume these two points of comparison are the same, but they can only be equivalent in a world of superabundance, in which all people have more of all resources than they want. In a world of scarcity, the two points of comparison are very different; a person who exists, but with whom you do not interact, takes up resources that you would be able to use if she did not exist.

It is hard to say whether "having nothing to do with each other" is truly definable in a world of scarcity, because any division of scarce resources requires some kind of interaction unless the parties are separated by a natural barrier. Therefore, the standard of "having nothing to do with each other," introduces uncertainty into what constitutes the proper basis for comparison: Should outcomes be compared to a position in which resources are distributed equally to everyone, or only to those who are willing to work with them, or to those who will take best care of them, or to those with first-come-first-served claims, or to people with claims from some other principle for the assignment of property rights?

Gauthier (1986) is also unclear on this point.[5] He discusses two possible initial situations: a noncooperative but noncoercive initial situation, and a coercive initial situation. Each situation corresponds to a given level of utility for both parties, but he does not discuss how to determine the levels of utility in these situations. Are the utility levels in the non-cooperative but non-coercive initial situation determined by scarcity? If so, how can a noncoercive, non-cooperative interaction bring about a distribution of scarce assets? This point is not comfortably ignored in a world of scarcity where there can be many different ethical standards by which one could define a non-cooperative, non-coercive situation. Therefore, either the initial situation must be one without scarcity or Gauthier must be employing some tacit ethical standard to it.

Of the many possible ways to define "having nothing to do with each other," I will focus on the one that seems to be the most simple and straightforward: the equal distribution of untradable assets (i.e., assets that are not allowed to be traded once distributed), or what Van Donselaar and many others have called the no-envy distribution. The comparison of the outcome of interaction between Crazy and Lazy to "if the other did not exist," involves the effects of two changes: Labor has become more abundant, and resources (land in this case) have become scarcer. But regarding the comparison of the outcome of interaction to the no-envy distribution, labor becomes more abundant but the per-person level of resource scarcity remains unchanged. That is, the difference between the two points of comparison is the level of resource scarcity caused by the size of the population.

The harm that Van Donselaar attributes to *exploitation* is attributable to this increase in scarcity. To see this, return to the Crazy–Lazy example. Suppose there are two consumption goods called "leisure" and "yams" and two resources called "labor time" (lost leisure) and "land." The island has four identical units of land.

Both people are equally skilled, and to produce one yam they must give up one unit of leisure and use one unit of land. One yam is the minimum requirement for subsistence. Lazy works just enough to reach subsistence, and after that always prefers to consume leisure rather than yams. Crazy always prefers consuming yams to leisure.

The comparison point for "if the other did not exist" is what each would do on the island alone with access to the *entire* island. Without Lazy, Crazy works all four units of land, enjoys no leisure, and consumes four yams. Without Crazy, Lazy enjoys three units of leisure, works one unit of land, and consumes one yam.

The comparison point for "if the two had nothing to do with each other" is what each would do with access to *half* of the island. Crazy works two units of land, enjoys two units of leisure, and consumes two yams. She is clearly worse off than if she has access to the entire island because although she now enjoys two units of leisure, by assumption she always prefers more yams to more leisure. Lazy, however, is in the same position as before. He enjoys three units of leisure and one yam. The increased scarcity caused by the increase in population hurts Crazy, but it does not hurt Lazy. Only Crazy is harmed because only Crazy has a use for more land than half the land. But it is hard to say that the decrease in Crazy's welfare is caused by Lazy's action or by anything but the increase in scarcity that results from having a larger population.

The example cited by Van Parijs has Lazy and Crazy starting from an equal distribution of property and making a deal in which Crazy works all the land, paying Lazy one yam as rent. Therefore, Crazy consumes three yams and enjoys no leisure, while Lazy consumes one yam and four units of leisure. Comparing this outcome to "if the other had not existed," Van Donselaar finds this outcome to be a clear case of Donselaarian exploitation. Lazy is better off (consumes the same amount of yams and enjoys more leisure) than he would have been if Crazy did not exist, and Crazy is worse off (consumes fewer yams and enjoys the same amount of leisure) than she would have been if Lazy did not exist. But comparing this outcome to "if they had nothing to do with each other" gives a different result. Lazy is better off (consumes the same amount of yams and enjoys more leisure), and Crazy is also better off: She consumes an additional yam (three instead of two) at the expense of two units of leisure; but we've assumed that she prefers even a small amount of yams to additional leisure. And we know that, starting from an equal distribution of resources, she would not have made this trade if it did not make her better off. Therefore, if "having nothing to do with each other" is defined as splitting natural resources equally without any trade, this trade is not exploitive even in the Donselaarian sense; and it cannot be exploitive as long as trades begin with an equal distribution of resources and all trade is voluntary.

To get the result that Lazy exploits Crazy, Van Donselaar has to use "if the other did not exist" as his point of comparison. Because the difference between the two points of comparison is the level of scarcity, he can only get his exploitation result by holding Lazy responsible for the level of scarcity his existence creates. Van Donselaar could respond that Lazy must be taking advantage of the level of scarcity; if the increased scarcity makes him better off at Crazy's expense surely something is wrong. But this statement is also a misattribution. It is not the increased scarcity of land that makes Lazy better off, but the increased abundance of labor. A change in price that makes land more expensive and labor cheaper will benefit those who sell land and buy labor, and will hurt those who buy land and sell labor; but it doesn't require any exploitation to make it happen.

Van Donselaar's point of comparison is also questionable because it condemns Pareto-improving exchanges of labor—the kind that he desires to promote. We don't need usurpation or usury to get Donselaarian exploitation using the "if the other did not exist" point of comparison. Suppose, starting from the no-envy distribution, Crazy and Lazy make the following agreement: "I'll scratch your back, if you scratch mine." Both of them equally enjoy this transaction, but Crazy does not enjoy it enough to compensate her for the scarcity that Lazy's existence creates. Because Lazy starts off no worse off than he would have been by himself, this trade clearly makes him better off than he would have been if Crazy did not exist. Crazy, simply because of her greater desire for land, begins worse off than she would have been if Lazy did not exist. Even though this trade is mutually beneficial in equal amounts to both parties, as long as she doesn't enjoy it as much as she would enjoy two more units of land, she is the victim of Donselaarian exploitation using the "if the other did not exist" point of comparison. Lazy hasn't done anything that seems wrong (no usury, usurpation, fraud, theft, or coercion), but he is an exploiter. Van Donselaar's point of comparison makes mutually beneficial trades exploitive unless the benefits are so great to make up for the scarcity that each individual's existence creates.

Van Donselaar might respond that this exploitation does not result from a property rights relation. But he is unclear about what he means by a property rights relation, and the ownership of property is integral to the exploitation result. The exploitation could be cured by taking away enough of Lazy's land so that after the exchange with Crazy, he is no better off than if Crazy did not exist, but it is hard to see what Lazy has done to justify this punishment.

Note that using Van Donselaar's preferred method for distributing resources (the X or the Q distributions, which give resources to those who want to work with them most) would not solve this problem. Even if Crazy started with three units of land and Lazy only one, Crazy would begin worse off than he would have been if Lazy did not exist, and thus any mutually beneficial trade risks leaving Crazy worse off and Lazy better off than either of them would have been if the other did not exist. Van Donselaar argues that his Q distribution does not cause Lazy to bear the burden of scarcity because it keeps him indifferent to where he would be if he were alone. It is true that this distribution (though not the X distribution) does not cause Lazy to bear *the burden of* scarcity, but Van Donselaar's definition of exploitation (using the nonexistence point of comparison) causes Lazy to bear *the responsibility for* scarcity.

3. Abuse of Rights, the Promotion of Work, and the Market Mechanism

Van Donselaar attempts to derive the responsibility to work without explicitly claiming that work is part of the best conception of the good life and should be promoted over other activities. Instead he attempts to derive this responsibility from principles such as "independent interests," "the abuse of rights," and "usury." But a nearly Calvinist veneration of work runs throughout *The Benefit of Another's Pains*. People who trade their labor for other goods are allowed to benefit themselves as much as they can by that trade. But people who trade assets or rights to jobs or anything else but their labor are entitled to receive only their reservation price (the amount that will make them indifferent to the trade), and they are labeled "usurpers" or "usurers" if they accept more. Why should this be different? Why not force workers to accept only their reservation price, and call any additional income "usury?"

All trades are made because of the gains from trade. People buy things because they believe they will be better off with the thing than with the cash. People sell things because they believe they will be better off with the cash (to buy other things) than with the thing. Van Donselaar believes the gains from trades belong only to people who trade their labor, and to benefit from the sale of anything else is to be a usurer. Certainly labor should be encouraged by making sure that laborers benefit from trades, but is there any reason (other than the veneration of work) that people who sell their labor should be entitled to *all* of the gains from trade and those who sell their right to labor or any other asset should gain *nothing* by trading?

The attempt to combine ensured efficiency with prohibitions on usury leaves individuals without control over the resources they need to sustain their lives. For example, imagine a subsistence farmer. A company or a cooperative wants to use the farmer's land to build a factory, which is far more productive than subsistence farming. If resources were tradable, the economy could reach efficiency while leaving the farmer to decide whether to give the land up for a factory. The Q distribution ensures that the factory must have the land. The prohibition of *usury* ensures the subsistence farmer gains nothing from the seizure of her land except the offer of a job in the factory. Under Van Donselaar's system, the farmer cannot decide whether or not to sell, or the price at which to sell. She must sell—and for no more than enough to leave her no better off than she would have been holding onto her land as a subsistence farmer. If the farmer believes she should not give up her land unless she shares in the benefits the factory will create, she is labeled a *usurer*. No one, in Van Donselaar's system, has the right to say, "this is my land to use as I want, and you cannot use it for your purposes unless I agree to it."

This problem with the Q distribution even runs afoul of Van Donselaar's own examples. He imagines an area of neighboring gardens. Some want to convert the gardens into a football field; others object. Van Donselaar concludes that the objectors should have their way as long as those who want to convert the land do not make a desirable offer, and he draws an analogy between home gardening and working part-time (p. 181). But this conclusion to this example conflicts with the conclusions of his Q distribution, which ensure that if the football field is more productive (in terms of sales), the land must be converted. The Q distribution concludes that those who lose their garden must not gain from this conversion unless they are willing to work on the football field. They can work part-time on the football field, but they cannot continue to garden; and any attempt to gain simply from giving up their gardens is usury. Presumably, Van Donselaar would put some mechanism in place to protect recreational assets from being seized by people who want to use them as inputs in the production process, but his prohibition against usury makes it impossible to use the market mechanism to determine the balance between personal and industrial uses of resources. Something is very wrong with the Q distribution if its conclusions conflict with its author's intuitions.

The abuse of rights (or buying low and selling high) is the lynchpin of capitalism. A categorical ban on it would end all fixed property rights (as Van Donselaar readily admits). There would be no private ownership of land, stocks, bonds, natural resources, or almost any other private asset. Suppose you buy a new car and you have *no use* for your old one anymore. You no longer have any independent interest in that car. Therefore you can't sell it without abusing your right to it. You could have sold it when you still wanted it, but only for the remaining use-value it had to you. It might be easy to make people think you still wanted a car you sold, but if you don't want to be a rights abuser, you must give the car away. Thus, the elimination of the abuse of rights and Donselaarian exploitation would require an enormous restructuring of the economy, if not the elimination of the market entirely.

To maintain efficiency in Van Donselaar's economy, tradable private property would have to be replaced by a system in which the government auctioned off such rights to the highest bidder, which in a perfect market, would ensure that resources were employed in their highest use-value. Van Donselaar then would distribute the proceeds or rents to workers in proportion to their willingness to work.[6] By doing so, he would put people in a situation in which no one had a claim to any resources unless they participated in this system that uses all of its resources in their highest market-valued use. Van Donselaar's "right and responsibility to work" is a strangely commerce-promoting version of socialism. Alternatively, an egalitarian distribution of resources (according people universal rights to property), ensures efficiency by allowing individuals to sell those rights to the highest bidder for their highest market-valued use. But it also allows them to keep their resources out of the market system and use them for whatever goals they believe are worthwhile instead. Such a system leaves it up to individuals to decide whether and at what price it is worth trading their rights to assets—just as it allows a worker to decide at what price to sell her labor for other assets.

4. Unknowable Information

Van Donselaar's argument against basic income relies on the belief that people who live on basic income and do not work are necessarily abusing rights and exploiting others, and the belief that those who work are necessarily contributing to others. But these conjectures are uncertain, and very likely their truth value is unknowable in many cases. His two points of comparison (if the other did not exist or if the two had nothing to do with each other) both hang tenuously on the subjunctive: One would be unable to judge the existence of exploitation without knowing what would have happened if things had not happened as they actually have happened. But we don't always know this information; and in many cases, we can't know it.

For example, what would 1,000 lazy surfers do if everyone else dropped off the face of the Earth tomorrow? Maybe they would live a barbarous life that was nasty, brutish, and short. Or maybe they would build an idyllic beach society: surf all day, pick fruit in the evening, and live much more happily than they would in an industrialized society even with a basic income. What would 1,000 lazy surfers do if they were forced by a social obligation to work? Would they all become Silicon Valley millionaires or would they get poorly paying, low-status jobs that make them miserable for the benefit of their bosses and customers? I do not know the answers to these questions. Therefore, how can I tell whether a surfer with a basic income is exploiting someone, or whether he is being appropriately compensated for the exploitation he would face in its absence and for the life he was denied through the appropriation of resources by others? I do not know the answer to this question, and I cannot know without rerunning the history of the Earth under controlled experimental conditions. If I do not know the surfer is guilty of something, what right do I have to force her to do anything? The accused exploiter would not even know if she was guilty. Does she exploit or doesn't she? Only her deity knows for sure.

Similarly, we do not know whether people who produce products are Donselaarian exploiters. For example, consider the advertising industry. In some cases advertising communicates useful information that benefits producers and consumers, and it represents a genuine contribution to society. But under some conditions advertising can be a zero-sum game that benefits advertisers at the expense of producers and consumers. To see how such exploitation is possible, assume there are two brands of soap. Assume, not knowing anything about either one, customers randomly select between the two. If one is advertised and the other is not, customers tend to select the one that is advertised. If both are advertised, customers go back to random selection. In cases in which these assumptions hold, competition forces both of the soap producers to buy advertising, driving up firms' costs and consumers' prices. Under such conditions advertisers are better off and consumers and producers are worse off than they would have been if they other did not exist (or if they had nothing to do with each other). Should we ban all advertising because in *some* cases it might be exploitative? Does it make any more sense to ban basic income because *some* recipients might be exploiters?

Similarly, exploitation can result from normal market interaction. Assume Joe would be a highly paid manager if Arnie did not exist. But Arnie is a better manager than Joe and outcompetes him for the management job. Joe then becomes a low-paid janitor and cleans Arnie's office, doing a better job than the next-best janitor would have done if Joe did not exist. Therefore, Arnie exploits Joe: He is better off and Joe is worse off than either of them would have been if the other did not exist.

If working does not prove that a person is innocent of exploitation, and if living off a basic income without working does not prove that a person is guilty of exploitation, Van Donselaar's connection between exploitation and the responsibility to work does not hold. In fact, by putting individuals in the position in which they have to fulfill conditions that benefit others before they can be as well off as they would be on their own, his conditions can actually cause the kind of exploitation they are designed to cure (see Widerquist 1999, 2001).

A similar informational problem exists with the abuse of rights. Imagine someone buys stocks, bonds, or commodity futures at a low price and sells them at a high price. She is clearly abusing her rights. The only motive for a speculator to buy financial assets is the hope that someone else will buy them again at a higher price. Speculators argue that their work provides an important service to the market by helping it reach an equilibrium price and by assuming risks that manufacturers are better off not carrying themselves. Critics argue that speculators simply skim off some of the profit for themselves. Others argue that some speculative markets are beneficial on balance and others are not. The abuse of rights might be exploitive or it might be beneficial. The information to know for sure is not always available.

In short, the information we need to draw definitive policy conclusions from Van Donselaar's principles is simply unknowable, and his connection between them and the responsibility to work is not valid.

5. Conclusion

This chapter has made three rebuttals to Van Donselaar's argument against the basic income guarantee. First, his definition of exploitation only succeeds in judging unconditional income recipients as exploiters by blaming them for the level of scarcity their existence creates. Second, he argues that those who sell a right to a job should receive only their reservation price or they are *usurers*, but those who sell their labor for a job are entitled to more than their reservation price without being labeled *usurers*. Third, the information needed to tell whether workers or basic income recipients are Donselaarian exploiters is often unknowable and not necessarily related to whether one works. Therefore, the link between his principles and the responsibility to work cannot be established.

Notes

1 Although neither Rawls nor Dworkin endorses unconditional basic income (UBI), Van Parijs uses Rawls's difference principle and Dworkin's resource egalitarianism in his case for a basic income guarantee.

2 Where not otherwise specified page numbers refer to Van Donselaar 1997.

3 The exact wording is, "A parasitic (property rights) relation exists between two persons A and B if in virtue of that relation A is worse off than she would have been had B not existed or if she would have had nothing to do with him, while B is better off than he would have been without A, or having nothing to do with her—or vice versa."

4 Assume that Crazy is female and that Lazy is male. The gender of the participants is not important for the issues discussed here, but being able to use two different personal pronouns (he and she) will add clarity.

5 Chapter VII, especially section 5.2.

6 If everyone were able both to work and to find work, proceeds would be distributed in proportion to their work.

References

Atkinson, A.B. (1996) "The Case for a Participation Income," *The Political Quarterly*, 67 (1): 67–70.

Dworkin, R. (1981a) "What Is Equality? Part 1: Equality of Welfare," *Philosophy and Public Affairs*, 10 (2): 185–241.

——— (1981b) "What Is Equality? Part 2: Equality of Resources," *Philosophy and Public Affairs*, 10 (4): 284–345.

Gauthier, D. (1986) *Morals by Agreement*, (New York: Oxford University Press).

Levine, A. (1995) "Fairness to Idleness: Is There a Right Not to Work?" *Economics and Philosophy*, 11: 255–274.

Nozick, R. A. (1974) *Anarchy, State, and Utopia*, (New York: Basic Books).

Phelps, E. (2001) "Subsidize Wages," in *What's Wrong With a Free Lunch?*, J. Cohen and J. Rogers (eds.), (Boston: Beacon Press).

Rawls, J. (1971) *A Theory of Justice*, (Cambridge, Mass.: Harvard University Press).

Van Donselaar, G. (1997) *The Benefit of Another's Pains: Parasitism, Scarcity, Basic Income*, doctoral dissertation, Department of Philosophy, University of Amsterdam. Also, forthcoming (Oxford: Oxford University Press).

Van Parijs, P. (1991) "Why Surfers Should Be Fed: The Liberal Case for an Unconditional Basic Income," *Philosophy and Public Affairs*, 20: 101–131.

——— (1992) "Basic Income Capitalism," *Ethics*, 102: 465–484.

——— (1995) *Real Freedom for All: What (If Anything) Can Justify Capitalism?*, (New York: Oxford University Press).

——— (1996) "Free Riding versus Rent Sharing. Should Even David Gauthier Support an Unconditional Basic Income?," in *Ethics, Rationality and Economic Behaviour*, F. Farina, F. Hahn and S. Vanucci (eds.), (Oxford: Oxford University Press), 159–181.

——— (1997) "Reciprocity and the Justification of an Unconditional Basic Income. Reply to Stuart White," *Political Studies*, 45: 327–330.

White, S. (1996) "Reciprocity Arguments for Basic Income," Paper presented at the Sixth International Congress of the Basic Income European Network, Vienna.

——— (1997) "Liberal Equality, Exploitation, and the Case for an Unconditional Basic Income," *Political Studies*, 45: 312–326.

——— (1999) "The Egalitarian Earnings Subsidy Scheme," *British Journal of Political Science*, 29: 601–622.

——— (2000) "Social Rights and the Social Contract: Political Theory and the New Welfare Politics," *British Journal of Political Science*, 30: 507–532.

——— (2003) "Fair Reciprocity and Basic Income," in *Real Libertarianism Assessed*, A. Reeve and A. Williams (eds.), (New York: Palgrave Macmillan), 136–160.

Widerquist, K. (1999) "Reciprocity and the Guaranteed Income," *Politics and Society*, 27 (3): 387–402.

——— (2001) "Who Exploits Who?," paper presented at the annual meeting of the Society for the Advancement of Socio-Economics.

Williams, A. (1999) "Resource Egalitarianism and the Limits to Basic Income," *Economics and Philosophy*, 15: 85–107.

Chapter 9

Perhaps There Can Be Too Much Freedom

Michael Anthony Lewis*

Ackerman and Alstott (AA) (1999) and Van Parijs (VP) (1995) justify their respective income policy proposals, in part, by appealing to the notion of real freedom. This is, roughly, someone's ability to do whatever she might want to do. AA, however, believe that the basic income would be less "real freedom promoting" than stakeholder grants would be. This is because the basic income would not allow people to capitalize their monthly grant into a large sum, say $80,000, to use for investment purposes or some other endeavor. Stakeholder grants, by providing people with an $80,000 lump sum, would allow for such endeavors. However, and this is the key point, people would also be allowed to use their $80,000 to purchase a lifetime annuity of some monthly amount. In short, stakeholder grants are regarded as more real-freedom promoting than basic income because although VP's version of the basic income could not be converted into a stakeholder grant a stakeholder grant could be converted into a basic income.

AA realize that some will be unable to make prudent use of the economic freedom an $80,000 grant would provide and will make very bad decisions. They suggest that requiring stakeholders to obtain a high school degree and refrain from criminal activity would help sift out those likely to make such imprudent choices. But if such sifting devices don't work, those who "blow" their grants should be held responsible for their decisions. If we chose not to adopt this course but to go with the basic income instead, we'd be holding those who'd make prudent choices "hostage" to the choices of the imprudent. That is, we'd be curtailing the freedom of most, simply to prevent the bad decisions of a relative few.

From a liberal or, perhaps more appropriate, libertarian point of view, AA's argument appears compelling. At first glance, it may seem that stakeholder grants would be much more real-freedom promoting than a basic income. Upon closer examination, however, one sees that for certain patterns of decision making, and perhaps, for those at certain developmental points in their lives, the basic income may be more real-freedom promoting than stakeholder grants would be. AA do not adequately consider this, and not doing so renders their argument for stakeholder grants more questionable than it first appears.

As I read AA's discussion, it appeared that the model of the actor they have in mind is the one that "populates" rational choice theory. This actor has a preference ordering and chooses the action he believes will result in his obtaining that which is ranked highest in this ordering, subject to any constraints he faces. Thus, to recast their points about freedom in slightly different terms, some recipients of a basic income might prefer receiving their money in a lump sum so they could invest it in some endeavor of interest. Some recipients of stakeholder grants might prefer their grants in monthly installments as opposed to a lump sum. The basic income is less real freedom promoting because it would not allow the first set of recipients to attain a more preferred outcome; that is, it would subject actors' choices to more stringent constraint than do stakeholder grants.

I think recasting AA's position this way allows one to more clearly see why it's questionable. Let's take an example they use in their book. AA acknowledge that one way people may blow their stakeholder grants is by gambling it all away. Their position is that if someone does this, they should be held responsible for, and therefore be required to live with, the consequences of this choice. Apparently, as AA see it, such is the "price" of promoting real freedom. The problem with this position is that it may not be real freedom promoting, from the perspective of the gambler, to let her gamble away her entire grant.

A behavioral phenomenon frequently discussed in philosophy is "weakness of will." If actor A can choose to do x or y,[1] believes it would be better for him (result in a more preferred outcome) if he chooses x, but ends up choosing y anyway, actor A has exhibited weakness of will (Elster, 1989). Let's take x to be using one's $80,000 grant to purchase a lifetime annuity that provides a monthly income and y to be gambling the $80,000 in a casino in Las Vegas. There are, no doubt, many who would exhibit weakness of will in this situation and, if they're unlucky, lose the entire $80,000 at the blackjack table. In fact, a lot of these people enjoy the "privilege" of having received a DSM III[2] diagnosis: pathological gambler.

We could, following AA, conclude that such unlucky gamblers ought to be held responsible for their decision to gamble; they've chosen to take their chances at the craps table, and if this has led to bad consequences, such is life. But if those who made or would make this "choice" did or would do so out of weakness of will, would facilitating it through stakeholder grants really be real freedom promoting?

My points about weakness of will regarding gambling are applicable to other situations. A pathological condition discussed in the social work and psychiatric literature is bipolar affective disorder. Persons suffering from this disorder have been known to go on shopping binges where thousands of dollars are spent in very short periods. Even though the concept of weakness of will isn't often found in discussions of bipolar affective disorder, I think it accurately captures some of the behavior of those afflicted with this condition. Juanita, while in a manic state, might think it would be better for her if she chooses to purchase an annuity with her stakeholder grant than if she uses it to buy that shiny new sports car, yet she might buy the sports car anyway. Is Juanita really enjoying real freedom through making this choice?

Alcoholics are also prone to weakness of will. John might think it would be better for him if he invested his stakeholder grant in some relatively low risk endeavor as opposed to blowing it all on parties and spirits, yet choose to spend his grant (over an extended period of time, given that it's $80,000) on booze. If we accept AA's position, we have to accept that alcoholics in this situation are enjoying real freedom.

Now there is no reason to believe that suffering from a pathological condition is necessary for someone to exhibit weakness of will. Thus, non-alcoholics, non-pathological gamblers, and non-affective-disordered persons may exhibit this decision-making pattern and may do so regarding decisions about how to allocate money.

A phenomenon related to weakness of will has to do with what are sometimes called "higher order preferences" or "metapreferences" (Goodin, 1995 and Elster, 1989). People not only have preference orderings but preferences (higher order preferences) about their preference orderings. A person may prefer the excitement expected to result from throwing loads of money on the black jack table, but prefer not to prefer this excitement. Someone may prefer driving at "break neck" speed in the new sports car purchased with her stakeholder grant but prefer not to prefer doing so. If someone were to blow her grant on these or other items in an effort to realize preferences she'd rather not have would this really amount to promotion of real freedom?

Another concern I have about AA's position is that it fails to seriously consider what social workers and psychologists call developmental issues.[3] Over the life-course, people typically become more prudent as they get older. Twenty-one-year-olds might decide to buy sports cars, hit casinos, or make other imprudent choices simply because they haven't fully matured. After reaching maturity, they may deeply regret having made such decisions. Given this possibility, stakeholder grants may be less real freedom promoting than may first appear.

VP's basic income proposal would, arguably, be a much better deal for those prone to make the kinds of imprudent decisions I have been discussing. If someone gambled away his weekly, monthly, or yearly basic income check, he'd receive another one the next period. Since it's unlikely that the periodic basic income allotment would be big enough for someone to blow it all on a sports car or some other extravagant item, these types of bad decisions would be constrained. If people are inclined to choose to gamble, but think it would be better for them if they choose to spend their money more wisely, and prefer not to prefer extravagant items, etc., the constraint of a basic income is exactly what they may require for their real freedom to be promoted.

This is not because the basic income would automatically abolish weakness of will, metapreferences, or the imprudent decisions of the immature. It is because those inclined toward weakness of will or making imprudent decisions for any of the other reasons discussed in this chapter would be given second chances under the basic income they would not get under the stakeholder approach.

If weakness of will were the result of pathological gambling or some other psychological problem, individuals who could convince themselves to do so would be able to obtain treatment for their condition. Assume all those who receive treatment would be *cured* of their condition. Under the stakeholder plan, this cure may come too late, after someone has blown his stake. Under the basic income, someone might have blown his monthly grant, but all wouldn't be lost since he'd remain entitled to another one. My experiences as a social worker suggest that *cures* for conditions associated with weakness of will often do not come easily (a point I'll return to later in the chapter). People frequently relapse several times before finally *beating* their condition, assuming they do finally beat it. During this process, basic income recipients would remain entitled to benefits. Stakeholders who've blown their stakes would not.

What I've said regarding those inclined toward weakness of will as a result of pathologies also applies to those inclined toward it for other reasons, as well as those inclined toward making bad decisions due to less preferred preferences winning out or to immaturity. The general point is that a basic income would give such people time to make the adjustments, with help from others if necessary, required for them to attain the capacity to act in accordance with their *true* preferences or the preferences of their mature selves. The stakeholder approach would not.

I stated earlier that AA realize that some will be unable to make prudent use of the economic freedom an \$80,000 grant would provide: AA attempt to address this problem in their proposal by requiring that stakeholders graduate from high school and refrain from criminal activity. I think there is a very good chance that these requirements wouldn't be stringent enough to disqualify those prone to the decision-making patterns discussed in this chapter. For example, I see no reason to believe that someone with a serious gambling problem couldn't graduate from high school or refrain from criminal activity.

At this point, I want to consider some possible responses AA could make to the points I've made. First, they might be open to the idea that 21 is too early for someone to be given an \$80,000 stake and entertain the possibility of raising the age at which one receives their stake. Depending on what this age would be and on human developmental patterns that none of us may understand very well, this would address the points I made about maturity. Let's assume that AA and I can agree on the *right* age at which young adults should receive their stakes. This still would not address the other problems I raised.

Next, AA might agree that their proposal *alone* could run into trouble due to weakness of will and to the other problems I discussed earlier. However, they could (and, no doubt, would) disagree that the proper response to this problem is to adopt basic income instead of stakes. They might argue that a better alternative would be to pair stakes with an approach that would enlist professionals, such as mental health workers and teachers, to help people deal with and overcome weakness of will, higher order preferences, etc. In many cases, mental health workers partnering with teachers could instruct people on psychological matters, such as weakness of will, metapreferences, etc., as well as strategies to combat the harmful effects of them. To the extent that these decision-making patterns were caused by pathologies, as a society we could construct a better system of getting professional help to those who need it. AA might argue that this approach would have the benefit of addressing the problems I raised earlier without curtailing freedom as a basic income would.

I think this alternative approach might go some way to addressing the problems I raised earlier but we should be careful not to be too optimistic here. The decision-making patterns I've spent most of my time discussing in this chapter are not well understood. We know people sometimes choose the course of action they themselves think will result in a worse outcome for them than some other available action, and we know people prefer not to prefer certain things. But we don't know much about what causes these phenomena or how to address them very well. This is why I made my earlier points about the relapses persons treated for weakness of will and other associated pathologies might experience before beating their condition.

Another consideration is the opportunity cost of mental health workers' and teachers' time spent trying to keep people from making bad decisions regarding what to do with their stakes. The time teachers spend teaching "Johnny" about weakness of will can't also be allocated to teaching Johnny how to read. Mental health workers' time spent working with people to prevent bad decisions due to metapreferences is time that can't be spent working with persons diagnosed with schizophrenia. Perhaps promoting real freedom is worth forgoing these other benefits. But if I'm right that we may not know enough to do a great deal to prevent bad decisions due to weakness of will, etc. through a mental health/teaching approach, we may end up forgoing these other benefits for not very much in return. Only a comparison of the social benefit of promoting real freedom versus the social benefit of these outcomes of mental health workers' and teachers' professional efforts would allow us to determine this. However, it would no doubt be very difficult to obtain the data that would be required to make such an assessment.

Another response AA could make to my criticisms is that they are based on only one possible *reading* of their perspective. I said above that AA's proposal appears to be grounded on rational choice assumptions. Another way to read their proposal is to see it, instead, as based on a model of the actor as a life planner. According to this model, actors are not preoccupied with choosing those actions they believe will result in their attaining what they most prefer but choosing how they will live their lives. In other words, actors are or, given certain circumstances, could become preoccupied with how they will spend the rest of their time in this world. This involves not a series of "one shot" choices of actions intended to attain what is most preferred (the perspective of the rational choice model) but a decision about what one wants to do with her life, and the carrying out of a plan to realize this vision. AA could argue that stakes would facilitate life planning to a greater extent than a basic income would and, therefore, would promote real freedom to a greater extent.

I'm skeptical about this. Life planners may be vulnerable to the same maladaptive decision-making patterns as rational choosers. Imagine Enrico is a 19-year-old high school graduate. He anticipates receiving an $80,000 stake at age 21. Enrico decides that when he receives this grant he will use it to start a small business and begins the steps necessary to realize his vision (begins reading about business, interviewing businesspersons, etc.). Now imagine that it's two years later and Enrico has just received his grant. At this point, though, Enrico also has his eye on a sleek $80,000 sports car. He believes that spending the $80,000 on capital for his business would result in his beginning to realize his life plan, while spending it on the sports car would allow him to experience the satisfaction of riding around in a cool car. He prefers beginning to realize his life plan to riding around in a cool car, but decides to buy the car anyway. It isn't clear to me how the life-planning reading of AA's proposal addresses this sort of problem.

A question that seems to be raised by AA's proposal is whether people can have too much freedom? However, this may be the wrong question to ask, or at least, not the only right one. The other is whether it can be more freedom promoting to actually constrain people's abilities to exercise certain choices and less freedom promoting to disallow such constraints. The phenomena discussed in this chapter suggest an affirmative answer. If so, then the choice between the basic income and stakeholder grants is not simply one between a less freedom-promoting plan versus a more freedom-promoting one. The extent to which one would promote or constrain freedom would depend on how people actually make decisions about how to allocate sums of money. Now this is an empirical question on which we don't have much data. No doubt, part of the reason we don't have much data is that we'd have to gain access to what's going on inside people's heads, which would be difficult to obtain. That is, we'd somehow have to be able to determine, for example, that an actor chose action x when he could have chosen action y, even though he *believed* that y would have resulted in an outcome preferred to the one he *believed* would have resulted from x. As a sociologist familiar with social scientists' attempts to study beliefs, I'm well aware of the problems encountered when trying to obtain data of this kind.

Given the lack of data on the extent to which people make decisions in the ways discussed thus far, in our choice as to whether we should adopt a basic income or a stakeholder plan, we face a policy decision in a situation of uncertainty. Thus, I think it might be instructive to model this decision using the tools of decision theory. Before doing so let me stipulate that the weakness of will and metapreference-based decision-making patterns discussed in this chapter will be called non-rational decisions.

Decision theorists typically model decisions under uncertainty by stipulating sets of acts, actions, and states of the world (states). This is often done using simple matrices similar to Table 9.1.

Table 9.1 Payoff table

	State 1	*State 2*
Actions	**Pervasive Non-rational Decision Making**	**Non-pervasive Non-rational Decision Making**
Enact BI	4	3
Enact Stakes	1	5

Table 9.1 contains two acts and two states. Neglecting hybrid versions of basic income and stakes, we can either choose to enact basic income or stakes. The possible states of the world are the following: one where the non-rational decision making patterns discussed in this chapter are pervasive (State 1), and one where this is not the case (State 2). I need to say a little about what I mean by "pervasive non-rational decision making."

For illustrative purposes, let "non-rational decision maker" refer to an individual at least 50 percent of whose decisions results from weakness of will or metapreferences. Then let the state of pervasive non-rational decision making obtain if at least 50 percent of 21-year-olds are non-rational decision makers. Thus, this state would not obtain if less than 50 percent of 21-year-olds are non-rational decision makers. Assuming that the probability of a 21-year-old being a non-rational decision maker is 50 percent, that being a non-rational decision maker and making a non-rational decision are independent events, and that blowing one's stake due to weakness of will or metapreferences is a non-rational decision, then the probability that a 21-year-old will blow his stake, given that he is a non-rational decision maker is 50 percent.[4] Thus, if State 1 obtains, then at least half of 21-year-olds would have a 50 percent chance of making a non-rational decision. But if we've enacted a basic income instead of stakes, it would be impossible for one of these decisions to be blowing their stakes. Let's give this outcome a payoff of 4[5] (see Table 9.1). If, on the other hand, we've enacted a stakeholder plan, then at least half of 21-year-olds would have a 50 percent chance of blowing their stakes. Using Table 9.1, let's give this a payoff of 1. Table 9.1 also shows that if non-rational decision making isn't pervasive and we've enacted a basic income, there'd be a payoff of 3; and if this state obtains and we've enacted stakes, a payoff of 5.

Given how I've defined pervasive non-rational decision making, the rankings in Table 9.1, and the fact that we have no information on which state is most likely to obtain; the question arises which of the two policies would it be optimal to enact? Decision theorists haven't reached agreement on what the *right* criterion to use for decisions made under uncertainty is, but one contender they regard as having intuitive appeal is the minimax risk criterion.[6] If we adopt this criterion in the face of the decision represented in Table 9.1, as I think we should, then the basic income would be the optimal policy. A matrix called the Risk Payoffs Matrix can be used to demonstrate this.

Table 9.2 Risk payoff table

Actions	State 1 Pervasive Non-rational Decision Making	State 2 Non-pervasive Non-rational Decision Making
Enact BI	0	2
Enact Stakes	3	0

The 0 entry in the 1 x 1 cell of the matrix is obtained in the following way. If State 1 turns out to be the true state and we've enacted a basic income, we wouldn't have forgone any gain by this choice because it would result in our gaining 4 utils (see Table 9.1), while if we'd chosen stakes we'd have gained only 1 util. I represent no forgone gain by "0." On the other hand, if State 1 turns out to be the true state and we've enacted stakes, then we'd gain 3 utils less than what we would have gained if we had gone with the basic income approach. This is why there is a 3 in the 2 x 1 cell of the matrix. The other entries in the matrix were obtained similarly. In decision theory, these entries are considered measures of the risk or regret of making the *wrong* decision. The minimax risk criterion stipulates that the action with the lowest maximum risk is the optimal one. The maximum risk of the basic income choice is 2, while that of stakes is 3. Thus, enacting basic income is the optimal choice.

Now I realize that AA and others might not agree with my choice of payoffs for the outcomes in Table 9.1, but this isn't that important. Using the same decision criterion, a sensitivity analysis can always be conducted using other payoffs. Depending on the payoffs assigned to the outcomes in Table 9.1, the risk payoffs might turn out to be such that the optimal policy choice would be stakes. I suspect that the major point of disagreement between those inclined toward stakes and those inclined toward a basic income would be around what payoffs to assign to the 2 x 1 and 1 x 2 cells of Table 9.1. That is, there'd be disagreement regarding which of the following two outcomes is worse: stakes in the presence of pervasive non-rational decision making or a basic income when non-rational decision making isn't pervasive. The usefulness of the decision theoretic presentation of the stakes versus basic income choice is that, given the uncertainty we face, it precisely represents the policy implications of this key point of disagreement.

I suspect many readers of this chapter, especially those sympathetic to some version of libertarianism, may still have a *nagging* concern about the whole tenor of my discussion. My belief that it may be more freedom enhancing to constrain people's choices may strike many as paternalistic. I admit to being guilty to the charge. I think this would be a fair characterization of the basic income and my sympathy for it. Given the bad name that paternalism appears to have among advocates of liberty (Goodin, 1995), it behooves me to try to defend it. The Goodin work cited in the previous sentence is instructive for this effort.

In a chapter entitled "In Defense of the Nanny State" (1995), Robert E. Goodin attempts to spell out the conditions under which paternalism on the part of government (state paternalism) is justified. First, he tells us that it is justified only for the "big decisions." He doesn't provide us with the kind of precise definition of "big decision" one might find in mathematics, but he does state that such decisions must at least involve life or death consequences, or substantially shape one's subsequent life prospects. If such decisions are "substantially irreversible," Goodin tells us that this, "further bolsters the case for paternalism" (Goodin, 1995, p. 124). Goodin then goes on to say, subject to the "big decision" constraint, that a necessary condition for public officials to refrain from paternalistic interference is that they must be convinced that one is acting on relevant preferences, settled preferences, preferred preferences, and (perhaps) one's own preferences. For present purposes, I will focus on only the middle two of these concepts.

By "settled preferences" Goodin means those that are not simply indicative of transitory phases people are going through. He appears to have in mind concerns similar to those I alluded to above when I discussed how the young might make choices in regard to how to allocate their stakes that they might later regret. By "preferred preferences" he appears to have in mind what, following Elster (1989), I called "metapreferences." It seems reasonable to me to believe that state paternalism is justified when, now using Goodin's language, a person's preferences are not settled or preferred, subject to the constraint that we are talking about for big decisions. The question is whether deciding what to do with one's stake is a big decision. The possibility of decisions and consequences like those I discussed above lead me to believe that it is; therefore, the more paternalistic form of promoting real freedom, BIG, is warranted.

At one point in their work, AA state that although they think people should be held responsible for how they choose to use their stakes, a decent society should not allow those who've blown their stakes to starve. I'm sure AA are aware that the United States is arguably not a decent one because many able-bodied indigent persons are not entitled to assistance and may very well starve. Given this context, I think stakes in the presence of pervasive non-rational decision making would be worse than basic income when non-rational decision making isn't pervasive, and this is why the payoffs in cells 2 x 1 and 1x 2 of Table 9.1 are as they are. This might be an overly pessimistic point of view but, pardon the play on words, given what's currently at stake, I think it's the right one.

Notes

* Reprinted with permission from Elsevier from *The Journal of Socio-Economics* (Feb. 2005) vol. 34 (1): 17–26.

1 When used in this chapter "or" will always be used in its exclusive sense. For the distinction between the "exclusive or" and "inclusive or" see Velleman (1994).

2 "DSM III" stands for the *Diagnostic and Statistical Manual of Mental Disorders,* 3rd ed. revised (American Psychiatric Association, 1987). It's essentially the "bible" of psychopathology.

3 I'd like to acknowledge Eri Noguchi for her input on this section.

4 This is a conditional probability. The formula for the probability of A, given that B has occurred is: $P(A/B) = P(A \cap B)/P(B)$. If two events A and B are independent, then $P(A \cap B) = P(A) \cdot P(B)$. Here A=the event that one blows his stake and B =the event that one is a non-rational decision maker. Thus $P(A \cap B) = .5 \cdot .5 = .25$. Thus, $P(A/B) = .25/.5 = .5$. For a discussion of probability theory, see Goldberg (1960).

5 Think of these numbers as interval utility levels.

6 For a discussion of this criterion, see Luce and Raiffa (1957).

References

Ackerman, B. and Alstott, A. (1999) *The Stakeholder Society,* (New Haven: Yale University Press).

American Psychiatric Association (1987) *Diagnostic and Statistical Manual of Mental Disorders,* 3rd ed. revised, (Washington, D.C.: American Psychiatric Association).

Elster, J. (1989) *Solomonic Judgments,* (New York: Cambridge University Press).

Goldberg, S. (1960) *Probability: An Introduction,* (New York: Dover Publications, Inc.).

Goodin, R. (1995) "In Defense of the Nanny State," in *Rights and the Common Good,* A. Etzioni (ed.), (New York: St. Martin's Press).

Luce, R.D. and Raiffa, H. (1957) *Games and Decision: Introduction and Critical Survey,* (New York: Dover Publications, Inc.).

Van Parijs, P. (1995) *Real Freedom for All,* (Oxford: Oxford University Press).

Velleman, D.J. (1994) *How to Prove It*, (New York: Cambridge University Press).

PART THREE: EVIDENCE

Chapter 10

Income Guarantees and the Equity-Efficiency Tradeoff

Steven Pressman

Introduction

This chapter examines the tradeoffs inherent in guaranteed income proposals. Its perspective is international, using standardized income data across nations and asking whether economic efficiency suffers when governments make greater efforts to protect the poor. It is recognized that this is not a perfect test of the guaranteed income plan, in large part because we are not actually testing anything about a guaranteed income plan. Nonetheless, we are testing one of the main issues surrounding guaranteed income plans, the equity–efficiency tradeoff raised by Okun—if governments do provide greater income supports, will economic efficiency suffer?

The first section provides a brief history of the rise and fall of guaranteed income plans. Then the Luxembourg Income Study (LIS), the main database for the empirical work of this chapter, is described. Using the LIS we see how governments of different countries affect income equality, and how this effort has changed over time. Section 4 examines whether those countries putting more fiscal effort into maintaining the incomes of its citizens operate less efficiently. Finally, Section 5 summarizes our findings and concludes.

1. Guaranteed Income and its Critics

Guaranteed income plans and the negative income tax first began to attract attention in the United States during the 1960s. Robert Theobald (1963, 1966) pushed for guaranteed incomes arguing that automation would make it impossible to create enough jobs with decent incomes for the large majority of the labor force. As technology made workers redundant, unemployment would rise. Even those able to keep their jobs would receive lower wages. For this reason, Theobald concluded, the government would have to make some basic income floor a right for all citizens.[1] It could do this in a number of different ways; but the main options were government transfer payments or tax rebates (leading to negative taxes owed) to low-income households.

Conservative economist Milton Friedman (1962: 177–195) gave a big boost to the negative income tax when he came out in favor of it. Friedman saw this policy as a way to end the stigma of welfare, mitigate the disincentives associated with the United States welfare system, and reduce the confusing panoply of welfare programs. The main objection to the negative income tax for Friedman was political rather than economic—people were unlikely to vote for a redistributive scheme whose main beneficiaries would be a small minority of citizens.

Not surprisingly, many liberal economists added their support. Keynesian James Tobin (1966), normally an adversary of Friedman, supported a guaranteed income for essentially the same reasons as Friedman. He even began to address some of the practical issues for designing such a plan (Tobin, Pechman and Mieszkowski 1967). Other economists supported the plan for pragmatic and humanitarian reasons—because it put income quickly into the hands of those who needed it (Hildebrand 1967) and because it helped to provide a decent and dignified existence to all families (Hayes 1969).

With the idea gaining increasing attention, President Johnson established a National Commission on Guaranteed Incomes in 1967. The commission, comprised of business leaders, labor leaders and other prominent figures, unanimously supported a guaranteed income to assist poor United States families.

But there was never unanimous support for a guaranteed income plan. Criticism came from both the left and the right; and much of this criticism involved the undesirable incentives that result from government income guarantees.

The right tended to focus on both the cost of a guaranteed income plan and the fact that the plan would destroy the American work ethic. There were also objections that the plan would make Americans overly dependent on government and that it treated the symptoms of poverty rather than the low wages that caused poverty (see Vadakin 1968).

On the left, Robert Lekachman (1971) noted that guaranteed income plans contained an important contradiction. These plans sought to help families in need, but they did not want to damage work incentives. However, the more help that needy families received, the less incentive they had to work and earn money. Lekachman thus anticipated the key issue set forth by Arthur Okun, who identified a big tradeoff between equality and efficiency. In a famous and much quoted passage, Okun (1975: 91ff.) had us consider a leaky bucket, which we use to transfer income from the wealthy to others.

> First consider the American families who make up the bottom 20 percent of the income distribution. Their after-tax incomes in 1974 were less than $7,000, averaging about $5,000. Now consider the top 5 percent of families in the income pyramid; they had after-tax incomes ranging upward from about $28,000 and averaging about $45,000. A proposal is made to levy an added tax averaging $4,000 (about 9 percent) on the income of the affluent families in an effort to aid the low-income families. Since the low-income group I selected has four times as many families as the affluent group, that should, in principle, finance a $1,000 grant for the average low-income family. However, the

program has an unsolved technological problem: the money must be carried from the rich to the poor in a leaky bucket. Some of it will simply disappear in transit, so the poor will not receive all the money that is taken from the rich. The average poor family will get less than $1,000, while the average rich family gives up $4,000. As we transfer incomes from wealthy families to poor families some of the water seeps out of the bucket. This is a net loss for society.

In the real world this loss is due to several factors (see Okun 1975: 96–100), but the basic problem is that guaranteed incomes reduce work effort and work incentives. First, with a guaranteed income, many people will opt for leisure rather than work. Less will get produced and therefore fewer goods will be available for all of us to share. Second, guaranteed incomes reduce the cost to workers of being fired. This threat serves as a "stick" that firms hold over workers and that forces them to work harder (Gordon 1996). With guaranteed incomes, workers should put in less effort since the financial consequences of losing a job is lower. Productivity is likely to suffer as a result. Third, generous benefits paid to those with low incomes will have to be paid for somehow. This means a rise in the top marginal tax rates, which reduces incentives to work, save and invest. Finally, redistribution may have psychological and sociological consequences. People dependent on government handouts become less self-reliant and more lazy (see Butler and Kondratas 1987; Murray 1984), causing productivity growth to suffer.

The death knell for guaranteed income plans, however, came in the late 1970s when results of the income maintenance experiments were made public. These experiments were conducted over a number of years in selected areas across the United States: New Jersey and Pennsylvania (1968–1972); rural areas in North Carolina and Iowa (1970–1972); Gary, Indiana (1971–1974); and Seattle and Denver (1970–1978). In each area, both a *control* group and an *experimental* group were selected. The experimental group received negative income tax payments and the control group did not. Payments to the experimental group varied so that it might be possible to measure the effect of greater income guarantees on work effort and other factors. The explicit purpose of this experiment was to see how behavior was affected by income guarantees.

As Robert Solow (1986) pointed out, the fact that these studies took place almost assured negative results. Economists know that giving people money will reduce labor supply. Both the income effect and the substitution effect guarantee this result. So, according to Solow, it was inevitable that the experiments would find that guaranteed incomes negatively affected work efforts; and it was also inevitable that the opponents of guaranteed incomes would use this to defeat any guaranteed income plan for the United States.

And this is exactly what happened. All of the four experiments found that a negative income tax reduced work effort. Husbands, on average, reduced their labor supply by 7 percent, while wives and female heads of house reduced their labor supply by 17 percent on average.

There are a number of problems, however, with these studies. First, as Burtless (1986) points out, because the experiments were temporary they may have caused more people to opt for leisure than would be the case with a permanent guaranteed income. For short periods of time people may be willing to give up some income for greater leisure and not work due to the income guarantee. But over longer periods, people may not be willing to sacrifice the lower standards of material living associated with lower pay and more leisure. Also, employment provides psychic benefits beyond income that people are less likely to part with in the long run.

A second and related problem concerns the selection of participants, and whether a true controlled experiment was conducted. In a real experiment, subjects in the control group and the treatment group would be identical. But the guaranteed income experiments required people who were willing to be part of the study. It is reasonable that those people wanting to take advantage of income guarantees would more likely agree to participate in such a study. Thus the results from the experiment would be larger than real world results due to this flaw in experimental design.

A third problem with guaranteed income experiments is that they failed to control for various important factors known to affect labor supply decisions. As noted above, Solow (1986) pointed out that higher income in the private sector leads to reduced work efforts, so they failed to distinguish income and substitution effects.

Finally, as O'Connor (2001: 221) points out, the experiments were designed to test only for the negative consequences of the program. Any positive effects on morale, productivity, health, social relationships, etc. were deliberately not examined. More specifically, guaranteed incomes might allow women to end abusive marriages or allow parents to spend more time with their children.

As these debates over the income maintenance experiments were taking place, there was also a resurgence of interest in guaranteed income plans.[2] This renewed interest was sparked by practical as well as theoretical and moral concerns. At the practical level, Clark and Healy (1997) developed a set of possible guaranteed income plans for Ireland. Nobel laureate James Meade (1995) suggested such a plan for the United Kingdom; and the former Finance Minister of New Zealand included a guaranteed minimum income as part of his recent reform proposals (Douglas 1995).

From a moral perspective, some of this renewed interest probably stems from concerns about rising poverty and inequality in the late twentieth century and a sense that something must be done about these problems. Rising productivity growth in the late 1990s as well as large budget surpluses also made these proposals more viable. They gave the government two key sources of funds to finance a guaranteed income plan—the higher incomes of its citizens and its own budget surpluses.

2. The Luxembourg Income Study

The Luxembourg Income Study began in April 1983 when the government of Luxembourg agreed to develop, and make available to social scientists, an international microdata set containing a large number of income and sociodemographic variables. Until that time, most cross-national studies of income distribution and poverty were plagued with data problems because the national data that they employed defined key terms differently. For example, transfer income and in-kind benefits can be treated differently by different nations when they gather and report income data. More importantly, different nations can define income differently. Likewise, different nations can have different notions of what constitutes a family or household (e.g., do you actually have to be married to be a family?).

One goal in creating the LIS database was to employ common definitions and concepts so that variables are measured according to uniform standards across countries. As a result, researchers can be confident that the cross-national income data and socioeconomic variables that they are analyzing have been made as comparable as possible.

By early 2002, the LIS contained information on 26 nations: Australia, Austria, Belgium, Canada, the Czech Republic, Denmark, Finland, France, Germany, Hungary, Ireland, Israel, Italy, Luxembourg, Mexico, the Netherlands, Norway, Poland, Russia, the Slovak Republic, Spain, Sweden, Switzerland, Taiwan, the United Kingdom, and the United States. Data for each country was originally derived from national household surveys similar to the United States Current Population Reports, or (in a few cases) from tax returns filed with the national revenue service. Datasets for additional countries are in the process of being added to the LIS.

Currently four waves of data are available for individual countries. Wave #1 contains datasets for countries for some year in the late 1970s or early 1980s. Wave #2 contains datasets for the mid-1980s. Wave #3 contains datasets for the late 1980s and early 1990s. Wave #4 contains country datasets for the mid-1990s. Wave #5, centered around the year 2000, just began to come online in 2002. Finally, historical data from the late 1960s and/or early to mid-1970s is available for a few countries.

LIS data is available for more than 100 income variables and nearly 100 socio-demographic variables. Wage and salary incomes are contained in the database for households as well as for different household members. In addition, the dataset includes information on in-kind earnings, property income, alimony and child support, pension income, employer social insurance contributions, and numerous government transfer payments and in-kind benefits such as child allowances, Food Stamps and social security. There is also information on five different tax payments. Demographic variables are available for factors such as the education level of household members; the industries and occupations where adults in the family are employed; the ages of family members; household size, ethnicity and race; and the marital status of the family or household head.[3]

This wealth of comparable information permits researchers to do cross-national studies of poverty and income distribution, and to address empirically questions about the causes of poverty and changing income distribution, with the knowledge that the cross-national data they are using is as comparable as possible.

This data provides a good *natural experiment* of the impact that guaranteed incomes will likely have on efficiency. Countries differ considerably in the benefits they provide to their citizens and the degree to which they reduce income inequality. The effort that individual countries have made in this direction also differs over time. Using the LIS we will test whether increased government efforts to increase equity and maintain incomes has had an impact on economic efficiency.

3. Government Policy and Income Distribution

There are various different ways to measure income inequality. The Gini Coefficient and the coefficient of variation are two of the most familiar and the most popular inequality measures. The Gini Coefficient measures the distance between the Lorenz Curve and the diagonal of perfect income equality. The coefficient of variation measures the standard deviation relative to the mean. But these two popular measures of income inequality, as well as other attempts at measuring income inequality, suffer from one defect or another. Some of these problems are conceptual; other are statistical. Statistically, the Gini Coefficient cannot be decomposed to distinguish between within group causes of rising inequality and changes in inequality due to changes in the size of various groups. Conceptually, the Gini coefficient gives greatest weight to the densest part of the income distribution while the coefficient of variation gives extra weight to the top part of the income distribution (Lyngstad et al. 1997: 13).

For purposes of evaluating guaranteed income programs, focus should not be on the entire income distribution; rather focus should be on those at the bottom of the distribution. These are the people most likely to be helped as a result of guaranteed incomes. And these are the people whose behavior will most likely be affected by a guaranteed income plan.

Guaranteed income plans differ in terms of who is affected and the extent to which they are affected by any program. We will examine the population receiving below 50 percent of *adjusted* income. This is the Organization for Economic Cooperation and Development (OECD) definition of poverty, and is also a reasonable goal for a guaranteed income program—bringing the income level of every household up to the poverty line.

Income must be adjusted to take account of the different income needs of households of different sizes. A family of four needs more income than a single individual. But does it need four times more, or are there economies of scale in consumption? If there are *no* economies of scale, we look at *per capita* household income. If there are some economies of scale, we need to make some adjustment for these. We employ the recommended Organisation for Economic Co-operation and Development (OECD) (1982) adjustments for family size in studies of income distribution and family size adjustment that are implicit in the Orshansky (1969) definition of poverty. That is, it is assumed that additional adults in the household need 70 percent of the income of the first adult and that each child requires 50 percent of the income of the first adult.[4]

Tables 10.1 and 10.2 begin by presenting some basic data on the size of the low-income population both before (Table 10.1) and after (Table 10.2) the government has impacted household income.[5] The 11 countries included in these tables were chosen because these are the LIS countries for which standardized manufacturing productivity data is available, and so will allow us to compare redistributive efforts with efficiency issues in a cross-national context.

Several things are noteworthy in these two tables. First, looking at just factor income (Table 10.1), poverty rates are both very high and relatively stable across nations. For our 11 countries, pre-fiscal policy, the average (unweighted) poverty rate is more than one-third. Over time there appears to be an upward trend in household poverty, not surprising given the rise in inequality over this time period. What is surprising, however, is the fact that the two countries (Canada and the United States) with the lowest poverty rates pre-fisc, or using factor income, have the highest poverty rates post-fisc or using disposable income (see Table 10.2). Tables 10.1 and 10.2 also show the greater fiscal policy efforts at reducing poverty over time. Although poverty rates still increase over time in Table 10.2, the magnitude of that increase has diminished. Based on factor incomes, average (unweighted) poverty rates rise by 4.8 percentage points from Wave #1 to Wave #4. But based on disposable incomes, the increase is only 1.5 percentage points. Thus fiscal policy throughout the world has countered a rise in income inequality at the lower end of the distribution.

Fiscal policy achieves this in two ways. First, governments tend to prop up the incomes of the poor through numerous spending programs, and second, governments employ progressive tax structures. In previous work (Pressman 2002), I have shown how these two redistributive tools differ from one nation to

Table 10.1 Poverty rates based on factor income (pre-fiscal policy)

Country	Wave #1	Wave #2	Wave #3	Wave #4	Average
Belgium	N.A	34.0%	37.7%	37.7%	36.5%
Canada	26.8%	29.6%	31.1%	33.7%	30.3%
Denmark	N.A	36.6%	38.9%	40.0%	38.5%
France	31.0%	35.2%	35.6%	36.5%	34.6%
Germany	33.8%	35.2%	32.0%	37.0%	34.5%
Italy	N.A	32.2%	30.7%	37.5%	33.5%
Netherlands	39.6%	39.8%	39.7%	39.4%	39.6%
Norway	33.0%	31.3%	33.0%	36.3%	33.4%
Sweden	35.0%	36.0%	38.2%	41.0%	37.6%
U.K.	33.5%	40.0%	38.4%	41.4%	38.3%
U.S.	29.7%	30.8%	32.0%	32.6%	31.3%
Average	32.8%	34.6%	35.2%	37.6%	35.0%

Source: Luxembourg Income Study.

Note: Column averages are unweighted averages.

Table 10.2 Poverty rates based on disposable income (post-fiscal policy)

Country	Wave #1	Wave #2	Wave #3	Wave #4	Average
Belgium	N.A	4.8%	5.5%	8.7%	6.3%
Canada	12.5%	11.8%	11.7%	11.7%	11.9%
Denmark	N.A	7.7%	6.9%	8.9%	7.8%
France	7.9%	12.7%	9.8%	8.4%	9.7%
Germany	6.6%	6.3%	5.9%	7.8%	6.7%
Italy	N.A.	9.8%	9.0%	12.8%	10.5%
Netherlands	7.3%	6.5%	6.2%	8.0%	7.0%
Norway	5.3%	4.7%	4.6%	5.8%	5.1%
Sweden	5.6%	8.0%	7.3%	8.7%	7.4%
U.K.	5.7%	7.1%	11.7%	10.6%	8.8%
U.S.	17.0%	18.6%	18.3%	19.0%	18.2%
Average	8.5%	8.9%	8.8%	10.0%	9.0%

Source: Luxembourg Income Study.

another; but despite these differences, in virtually every nation it is government spending more than taxes that achieves the largest part of any redistribution by the state.

Tables 10.3 and 10.4 attempt to summarize the data in Tables 10.1 and 10.2 by looking at the extent to which poverty was reduced across countries and over time. Table 10.3 is derived by subtraction from Tables 10.1 and 10.2. It shows the extent to which fiscal actions reduce national poverty rates in the aggregate. Table 10.4 takes a more microeconomic approach. After identifying particular poor households based on their factor incomes, it calculates what fraction of these poor households escape poverty due to fiscal actions.

Tables 10.3 and 10.4 tell an identical story. They show that the United States and Canada make the least effort at propping up the incomes of the poor, while the four Scandinavian countries make the greatest effort. In the aggregate, over time there is slightly greater effort at mitigating poverty by the use of fiscal policy. Table 10.3 shows that in Wave #1 fiscal policy reduced poverty on average by 24.3 percentage points. This slowly increased with each wave, so that by Wave #4 fiscal policy was reducing poverty by 27.5 percentage points. Table 10.4 also shows that over time fiscal policy has brought a greater percentage of households out of poverty—75.3 percent in Wave #1 versus 76.1 percent in Wave #4—although here the increase has not been continuous.

National efforts at poverty reduction also differ over time. Most European nations have exerted more effort at reducing poverty over time. Especially noteworthy is the large increase in Canada's fiscal efforts—from 14.3 percentage points in Wave #1 of the LIS to 22 percentage points in Wave #4 (Table 10.3). This is paralleled by the rising percentage of poor households removed from poverty due to fiscal policy—from 53.6 percent in Wave #1 to 66.8 percent in Wave #4 (Table 10.4).

Table 10.3 Poverty rate reduction due to fiscal policy

Country	Wave #1	Wave #2	Wave #3	Wave #4	Average
Belgium	N.A.	29.2%	32.2%	29.0%	30.1%
Canada	14.3%	17.8%	19.4%	22.0%	18.4%
Denmark	N.A.	28.9%	32.0%	31.1%	30.7%
France	23.1%	22.5%	25.8%	28.1%	24.9%
Germany	27.2%	28.9%	26.1%	29.2%	27.9%
Italy	N.A.	22.4%	21.7%	24.7%	22.9%
Netherlands	32.3%	33.3%	33.5%	31.4%	32.6%
Norway	27.7%	26.6%	28.4%	30.5%	28.3%
Sweden	29.4%	28.0%	31.9%	32.3%	30.4%
U.K.	27.8%	32.9%	26.7%	30.8%	29.6%
U.S.	12.7%	12.2%	12.7%	13.6%	12.8%
Average	24.3%	25.7%	26.4%	27.5%	26.2%

Source: Luxembourg Income Study.

Table 10.4 Percent of factor income: Poor who escape poverty due to fiscal policy

Country	Wave #1	Wave #2	Wave #3	Wave #4	Average
Belgium	N.A.	87.9%	86.5%	78.4%	84.3%
Canada	53.6%	61.2%	63.5%	66.8%	61.3%
Denmark	N.A.	80.4%	83.3%	80.7%	81.5%
France	78.7%	68.5%	76.9%	81.7%	76.5%
Germany	83.4%	84.0%	83.5%	81.6%	83.1%
Italy	N.A.	77.6%	79.6%	76.2%	77.8%
Netherlands	82.7%	86.9%	86.1%	80.7%	84.1%
Norway	84.9%	85.7%	87.4%	85.6%	85.9%
Sweden	89.3%	84.7%	84.0%	82.3%	85.1%
U.K.	84.3%	84.9%	71.7%	77.0%	79.5%
U.S.	45.1%	44.3%	47.8%	46.6%	46.0%
Average	75.3%	76.9%	77.3%	76.1%	76.8%

Source: Luxembourg Income Study.

4. Does Greater Equity Entail Greater Inefficiency?

We have seen that some countries put greater effort into equalizing incomes. And we have also seen that efforts at reducing poverty have generally increased over time. The big question raised by Okun (1975) is whether any relationship exists between such efforts and overall economic efficiency.

Productivity is the main measure of efficiency used by economists. As many people have pointed out (see Blinder 1990, Seidman 1990, Madrick 1995), more than anything else it is productivity that determines national living standards. And it is the growth of productivity that determines how much living standards will improve from year to year. Given the importance of compounding, higher rates of productivity growth over a long period of time will lead to much larger future living standards. Stagnant, or slowly growing productivity growth, in contrast, will lead to slow improvements in material well-being. Our children and grandchildren will do only slightly better than we do if our efficiency in production fails to grow by very much.

Secondarily, there is the question of whether work incentives will be affected adversely. Guaranteed incomes may reduce the willingness of people to work. In addition, the financing of any redistributive scheme may create an incentive problem as a result of the fact that taxes must go up to finance the redistribution.

This section focuses on whether a guaranteed income plan might adversely affect productivity growth.[6] We look at individual countries over time, comparing their productivity performance to their efforts at redistribution (as measured in the previous section). We also look at cross-country differences in redistribution in order to see whether or not those countries tending (over a long time) to make greater redistributive efforts suffer from any loss of efficiency.

Table 10.5 helps us in this endeavor. Due to the suspect nature of productivity measures in services, it presents data on productivity growth in the manufacturing sector only for our 11 nations over the time period covered by the LIS.

The data in Table 10.5 was constructed to make the comparisons with earlier tables as easy as possible to follow. For example, for Sweden the first data point in Tables 10.1–10.4 came from 1980, the Wave #1 LIS data set for Sweden. Since 1980 was used in Tables 10.1–10.4, 1980 was chosen as the focal point for Sweden in the column of Table 10.5 labeled "Wave #1." The productivity growth data reported there is the five-year average surrounding 1980 (the years 1978 through 1982). This was done for several reasons. First, productivity growth is known to vary over the business cycle (Basu and Fernald 2000), so taking five-year average growth rates will control for this. Second, tax and spending policies change only slowly over time. Thus, the programs in effect in Sweden in 1980 were likely to be quite similar to those in all the years between 1978 and 1982. Similarly, for Sweden in Wave #2, 1987 is our focal point, and the figure reported in Table 10.5 represents average manufacturing productivity growth rates from 1985 to 1989. All the figures in Table 10.5 were calculated in this manner.

Comparing Table 10.4 (as well as Table 10.3) with Table 10.5 it is hard to find any correlations between government income guarantees and productivity growth.

From a cross-sectional perspective, the two countries that do the least to assist poor households (the United States and Canada) do not experience greater productivity growth. The United States, which does the very least to help the poor, has slightly below average productivity growth rates. Canada does poorly on productivity growth as well as on redistributive fiscal policy. At the other extreme, three of the four countries that do the most to guarantee poverty-level incomes—Belgium, the Netherlands, and Sweden—also do very well in terms of productivity growth. The fourth country with strong redistributive efforts, Norway, actually does close to the worst in terms of productivity growth.

Examining the set of 11 countries over time also shows little relationship between income supports and economic efficiency. Between Wave #1 and Wave #2 government fiscal policy brings *more* households out of poverty while at the same time productivity growth rises substantially. Between Wave #2 and Wave #3 government income supports increase slightly but productivity growth declines slightly. Finally, between Wave #3 and Wave #4, income support declines (on Table 10.4) while productivity growth rises. However, the rise in productivity growth on average here is due primarily to the absence of data for Denmark, by far the worst performer in terms of productivity growth. Adding Denmark's average productivity growth over the period from 1985–1993 would have given us a figure of 2.9 percent at the bottom of the Wave #4 column, not substantially different from the Wave #3 average.

Looking at particular countries over time also reveals little equity–efficiency tradeoff. For Belgium, as government efforts to reduce poverty decline between Wave #2 and Wave #4, productivity growth first drops sharply and then rebounds somewhat. For Canada, government efforts to reduce poverty rise over time, but

Table 10.5 Productivity growth rates in manufacturing

Country	Wave #1	Wave #2	Wave #3	Wave #4	Average
Belgium	N.A.	5.8%	2.3%	3.6%	3.9%
Canada	1.7%	1.3%	2.4%	1.8%	1.8%
Denmark	N.A	0.7%	1.2%*	N.A.	0.9%
France	3.7%	3.2%	3.8%	3.5%	3.6%
Germany	1.9%	2.6%	2.6%	2.5%	2.4%
Italy	N.A	4.2%	3.5%	2.5%	3.4%
Netherlands	5.2%	2.5%	1.7%	4.6%	3.5%
Norway	1.3%	2.3%	1.8%	0.4%	1.5%
Sweden	3.9%	1.8%	4.4%	5.9%	4.0%
U.K.	1.4%	4.1%	4.8%	2.3%	3.2%
U.S.	1.1%	3.3%	2.5%	3.7%	2.7%
Average	2.5%	2.9%	2.8%	3.1%	2.8%

Source: U.S. Bureau of Labor Statistics website, international statistics.

there is little overall change in productivity growth. For the Netherlands and Sweden, a fall in government poverty-reduction efforts between Wave #3 and Wave #4 increases productivity growth. But similar declines in Germany have no impact on productivity growth, while in France it appears that greater government efforts at reducing poverty are associated with rising productivity growth rates.

Regressing our equity and efficiency measures from Tables 10.4 and 10.5 yields an R^2 of only .01, a regression coefficient of 1.16, and a standard error of 1.72. Although not statistically significant, this analysis points to a *positive* relationship between equity efforts and efficiency. We can conclude from this that there does not seem to be a noticeable equity–efficiency tradeoff across nations and over time.

Table 10.6 employs a slighter broader view of productivity growth. Table 10.6 is broader than Table 10.5 in several respects. First, it looks at the whole economy rather than just the manufacturing sector. Second, it indirectly takes account of some work disincentives in guaranteed income plans. If people prefer leisure to labor, greater redistribution should reduce labor and increases leisure.[7] Greater redistribution also requires higher taxes on the well-to-do, and people with high earnings may relocate to other countries that impose lower taxes. If raising the top tax rate causes workers with high and rising incomes to emigrate, GDP growth and GDP growth per worker will be adversely affected, since removing high income (and more productive workers) from an average will lower that average. Some possible real-world examples of this are Sweden and the United Kingdom in 1960s, where marginal tax rates over 90 percent may have led to talented individuals to leave the country. High tax rates can also lead people to focus on tax avoidance rather than production, and this too may adversely affect productivity growth.

Like Table 10.5, Table 10.6 was constructed to make comparisons with earlier tables easy to follow. The data reported are five-year averages for the year surrounding our LIS data points. Again, this was done on the assumptions that government tax and spending policies change slowly over time, and that the programs prevailing in any one year were similar in contiguous years.

Table 10.6 Growth of real GDP per worker

Country	Wave #1	Wave #2	Wave #3	Wave #4	Average
Canada	-0.2%	3.2%	0.4%	1.2%	1.2%
France	0.6%	0.8%	1.3%	1.4%	1.0%
Germany	0.3%	0.9%	1.8%	2.5%	1.4%
Italy	N.A.	2.5%	1.7%	2.3%	2.2%
U.K.	0.6%	3.8%	1.9%	1.6%	2.0%
U.S.	0.6%	2.8%	0.9%	1.3%	1.4%
Average	0.4%	2.3%	1.3%	1.7%	1.5%

Source: Penn World Tables; IMF, *World Economic Outlook*, May 1999.

Comparing Tables 10.4 and 10.6 indicates little correlation between the growth of GDP per capita and government redistribution efforts. The United States and Canada, which do the least to protect the living standard of its households, do not experience superior levels of economic growth per capita. In fact, both the United States and Canada perform below the average of the six countries in Table 10.6. At the other extreme, of the six countries for which data is available on GDP growth per worker, three made above average efforts in removing households from poverty: Germany, Italy, and the United Kingdom. Two of these had the highest growth rates in Table 10.6.

Looking at productivity growth and government income support over time also reveals little tradeoff between these two variables. When fiscal policy did the least to remove households from poverty (Wave #1) GDP growth per worker was the lowest. Higher income supports in Wave #2 led to higher GDP growth per worker.

Table 10.7 Equity efforts and efficiency

Country	Equity Efforts	Efficiency Measure
Australia	68.1%	1.04%
Belgium	87.2%	1.54%
Canada	59.4%	1.56%
Denmark	81.9%	1.29%
Finland	86.3%	3.00%
France	74.7%	1.31%
Germany	83.6%	1.04%
Ireland	77.4%	2.56%
Italy	78.6%	2.10%
Luxembourg	88.6%	2.56%
Netherlands	85.2%	0.60%
Norway	86.0%	1.69%
Spain	72.8%	1.79%
Sweden	86.0%	1.44%
Switzerland	46.0%	1.55%
U.K.	80.3%	1.93%
U.S.	47.7%	0.92%
Averages	75.9%	1.64%

Source: Luxembourg Income Study for Equity Efforts (% poor households removed from poverty by fiscal policy); Penn World Table for Efficiency Measure (% change in real GDP per worker 1979–1990).

Note: Equity Efforts from Wave #1 through Wave #3 only.

Looking at individual countries over time likewise provides little evidence that high income supports create productivity problems. The continual increase in Canadian income supports as we move from Wave #1 to Wave #4 are associated with mixed growth results. The increase in French income supports between Wave #2 and Wave #4 are associated with rising GDP growth per worker. In the United Kingdom, a sharp drop in income supports between Waves #2 and #3 is associated with a fall in GDP growth per worker, although an increase in income supports between Waves #3 and #4 is associated with a decline in the GDP growth per worker.

Supporting these observations, a cross-national and cross-temporal regression of data points in Table 10.6 with equity efforts in Table 10.4 finds little equity–efficiency tradeoff. Our R^2 is a mere .02 indicating that redistribution efforts can explain little of the changes in productivity growth. Moreover, the relationship between productivity growth and redistribution is a positive one, although not statistically significant (the regression coefficient is 1.09, and the standard error is 1.54).

Finally, Table 10.7 provides an even broader and more inclusive examination of this question. It relies on the Penn World Tables, which contains national income and population data for virtually every country throughout the world. As with the LIS, the Penn World Tables have been constructed to make data as comparable as possible across nations and across time.

One efficiency measure contained in the Penn World Tables is the percentage growth of real GDP per worker. This variable shows how much more each worker (on average) produces in each country. The figures reported in column 3 of Table 10.7 are country averages for the years 1979–1990, roughly covering the same time period as Waves #1 through #3 of the LIS. Column 2 of Table 10.7 reports the percentage of households in each country removed from poverty due to government fiscal efforts. The figures here were calculated the same way as the figures from Table 10.4, and averaged over Waves #1 through #3 of the LIS only (since the Penn World Tables don't have efficiency data for the Wave #4 time period).

Eyeballing Table 10.7, there seems to be little relationship between these two variables. Six countries make great efforts to support incomes, bringing more than 85 percent of factor income poor households out of poverty: Belgium, Finland, Luxembourg, the Netherlands, Norway and Sweden. Of these, two perform considerably above average on our efficiency measure (Finland and Luxembourg), three perform close to average (Belgium, Norway and Sweden) and one does poorly (the Netherlands). At the other extreme, all three countries making the least effort at supporting incomes (Canada, Switzerland, and the United States), by bringing less than two-thirds of poor households out of poverty, have below average records of real GDP growth per capita. The position of the United States is noteworthy here. The United States does just about worse than every other country in Table 10. 7 in bringing households out of poverty; but it does not seem to have gained anything in terms of productivity or greater labor force participation. To the contrary, the United States also scores close to the bottom when it comes to enhanced efficiency. Regressing our equity and efficiency measures in Table 10.7 gives us an R^2 of just .09 and a regression coefficient of plus .01, which although not statistically significant, indicates a *positive* relationship between the two variables rather than an inverse relationship. While certainly not conclusive, these empirical results all point to the absence of a big tradeoff between equity and efficiency as postulated by Okun.

5. Summary and Conclusions

The results presented above need to be interpreted carefully, with full awareness of the data limitations used to obtain them. First, the lack of a big tradeoff between efficiency and equity only apply within the limits of the income guarantees currently provided by developed nations. It makes good sense to worry more about the impact of redistribution the greater the amount of redistribution that takes place. If income guarantees were raised to the median level of income or above, there would likely be a large disincentive effect on work effort. Yet, for countries like the United States, it appears that equity efforts can be increased substantially without any serious negative efficiency effects.

Second, the lack of a tradeoff may be due to large and important cultural differences among nations. In an important study on income distribution, Christopher Jencks et al. (1972: 227) conclude that economic success depends on luck to a large extent. Yet, "those who are lucky tend...to impute their success to skill." In those countries where people tend to recognize luck as a major component of success in economic life, or where guaranteed incomes are accepted and believed to be part of a civilized society or a needed form of social insurance, income guarantees may result in smaller work disincentives. This possibility surely requires more research, which will involve serious inquiry into national attitudes and beliefs across nations.

Third, those countries that redistribute the most income may employ particular policies that have less effect on efficiency than those countries that redistribute little income. Haveman (1988: 24) has identified several such policies: refundable negative income taxes, guaranteed incomes for the elderly, programs that require absent parents to pay for the support of their children, employment subsidies, and capital accounts for youths to be used for training and education. The limits of this chapter prohibit an even cursory examination of the particular policies that different countries use to support incomes. But this too is a topic worth further exploration.

Fourth, the lack of relationship between redistributive effort and productivity growth may be due to missing variables that also affect productivity growth. The main such variables identified by economists are investments in physical human capital. But alternatively, there may be no big tradeoff. Clark and Healy (1997: 44f.) suggest why one reason why this might be so. Reducing the labor supply of married women may improve the educational attainment of women, thereby improving productivity growth in the long run. It also may result in less frantic and more productive married male workers. And more supervision of adolescents may reduce crime, reducing the number of workers firms must hire just to prevent crime. Meade (1995) and Esping-Anderson (1990) argue that a basic income program would add flexibility to the labor market by improving the efficient allocation of labor. Workers will be less likely to resist changes in employment practices and structures. There also may be positive effects on worker morale (Ayres 1966), or income guarantees may encourage risk-taking entrepreneurship because the costs of failure are lower. In addition, as Arrow (1980:8f.) and Galor and Zeira (1993) note, income supports may enable the poor to invest in human capital and be more productive in the future. Furthermore, by equalizing incomes, income guarantees should increase demand and employment, which also has efficiency effects since, as mentioned earlier, productivity growth is procyclical.

Finally, the empirical findings in this chapter are supported by a growing body of empirical research that fails to find any big tradeoffs between efficiency and equity. Although the overall results are still inconclusive (see Bertola 2000; Zweimüller 2000), a number of studies (Alesina and Roderick 1992, 1994; Perotti 1996; Garrison and Lee 1992; Persson and Tabellini 1992, 1994; Cory and Glyn 1994) have found that income equality does not harm economic growth. This should give some hope that efficiency concerns are not a fatal object to guaranteed income plans.[8]

Appendix

A10.1 Data years and data sources

Country	Wave #1	Wave #2	Wave #3	Wave #4	Source
Belgium	N.A.	1985	1992	1997	Penn Survey of the Centre for Social Policy
Canada	1981	1987	1991	1994	Survey of Consumer Finances
Denmark	N.A.	1987	1992	1995	Income Tax Survey
France	1981	1984	1989	1994	Family Budget Survey
Germany	1981	1984	1989	1994	German Transfer Survey (1981); German Social Economic Panel Study (1984, 1989, 1994)
Italy	N.A.	1986	1991	1995	Bank of Italy Survey
Netherlands	1983	1987	1991	1994	Socioeconomic Panel
Norway	1979	1986	1991	1995	Income and Property Distribution Survey
Sweden	1981	1987	1992	1995	Income Distribution Survey
United Kingdom	1979	1986	1991	1995	Family Expenditure Survey
United States	1979	1986	1991	1994	March Current Population Survey

Notes

1 Similar arguments have been made more recently by Jeremy Rifkin (1995).

2 See Widerquist and Lewis (1997); Reynolds and Healy (1995); Clark and Healy (1997); Murray (1997); Van Parijs (1992, 1995); Lerner et al. (1999); Groot and Vander Veen (2001).

3 For more information about the Luxembourg Income Study, and for information on how to access the LIS databases, see Smeeding et al. (1985, 1988) and the LIS homepage at www.lis.ceps.lu.

4 Some recent research (Ruggles 1990) has found that there are greater economies of scale in household living arrangements than is reflected in the OECD and Orshansky adjust-

ments. This work argues for using the square root of household members to adjust for household size. That is, adjusted household income, $Y_A=Y_D/\sqrt{n}$ where Y_A = adjusted income Y_D = disposable income and n = household size. Sensitivity analysis performed by the author indicates that the choice of an adjustment factor makes little difference for the overall results. Actual numbers differ, but relative positions remain pretty much the same. This is supported by other findings that cross-national measures of poverty are not very sensitive to equivalence scales used (Buhmann et al. 1988).

5 See Appendix 11.1 for data years and original sources of the data.

6 A companion paper (Pressman 2002–2003) looks in more detail at the labor force impact of income supports. In particular, it examines whether guaranteed incomes affect labor force participation and, thereby, economic growth. This paper finds little relationship between these two variables.

7 This impact is not discussed here, but it is discussed in Pressman (2002–2003).

8 The author thanks participants at the 2002 BIG conference in New York as well as Mark Setterfield for comments on an earlier version of this chapter. An earlier version of this paper was published in the *Journal of Socio-Economics*, 23 (2005): 83–100.

References

Alsenina, A. and Roderik, D. (1992) "Distribution, Political Conflict, and Economic Growth: A Simple Theory and Some Evidence," in *Political Economy, Growth, and Business Cycles*, A. Cukierman, Z. Hercowitz and L. Leiderman (eds.), (Cambridge: MIT Press), 23–50.

——— "Distributive Policies and Economic Growth," *Quarterly Journal of Economics*, 109: 465–490.

Arrow, K. (1980) "The Trade-off between Growth and Equity," in *Theory for Economic Efficiency and Essays in Honor of Abba P. Lerner*, H. Greenfield et al. (eds.), (Cambridge: MIT Press), 1–11.

Ayers, C. (1966) "Guaranteed Income: An Institutionalist View," in Theobald (1966), pp. 161–174.

Basu, S. and Fernald, J. (2000) "Why Is Productivity Procyclical? Why Do We Care?," Federal Reserve Bank of Chicago Working Paper #WP2000–11.

Bertola, G. (2000) "Macroeconomics of Distribution and Growth," in *Handbook of Income Distribution*, vol. 1, A.B. Atkinson and F. Bourguigon (eds.), (Amsterdam: Elsevier) 477–540.

Blinder, A., ed. (1990) *Paying for Productivity*, (Washington, D.C.: Brookings Institution).

Buhmann, B. et al. (1988) "Equivalence Scales, Well-Being, Inequality, and Poverty: Sensitivity Estimates Across Ten Countries Using the Luxembourg Income Study (LIS) Database," *Review of Income and Wealth*, 34: 115–142.

Burtless, G. (1986) "The Work Response to a Guaranteed Income: A Survey of Experimental Evidence," in *Lessons from the Income Maintenance Experiments*, A. Munnell (ed.), (Boston: Federal Reserve Bank of Boston), 22–52.

Butler, S. and Kondratas, A. (1987) *Out of the Poverty Trap*, (New York: Free Press).

Clark, C.M.A. and Healy, J. (1997) *Pathways to a Basic Income*, (Dublin: Conference of Religions Ireland).

Cory, D. and Glyn, A. (1994) "The Macroeconomics of Equality, Stability, and Growth," in *Paying for Inequality*, A. Glyn and D. Miliband (eds.), (London: Rivers Oran), 205–216.

Douglas, R. (1995) *Unfinished Business*, (Wellington: New Zealand Random House).

Esping-Andersen, G. (1990) *The Three Worlds of Welfare Capitalism*, (Princeton: Princeton University Press).

Friedman, M. (1962) *Capitalism and Freedom*, (Chicago: University of Chicago Press).

Galor, O. and Zeira, J. (1993) "Income Distribution and Macroeconomics," *Review of Economic Studies*, 60: 35–52.

Garrison, C. and Lee, F.Y. (1992) "Taxation, Aggregate Activity and Growth," *Economic Inquiry*, 20: 172–176.

Gordon, D. (1996) *Fat and Mean*, (New York: Free Press).

Groot, L. and Van der Veen., R.J., eds. (2001) *Basic Income on the Agenda: Policy Objectives and Political Chances*, (Amersterdam: Amsterdam University Press).

Haveman, R. (1988) *Starting Even*, (New York: Simon and Shuster).

Hayes, W. (1969) "The Guaranteed Annual Income: An Appraisal," *Review of Social Economy*, 27: 74–83.

Hildebrand, G. (1967) *Poverty, Income Maintenance, and the Negative Income Tax*, (Ithaca: New York State School of Industrial and Labor Relations).

Jencks, C. et al. (1972) *Inequality: A Reassessment of the Effect of Family and Schooling in America*, (New York: Basic Books).

Lekachman, R. (1971) "Can More Money End Poverty?" in *Poverty: Views from the Left*, J. Larner and I. Howe (eds.), (New York: William Morrow), 58–67.

Lerner, S., Clark, C.M.A., and Needham, W.R. (1999) *Basic Income: Economic Security for All Canadians*, (Toronto: Between the Lines).

Lyngstad, J. et al. (1997) "Poverty and Economic Inequality: Concepts Measures and Methods," in *Poverty and Economic Inequality in Industrialized Western Societies*, N. Keilman et al. (eds.), (Oslo: Scandinavian University Press), 3–34.

Madrick, J. (1995) *The End of Affluence*, (New York: Random House).

Meade, J. (1995) *Full Employment Regained*, (Cambridge: Cambridge University Press).

Murray, C. (1984) *Losing Ground*, (New York: Basic Books).

Murray, M. (1997) *"... And Economic Justice for All": Welfare Reform for the 21st Century*, (Armonk, N.Y.: M.E. Sharpe).

O'Connor, A. (2001) *Poverty Knowledge: Social Science, Social Policy and the Poor in Twentieth-Century U.S. History*, (Princeton: Princeton University Press).

OECD (Organisation for Economic Cooperation and Development) (1982) *The OECD List of Social Indicators*, (Paris: OECD).

Okun, A. (1975) *Equality and Efficiency: The Big Tradeoff*, (Washington, D.C.: Brookings Institution).

Orshansky, M. (1969) "How Poverty is Measured," *Monthly Labor Review*, 92: 37–41.

Perotti, R. (1996) "Growth, Income Distribution, and Democracy: What the Data Say," *Journal of Economic Growth*, 1: 149–187.

Persson, T. and Tabellini, G. (1992) "Growth, Distribution, and Politics," in *Political Economy, Growth, and Business Cycles*, A. Cukierman, Z. Hercowitz and L. Leiderman (eds.), (Cambridge: MIT Press), 3–22.

——— (1994) "Is Inequality Harmful for Growth?" *American Economic Review*, 84: 600–621.

Pressman, S. (2002) "The Gender Poverty Gap in Developed and Transitional Economies," *Journal of Economic Issues*, 36: 17–40.

——— (2002–2003) "Fiscal Policy and Work Incentives–An International Comparison," *Journal of Income Distribution*, 11: 51–69.

Reynolds, B. and Healy, S., eds. (1995) *An Adequate Income Guarantee for All*, (Dublin: Conference of Religious of Ireland).

Rifkin, J. (1995) *The End of Work*, (New York: Putnam).

Ruggles, P. (1990) *Drawing the Line: Alternative Poverty Measures and their Implication for Public Policy*, (Washington, D.C.: Urban Institute Press).

Seidman, L. (1990) *Saving for America's Economic Future*, (Armonk, N.Y.: M.E. Sharpe).

Smeeding, T.M., Schmous, G., and Allegraza, S. (1985) "An Introduction to LIS," LIS-CEPS Working Paper #1.

Smeeding et al. (1988) "Luxembourg Income Study (LIS): Information Guide," LIS-CEPS Working Paper #7.

Solow, R. (1986) "An Economist's View of the Income Maintenance Experiments", in *Lessons from the Income Maintenance Experiments*, A. Munnell (ed.) (Boston: Federal Reserve Bank of Boston), 218–222.

Theobald, R. (1963) *Free Men and Free Markets*, (Garden City, N.Y.: Doubleday).

———, ed. (1966) *The Guaranteed Income: Next Step in Economic Evolution?*, (Garden City, N.Y.: Doubleday).

Tobin, J. (1966) "The Case for an Income Guarantee," *The Public Interest*, #4: 31–41.

Tobin, J., Pechman, J., and Mieszkowski, P. (1967) "Is a Negative Income Tax Practical?" *Yale Law Journal*, 77: 1–27.

Vadakin, J. (1968) "A Critique of the Guaranteed Annual Income," *The Public Interest*, #11: 53–66.

Van Parijs, P., ed. (1992) *Arguing for Basic Income: Ethical Foundations for a Radical Reform*, (New York: Verso).

——— (1995) *Real Freedom for All*, (Oxford: Clarendon Press).

Widerquist, K. and Lewis, M. (1997) "An Efficiency Argument for the Guaranteed Income," Jerome Levy Economics Institute, Working Paper #212.

Zweimuller, J. (2000) "Redistribution, Inequality and Growth," *Empirica*, 27: 1–20.

Chapter 11

Have the 1996 Welfare Reforms and Expansion of the Earned Income Tax Credit Eliminated the Need for a Basic Income Guarantee in the United States?

James B. Bryan*

The Context

In the United States, a Basic Income Guarantee (BIG) faces a difficult barrier—the popular view that welfare should be tied closely to employment, and the perception that the 1996 welfare reforms and the Earned Income Tax Credit (EITC) have been great successes. The 1996 welfare reforms are frequently labeled "workfare" because of their employment requirements and time limits, while the EITC provides benefits as a subsidy to wages.

Whether the United States should consider moving to a BIG depends, in part, on the efficiency and equity of the reformed welfare system and the EITC. Washington legislators have been attracted to the EITC in recent years and, in general, have proclaimed the 1996 reforms a success. Shrinking welfare rolls plus poor (and previously poor) household heads with jobs can easily be interpreted as evidence of success.

Changes in Welfare and the EITC

The Personal Responsibility and Work Opportunity Reconciliation Act of 1996 (PRWORA) instituted the most significant changes to the United States welfare system since its inception. Blank (2002) identifies several major changes to welfare as a result of this legislation:

- **Transfer of authority to the states**. The primary federal cash assistance program for families, Aid to Families with Dependent Children Program (AFDC), was eliminated and replaced by a block grant to the states, Temporary Assistance for Needy Families (TANF). The result was to give the states the authority to set eligibility and payment rules.

- **State funding**. AFDC had a matching funding arrangement, where the federal contribution depended on the state's level of funding. Under TANF, the federal contribution was fixed and determined by funding levels prior to PRWORA. The main constraint was that state contributions could not fall below 75 percent of their previous AFDC contribution levels without jeopardizing federal matching funds.
- **Work requirements**. A radical change under PRWORA was the institution of a work requirement. By 2002 states were required to show that half of all welfare families and 90 percent of two-parent welfare families were working or in work-preparation programs.
- **Time limits**. Perhaps the greatest change under PRWORA was that recipients could receive benefits for no more than sixty months during their entire life. Current welfare recipients must now forecast their future needs for social insurance in deciding whether to receive benefits now. Part of the dramatic drop in the welfare rolls may be due to decisions by people to save their welfare for future gray days.

Recent changes in the EITC have been more modest. The EITC has three components, each of which is contingent on a family's composition and earned income. First, there is a phase-in range, where the transfer increases as earned income increases. Then, there is an income range where the transfer is constant (and is at its maximum). Finally, a phase-out range exists where the transfer is reduced with increased earned income, eventually reaching zero.

For 2001, the EITC worked as follows for a family with two children. In the phase-in range a family received an additional $0.40 for each dollar of earned income, from the first dollar through an income of $10,020. By the end of this phase-in range, the maximum transfer would be $4,008. There would be no change in this transfer as earned income rose from $10,020 to $13,090. The phase-out range extended from income of $13,091 to $32,121, with the transfer falling by just over $0.21 for each extra dollar earned.

The Tax Act of 2001 provides for three changes in the EITC, all pertaining to the phase-out range. From 2002 to 2004 both the starting and ending points of the phase-out range increase by $1,000. From 2005 to 2007, these points will increase by another $1,000, and in 2008 they will increase by another $1,000. This represents a nominal increase of $3,000 in the length of the constant range (since the starting point of the constant range is unchanged). Though the phase-out range does not change in length, its end point is extended by $3,000. These prospective changes imply no change in the maximum possible transfer (Hoffman and Seidman 2003: 30–31).

Changes in the EITC over the 1990s made the system more generous, but there were few changes to the basic program structure (Hoffman and Seidman 2003: 24–25). For a family with two children, between 1990 and 2000, the phase-in range endpoint grew from $6,810 to $9,750. The subsidy in this range increased from $0.17 to $0.40 on each dollar of earned income, and the maximum credit for a family with two children increased from $953 to $3,888, a nominal increase of 308 percent and a 214 percent increase after inflation.

The constant range of the EITC for this family actually diminished during the 1990s, from $3,920 to $3,070. The phase-out range almost doubled during the 1990s—increasing from $9,534 to $18,454. The endpoint of the range grew from $20,264 to $31,152, roughly a 50 percent nominal increase or an 18 percent real increase. During the same period, the phase-out rate (i.e., the benefit reduction rate or the increment in the effective marginal tax rate) more than doubled, from 10 percent to 21 percent.

During the 1990s the number of EITC recipients grew by about 50 percent. The average credit per family rose from $601 to $1,625, a nominal increase of about 170 percent and roughly doubling after inflation. Total credits quadrupled during the decade, rising from $7.5 billion to $30 billion, or slightly more than a tripling after adjusting for inflation (Hoffman and Seidman 2003: 26–28).

Some Implications of the Current Structure of Welfare and the EITC

The 1996 welfare reforms gave employment a central role in the ability to benefit from income transfers; and the growth of the EITC as a proportion of transfers has made its employment requirement all the more important to poor families. In the United States today, employment is the key to obtaining income transfers.

The transfer programs we have now, including TANF and the EITC, go to extraordinary lengths to induce recipients to work, probably to counteract the enormous work disincentives that flow from their contingency on income. To induce work, EITC provides its 40 percent wage subsidy over the first $10,000 of earned income, and TANF has work requirements and lifetime time limits on eligibility. These features, it was hoped, would counter the huge benefit reduction rates from TANF, Food Stamps, and other in-kind transfer programs that, in combination, can exceed 100 percent. Employment would have to have significant recreational value to be undertaken when it can take food off the table or clothes off the backs of children in poor families. PRWORA appears to be an attempt to shift the calculus from a continuous weighing of the benefits and the (prohibitive) costs of extra hours of work to an all-or-nothing choice—work or receive no benefits.

If, prior to 1996, one of the main efficiency costs of redistribution had been the reduction of work effort, PRWORA and the expanded EITC may appear to have been an effective antidote. If public sentiment is that welfare recipients can work and have a moral obligation to work, workfare would seem quite equitable. Superficial appearances, however, are far from sufficient in assessing either the efficiency or the equity implications of how we currently redistribute income. And there are problems with both PRWORA and the EITC on these grounds.

Even in the presence of stringent work requirements, high benefit reduction rates can alter work decisions and lead to an inefficient allocation of effort. Workers may work fewer hours than they would have worked without wage rate distortions. They may seek less demanding and lower paying jobs. They may acquire fewer new skills. Labor force participation decisions of additional adults in the family may be influenced. Finally, work requirements may induce some recipients to divert efforts away from the care of children, the elderly or disabled adults in the household to less valuable activity in the workplace.

The transfer of authority from the federal to state governments creates 50 different sets of TANF eligibility criteria and rules. This means that in the United States there can be as many as 50 definitions of who is sufficiently poor to warrant financial assistance, how much assistance will be given, and how long the assistance will last (within federal limits). A given family might be considered impoverished and worthy of cash assistance in one state but be deemed ineligible elsewhere. This is questionable on equity grounds.

The EITC penalizes work in its phase-out range. The benefit reduction rate of 21 percent represents a substantial increase in the effective marginal tax rate for families in the phase-out range. Families with earned income between $13,000 and $32,000 face federal and state income taxes and payroll taxes in addition to a transfer reduction of $0.21 on every dollar earned. Their effective marginal tax rate can easily fall in the range of 50 percent to 60 percent.

If the vast majority of EITC recipients were to fall in the phase-in and constant ranges of the program, work disincentives in the phase-out range would not be a problem. However, in 1996, 64.5 percent of the EITC population fell in the phase-out range, up from 50.2 percent just five years earlier. Also in 1996, only 25.6 percent of the EITC population fell in the phase-in range, which subsidized wages, down from 32.3 percent in 1991 (Hoffman and Seidman 2003: 49). In short, the EITC is work inducing for about one-third of its population and penalizes work for the other two-thirds. These proportions have worsened with time. Further, as noted earlier, the work penalty per dollar earned has increased. The benefit reduction rate in the phase-out range doubled during the 1990s. Combined with these efficiency concerns is the questionable equity of giving families in the constant range a credit that is more than double the average credit received by low-income working families in the phase-in range (Hoffman and Seidman 2003: 44).

Finally, the EITC excludes about 65 percent of poor families because they have no earnings or are demographically ineligible, failing the age or child tests (Hoffman and Seidman 2003: 41). Even if our concern with these programs were exclusively for the poor population under age 65, almost half are excluded. Of the non-elderly poor, 25 percent are excluded because they have no earned income and 22 percent because they are under age 25 and have no children (calculations based on Hoffman and Seidman 2003: 38).

The EITC, then, excludes almost half of the poor population under age 65, rewards poorer working families less than it rewards working families with somewhat higher incomes, and penalizes work for a large proportion of its recipients. Without question, almost any redistributive program will include work disincentives. In particular, a BIG could be structured with the same 21 percent benefit reduction rate as the phase-out range of the EITC, with the same $32,121 breakeven point, and provide a maximum transfer of $6,745; 68 percent higher than the EITC maximum transfer of $4,008. In 2008, the EITC breakeven point will increase to $35,121.Using this breakeven point, a BIG with a maximum transfer of $7,375 would be possible, a figure 84 percent higher than the maximum in the EITC. Even larger maximums and smaller benefit reduction rates would be possible for a BIG with a higher breakeven level of income. Under a BIG, the maximum transfer would accrue to families with no income, transfers could be structured to diminish consistently with income, and the net transfer could apply to the entire population within the applicable income range. Of course, a much larger budget would be required to finance a BIG.

Whether either efficiency or equity is served best by programs that have stringent work requirements, eligibility time limits, and wage subsidies (despite the many problems produced by these structural attributes) depends, in part, on the characteristics of the poor and the degree to which the poor are homogeneous. This is the impetus for the discussion in the next section.

Some Characteristics of Poor Households

Poor households are a more heterogeneous group than is often recognized. Very poor households, with incomes at or near zero, are distinct in many ways from the less severely poor with incomes above $15,000. To the extent that impoverished household heads are *unable* to work, welfare reform will not reduce their poverty and probably will increase it. Indeed, the income guarantee for workfare is zero in some cases and is at low levels in other cases. The EITC transfer for a household with zero earned income is zero. The TANF for some households with zero earned incomes begins at low levels, and is zero if time limits have been exceeded. Indeed, both programs raise serious questions regarding vertical equity, especially when one understands the characteristics of the poorest households. Social Security Disability Insurance (SSDI) addresses part of the equity problem produced by TANF and EITC, but it does so incompletely and with problematic work disincentives of its own.

To measure key differences among poor households, this research employs data generated by the Medical Expenditures Panel Survey (MEPS), compiled by the Agency for Healthcare Research and Quality in the Department of Health and Human Services. This survey data lets us obtain measures of health and disability across household heads at different income levels. The data comes from surveys of approximately 8,000 households containing about 22,000 individuals. To generalize from a non-representative sample, the survey designers developed weights that attach to each household. These weights adjust household responses so that sample statistics are representative of the United States population. Survey protocols allow the researcher some discretion in judging the credibility of respondents' answers and in adjusting those answers under specified conditions.

If the popular conception of very poor households is that they are headed by a group of able-bodied people who work less and earn less than households with higher incomes due to lack of motivation, opportunity, or training, the data suggest

Table 11.1 Health status of household head by annual household income level: Population under 65 years old (MEPS data, 1996)

Annual Household Income	Percent in Fair to Poor Health	Percent in Good Health	Percent in Very Good to Excellent Health
<= 0	37.1	22.9	40.0
1–5,000	22.0	31.2	46.8
5,001–10,000	25.4	32.0	42.5
10,001–15,000	20.0	27.2	52.9
15,001–20,000	14.1	29.4	56.5
20,001–25,000	14.3	24.1	61.5
25,001–30,000	8.7	29.6	61.6
> 30,000	6.9	22.7	70.4

Source: Author's calculations using the MEPS data.

that such a conception is flawed. Table 11.1 presents data on the health of household heads at different levels of household income. The definition of household income used in this table is all personal income, including transfers and excluding gains or losses from asset sales.

While more than one in three household heads have significant health problems among the very poor, one in seven heads have such health problems in households with income in the $15,000 to $20,000 range, and only one in twelve household heads have such poor health in the $25,000 to $30,000 income range. At household incomes of $30,000 and above, the comparable ratio is almost one in fifteen. Health status varies systematically and quite substantially with household income, and the ability to work differs by income.[1]

Ability to work, of course, is influenced by more than physical health. MEPS includes an assessment of the "complete inability to work," and contains other indicators that can be used to proxy a significant limitation on the ability to work. Using MEPS, I constructed a measure to indicate "some ability to work but with significant limitations." The binary indicator was coded "1" if the household head was not categorized as completely unable to work but had one or more of the following: poor physical health (the lowest of the five levels of health status), poor mental health (the lowest of the five levels of mental health status), significant cognitive impairment, significant impairment to social functioning. Table 11.2 displays the results.

More than 46 percent of the poorest households are headed by people with either a complete inability to work or a significant limitation on their ability to work. For households with incomes in the $15,000 to $20,000 range, the rate is about 19 percent; this rate falls to just under 11 percent for households with income above $30,000. Research using the National Survey of America's Families (Zedlewski and Alderson 2001) indicates that, despite TANF's incentives and requirements, a family's obstacles to work play a substantial role in whether the adults in a family do work. Obstacles in this study are defined as: education less than high school; having a child under one year of age; having a child receiving SSI; having a Spanish language interview (implying lack of fluency in English); either health limits or very poor mental health; and lack of employment for at least three years. Among adult TANF recipients in 1999, 20 percent had no barriers, 40 percent had only one barrier and 40 percent had two or more barriers. Of those with no barriers, 56 percent were working for pay and 26 percent were looking for work. Among those with one barrier, 33 percent were working for pay and 20 percent were looking for work. Of those with two or more barriers, only 20 percent were working for pay and 30 percent were looking for work (Zedlewski and Alderson 2001). In short, 80 percent of adult recipients faced significant obstacles to work, and 40 percent faced more than one such barrier. These barriers manifest themselves in much lower rates of employment.

States are allowed to exempt no more than 20 percent of their caseloads from time limits and as many as 50 percent from work requirements. More research is

Table 11.2 Limitations on ability to work of household head by income category: Population under 65 years old (MEPS data, 1996)

Annual Family Income	Complete Inability to Work (%)	Some Ability to Work, but With Significant Limitations (%)	Complete or Partial Inability to Work (%)
<=0	25.8	20.6	46.4
1–5,000	7.5	22.0	29.5
5,001–10,000	15.4	20.9	36.3
10,001–15,000	6.9	19.4	26.3
15,001–20,000	5.5	13.7	19.2
20,001–25,000	4.2	13.3	17.5
25,001–30,000	3.7	9.3	13.0
> 30,000	2.1	8.7	10.8

Source: Author's calculations using the MEPS data.

needed to see the extent to which states are exercising their options to grant these exemptions and to determine how problematic these constraints are. It is clear that it is not appropriate to try to put all of the poor to work, especially the very poor; and among those for whom it might be appropriate, it is not likely to be highly successful, even within a lengthy period of time.

Addressing Poverty

Poverty reduction is a primary goal of welfare policy in most countries. The question then arises: How have the poor in the United States faired in the periods before and after the welfare reforms of the mid-1990s? Recognizing that families in poverty are not all the same, it can be useful to look at the incomes and sources of income among some subsets of the poor. Of particular interest are single-mother

Table 11.3 Average family income by source (1997 dollars): Single-mother families in the poorest decile

	Poorest Decile			Absolute Changes		Percent Changes	
	1993	1995	1997	1993–1995	1995–1997	1993–1995	1995–1997
Earnings	820	973	862	153	(111)	18.7%	(11.4%)
EITC	123	250	261	127	11	103.3%	4.4%
Means-tested income	2,778	3,369	2,754	591	(615)	21.3%	(18.3%)
AFDC/TANF	1,191	1,209	1,112	18	(97)	1.5%	(8.0%)
Food Stamps	977	1,364	1,149	387	(215)	39.6%	(15.8%)
Other	1,167	1,095	996	(72)	(99)	(6.2%)	(9.0%)
Total Disposable Income	4,888	5,687	4,873	799	(814)	16.3%	(14.3%)
Earnings as Percent of Disposable Income	16.8%	17.1%	17.7%				

Source: Primus et al. (additional calculations by the author).

families in the two poorest income deciles. These are families whose after-transfer incomes range between 0 and 75 percent of the poverty line (Primus et al. 1999). Table 11.3 shows that, despite the new emphasis on employment, single-mother families in these deciles lost income as a result of the reforms. More notably, they lost ground in *earned* income—with reductions by 11.4 percent in the poorest decile and 10.0 percent in the second decile (see Table 11.4). On average, workfare did not put them to work.

Hardest hit were the single-mother families in the poorest decile. Their disposable income grew 16.3 percent between 1993 and 1995, helped by an 18.7 percent

Table 11.4 Average family income by source (1997 dollars): Single-mother families in the second poorest decile

	Second Decile			Absolute Changes		Percent Changes	
	1993	1995	1997	1993–1995	1995–1997	1993–1995	1995–1997
Earnings	1,722	2,438	2,193	716	(245)	41.6%	(10.0%)
EITC	220	549	685	329	136	149.5%	24.8%
Means-tested income	6,971	6,971	6,679	—	(292)	0.0%	(4.2%)
AFDC/ TANF	3,228	3,104	2,562	(124)	(542)	(3.8%)	(17.5%)
Food Stamps	2.360	2,377	2,547	17	170	0.7%	7.2%
Other	1,391	1,626	1,708	235	82	16.9%	5.0%
Total Disposable Income	10,304	11,584	11,265	1,280	(319)	12.4%	(2.8%)
Earnings as Percent of Disposable Income	16.7%	21.0%	19.5%				

Source: Primus et al. (additional calculations by the author).

increase in earned income, a 103.3 percent increase in the EITC, and a 21.3 percent increase in means-tested income. After the reforms, from 1995 to 1997, their disposable incomes fell by 14.3 percent, due to an 11.4 percent decline in earned income, a modest 4.4 percent increase in the EITC, and a decline in means-tested income of 18.3 percent (an 8.0 percent reduction in AFDC/TANF and a 15.8 percent reduction in food stamps). Before the welfare reforms, progress reducing poverty was made on grounds of both earned income and transfers, and it occurred at a rapid pace. After reforms, the very poorest lost income from both of these sources, and poverty reduction slowed considerably.

The effects in the second poorest decile were similar, albeit somewhat less bleak (Table 11.4). Single-mother families in the second decile saw their disposable income fall 2.8 percent from 1995 to 1997. Their 10 percent decline in earned income and 17.5 percent reduction in AFDC/TANF were offset by a 24.8 percent increase in the EITC and a 7.2 percent increase in the value of food stamps. For these households, workfare led to a decline in wage income and a significant increase in government wage subsidies (EITC).

It should come as no surprise that workfare is most effective among the least poor of the poor. More importantly, we should recognize that workfare can worsen the poverty of the poorest, those who can least likely improve their own lot and who are most deserving of help. It is difficult to find an equity criterion that would be consistent with this outcome. Interestingly, the levels of AFDC/TANF and Food Stamp transfers going to single-mother families in the poorest decile are less than half the levels going to such families in the second decile. It is expected that the EITC payments would be higher among families in the second decile, since EITC is a positive function of income; however, AFDC/TANF and Food Stamp transfers should be greater for the poorest families.

An examination of the income and its sources in the next two deciles (the third and fourth deciles) reveals a different picture. Table 11.5 shows that in the period just after the reforms (1995–1997), average family income managed to stay about the same, increasing less than 1 percent; however, the composition of that income was markedly different. Earned income and EITC transfers rose (18.2 percent and 41 percent, respectively), while means-tested income sources, such as AFDC /TANF and Food Stamps, fell (by 22.6 percent and 22.7 percent, respectively). In short, a significant reduction in means-tested transfers was largely offset by increases in earnings and the EITC. Those whose disposable incomes place them between 75 percent and 112 percent of the poverty line were able to do little more than tread water. On average, their poverty status did not change.

As with the lowest quintile, families in the second quintile saw much more progress in escaping poverty before the reforms than after; and the greatest progress in the 1993–1995 period (before the welfare reforms) had been in earned income (Table 11.5). After the reforms, progress from growth in earned income diminished, even in a period of robust national economic growth.

These statistics help us construct a picture of poverty before and after the 1996 reforms; however, a multivariate statistical analysis is required to draw inferences about the relative effects of the three major influences that were occurring simultaneously—the imposition of time limits via the welfare reforms; an expansion of the EITC; and a rapidly growing economy. One such study (Grogger 2001) finds that, for female-headed families, time limits on welfare eligibility reduced welfare participation substantially and led to lower family earnings and income. Grogger also suggests that time limits may hasten job search, leading to more mismatches and so shorter job duration and lower wages. His finds that the EITC reduced welfare rolls to a greater extent than the time limits, but that economic growth accounted for a substantial proportion of the decline in welfare use and the growth in employment.

The evidence available suggests that welfare participation and employment, while important, are quite incomplete as measures of the well-being of the poor. Further, favorable changes in these measures are attributable not simply to the 1996 reforms and the growth of the EITC but also to the growth of the economy.

Table 11.5 Average family income by source (1997 dollars): Single-mother families in the second quintile (third and fourth deciles)

	Second Quintile			Absolute Changes		Percent Changes	
	1993	1995	1997	1993–1995	1995–1997	1993–1995	1995–1997
Earnings	3,314	4,956	5,857	1,642	901	49.5%	18.2%
EITC	454	971	1,369	517	398	113.9%	41.0%
Means-tested income	7,621	7,587	6,124	(34)	(1,463)	(0.4%)	(19.3%)
AFDC/ TANF	3,533	3,248	2,513	(285)	(735)	(8.1%)	(22.6%)
Food Stamps	2,301	2,333	1,803	32	(530)	1.4%	(22.7%)
Other	2,044	2,233	2,507	189	274	9.2%	12.3%
Total Disposable Income	13,433	15,747	15,857	2,314	110	17.2%	0.7%
Earnings as Percent of Disposable Income	24.7%	31.5%	36.9%				

Source: Primus et al. (additional calculations by the author).

The Basic Income Guarantee Alternative—Framing Some Issues

BIG can be conceived either as an alternative to, or as an adjunct to, existing welfare programs. Conceiving it as an alternative provides the greatest likelihood that the BIG would be sufficient for a family to subsist. That is because, relative to existing welfare programs, the BIG would provide larger transfers to the poorest families; and the financing for a BIG can probably be maximized if it is funded as a substitute for current welfare programs. Conceived in either way, a BIG would be superior to our current welfare system.

First, in seeking to ensure everyone a minimum standard of living, a BIG is likely to rank first among the set of policy options. Insofar as a BIG would replace current programs, it would replace a system that increases benefits as income increases (at least over low levels of income) with one that aids the neediest the most. In so doing, it would improve the relative benefits and could improve the absolute benefits flowing to those who are unable to work. It would very likely represent an improvement in vertical equity.

Second, a BIG would provide cash benefits without the need for eligibility assessment, obviating most of the administrative expenses in existing welfare plans and allowing recipients to purchase the goods that most meet their needs.

Third, BIG would replace the large benefit reduction rates in existing welfare programs with a smaller benefit reduction rate. A family currently receiving some combination of TANF, EITC, in-kind benefits such as Food Stamps or Housing Subsidies, and SSDI (Social Security Disability Income) can face a cumulative benefit reduction rate exceeding 100 percent. Sometimes participation in even one or two of these programs implies a benefit reduction rate of 100 percent or higher. The current United States redistribution system thus chooses large work disincentives and probably a smaller national income in order to achieve the benefits of targeting. The costs of targeting may be larger and the benefits smaller than many perceive them to be.

Fourth, determining whether a recipient's efforts are more productively applied in the home or in the workplace would be left to that person rather than to government; and the recipient will choose to ensure an efficient outcome.

Fifth, horizontal inequities in the current mosaic of welfare programs and preferential tax treatments could be reduced substantially if these programs were replaced by a BIG.

Finally, the greatly simplified program entailed in a BIG, along with the absence of the stigma attached to current welfare programs, should result in a larger participation rate than with current programs such as Food Stamps and TANF.

The most telling arguments against a BIG include two that are substantive and one that is political. One substantive argument concerns the volume of transfers needed to achieve an acceptable income guarantee relative to the amount of transfers needed to finance more targeted programs. A BIG is often conceived as a gross transfer from the entire population to the entire population, resulting in net recipients and net donors. A program that distributes to each family in the population enough to constitute a minimum income guarantee is likely to imply a greater volume of transfers than programs that target much smaller subsets of the population. Insofar as a BIG involves a greater volume of transfers, a higher marginal tax rate will have to be applied to the net donor population in order to finance it.

A second substantive argument pertains to the benefit reduction rate. Keeping such a rate low means that work disincentives are low; however, a low benefit reduction rate implies a larger recipient population and a smaller net donor population. In turn, a smaller net donor population implies that a higher marginal tax rate would have to be applied to achieve the required financing, and this increases the work disincentive effects for net donors.

The political argument against BIG is the often-cited conclusion that it is easier to legislate a policy by making small, incremental changes to the status quo than to dismantle a very long list of existing programs and replace them with a costly alternative. The real and perceived losers in moving to a BIG could constitute a serious political obstacle; and it is unclear whether legislators could muster enough political support from the winners to make this cause worth their effort.

The National Tax Rebate Proposal

The Institute for SocioEconomic Studies has advanced a proposal by Leonard M. Greene for The National Tax Rebate (Greene 1998). It is designed to realize the advantages of a BIG and to minimize the inherent problems. This proposal has three major features: (1) Cash payments to individuals (annually about $4,000 to each adult and $2,000 to each child) regardless of income; (2) treating these payments as taxable income but not otherwise reducing benefits; and (3) financing the program by eliminating other welfare programs and tax expenditures, and by treating the transfer as taxable income.

These features yield a program that is sensitive to the fact that family need varies by family size; that keeps work disincentives to a minimum; and would claim no new resources for its financing. A family of two adults and two children would receive $12,000 per year. If we add the earnings from one full-time jobholder, even at the minimum wage, the family would be lifted above the poverty line.

Simulations of this plan (Garfinkel et al. 1997) forecast improvements in average after-transfer income in each of the bottom three quintiles of the population (relative to the then current set of transfer programs). The lower the quintile, the greater the improvement in disposable income. Further simulations suggest significant redistributions within each quintile, probably indicating an improvement in horizontal equity.

It is difficult to estimate the effects of this program on work effort. Relative to the pre-1996 set of programs, it is likely that the National Tax Rebate would have led to increased work effort. That is because it would replace programs having very large benefit reduction rates. However, the 1996 reforms brought work requirements and time limits. Work requirements turned welfare programs into all-or-nothing options for most potential recipients. Either the poor obtained at least part-time employment or they became ineligible for TANF. This countered the work disincentive effects for labor force participation, but it left in place work disincentives regarding decisions to find full-time work rather than part-time, decisions to work overtime, decisions to find better paying jobs; and decisions for an additional family member to work (Coe et al. 1998). However, as suggested earlier in this paper, increased work effort is not uniformly desirable across the poor population. Large proportions of the poor are unable to work, and still other poor individuals can better use their time in the home caring for children and the elderly.

Conclusion

The perception that the 1996 welfare reforms have been successful is probably unwarranted. Much of that perception rests on the faulty assumption that smaller welfare rolls imply reduced poverty and more gainful employment. Among the poorest of the poor (lowest quintile, single-mother families), total disposable income has fallen; and that decline has been in earned income as well as transfer income. Among the less poor, disposable income has changed little, but there have been notable changes in its composition. Earned income has increased but this has been offset almost entirely by decreases in transfer income.

United States welfare programs provide a very low safety net, with very low minimum incomes for the poorest segments of the populations. If accurately understood, this state of affairs likely would be perceived as inconsistent with common notions of vertical equity. Indeed, the situation may worsen in ways not fully anticipated as we experience more and deeper recessions and as time limits expire on welfare receipt.

In the wake of the 1996 welfare reforms and the rapid growth of the EITC, the United States has chosen to make income redistribution contingent on work. In so doing, it has chosen to exclude large proportions of the poor and subject large proportions of recipients to prohibitive benefit reduction rates. It attempts to counter work disincentives with wage subsidies, work requirements, and eligibility time limits that have problematic effects. Moreover, many of the poor cannot work, and some of the poor who are able to work can use their efforts more valuably in the household. A BIG would not be free of equity and efficiency problems; however, it is hard to imagine that its inequities and inefficiencies would be nearly so severe as our present problems.

BIG represents a valuable alternative to our reformed welfare system. Depending on its structure, it could yield a distribution of income that most people would consider superior to the status quo. In its simplicity, it would eliminate the wasted administrative resources now devoted to the income transfer process. It would reduce work disincentives. The stigma of receiving transfers would be eliminated, since everyone would receive them, thereby reducing many problematic participation effects that we have now. Finally, BIG would improve horizontal equity, treating equally needy people in similar ways rather than aiding them differently as the current mix of programs is likely to do.

Notes

* The author thanks Steven Pressman and two anonymous referees for helpful comments. Responsibility for remaining errors is the author's alone. Support from the Institute for SocioEconomic Studies is acknowledged with gratitude.

[1] Household income (Tables 11.1 and 11.2) is nominal and unadjusted for household size. While the average household size does increase systematically as household income increases, the change is small. In addition, it is common to assume that there are significant economies of scale in translating money income into household consumption. The equivalence income formula for comparing household incomes where household size differs that is recommended by Smeeding and Rainwater (2002) would do little to affect this table.

References

Blank, R. (2002) "Evaluating Welfare Reform in the United States," *Journal of Economic Literature*, 40: 1105–1166.

Coe, N. et al. (1998) "Does Work Pay? A Summary of the Work Incentives Under TANF," Urban Institute Discussion Paper.

Hoffman, S. and Seidman, L. (2003) *Helping Working Families: The Earned Income Tax Credit,* (Kalamazoo: W. E. Upjohn Institute for Employment Research).

Garfinkel, I., Huang, C.-C., Naidich, W. (1997) "Effects of Tax Rebates on Poverty and Income Distribution," Institute for SocioEconomic Studies.

Greene, L. (1998) *The National Tax Rebate: A New America with Less Government,* (Washington, D.C.: Regnery).

Grogger, J. (2001) "The Effects of Time Limits and Other Policy Changes on Welfare Use, Work, and Income Among Female-Headed Families," National Bureau of Economic Research Working Paper.

Primus, W. et al. (1999) *The Initial Impacts of Welfare Reform on the Incomes of Single Mother Families,* (Washington, D.C.: Center on Budget and Policy Priorities).

Primus, W. (2001) "Comment," in *The New World of Welfare,* R. Blank and R. Haskins (eds.), (Washington, D.C.: Brookings Institution).

Smeeding, T. and Rainwater, L. (2002) "Comparing Living Standards Across Nations: Real Incomes at the Top, the Bottom, and the Middle," Luxembourg Income Study Working Paper.

Zedlewski, S. and Alderson, D. (2001) "Do Families on Welfare in the Post-TANF Era Differ From Their Pre-TANF Counterparts?," Urban Institute Discussion Paper.

Chapter 12

Back to Work Incentives in a Dynamic Perspective: An Application to French Labor Markets

Thierry Laurent and Yannick L'Horty*

Introduction

Most European countries have adopted a "guaranteed minimum income" device that works on a purely differential basis. These mechanisms are efficient and cheap weapons to fight monetary poverty, as far as the level of guaranteed income is fixed above poverty line. On the other hand, these mechanisms can cause *work* incentive problems; especially when each additional Euro from wages implies one Euro less from minimum income transfers. This problem is magnified by other means-tested social transfers given to those at the bottom of the wage distribution. All in all, it leads to high marginal tax rates for poorer households (i.e., more than 100 percent), especially for parents with (many) children.

An institutional answer to these problems lies in making work pay. Of course, one can increase the minimum wage, but this won't be sufficient. Everywhere, the minimum wage is fixed on an hourly basis; it does not prevent low incomes for people who work a short time or with a labor contract that leads them to alternate between working times and unemployment during a year. For this reason, more and more European countries have adopted back to work allowances, following the example of the United State's Earned Income Tax Credit (EITC) or the British Working Families Tax Credit (WFTC). France is one of the European followers. Since autumn 2001, the Prime pour l'Emploi (employment bonus), a fiscal credit, has been given to 8.5 million low-wage households. Other examples include the Earned Income Tax Allowance created in 1991 in Finland, and the Labor Tax Credit introduced in 2001 in the Netherlands.

The present chapter discusses the capacity of such back-to-work allowances to solve work incentive problems. At the same time, it questions whether minimum guaranteed incomes always cause incentive troubles. Our starting point is that work incentive studies often rely on a static approach. This is particularly true in France (Laroque and Salanié 2000, Gurgand and Margolis 2001, Bourguignon 2001). However, a monetary loss associated with accepting a part-time job can be outweighed by favorable job prospects; symmetrically, an immediate monetary gain can lead to job immobility. In other words, work can pay immediately but not in the long run, or work can pay in the long run but not immediately.

We suggest modeling labor force participation decisions in an inter-temporal framework to better value back to work gains for unemployed people. These gains include worker mobility between jobs. We use the observed probabilities of transitions between different kind of jobs on the French labor market for different categories of workers (age, gender, skills, etc.), and the observed incomes associated with each kind of job, to identify the categories of workers that face inactivity or poverty trap problems.[1]

Our empirical results show that there is no obvious link between a static trap (work does not pay immediately) and long-run labor force participation problems (work does not pay at all, considering short- and long-run gains). In other words income guarantees *can* create a static trap, but this does not *necessarily* create work incentive problems. The labor force participation argument generally advanced against minimum income schemes is thus weakened.[2]

We first set forth a general framework and raise some questions about the static labor-force participation approach. Then we present a dynamic model of the labor decision. The last section presents some empirical results regarding the French labor market.

Static Analysis

From a static viewpoint, work incentive problems stem from a simple comparison between the revenues associated with work and non-work. The work decision depends on the marginal disutility of work and the revenue change associated with a transition between different states on the employment market: inactivity and employment, or part-time and full-time work, for example.

Formally, a static analysis requires us to build a revenue vector corresponding to the net gains of each labor market state. If the difference between net income associated with high and low employment levels is small relative to the marginal disutility of work, there is a work incentive problem: Work does not pay enough to induce an unemployed or underemployed worker to accept a job offer. To illustrate these effects in the French case, we first present the work incentive problem in the French system. We will then see that the facts from French statistical surveys do not support the existence of such a problem.

The French Back to Work Problem: An Overview

In the 1990s, French economic growth was low compared to that of the United States. Gross Domestic Product (GDP) grew 1.3 percent until the end of 1996, and unemployment reached 12.6 percent. Since 1997, GDP growth has been 3 percent, 1.7 million of jobs were created, and unemployment declined to 8.5 percent by the summer of 2002. Economic growth doesn't explain all this employment growth. New labor-market policies also helped create jobs. Since the beginning of the

Table 12.1 National Minimum Income (Revenu Minimum d'Insertion—RMI)

	RMI / month
Single	€405
Couple	€405 + 50%= €607
Couple with *n* children	€607 + $n \times 30\%$

1990s several French governments cut taxes on those with low incomes, and these targeted tax cuts were used to reduce working time to 35 hours a week.

To identify the main incentive problems in France we present a quick overview of the three main components of the French minimum income/minimum wage schedule.

First, the Revenu Minimum d'Insertion (RMI) was implemented in 1988. This guaranteed minimum income is given to the household without any conditions except that you are a French resident (there is no nationality condition) and at least 25 years old (18 is the European norm). Benefits increase with family size using an equivalence scale that replicates the Organisation for Economic Co-operation and Development (OECD) one (i.e., 150 percent of the single allowance for a couple, plus 30 percent for each child). By 2004, there were more than one million RMI recipients.

In the long run, there is a perfect substitution between the minimum income and wages; each Euro obtained from wages implies the loss of one Euro from the RMI, if people are still recipients of the RMI. In the short run, there is a temporary back to work allowance in France as well as in most European countries with a generous minimum income device: Recipients can cumulate half of their wage with RMI benefits during one year at most.

The RMI is a national social transfer. A second level in the French system occurs at the local level. Local transfers vary across areas. Unfortunately, we cannot compute the average local transfer; the only source available is a survey covering 10 areas in France including 3 major cities (Paris, Lyon and Marseille) and a few middle and small towns (Anne and L'Horty, 2002). From this survey, average Local Monetary Assistance is as described in Table 12.2.

Table 12.2 Local Monetary Assistance (LMA)

	LMA / month
Single	€136
Couple	€150
Couple, 1 child	€300
Couple, 2 children	€370
Couple, 3 children	€450

Finally, when former RMI recipients get jobs they usually get paid the minimum wage, the Salaire Minimum de Croissance (SMIC). Generally, they also get state aid labor contracts, and the SMIC is the main reference for such contracts. The calculations below give the monthly wage associated with full-time versus part-time jobs:[3]

SMIC is €5.4 / hour (after withholding), thus:

Full-time Jobs (39 hours/week)	=>	€969 / month
Part-time Jobs (20 hours/week)	=>	€484 / month

A single unemployed person with RMI and local aid earns on average €405 + €136 = €541/month (i.e., more than a 20 hour per week part-time worker). Such individuals should therefore refuse part-time job offers, and so we get a work incentive problem. Unemployed individuals would be *voluntarily* unemployed because they prefer income guarantees to part-time jobs. This is the so-called "inactivity" or "poverty trap": People get trapped into long-run unemployment with a decreasing probability of finding better jobs (due to loss of ability).

The main limitation of this approach is that it narrows the work incentive question to a comparison of the immediate gains associated with work and non-work. However, consumption/leisure choices are by nature inter-temporal.

What Can we Learn from Statistical Surveys?

In the French system, accepting a half-time job should be a very rare occurrence according to the static approach explained above. To examine this prediction, the best statistical source is the 1998 INSEE survey on Minimum Income Recipients. This survey raises many questions about the static analysis (see Afsa 1999 for details). First, nearly one-third of minimum income recipients who return to work claim no financial gain from doing so: 12.1 percent claim to be losing money, and 20.4 percent claim they are not gaining anything. Second, although minimum income beneficiaries generally claim to be looking for a full-time job, most say that they would accept a part-time job; moreover, among the January 1997 minimum income recipients who held employment one year later, nearly two-thirds had a part-time job.

Thus, the static analysis does not explain why France experienced a significant growth of low-wage part-time jobs in the 1990s. If these jobs do not pay, why do some people accept them? In addition, it seems that some workers accept jobs that do not pay. This chapter seeks to solve this labor market puzzle. We suggest that if some RMI-unemployed individuals accept low-wage, part-time jobs that do not pay immediately, it is because they think such a decision will pay in the future. Those people who do not accept these jobs think that, *for them*, it will not pay in the future. To test this hypothesis requires departing from the standard static analysis and developing a dynamic inter-temporal analysis of the work incentive problem.

Dynamic Analysis

In a dynamic framework, someone offered a job will not only consider the immediate benefits, but also the fact that job tenure increases the probability of a better job and higher wages in the future. A monetary loss from accepting a part-time job can be outweighed by favorable job prospects. In this case, unemployment income is higher than employment income (static trap), but this does not imply a dynamic trap: Work does not pay in the short run, but it pays in the long run. Similarly, a positive immediate gain can lead to unfavorable job prospects. In this case, one does not have a static trap but a dynamic trap: Work pays immediately, but it does not pay in the long run.

A dynamic approach includes all the components of a static approach, but adds a new one: the possibility of future income improvements (due to the accumulation of human capital, the increasing probability of access to a better job, etc.). One can identify five components in the trade-off facing an unemployed worker offered a part-time job: the net income earned by remaining unemployed, the immediate wage associated with the job, the probabilities of getting better jobs in the future, the wages associated with these future jobs, and the agent's preferences regarding present and future incomes.

Modeling

Consider an unemployed person facing a part-time job offer that does not pay as much as the income guarantee, and who needs to make a decision concerning the job offer. The problem is not to compare the immediate incomes, but the present value of the income flows (current and future) for the two choices. To make this calculation, the agent needs to know the probabilities of getting other types of jobs in the future, conditional on the strategy he chooses immediately (i.e., all the possible transitions on the labor market associated with a decision made now).

Table 12.3 Transition Probabilities in the French Labor Market

Situation in date T	Situation in date T+1			
	Job ≥ 35 h	20h ≤ Job < 35h	Job < 20h	Unemployment
Job ≥ 35 h	0.75	0.15	0.07	0.03
20h ≤ Job < 35h	0.35	0.50	0.10	0.05
Job < 20h	0.32	0.20	0.38	0.10
Unemployment	0.15	0.18	0.30	0.37

Source: Employment Survey, INSEE, 2000 and 2001.

Table 12.4 Average earnings

Job ≥ 35 h	R_{FT}	€1132
20h ≤ Job < 35h	R_{LT}	€715
Job < 20h	R_{ST}	€447
Unemployment	R_U	€541

Such transition probabilities[4] summarize labor market flows. There are many important flows—from unemployment to part-time or full-time employment, from part-time to full-time employment or unemployment, etc. These can be summarized with a matrix giving the probabilities of transition between different labor market conditions (Table 12.3). The example above distinguishes unemployment and three employment situations: full-time job, long part-time job and short part-time job (less than 20 hours a week). The matrix gives all the probabilities of switching, during one period of time, from one situation to any other one for men and women combined. The sum of probabilities over a whole line is equal to one.

We can easily compute the average earnings for each situation (see Table 12.4). For example, if the average weekly labor time for long part-time jobs is 24 hours and workers in this category are paid on average 20 percent above the minimum income, the monthly (23 days) wage will be: (24h / 5) × [€5.4× (1 + 20%)] × 23 = €715. A similar computation gives the monthly wage for full-time workers. Unemployed individuals get the sum of National Minimum Income and Local Monetary Assistance (€541 as seen above).

For short part-time job workers, we need to distinguish two cases. If the worker labors 15 hours and is paid 20 percent above the minimum income, a calculation similar to the previous one gives us average earnings of €447. As this is greater than the National Minimum Income (€405), such a worker will not receive any money from the National Minimum Income policy and will receive very little Local Monetary Assistance. But if the worker is employed only 10 hours a week, monthly income is €298, which is less than the National Minimum Income. Such a worker will receive a €107 national subsidy and will be eligible for Local Monetary Assistance of €136, so that their income reaches €541. The earnings matrix in Table 12.4 assumes the former of the two possible cases for short part-time workers.

This example contains a static employment trap; work does not pay, at least not immediately. The important question is does work pay in the long run? Does an unemployed individual have an interest in accepting a short part-time job that does not pay immediately, but will pay in the long run? If the answer is yes, we do not have any incentive problem or a dynamic trap, despite the existence of a static trap.

The transition matrix, and the corresponding earnings vector, allows us to calculate the payment associated with two strategies "*I accept short part-time jobs*"

Table 12.5 Static/dynamic traps

	$R_{ST} > R_U$ **Work pays immediately**	$R_{ST} < R_U$ **Work does not pay immediately**
$P(S_A) > P(S_R)$ **Work pays in the long run**	No Static trap No Dynamic trap	Static trap No Dynamic trap
$P(S_A) < P(S_R)$ **Work does not pay in the long run**	No Static trap Dynamic trap	Static trap Dynamic trap

(S_A) and "*I refuse short part-time jobs*" (S_R). The payments $P(\cdot)$ corresponding to each of these strategies are evaluated by calculating the discounted expected value, which indicates how the individual weighs immediate gains and future gains. Comparison of the respective returns gives the answer to our question: If the payment for the strategy "*I accept short part-time jobs*" is greater than the return corresponding to the other strategy, there is no incentive problem and no dynamic trap; work pays in the long run. Table 12.5 provides a quick overview of these results on static and dynamic traps.

Further Considerations

The dynamic analysis set forth above underlines the key role of labor force mobility. A static approach to work incentives only focuses on the difference between current income associated with work and unemployment. It suggests a way to solve the French labor market puzzle. Some people accept short part-time jobs that do not pay because they think in a dynamic rather than a static way. And different people make different decisions concerning job acceptance because they have different transition probabilities in the labor market and/or different discount rates.

It seems reasonable to assume that labor market transition probabilities are not identical for all individuals; different kinds of workers have different transition matrixes. These reflect differences in human capital accumulation (skill level), geographic inequalities (urban versus rural areas), and labor market discrimination (men versus women, French versus foreigners). The optimal strategy for one type of individual is thus not necessarily optimal for another type, and we need to analyze the work incentive problem for each category of worker.

Heterogeneity of discount rates is the other side of the coin that explains the occurrence of different job decisions among unemployed individuals. Let us assume for simplicity that the set of transition probabilities is such that the higher the current hours of work, the higher the probability of getting a "better jobs" and the lower the probability of returning to unemployment or "bad jobs."[5] In such a situation an unemployed individual facing a short part-time job offer may accept the offer, even if it does not pay immediately because it may increase future income. But this requires the individual have a low discount rate; only under this additional condition will the individual value future earnings enough to endure the current loss of income associated with the job offer. An unemployed individual with a strong time preference rate does not value future expected income enough to accept the temporary cost of accepting a job. Hence, the greater the discount rate for an individual, the greater the risk that there will be an incentive problem and lower labor force participation.

Thus, there are three factors that affect the dynamic trap and labor force participation problems: (1) the size of the static trap, or the gap between current income without work and earnings from various employment situations, (2) mobility perspective, as given by the transition matrix, and (3) the discount rate used by an agent to evaluate the present value of inter-temporal income flows.

Given (2) and (3), the greater the static trap, the higher the probability a dynamic trap will occur. This result is quite straightforward: If the static trap is large, future wage improvements are unable to outweigh the negative effect of the static trap on labor force participation.

There thus exists a link between the static and dynamic traps: For a given transition matrix and discount rate, there always exists a critical value of the static trap such that, under the critical value there is no incentive problem or dynamic trap, but beyond that value an incentive problem and a dynamic trap arise.

Testing for Static and Dynamic Traps in the Labor Market

Empirical Background and Choices

In order to test for work incentive problems in the French labor market, we need to obtain the mobility prospects and the associated average earnings vectors for different categories of workers, and we need to identify the transition matrices of different types of workers.

Concerning the first point, we used the French Labor Force Surveys (INSEE)[6] for 2000 and 2001, restricted to private sector wage earners except apprentices, government assisted workers, and students. With this database one knows the number of workers in each of the four employment situations (unemployment, short part-time jobs, long part-time jobs and full-time jobs) and the number of people that shift, during the year, from one situation to another one. We can thus compute the probability transition from, say, situation A to B, as the number of workers that move from A to B between 2000 and 2001, divided by the total number of people belonging to A at time 2000. Doing this for the 16 components of the matrix, we get the whole transition matrix.

Average earnings for the different job situations are also available from the database.[7] For short part-time jobs, we used either the average income from the database or the €541 associated with inactivity, depending whether or not the former is higher than the €405 National Minimum Income (see *Further Considerations* in the Dynamic Analysis section of this chapter).

We then built a transition matrix for different worker categories, corresponding to the intersection of three of the following five criteria:

- Gender: Male or female
- Skills: High school diploma or no high school diploma
- Age: Young (under 35) or old (over 35)
- Nationality: French or foreigners
- Marital situation: Single or not single

The three leading factors driving the transition matrix are gender, age and skills; so we selected these three criteria to define eight types of workers, each of them characterized by a specific transition matrix and earnings vector. The implicit hypothesis is that each individual uses the transition matrix of a reference group (all the people under the same category of age, skills and gender) as a proxy for his own mobility prospects.

Computations and Main Results

The problem is *(i)* to compute, for these eight types of workers, the present discounted values $P(\cdot)$ corresponding to the strategies S_A and S_R and *(ii)* to compare the two results. One expects to find $P(S_A) > P(S_B)$ and no incentive-to-work problems for some people, but $P(S_A) < P(S_B)$ and labor force participation problems and a dynamic trap for others.

The easiest way to make such comparisons is to compute, for each type of worker, the value of the Incentive Compatible Maximal (ICM) static trap and then compare it to the effective value of the static trap: *RU–RST*. One can then present all the results by putting the values (Static Trap, ICM Static Trap) for each category of worker on a graph, with the static trap value on the x-axis and the ICM static trap value on the y-axis. If the corresponding dot lies above the 45° line, the value of the static trap is lower than the computed value of the ICM static trap, and

Table 12.6 Characteristics of the different types of workers

	Gender		Age		Skills	
Type	**Men**	**Women**	**Young**	**Old**	**≥ High school**	**< High School**
1	✓	—	✓	—	✓	—
2	✓	—	✓	—	—	✓
3	✓	—	—	✓	✓	—
4	✓	—	—	✓	—	✓
5	—	✓	✓	—	✓	—
6	—	✓	✓	—	—	✓
7	—	✓	—	✓	✓	—
8	—	✓	—	✓	—	✓

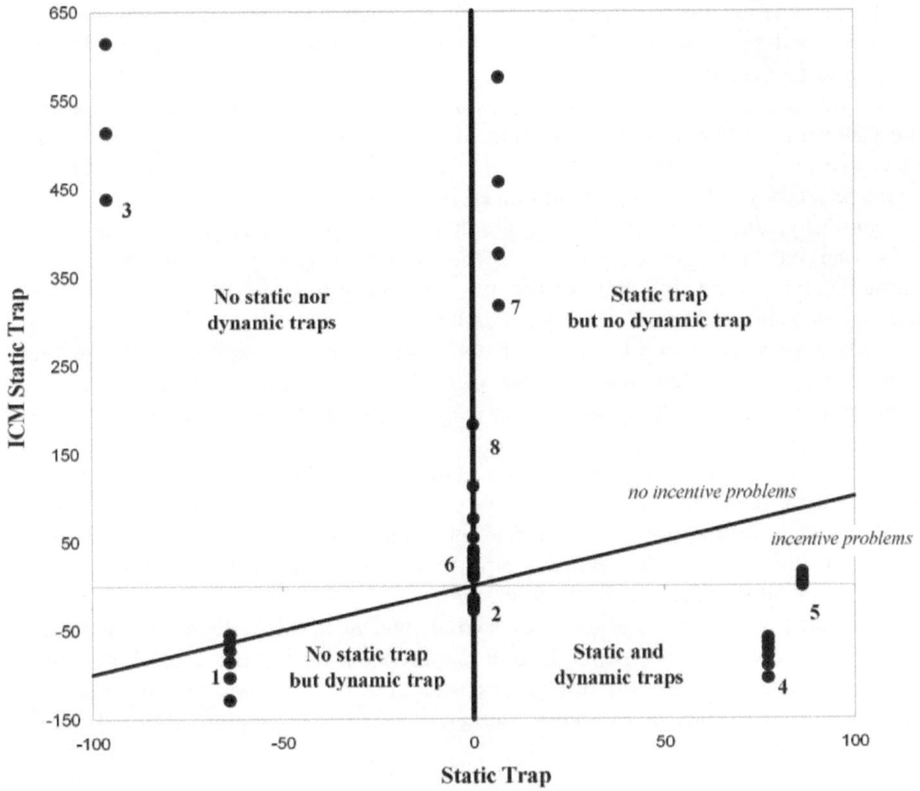

Figure 12.1 Static versus dynamic traps on the French labor market

there is no work incentive problem or dynamic trap. On the other hand, if the (Static Trap, ICM Static Trap) dot, lies below the 45° line, the value of the static trap exceeds the ICM static trap value, and we get a work incentive problem or dynamic trap. The graph in Figure 12.1 presents results for the eight types of workers depicted in Table 12.6.

Each worker category is not represented by a single dot, but rather by a set of six dots[8] that reflects the specific role played by the discount rate; one needs to remember that the discount rate is one factor that determines the present discounted value associated with job acceptance strategies and, consequently, the value of the ICM static trap. For each worker category one gets as many ICM static trap values as discount rate levels. Theoretically, for a particular type of worker, three results are possible:

- No dynamic trap; i.e., no incentive problems, whatever the level of the discount rate
- Dynamic trap; i.e., incentive problems, whatever the level of the discount rate
- Dynamic trap or no dynamic trap depending of the level of the discount rate

To investigate these different cases, we computed for each category the ICM static trap values corresponding to six different levels of the discount rate, from 1 percent to 50 percent.

As noted before, the 45° line divides the graph into two parts. Above the line, the static trap is lower than the computed ICM static trap value, and one has no incentive problems. The opposite arises in the area under the 45° line, which is characterized by a dynamic trap and incentive problems.

Similarly, the y-axis divides the graph into two parts. On the left side of the axis, one has a negative static trap, meaning that $R_{ST} > R_U$ and work pays immediately. On the right side of the axis, one has a positive static trap, meaning that $R_U > R_{ST}$ and work does not pay immediately.

This allows us to divide the graph into four areas, corresponding to the four traps configurations depicted in Table 12.5. All the possible static/dynamic traps configurations that might appear are shown in Table 12.7, and give us the following results.

First, the discount rate plays an important role concerning the computed value of ICM static trap (for the third category of workers this value goes from €438 to €1308) and is thus a potentially important parameter, to analyze work incentive problems. Furthermore, for the first type of workers, the existence of a dynamic trap depends of the level of the discount rate.

Second, for three worker categories (6, 7, and 8—all female categories) there are no work incentive problems despite the existence of a static trap. A part-time job does not pay in the short run (or is costly), but pays in the long run thanks to upward job transitions in the labor market. These results support those obtained

Table 12.7 Summary of the results

	Workers' characteristics						Traps configuration		
	Gender		Age		Skills		Static Trap		Dynamic Trap
Type	Men	Women	< 35	> 35	≥ High school	< High school	$R_U > R_{ST}$	$R_U = R_{ST}$	$P(S_A) < P(S_R)$
1	✓	—	✓	—	✓	—	—	—	✓*
2	✓	—	✓	—	—	✓	—	✓	✓
3	✓	—	—	✓	✓	—	—	—	—
4	✓	—	—	✓	—	✓	✓	—	✓
5	—	✓	✓	—	✓	—	✓	—	✓
6	—	✓	✓	—	—	✓	—	✓	—
7	—	✓	—	✓	✓	—	✓	—	—
8	—	✓	—	✓	—	✓	—	✓	—

**Note*: Occurrence of the dynamic trap depending on the discount rate.

from the 1998 INSEE survey on minimum income recipients, which stressed that more than 30 percent of beneficiaries of the minimum income support, who return to work, claim no financial gain.

Third, for one worker category (young skilled men) there is a work incentive problem despite the fact that a part-time job pays in the short run (no static trap). The corresponding transition matrix tells us that for these people the probability of getting a full-time job is higher when unemployed than as a short part-time worker; the probability to shift from unemployment to full-time is around 52 percent against 42 percent if coming from a short part-time job. Thus, for young skilled men it is better to refuse short part-time jobs because by accepting such jobs they can be trapped in them. They waste time that could be better used finding a full-time job, and they signal to employers a lack of self-confidence regarding their ability to find a full-time job. In brief, it is better for young skilled men to spend their time searching for a lucrative full-time job than to waste it by accepting a part-time, low-wage job.

Fourth, unskilled workers should accept short part-time jobs that do not pay immediately. Without a diploma, employers cannot observe their abilities, and a part-time job can signal their own productivity; such workers see part-time jobs as a first step that will allow them to move upward.

Fifth, in four categories the static and dynamic results match. For three of them (2, 4, and 5—unskilled men and young skilled women), the static trap is too large to be balanced by future upward labor market mobility and so we have both static and dynamic traps. In one category (3—old skilled men) there is no static trap and no dynamic trap.

Analyzing the transition matrices helps us understand the difference between categories 6, 7 and 8 (no dynamic trap despite a static trap) on one side and 2, 4 and 5 on the other side (both static and dynamic trap). In categories 2 and 6 the static trap is the same and equal to 0, meaning that there is no difference between income associated with unemployment and with a part-time job. Nonetheless, the optimal strategy is not the same for the two different types of workers; type 6 picks SA and accepts part-time jobs that do not pay in the short, but type 2 picks SR and refuses part-time jobs that do not pay in the short run.

This phenomenon highlights the key role played by mobility perspectives in a dynamic framework. For type 6 individuals, the probability of getting a full-time job when coming from unemployment is low (23 percent); thus the best way to get a full-time job is to accept a short part-time job (strategy SA), giving them a high probability of getting a long part-time job (44 percent) and a high probability of getting a full-time job (34 percent). For type 2 individuals, the probability of getting a full-time job when coming from unemployment is quite high (42 percent); and is higher than when coming from short part-time job (35 percent). For this type the best way to get a full-time is to refuse short part-time job (pick strategy SR) in order to jump directly from unemployment to a full-time job.

Conclusion

This chapter stressed the weakness of a static approach to labor force participation analysis and developed an inter-temporal approach to work incentive problems.

Concerning the first point, we have seen that there is no obvious link between the short- and long-run work incentive problems; for four of the eight categories analyzed, we find either a static trap but no dynamic trap or no static trap but a dynamic one. This underlines the limits of the static approach; a minimum income scheme is not a sufficient condition, nor a necessary condition, for incentive problems to arise. Some people will accept jobs that do not pay immediately because they will pay in the future, and others will refuse part-time jobs even if they do pay immediately (to avoid being trapped in part-time employment).

Turning to the second point, we think that the dynamic modeling proposed in the chapter offers a way to test for labor force participation problems and whether they exist in minimum income schemes. It allows us to distinguish between different kinds of individuals, and to analyze labor force participation decisions from a microeconomic point of view.

Notes

* We thank participants of the US BIG session at the 2003 Eastern Economic Association meeting and the 2003 European Association of Labor Economists meeting for helpful comments.

1 Burdett and Smith (2002) show that such traps can occur within a simple matching model, resulting in low-wage, low-skill workers.

2 This is also the main conclusion of Eissa and Liebman (1996) when looking at the US labor force response to the EITC.

3 If people get full-time jobs, they don't automatically work 35 hours a week, especially when employed by a small firm. For this reason we kept a 39-hour week for our calculations.

4 For examples using theses probabilities see Magnac and Robin (1994), Stewart and Swaffield (1999) or Dickens (2000).

5 The expressions "better job" and "bad job" refer here to just the following ranking: short part-time job < long part-time job < full-time job; we thus assume that people prefer to work more in order to earn more.

6 National Statistics and Economic Studies Institute. This survey is the official French source for computing employment and unemployment.

7 Earnings include all monetary bonuses and exclude social taxes on wages.

8 Upper dots corresponding to categories 3 and 7 lie out of the graph: ICM static trap values corresponding to type 3 workers lie between €438 and €1308; between €317 and €1081 for type 7.

References

Afsa, C. (1999) "L'insertion professionnelle des beneficiaires du revenu minimum d'insertion, Etudes et Statistiques", DREES, Ministère des Affaires sociales.

Anne D. and L'Horty Y. (2002) "Transferts sociaux locaux et retour à l'emploi," *Economie et Statistique*, 357–358: 49–70.

Bell, L. and Freeman, R. (2001) "The Incentive for Working Hard: Explaining Hours Worked Differences in the US and Germany," *Labour Economics*, 8: 181–202.

Bourguignon, F. (2001) "Revenu minimum et redistribution optimale des revenus: fondements théoriques," *Economie et Statistique*, 346–347: 187–204.

Burdett, K. and Smith, E. (2002) "The Low Skill Trap," *European Economic Review*, 46: 1439–1451.

Dickens, R. (2000) "Caught in a Trap? Wage Mobility in Great Britain: 1975–1994," *Economica*, 67: 477–497.

Eissa, N. and Liebman, J. (1996) "Labor Supply Response to the Earned Income Tax Credit," *Quarterly Journal of Economics*, 111: 605–637.

Finnie, R. and Gray, D. (2002) "Earnings Dynamics in Canada: An Econometric Analysis," *Labour Economics*, 9: 763–800.

Gurgand, M. and Margolis, D. (2001) "RMI et revenus du travail: une évaluation des gains financiers à l'emploi," *Economie et Statistique*, 346–347: 103–121.

Laroque, G. and Salanié, B. (2000) "Une décomposition du non emploi en France," *Economie et Statistique*, 331: 47–66.

Magnac, T. and Robin, J. (1994) "An Econometric Analysis of Labour Market Transitions Using Discrete and Tenure Data," *Labour Economics*, 1: 327–346.

Stewart, M. and Swaffield J. (1999) "Low Pay Dynamics and Transition Probabilities," *Economica*, 66: 23–42.

Chapter 13

Social Minima in Europe: The Risks of Cumulating Income-Sources

Stephen Bouquin*

Introduction

"Social Minima and Wage Labor: Europe Viewed From Below" is the title of a collective research project conducted between 1998 and 2001 in France, Germany, the United Kingdom and Belgium. The other researchers and I studied the benefit recipients of social minima, as well as low-wage workers, the unemployed, and the poor. The overview of the evolution of social minima can be summarized as a three-fold tendency toward the following:

- a reduction of the amount, the availability and the duration of entitlement.
- the generalization of minimal social benefits with universal access on the one hand and higher conditionality on the other.
- the possibility of drawing several incomes from social benefits and from working (not necessarily in wage labor).

These tendencies are part of and are driving forward the recommodification of wage labor (Jessop 1994; 2000; Pierson 2001), i.e., imposing greater market discipline on work, which transforms labor into a simple commodity that can be bought or sold without social constrains. On the sociological level, this process expresses itself through the fragmentation of the post-war "employment standard," i.e., fulltime work with unlimited contracts; and the equivalent "income standard", i.e., a high (household) wage assumed to be earned primarily (but not uniquely) by "male breadwinners." This fragmentation encompasses the following:

- mass unemployment with a growing portion of long-term unemployed people (an important, although unequal factor, in the countries in the study).
- an increase in poverty among unemployed, retired, and working people.
- a growing layer of "casual", "precarious" workers—those with uncertain work and income, and those with part-time and temporary contracts (see Tables 13.1 and 13.2).

- a layer of "stable" (well-qualified or knowledgeable) workers bound to employer-centered insurance schemes for health, unemployment, and pensions.

The figures in Tables 13.1 and 13.2 show how the workforce became more segmented between 1994 and 1998. In some countries (Spain and the United Kingdom) both male and female unemployed found less temporary work than before, while in other countries women account for most of the increase.

The transformation of social security systems has tended to reduce the distinction between the Anglo-Saxon, Scandinavian and continental models with a general dynamic toward segmented labor markets. A dualistic social security system has been created with a basic minimal (some are saying "universalist"), publicly funded "solidarity" scheme (more taxes and fewer contributions based on wages) in case of unemployment, sickness and retirement on the one hand, and private or mixed saving funds or insurance schemes for additional income guaranties on the

Table 13.1 Proportion of unemployed women who found a part-time job

	1990	1994	1998
Belgium	49	48	54.5
France	36	55	53.0
United Kingdom	54	56	60.0
Germany	47	45	40.0
Netherlands	57	78	75.6
Spain	14	23	27.0
European Union	30	42	40.0

Source: (Commission Européenne, 2000, 39).

Table 13.2 Proportion of unemployed population finding a temporary job

	Men		Women	
	1994	1998	1994	1998
Belgium	50	52	30	53.0
France	52	60	58	62.0
United Kingdom	22	20	23	19.0
Germany	36	43	40	48.0
Netherlands	37	48	41	47.5
Spain	92	89	89	83.0
European Union	23	20	50	55.0

Source: (Commission Européenne, 2000, 42–43).

other hand. Greater conditionality of social rights and the use of workfare are secondary aspects that appear in response to different elements that include the following:

- The "individualist revolt" of the "active" and higher-qualified population for whom the fiscal burden seems to be high and the system seems to be ineffective; the imposition of conditions and compliance policies makes the fiscal burden more politically *acceptable* to this group.
- "Benefit traps," in which unemployed people are discouraged from accepting work outside of their normal social and professional expectations because of the risk of losing their benefits.
- "Labor market dysfunction" forcing an increased availability of reserve workers on the supply side.
- Since the late nineties, governments have implemented "active policies" for which earning income from work is most important. These active policies were justified as a two-fold approach: "Making work pay" by using financial incentives to stimulate labor market entry; and reducing labor costs by making less-qualified workers attractive to employers.

Sometimes, these active policies are combined with compliance policies (workfare), and sometimes they include "in-work benefits," which allow recipients to combine public benefits with income from wage labor.

The semantic use of a distinction between "active" and "passive" policies makes it possible to stigmatize the traditional social welfare system as producing rigidities and keeping the unemployed out of the labor market by paying them for inactivity. Of course, there could be a correlation between these qualitative characteristics of social protection and the level of poverty, but recent research comparing social security systems has demonstrated that there is no causal link between the amount of benefits and the length of their grants to the level of unemployment (Gallie and Paugam 2001).

In this chapter, I present results of research on the effects of tax-credit systems and in-work benefits on the social situation of individuals and on the structure of the labor market. The underlying question of the analysis is whether we can speak of a "Speenhamland effect" on wages, by which I mean the negative impact that combining benefits with wage income can have on real wages.

Speenhamland was a county in Berkshire (England) where in 1795 judges decided to extend subsidies for infirm people to workers, as an "allowance system" against poverty (Polanyi 1974). This policy was a response to the increase in poverty that accompanied the second round of the enclosure movement (1790 to 1830), which privatized previously common land. The Speenhamland policy replaced other forms of social protection, and after a while, was extended to the manufacturing sector where employers reduced the wages by the exact amount of the allowances, considering them as part of the wage. This is what Polanyi calls the "ironic result that the financially implemented 'right to live' eventually ruined the people whom it was ostensibly designed to succor" (Polanyi 1974: 81). The deflationary pressure on wages was so high that it caused, "pauperization of the masses, who almost lost their human shape in the process" (Polanyi 1974: 82). Workers who once had the opportunity of getting some income or food (by laboring on common land) became dependent on wage work, and therefore, unable to object to employers who were then able to reduce wages by the amount of Speenhamland's allowances. Therefore, the Speenhamland system played a key function in helping to generalize the labor market and to increase the acceptance of economic coercion in the wage relationship. It was only abandoned when it became clear that it couldn't guarantee social peace anymore. "In the long run, a system as uneconomical as that was bound to affect productivity of labor and to depress standard wages, and ultimately even the scale set by the magistrates for the benefit of the poor" (Polanyi 1974: 97). The Act of Speenhamland was abolished in 1834, pushing the English working class into a struggle for wages at decent living standards.

This historical precedent is important enough to catch our attention regarding the possible side effects of today's "incentives to work," which increasingly use the strategy of in-work benefits. Indeed, evidence presented below suggests that employers tend to integrate benefits into the calculation of wage while individuals tend not to push for wage increases that may provoke a (partial) reduction of their in-work benefits. The "Speenhamland effect" here is not a mechanical but rather a dynamic process, which is part of the more global process of recommodification of wage labor. Nowadays—especially in the European countries where a strong social protection was built up on a national level during the post-war period—the consequence of the "Speenhamland effect" is a reduction in the living standards of unskilled workers.

Part 1 looks for evidence of Speenhamland effects in the labor market policies of three European countries that have been increasingly relying on in-work benefits, including the United Kingdom (Working Tax Credit, Income Support), France (Tax Credit), and Belgium (several policies). Part 2 concludes with a discussion of alternative policies that are needed to avoid this perverse effect.

1. Experiences of In-Work Benefits in Three Countries

1.1 United Kingdom

After the United States, the United Kingdom was one of the first countries to introduce workfare into its social security system. Programs such as New Deal, Jobseekers Agreement (JSA), Income Support, and Jobseekers Allowance don't generate or lead to quality work, but most of the time, they produce temporary and casual jobs with part-time hours and part-time incomes. Our fieldwork gave evidence to illustrate this phenomenon. Most of the New Deal jobs pay less than £3.50/hour; 25 percent are part-time, and 47 percent are in small organizations or firms without any control over the content of the work or over other activities. In the JSA, 35 percent of jobs were part-time, and 28 percent were temporary (less than six months), while this kind of job represents only 10 percent of the private labor market. People who don't accept these kinds of occupations are given sanctions, such as temporary or—after a while—permanent benefit reductions. The number of persons sanctioned decreased from 166,000 in 1998 to 90,000 in 2002. This is not an effect of reducing the policy's "toughness" but it reflects a change in the recipients' behavior. The New Deal system seems to be more compulsory. Sanctions are very short, involving reduction of 60 percent of the benefit for two, four, or more weeks, when the unemployed person refuses an offer or quits his job. Exception is made for single parents, for whom the program is voluntary.

More significant from a quantitative standpoint are the combined forms of income support, including Working Families Tax Credit (WFTC), introduced during the autumn of 1999 as a substitution for the "Family Credit." WFTC is granted by the tax center of the state. The credit is used by 22.4 percent of households; a strong increase in comparison to the 15.4 percent that used the Family Credit (Bruegel and Gray 2001). However, even after a slight increase in the amount of tax credit, WFTC doesn't enhance the work incentive for all parents. In households with only one wage income benefiting from WTFC, the employment of a second household member signifies a reduction in the amount of WTFC. This discourages many married women from employment because their husband is getting the tax credit. It also encourages the formation of single-parent households. Economic inquiries proved that the credit system tends to reduce participation of women in the labor market, whereas the official arguments for it promised the opposite effect. In response, the government raised a supplementary benefit for childcare and modified the decrease of the tax credit relative to income from work (subtracting £0.55 for each additional £1.00 of private income). The New Deal of London offered participants the choice between a wage on the one hand and keeping their benefit with a supplement of £15.38/week on the other hand. It is significant that 75 percent preferred to keep their benefit with the supplement, probably because of high housing prices and the possibility of combining the housing benefit with other benefits, but not with wages. In other areas, such as Tees-side in the North, the choice was exactly the opposite. Recognizing the risk of benefit traps for single persons and childless households, the government reformed the WTFC system for these categories until 2003.

WFTC is only one of the three main measures designed to "make work pay." Another is the introduction of a special low tax rate of 10 percent instead of the normal 22 percent. A third measure concerns the increase of the ceiling on the wages that one may earn before having to pay for national health insurance. The difference between the wage ceiling and the lowest weekly wage level has been increased from £2.54 to £7.05 for men and from £3.82 to £4.19 for women. But this still remains very small. Indeed, because of the use of income levels in the tax-credit system, people who draw a salary above £400 per month lose the credit income of £240 (Gray 2001; Delarue 2000).

To be eligible for the WFTC, one has to be employed for at least five weeks or be employed by a temporary work agency. The entitlements are given for a six-month period during which changes in social situations, except divorce, don't affect the tax credit. Both partners may initiate a request for WFTC, which was not the case with the older Family Credit. For the first six months, the tax credit is granted directly to the employee; but afterwards, the employer integrates it into his or her pay. The most recent step was the introduction of ICC (Integrated Child Credit) in 2003. This breaks the WFTC granted for children into two parts. If the household head is employed, he or she receives the WFTC with his or her wage, while the ICC is granted to the unemployed parent.

Recent field research (Bruegel and Gray 2001) suggests that the tax credit system and other forms of benefits combined with wages can facilitate the employers' recruitment of low-wage workers, when otherwise they would have been obliged to recruit higher-qualified and better-paid workers. In Northern Ireland, research on the effects of these systems confirmed this hypothesis. Unison, an important trade union, concluded, "WFTC will result in a lesser responsibility for employers to provide a decent living wage." Moreover, the existence of the tax credit system restrains wage demands among the recipients because workers don't want to lose the tax credit (which is an additional income) by receiving a slight wage increase. As a result, a convergence of interests between employers and employees appears to keep wages just below the wage ceiling set by WFTC.

The Low Pay Unit (LPU) conducted several inquiries concerning the National Minimum Wage (NMW) and the WFTC. One of their main observations was that women didn't experience significant wage increases despite the introduction of NMW. WFTC can foster a reduction of wages or the extension of low wages, because it gives people a higher tolerance for low income. The introduction of NMW at least had the effect of stopping a *downswing* tendency of wages while WFTC restrained an upswing of them. This is especially the case in poor regions of the United Kingdom. The fact that NMW isn't applicable to people younger than 22 stimulates the recruitment of individuals under 22 years of age, which in turn provokes less job opportunities for adult women unless they engage in wage competition. The majority of the interviewed workers said that they dislike the fact that employers are joining the tax credit with the wage, and thus taking the opportunity to pay employees less.

Another group of people interviewed during our research project's field enquiry (Gray 2001) argued that the informal economy of undeclared workers is disturbed by the WFTC system: By being obliged to officially declare all of the workers to be employed, employers were actually pushed towards paying less for the work because they have to pay taxes and national insurance contributions. This drives workers into a more separated semi-legal and totally unregulated economy instead of toward legalizing their situation. The Grabiner report (Grabiner 2000: 9) on the informal economy for HM Treasury counted more than 120,000 persons who combine benefits and "informal work". But how is it possible to change this reality without a countervailing power inside firms? Official discourses explained effectively that credit systems such as WFTC and Family Credit were designed to hold back wages and act as an auxiliary of the workfare system. Indeed, there seems to be substantial evidence of a Speenhamland effect from activist labor-market policies in the United Kingdom.

1.2 France

In 1970, with an unemployment rate of 1 percent, the insurance-based income system guaranteed 80 percent of the claimant's last wage[1] and 110 percent when an unemployed person engaged in a training and education program. In 1992, the unemployment rate was as high as 12 percent (3 million people) but only 55 percent of them were covered by the insurance system. The introduction of a Revenu Minimum d'Insertion (RMI) minimal integration income in 1988 was a first step toward a social help system parallel to the insurance-based one. During the following decade, the RMI provided 10 to 25 percent of unemployed people with a fixed-rate income between 380 and 420 Euros. Several benefits were created in between the RMI and the insurance-based Allocation Unitaire Dégressive (AUD) such as benefits for single parents and "solidarity" benefits. Although workfare policies are barely present in France, there is a link between the growth of social-aid oriented and fiscally funded benefits and the contractualization of social rights. That is, the individual must engage in training and accept any job offer. The recent introduction of Plan d'Aide de Retour à l'Emploi (PARE, Plan to Aid the Return to Employment) is an example of this.

The possibility of combining public benefits such as RMI (social help) with part-time work was introduced in 1998. This system *stimulates activity* by maintaining benefits after the individual finds work, then progressively reducing it to 33–50 percent, depending on the wage. In less than two years, more than 20 percent of RMI recipients used this combined system. There are no concrete longitudinal results about the specific impact of the combined income. More generally, the longitudinal analysis of unemployment shows the deep segmentation of the labor market. Out of a representative sample from 1996, only 26 percent left the RMI, 17 percent were still inside the RMI system and 57 percent were "back on the dole" after temporary employment (Rioux 2001).

Obviously, the segmentation of the workforce is as profound as the difficulties of going back to work are strong. In order to stimulate the outflow of the RMI system, a tax credit was given in 2001 as a second measure, to make part-time work more attractive. The report written by Pisani-Ferry (2000) states,

> this tax-credit system should be maximal when leaving the RMI for a job and decrease until the person reaches the minimum wage. The purpose is to cease any support of inactivity before part-time work.

The huge mobilizations of the unemployed during the winter of 1997–1998 had a trivial impact on the situation in France: Conditionality and workfare were less developed, but a significant increase of social minima was refused, with market-oriented arguments (such as traps and disincentives). According to the leftist government, the reduction of poverty and unemployment had to be solved by a combination of Keynesian and neo-liberal strategies. Half a million jobs were created in the public sector to reduce youth employment, and the combination of incomes and tax credits was allowed in order to "make work pay." The second type

Table 13.3 Short-term transitions

January 1998	September 1998	Percent
Employment	Employment	20.12
Employment	Unemployment	5.34
Unemployment	Employment	9.24
Unemployment	Unemployment	45.12
• Inactivity • Employment, unemployment, inactivity	• Employment, unemployment, inactivity • Inactivity	20.16

Source: Rioux (2001, p. 16).

Note: In January and September of 1998, 20.12 percent of the December 31, 1996 RMI recipients were employed.

of measure was put into effect during the early period of the research project; it is difficult to verify any Speenhamland effect, but there are some reasons to support the hypothesis. According to some economists (L'Horty and Parent 1998), there was no such effect possible as long as (a) recipients could not combine RMI with wage work and (b) the minimum wage was still the main reference. RMI did not allow in-work benefits until 1998. At that time, it is clear that the minimum wage had partially lost its structuring power through the development of part-time work and its strong effect in reducing income. Indeed, between 1988 and 1995, the proportion of low-wage workers[2] increased from 13.2 percent to 15.3 percent, especially among part-time workers. According to Concialdi (1997), these figures confirm that the phenomenon of the working poor was at first driven by the development of part-time work. Thereafter, the small difference between part-time income and RMI created a benefit trap. The neo-liberal *solution* is to "make work pay" by opening the possibility of combining the benefit (RMI) and a (very) low part-time wage.

Table 13.4 Employment–unemployment transitions between January 1997 and September 1998

Permanent Employment	8.6%
Single Transition Between Employment and Unemployment	19.1%
Double Transition Between Employment and Unemployment	11.4%
Three or More Transitions	10.3%
Permanent Unemployment	50.6%

Source: Rioux (2001, 16).

1.3 Belgium

In Belgium, for the year 2001, about 25 percent of the 700,000 unemployed people combined benefits and wage income. This figure is based on a wide range that includes older unemployed people who are not considered to be disposed to enter the labor market as well as pre-retirement workers. I briefly present some of the systems of combined income.

Benefits and part-time work in the 1980s

During a short period in the 1980s, Belgium distinguished itself by extending an unemployment benefit to part-time workers. Reflecting that full-time work was still the norm and following the idea that people were involuntarily in part-time work, a "part-time benefit" was created to replace the partial loss of income. Not surprisingly, part-time work increased very rapidly—from 7.7 percent in 1983 to 15.7 percent in 1998. The proportion of involuntarily part-time workers combining a wage with a benefit increased from 14 percent in 1983 to 51 percent in 1990. After that year, the distinction between "involuntarily" and "voluntarily" vanished and the additional benefit was reduced to an insignificant amount and also changed to restricted access. Only 5.1 percent of part-time workers still receive a combined income.

This *double-dipping* made part-time work very popular, which in return undermined its involuntary characterization. Because this *atypical* labor was almost totally female, it gave weight to a discourse about *conciliation* between work and family. The involuntarily dimension of part-time work could then be denied because of the so-called family-friendly effect of part-time work on mothers' time.

Because in-work benefits made insufficient part-time wages acceptable with a benefit, they paralleled a downscaling of both wages and benefits. But at the same time, the social security system introduced administrative categories (with different benefit rates) for the unemployed population. These included household head, cohabitant, and single. Cohabitants constituted 67 percent of part-time workers, and they received a much lower unemployment benefit because of this status. Therefore, they had a big interest in working part-time, while keeping part of their benefit. The right of combined incomes coincided also with the introduction of fixed contractual benefits linked with the family situation. Since that period, the growing feminization of the labor-force corresponded with part-time, "precarious" work and low wages. But this reality was kept outside the official and dominant academic analysis because of the pro-family viewpoint considering one (male) and one half-time (female) income as the standard. Therefore, it cannot be denied that the social security system sustained a segmentation of the labor market along gender divisions. Unemployed single parents hold the "household head" status and receive a benefit of 850 Euros, which is not much below the minimum wage (about 1,000 Euros) and far above the average part-time wage (650 Euros).

Local employment agencies

A second possibility for combining work and benefits was created with the Local Employment Agencies (LEA) organizing paid services for both individuals and organizations. Long-term unemployed people are permitted to keep their benefits in combination with a maximum amount of 45 hours of paid work per month. Employers who use the services pay a check, of which one portion goes to the individual worker and the other to the agency. This system is now used by about 10 percent of unemployed people (about 42,000 in 2000). The LEA system is very popular among unemployed people because they can increase their monthly incomes with officially recognized work. Women constitute 82 percent of LEA workers. This system doesn't push people back into the normal labor market, because the average monthly income is equal to or above a part-time wage and stability is much higher inside this neo-domestic labor market system than outside it. The fact that social benefits haven't increased since the beginning of the 1980s is not unimportant to the popularity of these systems.

"Activation" of benefits in the late 1990s

Between 1997 and 2000, the government introduced "activated jobs" in the service sector compelling the unemployed to search for work, using their benefits as a direct reduction of the wage cost. This system gave work to 18,000 people, of which 70 percent received part-time jobs. The purpose was to subsidize social and environmental activities that a *traditional* market activity would not support because of low productivity or added value. The fact that a rather stringent control system refused more than half of the employers' demands, citing substitution and cannibalism of existing jobs, indicates how strong the logic of profitability can be. Casual work and bad jobs are chasing away decent work and pay.

Social security funds used to finance competitiveness of firms

On a collective level, employers and governments have put a strain on the social security system by reducing direct contributions. Lack of resources is only partially compensated by fiscal means. Some of these reductions are unconditional and apply, in general, to the sectors exposed to global competition; others are linked with some target groups such as the unskilled, low-wage workers, the long-term unemployed, and youth. In both cases, the principle is the same: Reduce labor costs to stimulate recruitment or to sustain the competitiveness of firms as a condition to keep up employment levels. During our fieldwork, we saw how this system made it easier to find a job after one year of inactivity—"after that, I became cheaper"; or simply inverted the order in the unemployment lines without reducing its length.

From a neo-liberal viewpoint, these reductions of resources are consistent with the freezing of expenditures on welfare (health, retirement, and entitlements). To understand the scale of this, note that the €3.75 billion reduction of 2001 represents almost four-fifths of the €4.25 billion expenditure on unemployment benefits.

Table 13.5 Reductions of employer contributions to social security system in Belgium

	Reduction of Contributions (billions of Euros)	As Part of Social Security Contributions (%)	Part of Contribution Reductions in the Global Labor Cost (Private Sector) (%)
1994	1.06	4.20	1.0
1996	1.42	7.80	1.7
1998	1.85	8.20	2.8
2000	3.10	9.60	5.2
2001	3.76	11.05	6.3
2002	3.80	10.80	6.1
2003	3.90	10.60	6.4
2004	4.40	11.70	6.5

Sources: Bouquin (2001), Social Security of Belgium (2004), Bureau Fédéral du Plan (2004).

Therefore, the tendency toward a minimal public security system with fewer resources translates into a push of least-skilled workers toward subsidized (casual) work and a push of the higher-skilled workers toward purchasing additional health-insurance and private-pension schemes. Concerning the unemployed, the reduction of resources for social expenditures is strongly correlated with the duration and amount of benefits, restricted rights, and the growing compulsory character of social policies. The social security system had to become economically effective; this could be achieved through the individual use of benefits in the labor market to make part-time, temporary or casual work socially acceptable and financial attractive. These are the two faces of the same neo-liberal agenda. Using the resources of social security to reduce labor costs is justified as an effort "to protect" the employment of the more productive workers, but in reality, these resources mainly serve the competitiveness of firms while the wages are disconnected from productivity growth (Bouquin 2001).

1.4 In-Work Benefits as Part of the Process of Recommodification and Casualization

According to G. Esping-Andersen (1996), the different welfare regimes and social policies developed a logic of decommodification, because workers can hold a level of welfare independent of their immediate activity in the labor market. In this perspective, workfare is developing a logic of recommodification and combined incomes aren't. But, isn't there a common logic between in-work benefits and the use of social security resources to regulate the labor market, to reduce labor costs, and to increase competitiveness? For Bob Jessop (1993), it is essential to recognize the link between the new active social policies oriented towards employment "at any expense" and the evolution toward an economy based on flexible accumulation and neoclassical principles. By subordinating social rights in one way or another to economic objectives (reducing inactivity, making work pay or reducing labor costs), welfare provisions and benefits are becoming part of the tendency toward recommodification of labor. Taking into account that the dominant discourse isn't focusing on too high benefits and reservation wages anymore, but more on the problem of poverty, low wages and part-time work, the evident solution consists in "making work pay" by *in-work benefits* giving someone the possibility of drawing a salary and earning an income from the social security system at the same time. This kind of social policy seems much less compulsory and disciplinary, just because it gives people more financial margins. But at the same time, as we saw above, these systems participate in the extension of precarious, casual-work situations, making them acceptable or less unacceptable by removing the autonomy social security guaranteed against one's dependency on the labor market. For this reason, the existence of a Speenhamland effect cannot be denied. Nowadays, even if the amount of this additional income is not defined by the dynamics of the market, it acts upon the price definition of wage labor and enforces the process of recommodification. Of course, the way it does depends on the reality of collective bargaining, unemployment, minimum wage, unionization and the scarcity of qualifications.

In-work benefits reduce casualization and bad work situations, and recommodification in general, under the sole condition that they are high enough to lose their "additional" character. But to what extent is this different from high unemployment insurance? The only difference is that the latter doesn't provide a way to combine work and benefits, but this difference is far from negligible. In one case, employers face workers' unwillingness to accept low-wage work because a benefit is better (and it is indeed). In the other case, they found a certain willingness to accept this bad work, which with the actual social and sexual division of labor is certainly not easy to escape.

2. No Shortcuts But an Alternative Route

Returning to the issue of in-work benefits, we might say that only a universal right to a decent living income—a universal social wage (*salaire universel*)—will not reproduce Speenhamland effects in the labor market. B. Friot (2000) defined a "universal social wage" as the right for everyone to earn a decent living wage as a student, as a worker, as a part-time volunteer, as a retired person, or as caretaker of children or of the infirm. A universal social wage necessarily tackles the systemic components of the question, in place of relaying upon a sole measure to solve a vast and heterogeneous social crisis of which unemployment is only one aspect. As I've said, these systemic aspects not only concern the need for financial resources (taxing much more of the added value of private corporations and financial markets), but they also imply a democratic allocation of human resources in order to satisfy actual (and extending) needs of the population. This allocation cannot be organized only by market mechanisms since they only recognize high productivity and added-value labor, which in turn underlines the need of public sector services (education, health care, etc.). If the term "full employment" must be avoided, it cannot be replaced by "full activity in a dual society." Defending a universal social wage implies another social and economic organization of society, which basic income in its minimalist version does not.

I would like to conclude with a discussion of three issues: first, practical answers to job insecurity and poverty; second, new collective guarantees; and third, the role of the state.

2.1 A Universal Wage in a Full Employment Society against Poverty and Job Insecurity

The existence of widespread poverty in Europe today is an accepted fact. In 2000, 18 percent of the population had income of less than 60 percent of the average in the 15 European Union member nations; there were 60 million poor people and 15 million unemployed. The existence of job insecurity is beginning to be admitted, but we still do not know whether efforts to create "flexicurity"—transitional markets and forms of contract combining social guarantees and flexibility—can respond sufficiently. To combat job insecurity, it is necessary to guarantee sufficient income to live in dignity, to reintroduce employment standards that guarantee well-paid work, or to combine the two approaches.

Guaranteeing sufficient income would act effectively on the availability of labor and reduce individuals' "tolerance threshold" for job insecurity. This approach acts directly on social situations through supply and demand in the labor market. At the same time, by combining social security benefits and income from work, this option could also further the trend toward the devaluation of labor and lower wage costs. In cases where this additional income is relatively generous, it also favors a "tax revolt" on the part of contributors and households carrying a large part of the tax burden through full-time work. This in turn, for reasons of political legitimacy, leads to the repressive trend of *workfare*. If it remains insufficient, such additional income runs a high risk of locking individuals into job insecurity and rendering that insecurity socially acceptable.

For these reasons, I favor a universal social wage. This proposition is exactly the opposite of the one that considers a wage as only a payment for a hired laborer as determined by the laws of the labor market. Because work is more and more procedural, collective, dependent on education, and cognitive, a wage needs to be understood as a collective payment, more and more disconnected from the immediate mobilization during the constrains of time (working time) and space (the firm). Moreover, it is impossible to combine the principle of equal pay with an individualistic approach to wages, based on one's added value to global productivity. Therefore, the universal wage means a further socialization of wage labor, not based on fiscal funding sources, such as taxes, which leave all the power to private corporations, but based on a direct socialization (of part) of the surplus value. Until now, the best expression of such a kind of socialization is, indeed, a repartition between wages and profits, not in the sphere of circulation but in production itself. This means that historically the social protections generalized in Europe since World War II express, in an unachieved way, the movement toward socialization—even if, in each of the different models, we can criticize its pro-work, undemocratic (controlled by state or union apparatus) and discriminating dimensions toward women, the unskilled, and foreigners. To open a new social horizon on a global scale, we must understand this, build on what exists, and not destroy these social protections, as the currently unfolding pro-market policies are doing.

The resolution of the actual social crisis cannot be reduced to the sole issue of income. There is also need for a new employment standard. This norm should be based on the idea that not all work is a job; that we must combat situations where people are called on to work too many hours a day, or where the working conditions are intolerable for one's health and social life. Therefore, this means abandoning the paradigm of "employability," which tends to individualize the cause of non-employment and reduce resolution of the unemployment question to a qualitative adjustment of the supply and demand of labor, when in fact there are many other parameters (productivity, working hours, productive choices of capital, and public macroeconomic policies). Working toward a new employment standard cannot be separated from working toward "full employment", which Beveridge defined as "having more vacancies for workers than there are workers seeking vacancies" (Beveridge 1967: 2). Unlike the common representation of the "golden sixties," full employment has never been determined by economic development alone, but also by political choices. Claimed by Beveridge as indispensable for a democratic society and the minimum application of state functions, full employment also meant a different order of priorities. One may retort that full employment means the end of trading in labor and that inflation will return with a vengeance. I would reply that we must reopen the path to a different development rationale. Why should there be no other healthy future than the tyranny of markets favoring deflation, stop-start growth, and growing social polarization within populations and regions? Why would it be impossible to guide the future of humanity toward the development of an economy of services and work liberated from the valorization and accumulation of capital? If this requires the extinction of financial markets and the socialization of wage labor, is this the worst thing that could happen?

In the current state of progress with globalization, European integration and an ideological climate still enamored with the dogma of neo-liberalism, it remains difficult to link the issue of full employment with that of the role of the state and political intervention. Moreover, as I pointed out earlier, the liberal nature of European construction—in terms of both orientations and the hardly democratic functioning—makes this debate somewhat elusive. Nevertheless, the formulation of an alternative route cannot cut corners in defending the real harmonization of certain regulatory frameworks: first, a common minimum wage standard; second, a minimum guaranteed income for retired people and social minima in general; third, an employment standard. With regard to this last aspect, can we shore up a standard (full-time employment for an indefinite period) that has become increasingly vulnerable? I don't think so, because the modern forms of hiring labor (temporary, fixed-term contracts, call contracts, bogus freelancers) play a growing part. Therefore, it is becoming a matter of urgency to reconstruct a common foundation for all segments of the labor force: both casual workers and those who are not (yet) casual workers.

2.2 New Collective Guarantees

Faced with increasing job insecurity and the renewed negotiability of the workforce, the debate on new collective guarantees is still in its infancy. At this level, the creation of a "professional status" merits our attention. The first objective of this professional status is to reunify the fragmented situation surrounding the right to individual social security benefits in terms of annual holidays, training, credit hours, children's education and engagement in associations (Supiot 1999). This proposal forms part of a larger picture, including the "activity contract" (Boissonnat 1995) and work on the subject of "transitional markets". The common denominators linking them are employment instability and the desire to reconstruct statutory guarantees for marginal, precarious, or atypical labor. From this standpoint, the labor market is seen as inherently unstable because the individual no longer has a fixed employer and because the individual often now gives priority to inter- or trans-professional mobility. Therefore, these "transitions" must be addressed by regulatory political action with the aim of procuring new social guarantees in terms of training, free time, and domestic or associative activities.

Alain Supiot proposes the reconstruction of a common foundation based on both law and convention, in contrast to contractualization (in the civil law sense) and the movement toward making the workforce a negotiable item. In his view, professional status should no longer be linked to employment (and therefore attached to the employer), but would be placed "beyond" the employer by basing it on "work in general", in other words on all activities including training, domestic work and activities with associations:

> The paradigm of employment would thus be substituted by a paradigm of the professional status of persons, which would not be defined by the exercise of a given profession, but would encompass the various forms of work that any person might accomplish during his existence (Supiot 1999, 89–90).

However, Supiot is opposed to the idea propounded by the Boissonat Report—of using the term "activity contract" for this new common legal basis, since activity is indefinable and too broad for use as the basis of specific but uniquely universal rights. Such universal rights would have to be developed largely in the form of rights to social benefits "facilitating the changeover from one type of work to another…to avoid the risks of becoming locked into a given work situation" (Supiot 1999, 90). A worker could thus obtain training, elect to invest his efforts in an association, or take up work as a freelance worker.

This approach has the merit of reopening the debate, but it remains blind to the labor force management methods of the neo-liberal era. In effect, these proposals are based on the practice of the externalization of social rights from the application of all or part of labor law and collective guarantees. Having first affected the most unstable segments (low skilled, categories discriminated against—such as women, immigrants, etc.), this sidelining of a norm for protection has progressively embraced all categories from skilled workers to technicians, engineers and managers. These reorganizations contribute primarily to a return of the workforce as a negotiable item, even though the most skilled categories can "play the system." However, Supiot's analysis tends to take into account only the obvious elements, comparing the unfortunate precariousness of non- and low-skilled workers with the fortunate self-employed in the higher strata. It follows that there are "positive transitions" as well as "negative transitions". The first applies to the "labor market nomads" who enjoy a situation guaranteed by their high level of "employability", while the "negative transitions" apply to the various forms of relegation to job insecurity, unemployment and social marginalization. Such a dualist representation of these transitions seems to hamper discussion of how instrumental rationality dominates individual behavior and tends to make the use of oneself—as a depository of human capital—subject to the make-believe world where the customer is king.

The analysis suggests certain reforms. Note that Supiot sees a close link between labor law drafted during the post-war period and Fordism. But, is it a systemic link or just the historical expression of the changing balance of forces between labor and capital? Since he doesn't answer this question, we may think that the proposed "professional status" represents more a judicial but very similar approach to a basic income.

On the subject of a universalistic approach involving the acquisition of new personal rights, Robert Castel (1999) wonders whether collective protection and guarantees for a part-time cashier would have to pass through haphazard mediations external to the working relationship, which would not be included in actual employment conditions? He goes on to ask, "How, by displacing the constraints of employment rights to the person, can we institute strong constraints on the employers' side?" Bringing back "gray areas" of employment must not lead to chasing shadows. According to Castel, it will be necessary to continue to use working relationships and employment conditions as a basis for collective action in this area.

Since the nineties there have been several signs of the reemergence of collective mobilization and union activity. Restructurings (such as layoffs, bankruptcy, and relocation) remain essentially defensive moves; but several indicators point to growing resistance to deteriorating working conditions in new sectors (e.g., call centers), highly "unstable" sectors (e.g., food industry and retail trade), and strategically important sectors (e.g., road, air, and rail transportation). Union membership is on the increase accompanied by a rising number of work disputes. This trend toward remobilization remains rather patchy but affects almost all European countries. The level of trade union membership is rising in expanding sectors (e.g., health care, nonprofit, and retail); and many small conflicts are arising.

The aim of a new employment standard is not as unfashionable as we may think. Following an opinion poll published in the French daily newspaper *Libération*, 79 percent of people between 20 and 30 years old said that they were strongly in favor of long-term employment contracts and a secure income, and only 11 percent want temporary work (*Libération* 2000). Because the work experienced by this generation is marked by job insecurity, 50 percent of employed people less than 25 years old receive a wage below the statutory minimum; in one generation the wage gap between 25-year-olds and 40-year-olds has multiplied by three; 30 percent of people under the age of 30 have a temporary job compared with 6 percent of those over 30; part-time work is twice as common among young people as among older people. Facing such a vast insecurity, it is far from surprising that these same young people express the need for a continuous income and secure work situation even if a majority (70 percent) is willing to change jobs several times. In a situation where the aspirations of wage earners are going to test working relations, new militant energies are feeding collective action. The key question remains how to reconstruct a social outlook in which the positions of low-paid and precariously employed workers as well as "stable" ("core") workers converge toward a better quality of life for all. The weight given respectively to "universal" or "specific" social rights also, no doubt, depends on the regulatory power of union organizations, how representative the unions are, and the unions' capacity to promote claims, as well as on the place accorded to legislative intervention. This brings us to the last question—that of the state.

2.3 Recognizing the Political Character of the Economy in Order to Democratize it

At this turning point in history, still marked by neo-liberal dogma, the role of the state oscillates between that of a stimulator of the new economy and a *regulator* of social tensions. In parallel, the concentration of economic power in the hands of the major monopolies and of those seeking returns on capital has never been greater. The fact that the turnover of certain multinationals exceeds the budget of small and even medium-sized countries is typical of this development. Classification of the 50 largest economic entities reveals that half of them are multinational firms. The forms taken by enterprises have certainly changed, becoming networked firms with the phenomena of outsourcing and externalization; no less than 50 percent of world trade concerns intra-group trading. There is a phenomenal concentration of power over regional development, the environment, and—even more—over the social and economic fabric. The choice of investments; where they are made; their nature; redundancies; and training (fashioning populations in relation to their work) are all precipitating factors in the neo-liberal rebuilding of society.

As for the labor movement, and even for society itself, it is becoming imperative to extend democratic control over large corporations—without which control, democracy itself will be wiped out before the tyranny of the financial markets and major companies. The debate must focus on the state and on the counterweight of unionism.

Any analysis that sets the state against the market and tends to represent regulation as an alternative to a full market is very likely to turn out to be an impasse. The state has an important role in ensuring the success of capitalism, whether it is the monetarist policy initiated by Reagan in the early eighties or the orientation of European construction; any neo-liberal counter-reform without state intervention would be impossible. The creation in Europe of a single market and a new currency are living proof of this. We therefore have to dare to change the debate to discuss the nature of public and state intervention, without which the current wave of globalization threatens to make all spheres of social life subject to market expansion.

The union counterweight should be released from its confinement within enterprises and nations. Sidelined by social reorganizations, mergers and internationalization, fragmented by the breakup or segmentation of working groups, unions can only regain lost ground by founding its efforts on general political principles. The economic and social responsibility of enterprises goes beyond their "responsibility in company matters". With the use of public grants and a wide variety of exemptions, companies must provide accounts; this right of oversight cannot exist without union action. Therefore, all rules enjoyed by unions inside firms—at local and global level—need to be reviewed. Conversely, recommending solutions such as social responsibility and a "citizen enterprise" with ISO 8000 series certification means admitting that certain firms would not exist. In addition, with a cascade of subcontractors and other forms of externalization, it is becoming easy to obtain an ethical or "citizen" label for brands while core and peripheral production activities are carried out using forced labor (Klein 2000).[3]

In this era of mergers, concentrations, the formation of near monopolies, and ever fiercer competition, one might wonder how consumer action could influence production choices and impose respect for social norms. At a time of hyper-industrialization of agriculture and food production, the debates driven by various health crises have revealed the obstacles to formulating regulations that guarantee health security and preserve the profit motive. Although resolving these problems means posing the question of social forms of ownership, it also implies a transformation of working relations. Indeed, under the current wage regime, the constraint of selling labor at a discount is omnipresent. It is always possible to find available labor even for the most onerous or dangerous tasks (such as industrial cleaning at nuclear power stations carried out by subcontractors employing clandestine workers), thereby fragmenting the alternative based on a single work place. Simultaneously, at the global level of the company, consumption also remains subject to purchasing power; it comes as no surprise to see the development of cheap but poor quality food, of insalubrious accommodation and of lack of education for poor people and other "unemployables". The actions open to trade unions and citizens cannot profoundly change the course of events. For this reason, the question of an alternative must go beyond the issue of concrete measures and the rebuilding of unions and social movements at local and international level; it must also question the role of the state and its field of action in a political way.

Notes

[*] This research project was financed by the European Commission–TSER Program. Members of the research team are Anne Gray (South Bank University, London), Martin Güeck (Heidelberg University–Kairos Europa), Estelle Krzeslo (Université Libre de Bruxelles), Stephen Bouquin (University of Amiens, CNRS); it was coordinated by Catherine Lévy (CNRS Center G. Friedmann, University Paris I).

[1] The "last wage" means the wage someone received from his or her last employer. France has a Bismarck-type social security system, in which benefits are not funded by taxes, but by the contributions part of the total wage. In this case, the total wage is divided between a net wage from which the state takes taxes and a second part (which we may call the social wage) from which contributions are taken for unemployment, retirement and health. These contributions go to the social security funds that are managed by social partners (unions and employers' organizations). This system has a (stronger) link between the last wage and the level of benefits than a Beveridge system.

[2] Defined as workers who make below 50 percent of the median wage.

[3] This illustrates that neither the new technologies nor the new economy transform the nature of labor by virtue of their intrinsic qualities alone, but that on the contrary, under the regime of the accumulation of capital, "old" forms of labor sometimes reappear. This also applies to the *sweatshops* in Asia, the *maquiladoras* in Central America and forced labor in prisons in the United States. In the latter case, note that almost one million prisoners are, to varying degrees, forced to work for an hourly sub-wage that does not exceed $1.50. Microsoft had a large portion of the packaging for Windows 95 carried out by the company Exmark, which specializes in employing prisoners (Burton-Rosen 1996). See also http://www.prisonlegalnews.org.

References

Beveridge, W.H. (1967) *Full Employment in a Free Society,* (London: Allen and Unwin).

Boissonnat, J. (1995) *Le travail dans vingt ans*, (Paris: La Documentation Française and O. Jacob).

Bouquin, S. (2001) "Lonen en Winsten in het neo-liberaal tijdperk," *Vlaams Marxistisch Tijdschrift*, 35 (4): 69–92.

Bruegel, I. and Gray, A. (2001) *The Impact of the Working Families' Tax Credit*, (London, mimeo).

Bureau Fédéral du Plan (Jul. 16, 2004) "Figures & Facts," http://www.plan.be.fr/db/ActieveDB/Data-php?DB=mod&Page=wage.htm.

Burton-Rosen, D. (1996) *Le Goulag Américain: Le travail forcé aux Etats-Unis,* (Paris: l'Esprit Frappeur).

Castel, R. (1999) "Droit du travail: redéploiement ou refondation?," *Droit social,* 5: May.

Commission Européenne (2000) *L'Emploi en Europe 1999, DG Emploi and Affaires Sociales,* (Brussels: EU).

Concialdi, P. (1997) *Les bas salaires en France,* (Paris: IRES Publications).

Delarue, V. (2000) "Le Working Families Tax Credit, un nouveau crédit d'impôt pour les familles de travailleurs à bas revenus," *Economie et Statistiques* 305 : 47–61.

Esping-Andersen, G. (1996) "After the Golden Age," in *Welfare States in Transition,* G. Esping-Andersen (ed.), (London: Sage).

Friot, B. (2000) "Le salaire socialisé", *Revue Française des Affaires Sociales*, no. 3 (Paris: La Documentation Française).

Gallie, D., Paugam S. (2001) *The Employment Precarity, Unemployment and Social Exclusion Research Program*, TSER–EU final report (Brussels: European Commission).

Grabiner, A. (2000) *The Informal Economy,* (London: HM Treasury).

Gray, A. (2001) "European Perspectives on Welfare Reform," paper presented at Glasgow Conference.

Jessop, B. (1993) "Towards a Schumpeterian Workfare State?" *Studies in Political Economy*, 40: 7–39.

——— (1994) "The Transition to Post-Fordism and the Schumpeterian Workfare State," in *Towards a Post-Fordist Welfare State?,* R. Burrows and B. Loader (eds.), (London: Routledge).

——— (2000) *The Future of the Welfare State,* (Cambridge: Polity Press).

Klein, N. (2000) *No Logo,* (U.S.A.: Picador).

L'Horty, Y. and A. Parent (1998) Deux études sur le RMI, working papers, Université d'Evry–Val d'Essonne.

Libération (2000) "Les jeunes et le travail," Monday, February 28, employment section, p. IV.

Pierson, P. (2001) "Coping With Permanent Austerity: Welfare State Restructuring in Affluent Democracies" in *The New Politics of the Welfare State*, P. Pierson (ed.), (Oxford: Oxford University Press), 410–456.

Pisani-Ferry, J. (2000) *Plein emploi,* (Paris: La Documentation Française).

Polanyi, K. (1974) *The Great Transformation,* (Boston: Beacon Hill Press).

Rioux, L. (2001) "Recherche d'emploi et insertion professionnelle des allocataires RMI," *Economie and Statistique*, 346–347: 13–24.

Social Security of Belgium (2004) "Budget 2004," "Parametres macroeconomiques 2000–2004," http://socialsecurity.fgov.be/vademecum/index.htm.

Supiot, A. et al. (1999) *Au-delà de l'emploi: Transformations du travail et devenir du travail en Europe*, (Paris: Flammarion).

PART FOUR: PROPOSALS

Chapter 14

The Political Economy of the Basic Income Grant in South Africa

Nicoli Nattrass and Jeremy Seekings

Introduction

"Welfare reform" in much of the world entails a process of managed retrenchment, as benefits are cut back in the face of political, demographic or economic pressures. South Africa is one country where debates about welfare reform in the early 2000s have revolved around the expansion of the welfare system, i.e., around extending the coverage of social assistance to groups of the poor who have been excluded hitherto. Central to this debate have been calls for the introduction of a basic income grant (BIG), guaranteeing a minimum, unconditional income to all citizens. Although South Africa is hardly an affluent country, calls for a BIG grew loud in the early 2000s. Trade unions, churches and nongovernmental organizations (NGOs) joined together in a "BIG Coalition"; an official government commission recommended (with conditions) the introduction of a BIG; several thousand people marched to Parliament in support of a BIG; and even the official opposition party in parliament supported the introduction of means-tested income support as an alternative to a universal BIG.

One might imagine that this discussion of a BIG is a product of democratization in South Africa. After all, South Africa under *apartheid* was rightly infamous for systematic racial discrimination against its black majority. Black South Africans were politically excluded, economically disadvantaged and socially marginalized. The result was inequality in the distribution of incomes as high as anywhere else in the world. In 1994, after a long struggle for democratization, the African National Congress (ANC) won a large majority in the country's first democratic elections. The ANC's election manifesto, the *Reconstruction and Development Programme* (RDP), included a clear commitment to poverty reduction through the public provision of welfare as well as through employment growth, land reform and other measures. The RDP included the promise, largely downplayed in public, that welfare policies would ensure that everyone received a minimum income. The poor voted overwhelmingly for the ANC. Two years later in 1996, South Africa adopted a new constitution that included a Bill of Rights encompassing social and economic, as well as political and civil, rights. In 1999, the ANC was re-elected, again promising "A Better Life For All," and in 2004 it won a third successive election with further promises to reduce poverty and inequality. A BIG is an obvious way of redistributing from rich to poor, undoing some of the inequities of the apartheid era.

But the ANC leadership has, in fact, been opposed to the introduction of a BIG, and has sought to dampen demands for, and even discussion of, a BIG. The calls for a BIG have certainly come from groups that were at the forefront of the struggle for democratization and have been broadly supportive of and aligned with the ANC since 1994, but they have not come from the ANC itself. These calls for a BIG are being made on the foundations of a welfare system that, surprisingly, substantially predates 1994. The post-apartheid state inherited a remarkably generous system of public welfare, financed through a remarkably efficient and progressive tax system. The roots of South African exceptionalism in the public provision of welfare prove to be much more complex than one might have imagined.

In South Africa, a BIG has been on the agenda because of the coincidence of four main factors. First, the country already has a system of public welfare that is unusually extensive in its coverage, unusually generous in its benefits and unusually redistributive in its effects. In South Africa, a BIG involves an extension of the welfare system rather than an entirely novel innovation. Secondly, poverty persists due to unemployment and the absence of any real subsistence agriculture—both products of public policy under apartheid—and there is little prospect of reducing poverty through job creation or land reform in the short- or even medium-term. Thirdly, the existence of an extensive system of private welfare, through remittances sent by employed workers to mostly rural kin, means that it is in the interests of the powerful trade union movement to support a BIG. And, fourthly, the extent of inequality paradoxically makes it easier to finance a BIG based on redistribution from the rich to the poor.

The South African Debate

Calls for a BIG arose in South Africa in response to the country's huge and persistent unemployment problem, which exposed a huge hole in an otherwise generous welfare system. In 1998, under pressure to show that it was taking unemployment seriously, the South African government convened a Presidential Jobs Summit to discuss the policy challenges caused by high unemployment. Representatives of business argued (*inter alia*) for greater labor-market flexibility, whereas the labor unions, NGOs and community organizations called for more labor market protection and an expanded welfare system that included income support for all.[1] For the first time, the idea of providing a BIG was placed on the policy agenda. The government responded cautiously by promising to investigate the issue.

In March 2000, the government appointed the Committee of Inquiry into a Comprehensive System of Social Security for South Africa (known as the "Taylor Committee" after its chair, Professor Vivienne Taylor of the University of Cape Town), with the task of examining "options for the establishment of an integrated and comprehensive social security system."[2] The Congress of South African Trade

Unions (COSATU), churches and NGOs called for a BIG as part of an expansionary "People's Budget", and in 2001 formed the BIG Coalition. In March 2002, after repeated delays, the Taylor Committee handed its report to the government, although it was not published until May 2002. The report, *Transforming the Present, Protecting the Future* (South Africa 2002), called for the introduction of a BIG set at R100 (or about $15) per month. But the committee proposed that the introduction of a BIG should depend on improved technology and hence lower administrative costs. In the meantime, the existing child-support grant (providing means-tested income support for poor children) should be extended to older children, up to the age of 18.

The opposition Democratic Alliance, eager to demonstrate that it was not a party of the privileged only, called for a means-tested income grant. Under the Democratic Alliance's plan, the grant would be payable only to people with annual incomes below R7,000 (i.e., about $1,000), and to a maximum of four people per household. This would exclude most households with members in formal employment. Unsurprisingly, the trade union movement strongly denounced the Democratic Alliance's proposal.

The unions' own allies in the ANC and government, however, responded much more negatively to the Taylor Committee. The ANC leadership sought to suppress discussion at the party's pre-election conferences in 2003. Officially, the government simply deferred making any decision, but spokesmen made the government's opposition quite clear. The cabinet, one spokesman said, had a rather different philosophy than the Taylor Committee; it was opposed to "hand-outs." The government did extend the child support grant (but only to the age of 14), but its main emphasis was on addressing poverty through public works programs rather than welfare. Nonetheless, as of 2004, the BIG is still clearly on the national agenda, with the BIG Coalition continuing to exert pressure. It remains on the agenda because so little is being done for the many poor people in the country.

Inequality and Public Policy Under Apartheid

Inequality, under and after apartheid, has been shaped profoundly by a mix of labor market and welfare policies, as well as other policies shaping the economic "growth path"; i.e., the character as well as the overall rate of economic growth. Under apartheid, labor and welfare policies ensured minimum incomes for white people, in part through comprehensive racial discrimination. White peoples' incomes were bolstered primarily through labor market policies, with racial job reservations (i.e., the reservation of better jobs for white people) in both the public and private sectors. These policies served to secure almost full employment for white workers. Education, health and housing benefits were all massively biased towards white people. Public welfare was limited to people who could not support themselves through work: the elderly (through a means-tested, noncontributory old-age pension system), children in one-parent families (through means-tested, noncontributory child-support grants) and the short-term unemployed (through the contributory, but subsidized, Unemployment

Insurance Fund) (Nattrass and Seekings 1997). Economic policies also promoted an economic growth path favoring semiskilled and skilled, i.e., white, workers. In these respects, the apartheid state was a racially exclusive variant of the Australian "wage earners" welfare state—i.e., a welfare state that sought to ensure a certain standard of living for Australians as wage earners rather than as citizens (Castles 1985).

By contrast, black South Africans were subjected to extensive labor-market discrimination and disadvantage. Inferior education, restrictions on geographical movement and constraints on business activity undermined black peoples' incomes (and hence partially compensated employers, particularly in mining and agriculture, for the high costs of white labor). Given the chronic labor shortages that plagued low-wage sectors (notably agriculture and mining) during the postwar period, the apartheid government was averse to providing any alternative means of subsistence for African job seekers. Instead, it relied on coercive labor legislation to channel African labor to where it was most needed.

The apartheid state, did, however, provide a universal welfare net in the form of the old age pension—although the value of the pension varied between regions and racial groups. The noncontributory old-age pension had its origins in the peculiar circumstances of the Second World War (see Seekings 2000b), but survived the election in 1948 of the National Party and the implementation of apartheid. The apartheid state discriminated (increasingly) in the benefits it paid, with the maximum pension payable to African people falling to just one-seventh of the value of the white pension, but never abolished the system entirely. When, in the 1970s and especially 1980s, the apartheid state sought to remove racial discrimination from the statute books, it was required to increase benefits to the levels enjoyed by white pensioners, achieving parity on the eve of democratization. The old age pension proved to be an important lifeline for poor African families, particularly from the 1970s onwards, as unemployment rose and as the real value of the pension increased. Even in the heyday of apartheid, African people probably benefited from government social expenditure more than they paid in taxes (McGrath 1983)—a situation made possible by the fact that white South Africans benefited so greatly from other forms of government intervention, notably in the labor market. By the end of the apartheid period, with rising expenditures on pensions, education and health care, the budget had become a mechanism for massive redistribution from rich to poor, and from white to black South Africans, as we shall see below.

The late-apartheid period also saw the erosion of racial discrimination in labor market policy. The state could abolish job reservation because white South Africans were no longer dependent on this kind of discrimination to protect their living standards. What changed the position of poorer white people was the apartheid state's extraordinary investment in public education in the 1950s and 1960s, which ensured that the children of unskilled white parents were not themselves unskilled. By the 1980s white peoples' earnings were largely dependent on skills, not on direct discrimination. The development of the labor–welfare policy nexus under apartheid reflected the changing class interests of powerful white constituencies. The changing interests of key white constituencies even allowed the state, faced with industrial action by black workers, to deracialize the institutional framework for wage determination. The contribution of racial discrimination to wage determination declined significantly between 1980 and 1993, dropping from 20 percent to 12 percent of the African wage (Moll 2000). A racial wage gap persists in post-apartheid South Africa, but it is now predominantly explained by factors other than discrimination, such as differences in education and skill, location (urban or rural), and economic sector. African workers have the lowest educational qualifications, live predominantly in rural areas, and are more likely to work in low-paying sectors such as agriculture (Schultz and Mwabu 1998a, 1998b; Moll 2000; Butcher and Rouse 2000). Education is particularly important. According to Schultz and Mwabu (1998a) half of the difference in racial earnings can be attributed to differences in educational qualifications. Those with qualifications typically find work at reasonable wages; those without either find low-wage jobs or more commonly, do not find work at all (see also Anderson et al. 2001).

Policies may have been deracialized, but inequality remained stubbornly high in the newly democratic South Africa. In 1993, the poorest four deciles (40 percent) of households, comprising 52 percent of the population, accounted for less than 10 percent of total income, while the richest decile (10 percent) of households, comprising just 6 percent of the population, captured well over 40 percent of total income. The mean household income in the top decile was about one hundred times the mean household income in the bottom decile. There was still a correlation between race and household income as 95 percent of those in the bottom decile were African, and 77 percent of the richest decile were white (Seekings 2000a). But upward occupational mobility among black South Africans meant that interracial differences were declining rapidly. By the mid-1990s, intra-racial inequality was contributing more to overall inequality than interracial inequality (Whiteford and Van Seventer 2000; Leibbrandt et al. 2001).

Public and private welfare systems serve to mitigate the extent of inequality. The public welfare system is highly redistributive, as taxes paid by the rich are transferred to the poor through old-age pensions and, to a lesser extent, child support grants and disability grants. The private welfare system is also highly redistributive, as many working people remit a share of their earnings to poorer kin. Overall, redistribution through public transfers in 1993 was about 1.7 times larger than the total value of redistribution through private transfers (remittances). The noncontributory old-age pension system has a major effect on poverty not only for the elderly, but also for poor children, because so many children live in three-generation households dependent on a grandparent's pension (Ardington and Lund 1995; Case and Deaton 1998; Duflo 2003).

The pattern of redistribution through public and private welfare systems has two important implications affecting possible reforms of public welfare. First, households spread across a wide range of deciles benefit from redistribution through the budget—including through old-age pensions. Although old-age pensions are means tested, only the individual applicant's income is taken into account, so there are many recipients of old-age pensions living in households in richer deciles, i.e., living in the same households as (typically) children with well-paid employment. Public transfers are not only substantial, they are also broad in their coverage, resulting in a powerful coalition of groups in favor of increased public welfare financed in similar ways to the existing public welfare system. The public welfare system can redistribute from a small base (the top two deciles) to such a wide range of beneficiaries, and at quite generous levels, because South Africa has a very efficient and progressive tax system, comprising primarily income taxes levied on the rich.

Secondly, the private welfare system serves to redistribute income from a much wider range of households to a narrower range of households. Crucially, the deciles that encompass the industrial working-class and public sector employment—i.e., the bases of the trade union movement—are net beneficiaries of public welfare transfers but net disbursers of private welfare transfers. These are households with, typically, incomes above the median but below the mean for South Africa, i.e., in deciles six through eight especially. There is some evidence that public welfare has a crowding-out effect on private welfare, i.e., workers send fewer remittances to relatives if those relatives receive old-age pensions (Jensen 2003). The South African trade union movement thus has a clear interest in increasing the public welfare system, because its members would both share in the direct benefits and be able to reduce their remittances to poorer kin, benefiting indirectly.

South Africa's welfare systems may be redistributive, but they are incomplete. Large numbers of households receive no old-age pensions, because they have no members of eligible age, and receive no or negligible support in the form of remittances. These households either have members in low-wage jobs, especially in agriculture, or have no employed members at all. Whereas inequality until the 1970s was determined largely by the gap between white and black incomes, inequality in the 1990s is primarily driven by (a) inequality within the distribution of wages, and (b) by the fact that 30 percent of households had no wage income at all. As Leibbrandt et al. (2001: 34) point out, "access to wage income is central to determining which households are able to avoid poverty and even the depth to which poor households sink below the poverty line." Not only are poor households likely to have more unemployed adults than richer households, but they are also likely to have more adults who say they are not available for work. Labor force participation rates rise steadily up the income deciles (Seekings 2000a). The dual correlation between unemployment and income, and labor force participation and income, suggests that low-income households are significantly marginalized from the labor market.

Poverty and Inequality after Apartheid

In the decade following the end of apartheid, inequality has remained high and has probably even risen somewhat, while poverty has clearly grown. The comparison of the 1995 and 2000 Income and Expenditure Surveys suggests that the Gini coefficient for the distribution of income rose from 0.65 to 0.69. Interracial inequality has declined, while intra-racial inequality has grown. These trends reflect, above all, trends in the labor market. Unemployment has continued to rise, reaching 30 percent by the official, *strict* definition (that only includes active job seekers) or 40 percent (if discouraged job seekers are included). Working people in formal employment have prospered, however, as real earnings have risen for the employed. Growth has been slow; but formal employment has fallen and all economic sectors have continued to move toward more skill-intensive and capital-intensive production (Seekings et al. 2004).

The post-apartheid state did reform social spending in apparently progressive directions. Taking into account government spending on welfare transfers, public education, public health, subsidies for housing, and capital expenditure on the provision of water, Van der Berg (2001) estimates that spending on the poorest 40 percent of households (i.e., quintiles 1 and 2) rose by about 50 percent between 1993 and 1997. A small part of this was made possible by reduced spending on the rich, in that spending *per capita* on the top quintile actually declined. But the main share of extra spending on the poor during the mid-1990s came from increased and well-targeted spending by the government. This targeted expenditure entailed not *cash* income, in the form of government welfare transfers, but rather benefits *in kind*—especially in terms of public education. Unfortunately, there is little evidence that spending more on the teachers who teach poor children has resulted in actual improvements in the quality of schooling for poor children.

Trends in cash welfare transfers in the first post-apartheid decade were similarly ambiguous. Between 1993 and 2000, the real value of the old age pension declined by an average of about 1.5 percent per year, or a total of about 20 percent. In the early 2000s, it rose somewhat, but remained far below its 1993 value. The old-age pension continues to account for the bulk of welfare spending, but disbursements through child support grants and disability grants have grown steadily. The AIDS pandemic has fueled the need for disability grants (although the provision of antiretroviral drugs from 2004 might mitigate this). Expenditure on child support grants has risen due to rapid increases in coverage. The post-apartheid state inherited a system of State Maintenance Grants paid to low-income single parents; these were very generous, but coverage was limited, primarily to colored (i.e., mixed race) mothers in one province (the Western Cape). In 1998, the government replaced the State Maintenance Grants with parsimonious Child Support Grants, set initially at R100 per child per month; whereas the former had been payable to the age of 18, the new grants were payable only until a child turned 7. This "reform" was defended on the grounds that the state could not afford the cost of extending the existing grant. Take-up rates for the new grants rose rapidly in the early 2000s. In April 2003, the government extended the grants to children up to the age of 14 (although this extension would be phased in over 3 years). By September 2003, 3.6 million children were registered to receive the Child Support Grant.

One important shift was the extension of unemployment insurance to cover workers in sectors that had previously been excluded. The Department of Labor extended the compulsory, contributory unemployment-insurance system to protect all workers in the private sector—including domestic, seasonal and other informal workers. The benefit schedule was also revised to provide higher proportional benefits for low-income workers than high-income workers. But these reforms did nothing to help the many unemployed who had never contributed to the insurance fund, and who were therefore ineligible for benefits.

After ten years of democracy, therefore, the patterns of poverty and inequality remained much as they had prior to 1994. Economic and labor market policies buttress the earnings of the formal working class, especially the more skilled sections thereof, while reducing the prospects that the unemployed will secure employment in the short- or medium-term (Nattrass 2000b, 2001). The welfare system provides generous assistance to old-age pensioners and limited assistance to single parents, but none to the many poor whose poverty is the result of unemployment rather than age. There is no provision for the long-term unemployed, or for people who have never been employed. South Africa's welfare system was designed at a time (the middle of the twentieth century) when there was little or no unemployment, and the challenge was to assist people who were unable to work on grounds of age, infirmity or the need to care for children. At the beginning of the twenty-first century, South Africa had essentially the same welfare system, but amidst massive unemployment. It was unsurprising that the Taylor Committee, borrowing a phrase from Samson (2002), described South Africa's social safety net as having "a very loose weave" (South Africa 2002: 59).

Arguments for a Basic Income Grant

The debate over poverty reduction is all too often reduced to a choice between growth or redistribution. Economic growth is said to require conservative fiscal and monetary policies, investor-friendly liberalization of trade and financial markets, privatization, and perhaps astute industrial policies by a developmental state. But this kind of growth has not delivered jobs and reduced poverty in the past. Economic growth might be a requirement for poverty reduction in the long run, but even strong economic growth has little effect on poverty if current patterns of inequality remain changed. Few of the benefits of growth "trickle down" to the poor. If the choice is between "distribution-neutral growth" (i.e., growth that does not affect current patterns of distribution) and active redistribution (for example through a BIG), then it is easy to show (as does Meth 2003) that the poor benefit more from the latter, even if redistribution erodes the rate of growth.

Most of the proponents of a BIG point to the immediate poverty-reducing effects that direct monetary transfers would have on the poor. One way of measuring the impact of a BIG is to see what effect it has on the "poverty gap," i.e., the aggregate of the difference between a selected poverty line and the incomes of households with incomes below that line. Samson (2002) estimated that South Africa's current social security system (before the recent extension of the child support grant) reduced poverty by about one-quarter, and would reduce it by one-third if take-up rates were 100 percent. But a BIG, set at R100 per month, would eliminate destitution and fill three-quarters of the poverty gap. Bhorat (2003) similarly calculates that the grant would reduce the number of people living in poverty by half, and the poverty gap would shrink by two-thirds. More speculatively, and optimistically, Samson suggests that a BIG would help build social capital and improve health among the poor, would result in expanded supply of labor and demand for labor, and would stimulate economic growth (see also Coleman 2003).

Efficient transfers of cash from richer to poorer citizens will, of course, reduce poverty faster in the short- and medium-term than economic growth. But are there other alternatives to both a BIG and distribution neutral growth? Most importantly, is it possible to limit the numbers of those needing welfare support by expanding employment, not so much through faster growth as through promoting an economic growth path that entails job creation rather than job destruction? It has been argued that South Africa's system of industrial-level collective bargaining (whereby wages in organized and typically larger and better-paying firms are extended to nonparty firms) constrains the growth of relatively low-wage, labor-intensive firms (Moll 1996)—although others have doubted the overall importance of labor-market institutions in shaping employment patterns (Standing et al. 1996). Whatever the relative merits of the argument, substantial labor-market reform is not on the agenda in South Africa because of the institutional and political power of the trade union movement. Any such proposed measures have been, and will continue to be, resisted by the trade unions and by those arguing that South Africa is better off attempting to compete through upgrading the skills of the workforce (Nattrass 2001), rather than allowing more low-wage labor-intensive employment patterns to emerge. Unable to reform labor market policy to expand the demand for low-wage, unskilled labor in the private sector, the state has opted instead for public works programs that pay low wages to unskilled workers.

It is difficult to imagine how either public works programs or the limited labor-market policies that are politically feasible could make much of an impression on the massive unemployment facing South Africa. Under these circumstances, there is clearly a compelling case for poverty reduction through redistribution, i.e., through a BIG. But it is important not to ignore the detrimental indirect effects and financial costs of a BIG.

First, it is likely that some of the benefits of public redistribution to the poor would "trickle up" to the less poor, through crowding-out effects on private redistribution. Jensen (2003) shows that poor people receive less in private remittances than one would predict, if they receive a government old-age pension. The trade union movement recognizes this, arguing strongly in favor of a BIG in part on the grounds that the state should relieve working people of this responsibility for the welfare of poor kin.

Secondly, a BIG is not costless. In the first instance, according to calculations in 2001–2002, it would cost a minimum of R52 billion, or 21 percent of (current) government spending (and more than the government currently spends on education, which is the biggest item in the budget at present). The devil, as ever, is in the details, especially when it comes to financing. Samson et al., in unpublished work for the People's Budget and the Taylor Committee, proposed that about half of the cost be raised through higher income tax rates on the richer half of the population, with the other half funded through other taxes (including value-added and capital gains taxes) and borrowing. The People's Budget itself proposed raising half of the cost through a "solidarity levy" in the form of a 17.5 percent surcharge on income tax for the top two quintiles, but had little to say about how the rest of the money might be raised. Overall, as COSATU put it bluntly in a resolution, the cost of the BIG must "fall on the rich."[3] Initially, COSATU appeared to envisage a more broadly based tax base for the BIG. In its 1998 submission to the Jobs Summit, COSATU suggested that a BIG be financed in part by those earning over R3,000 a month paying back the amount they receive as tax, and those earning over R5,000 per month paying double the amount back.[4] A high proportion of COSATU workers (particularly those in the government sector such as teachers and health workers) would fall into the R5,000 per month bracket. In this regard, the proposal has clear social democratic aspects to it. By the early 2000s, however, COSATU's position had hardened into a discourse that talked only of taxing "the rich," meaning the *very* rich, rather than taxing a wide spectrum of income earners.

The most compelling proposals for financing the BIG have been made by Le Roux (2002). Le Roux proposes that sales taxes be increased by about 50 percent. This means that Value-Added Tax, which accounts for the lion's share of sales taxes, would be increased from its current rate of 14 percent to 21 percent. "Sin" taxes on alcohol and tobacco and other excise taxes would be increased proportionately. As Le Roux shows, financing a BIG through indirect taxes in a highly unequal society is highly redistributive, even if the poor spend a slightly higher proportion of their income in sales taxes than the rich (which is especially true for the sin taxes). Under Le Roux's proposals, people in the bottom income decile end up paying about R34 per person per month more in tax as a result of the tax increases. If the BIG is set at R100 per month, they benefit by a net R66. Individuals in the poorest half of the population all benefit substantially. Individuals with incomes above the median and up to the mean, i.e., in the sixth, seventh and eighth income deciles, come up about level, paying about as much (R100) in extra tax as they gain from the BIG. The richest fifth of the population pay more in extra taxes than they receive from the BIG. Financing a BIG in this way means that substantial sums are redistributed from the richest fifth of the population to the poorest half.

The difference between the COSATU and Le Roux proposals for financing a BIG boil down to the position of the typical trade union member. If the BIG is financed solely out of income taxes on the very rich, most trade union members would pay little extra tax but all would receive the benefit of the grant (as well as the possible indirect benefits arising from a reduced need to support poorer kin). If the BIG is financed out of sales taxes, the direct benefit of a BIG to trade union members would be offset by the extra taxes they would pay. Under one system, they would be net direct beneficiaries, under the other they would not (although many would still be indirect beneficiaries).

The Politics of and Prospects for the BIG in South Africa

It is unusual for a proposal as radical as a BIG to be on the agenda at all in a developing country. In most developing countries there is no social assistance for even the most deserving poor: the elderly, the disabled and sick, or children unfortunate enough to be born into disadvantage. In several countries—including Botswana and India—there has been a recent expansion of public responsibility for the provision of welfare, largely because it is clear that in too many cases the family no longer provides the kind of support that it was assumed to do. In Brazil, municipal and state administrations controlled by the Workers' Party or other progressive coalitions have expanded public support, especially for children from low-income families (and tied to attendance at school). But South Africa is unusual in having already an extensive system of public welfare support. This is precisely why a BIG is so easily put onto the agenda. In the South African case, a BIG is not such a radical proposal: it entails the extension of the existing system of support for the young, the infirm, and the old to the able-bodied, working-age population. If a BIG is introduced, it will have been almost "through the back door."[5]

South Africa is also unusual in having a powerful organized constituency with a clear interest in welfare expansion: the trade union movement, including especially COSATU. Most COSATU members stand to gain indirectly, through a reduced need to support poor kin, and directly, if the BIG is financed through higher income tax on people earning more than COSATU's own members. For the semiskilled and skilled working class, poverty reduction through a BIG is greatly preferable to poverty reduction through the reform or partial deregulation of the labor market. But how hard will COSATU push for a BIG? In the face of skepticism (Matisonn and Seekings 2003), the general secretary of COSATU describes the BIG as "a critical component of the social wage, the defense of which is a nonnegotiable plank in COSATU's programme for socioeconomic transformation" (Vavi 2003: ix). Defending the social wage is indeed important to COSATU, in part because the lion's share of the *social wage* is paid in salaries to the large number of public sector workers who are members of COSATU-affiliated unions. The teachers' and municipal workers' unions, most obviously, have a massive and direct interest in the budgetary allocation to education and local government respectively. But few COSATU members depend on the welfare budget for their employment. COSATU's interest in the welfare budget is much less direct than its interest in the education budget. In 2004, COSATU actively supported the ANC in the country's third democratic elections, despite the ANC-led government's opposition to the BIG. But is the BIG sufficiently important for COSATU to treat it as *nonnegotiable*?

It is unclear why the ANC leadership is opposed to a BIG (Matisonn and Seekings 2003). The reason might be, at least in part, narrowly institutional: Other ministers in the cabinet are unlikely to favor a massive budgetary reallocation to the jurisdiction of the Department of Social Development, which is responsible for welfare policy. The ANC leadership certainly has little immediate *interest* in a BIG. In 2004, it won handsomely its third consecutive election, without having to make populist promises about a BIG. There is no credible party to the left of the ANC that is threatening the ANC's support base among the poor. If such a threat does emerge in future, then it is possible that the ANC leadership would turn to a BIG to boost its support. Even this is unlikely, as the partisan interests of the ANC might be strengthened more by discretionary antipoverty spending, and a strengthening of patronage politics, than through programmatic expenditure that recognizes *rights*. For the moment, however, there is little reason for the ANC leadership to shift from its ambivalence or opposition to BIG.

If the ANC-led government is pushed toward a BIG, it would be sensible for it to package this as part of a broader social accord with the unions. Under such an accord, redistributive welfare policies might be offered in return for union assent to reforms that the unions have opposed hitherto, including reforms to labor-market policies to facilitate the creation of low-wage jobs for unskilled workers. A BIG might also be financed through sales taxes, as proposed by Le Roux, rather than income taxes. Such an accord would entail a social democratic compromise in a context in which having employment is a privilege. The employed, rather than just the more narrowly defined *rich*, would compensate the unemployed for their unfortunate circumstances. This kind of accord would certainly be easier to sell to the very rich themselves as well as domestic and foreign investors. If the government were to propose a BIG financed in this way, and accompanied by some labor market reforms, it is hard to see how COSATU could easily oppose it. This, perhaps, is the most optimistic scenario for a BIG in South Africa, and thus in the developing world in general.

Notes

1 See summary documents at www.polity.org.za/govdocs/summit/ jobsummit.html.

2 Statement by Minister of Welfare, Population and Development, on the appointment of a ministerial committee of inquiry into social security, March 31, 2000.

3 Available at http://www.cosatu.org.za.

4 Available at http://www.polity.org.za/govdocs/summit/jobsummit. html.

5 This phrase was used by Anthony Atkinson to refer to the possibility of a BIG in developed countries, in a presentation to the Congress of the Basic Income European Network, Geneva, September, 2002.

References

Anderson, K.G., Case, A. and Lam, D. (2001) "Causes and Consequences of Schooling Outcomes in South Africa: Evidence From Survey Data," *Social Dynamics*, 27 (1): 37–59.

Ardington, E. and Lund, F. (1995) "Pensions and Development: Social Security as Complementary to Programmes of Reconstruction and Development," *Development Southern Africa*, 12(4): 557–577.

Bhorat, H. (2003) "A Universal Income Grant for South Africa: An Empirical Assessment," in *A Basic Income Grant for South Africa*, M. Samson and G. Standing (eds.), (Cape Town: University of Cape Town Press).

Butcher, K. and Rouse, C. (2000) A Study of Wage Impacts of Unions and Industrial Councils in South Africa, Working Paper no. 442, Princeton University.

Case, A. and Deaton, A. (1998) "Large Cash Transfers to the Elderly in South Africa," *Economic Journal*, 108 (450): 1330–1361.

Castles, F. (1985) *The Working Class and Welfare: Reflections on the Political Development of the Welfare State in Australia and New Zealand, 1890–1980,* (Sydney: Allen and Unwin).

Coleman, N. (2003) "Current Debates around BIG: The Political and Socio-Economic Context," in *A Basic Income Grant for South Africa*, M. Samson and G. Standing (eds.), (Cape Town: University of Cape Town Press).

Duflo, E. (2003) "Grandmothers and Granddaughters: Old Age Pension and Intrahousehold Allocation in South Africa," *World Bank Economic Review*, 17 (1): 1–26.

Jensen, R. (2003) "Do Private Transfers 'Displace' the Benefits of Public Transfers," *Journal of Public Economics*, 88: 89–112.

Le Roux, P. (2002) "Financing a Universal Income Grant in South Africa," *Social Dynamics*, 28 (2): 98–121.

Leibbrandt, M., Bhorat, H. and Woolard, I. (2001) "Understanding Contemporary Household Inequality in South Africa," in *Fighting Poverty: Labor Markets and Inequality in South Africa*, H. Bhorat et al. (eds.), (Cape Town: University of Cape Town Press).

Matisonn, H. and Seekings, J. (2003) "The Politics of a Basic Income Grant in South Africa, 1996–2002," in *A Basic Income Grant for South Africa*, M. Samson and G. Standing (eds.), (Cape Town: University of Cape Town Press).

McGrath, M. (1983) *The Distribution of Personal Income in South Africa in Selected Years Over the Period 1945 to 1980*, unpublished Ph.D. thesis, University of Natal, Durban.

Meth, C. (2003) "Mass Poverty, Slow Economic Growth and Redistribution," *Social Dynamics*, 29 (1): 99–130.

Moll, P. (1996) "Compulsory Centralization of Collective Bargaining in South Africa," *American Economic Review: Papers and Proceedings*, 82 (2): 326–329.

——— (2000) "Discrimination Is Declining in South Africa but Inequality Is Not," *Studies in Economics and Econometrics*, 24 (3): 91–108.

Nattrass, N. (2000a) "The Debate About Unemployment in the 1990s," *Studies in Economics and Econometrics*, 24 (3): 73–90.

——— (2000b) "Inequality, Unemployment and Wage-setting Institutions in South Africa," *Studies in Economics and Econometrics*, 24 (3): 129–142.

——— (2001) "High Productivity Now: A Critical Review of South Africa's Growth Strategy," *Transformation*, 45: 1–24.

Nattrass, N. and Seekings, J. (1997) "Citizenship and Welfare in South Africa: Deracialisation and Inequality in a Labor-Surplus Economy," *Canadian Journal of African Studies*, 31(3): 452–481.

——— (2001) "'Two Nations': Race and Economic Inequality in South Africa Today," *Daedalus*, 130: 45–70.

Samson, M. (2002) "The Social, Economic and Fiscal Impact of Comprehensive Social Security Reform for South Africa," *Social Dynamics*, 28 (2): 69–97.

Schultz, T.P. and Mwabu, G. (1998a) "Wage Premia for Education and Location, by Gender and Race in South Africa," Discussion Paper no. 785, Economic Growth Center, Yale University.

——— (1998b) "Labor Unions and the Distribution of Wages and Employment in South Africa," *Industrial and Labor Relations Review*, 51 (4): 680–703.

Seekings, J. (2000a) "Visions of Society: Peasants Workers and the Unemployed in a Changing South Africa," *Studies in Economics and Econometrics*, 24 (3): 5–72.

——— (2000b) "The Origins of Social Citizenship in South Africa," *South African Journal of Philosophy*, 19 (4): 386–404.

Seekings, J., Leibbrandt, M. and Nattrass, N. (2004) "Income Inequality after Apartheid," CSSR Working Paper no. 75, Centre for Social Science Research, University of Cape Town.

South Africa (2002) *Transforming the Present, Protecting the Future: Report of the Committee of Inquiry Into a Comprehensive System of Social Security for South Africa,* (Pretoria: Government Printer).

Standing, G., Sender, J. and Weeks, J. (1996) *The South African Challenge: Restructuring the South African Labor Market,* (Geneva: International Labor Organisation).

Van der Berg, S. (2001) "Redistribution through the Budget: Public Expenditure Incidence in South Africa, 1993–1997," *Social Dynamics*, 27 (1): 140–64.

Vavi, Z. (2003) "Comment," in *A Basic Income Grant for South Africa*, M. Samson and G. Standing (eds.), (Cape Town: University of Cape Town Press).

Whiteford, A. and Van Seventer, D. (2000) "Understanding Contemporary Household Inequality in South Africa," *Studies in Economics and Econometrics*, 24 (3): 7–30.

Chapter 15

The Approval of the Basic Income Guarantee in Brazil

Eduardo Matarazzo Suplicy

When I was elected senator for the first time in 1990, representing the State of São Paulo, I decided to promote a basic income guarantee in Brazil. First, in 1991, through a negative income tax, every citizen 25 years of age or over with a monthly income below the equivalent of US $150.00 would receive an income supplement of between 30 percent and 50 percent of the difference between US $150.00 and his or her income. The executive (the president) would decide, taking into account the availability of resources and the ongoing results of the program, where to set the rate within the range of 30 percent to 50 percent. The program would be introduced gradually over eight years, starting with individuals aged 60 years or over, then 55 years or over, and so on, from 1995 to 2002. The proposal was unanimously approved by the Brazilian Senate in December 1991, went to the Chamber of Deputies in 1992 where it got a favorable report in the Finance and Fiscal Committee in 1992, then it stopped there ready to be voted on.

The initiative also launched a very productive debate; and numerous partial basic income guarantee programs related to education and health, known as the Bolsa-Escola and Bolsa-Alimentação programs, were proposed. During the 1990s, while discussing ways of providing BIG programs, I became more and more aware of the concept of an unconditional basic income and its advantages, even with respect to the negative income tax version of BIG. A negative income tax guarantees income by paying only those with low incomes, while a basic income pays everyone a small amount regardless of their income from other sources.

Accordingly, in December 2001, after being re-elected in 1998 for another eight-year term as senator, I decided to present a new project to institute BIG in Brazil from the year 2005 onward. Today, I am quite convinced that an unconditional basic income is a common sense proposal for the purpose of eradicating poverty, building a more equitable society, and providing real freedom for all the people; just as the common sense way for a person to leave his home is by going out through the door. This was pointed out by Guy Standing at the International Conference on Minimum Income held in the Brazilian senate in 1998. As Confucius explained 520 years before Christ, "Can anyone go out from his home except through the door?"

This initiative was approved unanimously by the Brazilian Senate in December 2002 and was approved by the Brazilian Chamber of Deputies in December 2003, and therefore, by the Brazilian congress. A few weeks later, on January 8, 2004, in a moving ceremony with Professor Philippe Van Parijs present, President Luiz Inácio Lula da Silva signed the bill into law. Brazil then became the first national government in the world to institute a basic income guarantee.[1]

The Brazilian Senate also recently approved President Lula's initiative for a constitutional amendment on fiscal reform that includes for the first time the principle of a basic income guarantee. Article 203 states, "the Union will institute a minimum income program to provide the necessary subsistence to persons and families, giving priority first to those most in need, [in a manner] that may be coordinated in collaboration with the states, the Federal District and the municipalities, according to the Law." The Chamber of Deputies will vote on it soon.

In December of 2003, I had the opportunity to address the Congress of the South Africa Coalition for a Basic Income Grant in Gauteng. At the time, I told them it was encouraging for me to know that in South Africa 27 organizations (including trade unions; churches; and several organizations dealing with issues such as youth, children, HIV/AIDS, the aged, and human rights) representing more than 12 million people have joined a coalition to promote the basic income grant (as it is called in Brazil). South Africa and Brazil have many common problems. Both are industrialized developing nations with huge inequality and acute problems of poverty, crime, and violence. But both nations have extraordinary human and natural resources that may help solve these problems. Very importantly, both nations have governments elected democratically by their people, raising great expectations that they would be able to eradicate hunger and absolute poverty, promote growth and job opportunities, and build a more fair society.

In South Africa and in Brazil, we hold as a common objective the desire to build a just and civilized society. We have learned that to achieve this ideal, we need to consider values other than narrow self-interest, which seeks personal advantage in everything even at the expense of our neighbors. Of course, it is natural to seek our own progress and the progress of our children. However, we also need to look at values such as the search for ethical behavior, truth, solidarity, fraternity, freedom and democracy. In fact, those values are present in the history of all peoples. They constitute the fundamentals of all religions such as Buddhism, Judaism, Christianity, and Islam.

We need to apply economic policies consistent with these values. In Brazil, for example, in order to eradicate hunger and absolute poverty, to stimulate economic growth and job creation, and to improve our distribution of income toward a more equal society, President Lula is emphasizing several programs: agrarian reform, the expansion of micro credit, the strengthening of cooperatives, the support of family farms, the expansion of public educational opportunities and public health services, and an expansion of income transfer programs related to the Zero Hunger target.

During the 1990s, we have developed several kinds of income transfers mainly with the objectives of eradicating absolute poverty, ending child labor, and stimulating poor families to have their children go to school. Last October, President

Lula decided to announce the unification, rationalization and better coordination of four of the existing programs in the so-called Bolsa Família Program. Accordingly, all families with income per person below R $50.00 (US $1.00 is about R $3.00) per month will have the right to receive a complement of income equal to R $50.00, with an additional R $15.00, R $30.00 or R $45.00, respectively, if the family has one, two, three or more children. If the families receive a monthly income per capita between R $50.00 and R $100.00, they will have the right to receive only the R $15.00, R $30.00 or R $45.00, depending on the number of children. The families will have to show that their children aged 0–6 years are having the recommended vaccines, according to the Health Minister calendars; that they are from time to time being weighed and following the nutritional instructions, that their children aged 7–15 years are really going to school, and that the adults are enrolled in some literacy or skills-building course.

The following four programs were unified: the Minimum Income Program related to Education or Bolsa Escola Program; the Minimum Income Program related to Health or Bolsa Alimentação; the Auxílio Gás or Gas Help Program (these three were already in practice, instituted by Fernando Henrique Cardoso's administration), and the Cartão Alimentação or Food Card Program, related to the Zero Hunger Program (began in February 2003 as a new program of the present administration one month after President Lula took office). The first two programs offered a benefit of R $15.00, R $30.00 or R $45.00 to families with income per capita up to half the minimum wage and with children aged 7–15 years and 0–6 years, respectively, in the Bolsa Escola and in the Bolsa Alimentação Programs. The Gas Help Program provided a monthly benefit of R $7.50 for families to buy cooking gas. The Food Card Program distributed a monthly card of R $50.00 to families with income per capita below half the minimum wage, with the limitation that the money could only be spent on food. After the first eight months of the program, the government decided that it would be better for the beneficiaries to have freedom to spend their Bolsa Família benefit as they wish, with no requirement to spend it only on food. This is a step in the right direction. Today, 3.6 million families are beneficiaries of the Bolsa Família Program, which is first being applied in the poorest regions of the country, such as the Northeast.

The new law stipulates that the basic income will be instituted gradually from the year 2005 onward, starting with those most in need. The executive will determine the amount that will be paid and the velocity of gradual implementation until it reaches the whole population. It will always consider the economic progress of the nation and the availability of resources.

By the year 2006, 11.4 million families or about 46 million people (one-fourth of the Brazilian population of 182 million) are expected to be enrolled in this program. Ana Fonseca, executive secretary of the program, mentioned in an interview last January that the Bolsa Família is the beginning of the Citizen's Basic Income. I suggested to President Lula that his government should evaluate continuously the results of this program, especially checking to what extent this design is avoiding the phenomena of the so-called unemployment and poverty traps that are often analyzed in the literature on guaranteeing income to all. We might see this unification of income transfer program as a step towards the institution of a basic income guarantee. This is defined as a modest income that will be sufficient for the subsistence of each person, which will be paid by the nation to everyone regardless of origin, age, sex, race, civil, and socioeconomic condition.

But are we going to pay this basic income even to the wealthiest people, those that are not in need? Yes. But of course, they will contribute relatively more in taxes and, just as everybody else, they have the right to receive the grant. What are the advantages of giving the basic income to everyone? First, basic income eliminates the tremendous bureaucracy involved in determining how much each person receives in the formal and informal market before we can determine who is eligible for aid. Therefore, basic income creates more certainty that all the poor will really have access to aid. Second, we will extinguish the stigma or the shame that someone may feel when forced to say that he or she earns only so much and therefore deserves an income supplement. Third, and more importantly, from the point of view of each person it will make a tremendous difference if he or she knows that from now on every citizen has the right to receive an amount of the national product as the nation progresses more and more; a right that is equivalent to the right of anyone in South Africa or in Brazil, rich or poor, to walk and swim at South Beach in Durban or at the Copacabana beach in Rio de Janeiro, respectively.

The basic income guarantee has been defended by a wide spectrum of economists, social scientists and philosophers: from James Tobin to Milton Friedman, from Joan Robinson to John Kenneth Galbraith, from James Edward Meade to Jan Tinbergen, and from Martin Luther King to Philippe Van Parijs and Guy Standing. Is there a place in the world where it has been applied? Yes, and with great success, in the state of Alaska in the United States. During the early sixties, Jay Hammond, the mayor of a small fishermen's village (Bristol Bay, Alaska), observed that although a huge amount of wealth came out of Bristol Bay, many of its residents still remained poor. He proposed a three percent tax on the value of fish to create a fund that would belong to everyone. He had much trouble persuading people of soundness of his idea. It took five years. But it was so successful that ten years later he became the governor of Alaska.

In 1976, when the Alaska pipeline was under construction, Governor Jay Hammond told the 300,000 Alaskan residents:

> We should think not only of our generation but also of the future generations. Since oil and other natural resources are nonrenewable, let us separate 50 percent of the coming oil royalties into a fund that will accumulate and that will benefit all Alaskans from now on.

The Alaska Permanent Fund was approved by the state assembly and also by a popular referendum; 76,000 voted in favor of it and 38,000 against it. Today it is considered political suicide for any Alaskan leader to oppose the Permanent Fund. I visited Alaska in 1995. For seven days I asked everyone in all the places I went how they evaluated that dividend system. I could see very strong and widespread support among the people for the fund.

The oil royalties are invested in U.S. Bonds; shares of Alaskan, United States and international corporations; and real state investments. Since 1980, the net worth of the fund has grown from US $1 billion to US $28 billion. Everyone living in Alaska for the previous year has the right to receive the annual dividend that has varied from a value from US $300.00 in the 1980s to US $1,107.00 in 2003. The largest dividend, almost US $2,000.00, was paid in 2001.

The Alaska Permanent Fund dividend system has made Alaska the most equal of all the American states. During the period 1989–1999, Alaska distributed six percent of its Gross Domestic Product equally to all of its citizens, today around 660,000 people. As a result, during the last decade, while the average income of the poorest families in the United States grew 12 percent and that of the richest families grew 26 percent, in Alaska the average income of the poorest families grew 28 percent whereas the average income of the richest grew 7 percent. Q.E.D., as we normally say when we prove a mathematical theorem.

This serves as an example for all nations of the world and is especially valid for countries like Brazil, the Philippines, South Africa, Colombia and Iraq that greatly need to eradicate poverty and to improve their income distribution in the direction of greater justice. The economists and social scientists of the Basic Income European Network (BIEN), founded in 1986, have more and more demonstrated the rationality of the basic income approach, as have their counterparts in other continents.

In fact, although Jay Hammond does not refer to Thomas Paine in his autobiography (Hammond 1995), the Alaskan initiative echoes the proposition that this leader of the American Revolution presented to the French National Assembly in 1795 in his pamphlet “Agrarian Justice.” Paine argued that poverty is something related to private property and civilization: Since property was held in common among Native Americans, destitution did not exist among them, as it did in the villages and cities of Europe in his time. But he said it was common sense that someone who cultivates the land and makes benefits to it should have the right to the income resulting from his work in his property. However, it was Paine’s plan that everyone who cultivates land should contribute a portion of income to a fund that would belong to everyone in that nation. From this fund, once it has accumulated, he argued, we would pay a basic capital and income equally to everyone in the nation—not as a gift but as a right that was taken from the person when private property was instituted in that society. He emphasized that this proposition should be applied in all nations (Paine 1920).

On May 26, 2003, when the Brazilian Sérgio Vieira de Melo was nominated to be the coordinator of the United Nation’s actions in Iraq, I wrote a letter describing the Alaskan example and suggesting that he propose to the Iraqis that they follow it so that all the people of that nation can share in the ownership of its wealth. On May 30th, he answered that he took good note of the proposition and that he would tell those responsible for administering Iraq about it. On June 23rd, at the World Reconciliation Summit in Jordan, Ambassador Paul Bremer III, the Chief Administrator in Iraq, gave a speech, “What are the Next Steps?,” in which he said the following:

> One way to share Iraq's blessings among its people would be with a special program funded with oil revenues. Some profits from oil sales could be distributed to Iraq's citizens as "dividends," along the lines of the system used by the State of Alaska. Alternatively, oil revenues could be deposited in a national "trust fund" used to finance public pensions or other elements of a social safety net needed to ease the transition from a state-dominated to a private sector economy. In either case, every individual Iraqi would come to understand his or her stake in the countries economic success. I believe this type of proposal could be profitably debated when an interim Iraqi authority is convened in the months ahead.

On the first of August, I spoke for about fifteen minutes on the telephone with Sérgio Vieira de Melo while he was working at the UN in Baghdad. He then told me that the proposal had been very well accepted among the people there and that a mission of the World Bank in Iraq said that it was feasible. Unfortunately, Sérgio was killed on August 19th, 2003 by someone who didn't understand that he was there only for the benefit of the people.

In Brazil, South Africa, and many developing countries, a huge portion of the population lives in absolute poverty. In Brazil we also have a large public debt. The Brazilian public sector (including the municipalities, the states and the union) paid R $145 billion in interest in 2003 from an estimated GDP of around R $1.5 trillion. Therefore, we are paying almost 10 percent of our GDP in the form of interest to both internal and external owners of the Brazilian public debt. Thanks to the efforts of Lula's government, in 2004 this amount diminished to R $128 billion. This is still a tremendous burden compared to the Bolsa Família program that will benefit 3.6 million families in 2004 at an expenditure of only about R $5.3 billion.

If Alaska has an income per capita of around US $35,000 per year, ten times that of Brazil, then we could think of a modest basic income to start with of around R $480.00 per year, R $40.00 per month per capita (US $1.00 is around R $3.00). This would mean R $240.00 per month for a family of six, or around US $80.00, the equivalent of the minimum wage in Brazil today. It would cost R $83.5 billion or about 5 percent of GDP. An amount of this magnitude cannot be considered in the short run, but we can think of gradually attaining this objective when we fully understand the extent of its benefits to the whole society.

Some people have difficulty accepting the idea of a basic income guarantee either in the form of a negative income tax or a basic income payment because of its possible effects on the attitude toward work and the risk of stimulating laziness. Let us think about the fact that there are so many activities that are so important for humanity, such as parents taking care of their children, or activities that we like to do in our communities for no remuneration. Most national constitutions establish the principle of respect for private property, which means that those who own capital may receive income in the form of interest, rent, and profit without any obligation to work. However, normally they send their children to school, and they work. Why? Because it is natural for human beings to want to progress. Therefore, if we allow the rich to receive income even without the obligation to work and they do work, why not extend the right to both the rich as well as the poor to receive a modest income sufficient for survival, for everyone to be a partner of the nation and of the planet Earth?

There is one point that workers, entrepreneurs, and members of the government should be aware of, especially in developing countries. We must take into consideration that most developed nations today have income transfer programs to alleviate poverty and to complement the incomes of their population that have the effect of making their economies more competitive towards ours if we don't apply a form of income transfer.

For example, in the United States, in addition to the Food Stamp Program and Temporary Assistance to Needy Families (TANF), the government has introduced and expanded significantly during President Bill Clinton's years, the Earned Income Tax Credit (EITC), which is a form of negative income tax. During 2003, the United States government paid about US $35 billion to more than 20 million families or more than 50 million people. Since the United States economy increased the EITC, the United Kingdom introduced a similar form of negative tax with the Family Tax Credit. Almost all European countries have some kind of guaranteed income program with similar effects. These programs mean that developed countries have decided to pay their workers an extra amount of money to keep them above the poverty line. Of course, these programs make it possible for firms to pay somewhat less than they would otherwise. Because these programs cause the economy to function at a higher level of activity, the final result is that growth rates, levels of employment, and wages will end up even higher.

In the developing countries, we must be conscious that we should also apply a form of income transfer, either in the form of a negative income tax or a basic income, to make our economies more competitive. The most rational form, I am firmly persuaded, is the unconditional basic income. The results shown above for the development of Alaska, when compared to the average for all 50 American states, are strong evidence that this is the case.

The basic income guarantee will have a tremendous impact on the freedom of everyone, as Philippe Van Parijs (1995) argues so brilliantly in *Real Freedom for All: What (If Anything) Can Justify Capitalism?*. It is the instrument that is so compatible with the objective stated by Amartya Sen (2000) in his *Development as Freedom*, when he argues that you have real development when it really means the amplifying of choices for everyone in society. Because basic income guarantee gives people the alternative to survive with dignity, it will free them from the humiliation of having to sell their bodies, to participate in narco-traffic gangs, or to accept work conditions tantamount to slavery, which still exist in many parts of the world today. Let us join forces to implement a basic income guarantee in all nations of the world. It will be a way for all the people to participate effectively in the table of fraternity, and for peace to prevail everywhere.

Note

[1] A more complete bibliography on the theme may be found in my book: *Renda de Cidadania. A Saída é pela Porta. Perseu Abramo Editora e Editora Cortez*. 2002. Segunda Edição.

References

Hammond, J. (1996) *Tales of Alaska's Bush Rat Governor: The Extraordinary Autobiography of Jay Hammond Wilderness Guide and Reluctant Politician,* (Kenmore, Wash.: Epicenter Press).

Paine, T. (1920) [1795] *Agrarian Justice,* (London: Bell).

Sen, A. (2000) *Development as Freedom,* (Oxford: Oxford University Press).

Suplicy, E. (2002) *Renda de Cidadania. A Saída é pela Porta. Perseu Abramo Editora e Editora Cortez*, (São Paulo: Segunda Edição).

Van Parijs, P. (1995) *Real Freedom for All: What (If Anything) Can Justify Capitalism?*, (Oxford: Oxford University Press).

Chapter 16

The Basic Income Guarantee in Europe: The Belgian and Dutch Back Door Strategies

Yannick Vanderborght*

Introduction

Since the early 1980s public discussions on the basic income guarantee (BIG) have been intense in various European countries. First advocated by intellectuals and a few social movements, the proposal has gained increasing credibility and has even been propelled onto the governmental agenda in two countries, Ireland and the Netherlands. In Ireland, a tremendously influential lobby has managed to push for an official green paper on BIG, which was published in October 2002 (see Ireland 2002). In the Netherlands, as is explained in some detail below, the idea was considered a worthwhile alternative in political circles during the 1990s, but was finally dropped. However, through incremental tax reforms, a modest negative income-tax system has gradually been introduced.

Although most BIG proponents are defending the idea as a national welfare reform, some have already considered the possibility of creating a true European dividend (see for instance Van Parijs and Vanderborght 2001). In 1986, academics interested in BIG launched the Basic Income European Network (BIEN), which aims at fostering the discussion of the idea throughout Europe.[1] With the passing of time, BIEN has become a well-developed network involving researchers and activists from five continents. In September 2002, it organized its ninth international conference at the International Labor Organization (ILO) in Geneva. In his enthusiastic opening speech, Juan Somavia, Director-General of the ILO, said to the participants, "the moment may be nearing when [their] ideas will become common sense" (Somavia 2002). In Europe, however, there is still much work to be done, and BIG is nowhere considered a short-term alternative.

Regarding the prospects of a transformation of income-security programs into a universal and unconditional minimum-income scheme, Belgium and the Netherlands are of particular interest. Since the early 1980s, one can find in the "low countries" some of the most prominent proponents of an unconditional BIG. In no other advanced European welfare state has the BIG debate been so broad and lively as in the Netherlands. Since 1975, the idea of a *basisinkomen* has been discussed within many Dutch political parties, trade unions, social organizations, and even at the governmental level. It was at the core of various official reports that progressively increased its respectability in political circles. Belgian political actors have always been more reluctant to consider it, with the noteworthy exception of the two green parties. But the academic discussion has been quite extensive. The founding congress and second international conference of BIEN were held in Belgium, respectively, in 1986 and 1988. In 1999, a Belgian political formation named Vivant was launched as the first European single-issue party entirely focused on BIG. Although Vivant remains a tiny player in Belgium's political game, it managed to attract public attention on the proposal through eye-catching posters in the country's main cities.

In this chapter, I scrutinize the political chances of a BIG in the low countries and the probability of incremental steps in that direction. In section 1, assuming that a BIG would replace most existing means-tested minimum income schemes, I briefly review the main social assistance programs of both countries. I shall try to demonstrate that a paradigm shift is underway that may at first sight seriously undermine the progress to a more universal and unconditional income-security system. Partly based on interviews and an extensive review of the press, section 2 is devoted to a brief account of more than twenty-five years of BIG debate in both countries. Section 3 focuses on the reasons of this failure to gain support, which are of paramount importance for the future prospects of unconditional minimum income schemes. As is argued in some detail, the moral objection to an income by right without a related duty to work seems to be the most decisive impediment. Finally, in section 4 I shall try to clarify why, given the obstacles and objections they encountered, most Dutch and BIG proponents have adopted an incremental approach. Refundable tax credits or a "participation income" constitute two possible steps that may prove to be far more promising than the strategy of going all the way to a full BIG.

1. A Paradigm Shift in Welfare

In the literature, both Belgium and the Netherlands are generally classified as corporatist or Christian-Democratic welfare states. Trade unions and employers—the so-called "social partners'—play an important role in the shaping and administration of social security. Most benefits are insurance based and financed through payroll contributions. Tax expenditures play only a modest role in the field of social policy, mainly in the form of tax allowances for children, even though things have been changing in the late 1990s—in particular in the Netherlands. To sketch the broad context of the basic income guarantee (BIG) discussion, this section briefly considers the main characteristics of both the Dutch and the Belgian welfare states and focuses on minimum income schemes as well as recent trends in social assistance. It is not part of the purpose of this chapter to develop a detailed scenario for the concrete implementation of a BIG in Belgium and the Netherlands. I shall assume here, without argument, that a generous BIG scheme would replace existing means-tested minimum-income schemes, the bulk of tax credits and exemptions, and be integrated with family allowances and, in the Dutch case, the basic pension scheme. In the field of social insurance, a BIG would replace the bottom part of the earnings-related unemployment, disability and pension benefits; the income floor it provides would remain supplemented by earnings-related benefits, designed to make up the difference between the guaranteed minimum and current benefit levels.

Dutch "Miracle" and Belgian "Status Quo"

Since the mid-1990s, many scholars have expressed admiration at what has come to be called "the Dutch Miracle." During the 1980s the Netherlands had been stigmatized as an exemplary case of "welfare without work," and the Dutch themselves were moaning over the "Dutch disease." In the second half of the 1990s, the Netherlands became, instead, a model for European decision makers. The economy seemed to have fully recovered: real Gross Domestic Product (GDP) growth was nearly four percent on average over the 1997–2000 period.[2] Above all, the standardized unemployment rate had dropped from a peak of almost 10 percent in 1983 to 2.4 percent in 2002 (OECD 2002b). According to the usual interpretation, the 1982 Wassenaar agreement between unions and employers inaugurated a long period of wage moderation and working time reduction, which in turn resulted in the creation of many jobs. Significantly, social rights of part-time workers were gradually strengthened, and the trade unions did not oppose the massive creation of temporary jobs.

Compared to the Dutch transformations, Belgium is sometimes said to have been stuck in a kind of *immobilism* (Hemerijck and Visser 2000). Belgian unions and employers, unlike the Dutch ones, had not been able to strike a deal at the national level during the 1980s, and they failed again to do so in the mid-1990s. The discretionary power of the federal state in industrial relations has therefore increased, but has proven to be more efficient in neutralizing the social partners than in combating unemployment (Vilrokx and Van Leemput 1998: 342). From about 10 percent in the mid-1990s, the standardized unemployment rate dropped to 6.8 percent in 2002, under the European average (7.6 percent) but still far above the Dutch level (OECD 2002b). Part-time work is not considered as a viable alternative by unions and has never been fostered by the government. Hemerijck and Visser (2000: 253) harshly conclude that there is no other country "where governments designed so many pacts, proposals and plans to coax unions into accepting wage restraint and employers into creating jobs, with so little success." A crucial explanation may lie in the fact that in Belgium innovative policy making has long been ruled out by the linguistic clashes that occurred between the Flemish and French-speaking communities. But one must remember, too, that Belgium is the oldest industrial country of continental Europe. It specialized in the production of coal and steel whose profitability began to decline in the 1960s. By contrast, the Netherlands has never been a true industrial nation, and the adaptation of the Dutch economy to new international pressures proved to be far less painful. One should also stress that in Belgium the slow shift to services has mainly benefited Flanders, whose economic situation is far better than that of Brussels and the Walloon region. Consequently, even if speaking of a relative *status quo* in terms of outcomes at the federal level is correct, one should pay attention to the regional differences. For instance, whereas in 1999 the unemployment rate in Flanders was 7.5 percent, it was 17.3 percent in the Walloon region and 18.1 percent in Brussels (OECD 2001: 61–63).

Minimum Income Schemes

The core transfer programs of the Belgian and Dutch welfare states are earnings related. Social insurance, financed through social contributions of workers and employers, provide various benefits covering such social risks as unemployment, sickness, disability, and old age. In the case of unemployment, workers are expected to register as unemployed and stay available for work. Whereas benefit duration is dependent on work history in the Netherlands, they are theoretically payable without time limit in Belgium. However, an unemployed person can be denied the right to benefit if she is in an "abnormally long period of unemployment," i.e., if this period is twice as long as the regional average for the same sex and age category.

Both countries already have universal schemes, which are nevertheless far removed from a true basic income guarantee for all as they are restricted to specific age categories. Family allowances are flat rate, and granted without means or income test. The first tier of the Dutch pension system is a universal non-means-tested basic pension, financed through general taxation. Since it guarantees every citizen over age 65 a flat-rate income floor, it has sometimes been described as a first step towards a comprehensive BIG scheme for all.

Finally, a residual tier provides social assistance for those who cannot benefit from the other two tiers. The Belgian and Dutch minimum income guarantees are financed through general taxation and are designed to provide a safety net for those who have lost other entitlements or have no other means of subsistence. People older than 18 whose resources are below the prescribed limit are entitled to the minimum income. The amount is adjusted according to the means of the beneficiaries and as a function of the resources of possible cohabiting partners. Both schemes make up the difference between these resources and the prescribed maximum amount. In Belgium the level of the guarantee (€595 for a single individual[3]) is calculated without any reference to the average disposable income or the minimum wage legislation, but is linked to the retail price index. By contrast, the Dutch minimum income level (€578 for a single in 2004[4]) is fixed as a proportion of the legal net minimum wage. A single person is entitled to 70 percent of the net minimum wage, single parents to 90 percent, and a couple to 100 percent. As in the Belgian scheme, handling of cases of social assistance is individualized.

From De-Commodification to Active Policies

Since the mid-1990s, social policy reforms have been changing the face of the Belgian and Dutch income security programs. Unemployment benefits and minimum income schemes are said to discourage *self-sufficiency*, and therefore have been transformed by actively linking benefits to work requirements. Partly under the influence of European guidelines, ambitious reforms have already been implemented. New obligations are imposed on beneficiaries, while eligibility criteria have been tightened and sanctions applied more strictly. In this respect, one can argue that both countries are in the incremental process of a true paradigm shift in welfare.

Belgian Minister Frank Vandenbroucke[5] is probably the policy maker who voiced most explicitly the normative core of the new conception of social rights in the Belgian-Dutch context. In an official speech he gave in the Netherlands in June 1999, he explained in detail his vision of the role of a reformed welfare system, which he called "the active welfare state." In his view, contemporary social security programs should not only provide income security, but also

> increase opportunities to participate in social life, so that the number of active persons in society is increased.... It would be proper to suppress or correct, as much as possible, the current social security system mechanisms which discourage people instead of giving them incentives to be active (Vandenbroucke 1999: 5).

The role of the *active welfare state* should essentially, therefore, be that of fostering participation, in various ways.

It would be, by far, an exaggeration to assert that Vandenbroucke supports US style workfare schemes. To the contrary, in his view, social-democratic activation policies should be aimed at dealing with exclusion, not at stigmatizing beneficiaries. But he nevertheless favors an individualized approach to social welfare, meaning that individuals could be held responsible for staying out of the labor market. The "active welfare state," he wrote in an academic paper, "is bound to address questions of *individual responsibility*" (Vandenbroucke and Van Puyenbroeck 2000: 87). In this sense, his conception of welfare is no doubt part of the same ideological family as American workfare. Within this framework, the importance attached to individual responsibility increases, whereas emphasis on collective responsibility—which forms the historical core of European social security systems—loses its importance. Vandenbroucke's views have exercised considerable influence over the Belgian social policy debate. As such, they were the first explicit formulation of a diffuse political climate, which had also impregnated the Dutch public debate. The notion of an *active welfare state* was prominent in the Belgian liberal-socialist-green coalition's governmental agreement, published in July 1999. But it was already underlying initiatives in the field of social assistance and unemployment policy since the late 1980s, in Belgium as well as in the Netherlands. Interestingly, the need to create such an *active welfare state* was also strongly emphasized at the special meeting of the European Council in Lisbon in March 2000 (Rhodes 2002: 329).

The shift from passive to active social assistance is one of the most important developments of the 1990s in Belgian welfare reform (Vranken 1999: 181). The social right to an income in case of need has been progressively replaced by a social right to reintegration through work or training.[6] The new legislation on minimum income, which replaces the 1974 law and took effect in October 2002, is particularly illustrative. Opposed by various social movements, including the main trade unions, it perfectly conveys the ambitions of Belgium's political circles in terms of active social policy. Whereas the initial legislation's first article guaranteed the needy a right to means of subsistence, the new law subtly stipulates that everyone has "the right to social integration" (Belgium 2001a). As it clearly appears in the text, social integration will preferably take the form of paid work. To be entitled to the new "integration income," the claimant will be enrolled in an "individualized integration project," which consists of training and job counseling. For recipients under 25, it is compulsory and must lead to a job contract within a fixed term.[7] The new right to social integration then becomes an explicit "right to social integration *through employment*" (art. 6). In the preamble including the grounds for the adoption of the new bill, integration through paid work is presented as the norm. Social policies, it is said in the document,

> have to develop from strictly financial assistance to social action.... Everyone should be able to find his/her own place in our society, jointly contribute to its development, and benefit from the guarantee of the right to personal emancipation (Belgium 2001b: 2).

In the Netherlands the shift to active social assistance appears even more powerful and radical than in Belgium. When the first liberal–labor coalition came into power in 1994, the unambiguous leitmotiv was "work, work, work." In 1996, the new General Social Assistance Act introduced various work-related conditions into the social assistance scheme. One of the most controversial of these elements is the introduction of a work requirement for single mothers with children of school age, i.e., more than five years. According to Knijn and Van Wel (2001), this particular reform constitutes an "enormous ideological shift," rather than a useful tool for helping single parents to get off welfare. In 1998 a number of training and employment programs for the young and long-term unemployed were merged into the Job-seeker's Employment Act (Wet Inschakeling Werkzoekenden). It includes three main schemes, each designed as a single pathway to the regular labor market: subsidized jobs with a regular employer, subsidized jobs with local employment organizations, and training or "social activation" through unpaid work (Spies and van Berkel 2000). For the young unemployed, if no subsidized job is available, participation in training and social activation is compulsory. After various warnings, recipients who regularly drop out of one of the three schemes or refuse to participate in training activities can ultimately be sanctioned by withdrawal of the benefit. In October 2001, the Dutch Minister of Social Affairs, Vermeend, firmly stated in an official order that possible exemptions from the duty to work had to be granted very carefully: "the obligation to work is the rule" (Vermeend 2001). The latest reform of the assistance law took effect in January 2004. Within the framework of the Wet Werk en Bijstand (WWB), claimants must accept job offers even if they do not match their qualifications or past work experience.

These reforms are constructing a new ideological framework within which any chance of a promising and dispassionate debate on the basic income guarantee appears at first sight to be jeopardized. How could one imagine that the idea of an unconditional minimum income could be taken seriously, while conditionalities in social assistance and unemployment insurance are gradually tightened in both countries? Whereas in the 1980s and early 1990s the Dutch BIG debate was comparatively broad and lively, the proposal now seems to have dropped from the public attention. In Belgium, it has gained increasing visibility during the 1990s, but it still lacks any broad political support. I shall briefly concentrate, in Section 2 of this chapter, on the Belgian and Dutch political history of this idea.

2. The Basic Income Guarantee Debate

Belgium: From the Green Parties to a High-Tech Businessman

While, in Belgium, the idea of a comprehensive negative income-tax system was discussed during the 1970s, the concept of universal basic income didn't arise there until the mid-1980s, almost ten years later than in the Netherlands. From the very beginning, it has always been in some way related to the green movement. In January 1983, Philippe van Parijs, a philosopher and member of the French-speaking green party Ecolo, had suggested that the party should endorse the idea of a universal basic income guarantee (BIG). At the time that he wrote the first versions of his proposal, Van Parijs did not know that the idea had already been discussed in many countries, including the nearby Netherlands—under the label "*basisinkomen.*" In 1986, however, he organized in Louvain-la-Neuve the founding congress of the Basic Income European Network (BIEN).[8]

The Mid-Eighties as Starting Point

The Belgian debate, which had already been opened within the green parties, broadened to the public sphere in April 1985. A collective (the so-called Collectif Charles Fourier) led by Van Parijs edited a special issue of the Christian-democratic monthly *La Revue Nouvelle*, in which it suggested a comprehensive reform of the Belgian welfare state and the introduction of a BIG. In the following months, many harsh reactions were published in newspapers and magazines in all parts of Belgium. The severity of commentators was undoubtedly due to the provocative nature of the initial proposal. In the opening article, the members of the collective had designed a radical implementation program for their BIG, implying the suppression of most existing benefits and the deregulation of the labor market (Collectif Charles Fourier 1985: 345). Needless to say, this way of presenting the idea, despite the more sober arguments developed in the journal, aroused considerable opposition from the left, to which the Collectif Charles Fourier claimed to belong. In a sense, it also negatively influenced the debate on a long-term basis, creating obstacles that have proven difficult to remove afterwards. On the other hand, the strong impact of the proposal was clearly due to this very innovative and radical way of tackling the issue of social policy reform.

In the Flemish part of Belgium, the debate had naturally been influenced by the Dutch discussion, launched in the mid-1970s. The right–liberal Freedom and Progress Party (Partij voor Vrijheid en Vooruitgang—PVV) was then in favor of a negative income tax system à la Friedman, which had also been discussed within the Flemish employer's organization, the Flemish Economical Association (Vlaams Economisch Verbond—VEV). The simultaneous publication of a Dutch official report on BIG (see *infra*) and of the Collectif Charles Fourier's proposal contributed the most to boost, be it very briefly, the Flemish debate on the topic. In 1985 the Flemish left-wing journal *Komma* published a comprehensive analysis of basic income as a way of "uncoupling work and income" (Abicht 1985). However, aside from the discussions that took place within the green parties, from its very start the BIG debate remained confined mainly to a few academic circles.

Political Forces: The Green Parties and "Vivant"

In Belgium, the only genuine political forces that have explicitly and somewhat continuously supported BIG are the two green parties, Agalev (Flemish) and Ecolo (French-speaking). Created in the early 1980s, both parties were still very small organizations at the time discussion over a BIG was launched by Van Parijs. However, they quickly became an integral part of the Belgian political landscape. Following strong progress in votes during the 1990s, particularly at the June 1999 general elections, they took part in the federal coalition with socialists and right–liberals.

For the greens, a BIG appears to be conceived of as a long-term objective, as an analytical tool to be used in thinking about social security reforms. According to both parties, various incremental adjustments should be seen as steps towards a true BIG for all. Family allowances, for instance, should become an equal right for each child, and their amount fixed irrespective of birth order or age. A universal basic pension should be established as it exists in the Netherlands (Agalev 2001). While Ecolo officially but cautiously endorsed the idea at its first Socioeconomic Congress in 1985, it hastened to stress that a BIG "could not been directly implemented."[9] The idea has long been in contention among its members, but since the early 1990s there seems to be a consensus regarding the approach of the BIG as a long-term objective. For instance, green Walloon minister, Detienne, who felt worried about the radical and unpredictable effects of the uncoupling of work and income, agrees that the BIG idea is interesting because it can give "guiding principles." In his opinion, Ecolo's priority should consist in acting so that those principles, including universality and individualization of social rights, go forward.[10]

One could not end this very brief survey of the Belgian BIG debate without mentioning the Vivant experiment. It is a unique case of a political party whose platform is almost entirely focused on implementing a full BIG.[11] Even compared to the green parties, Vivant is a tiny player in the Belgian electoral game. Founded in 1997 by high-tech businessman and life-member of the Basic Income European Network, Roland Duchâtelet, the party took part in the general elections for the first time in June 1999. On average, its results varied between 2 and 2.4 percent. Although these percentages were small, they made Vivant the most successful among the parties not represented in the Federal parliament. But this experiment was particularly instructive because of the public visibility it gave to the idea of an unconditional income. With no public funding or elected representative, the party had made its name in 1999 through a large-scale electoral campaign. Through huge posters in the Belgian cities and massive doses of leaflets, Vivant had been very successful in attracting attention to its central proposal: the introduction of a basic income guarantee for every citizen. "You will receive an income at the age of eighteen," "Free yourselves with the basic income," "Choose your liberty with basic income," were some of the eye-catching slogans used by the party.

Even if the emergence of Vivant on the political scene has contributed to the spreading of the idea, it cannot be said to have boosted discussions about BIG in Belgium. Since the 1999 elections, the party has dropped out of public attention. In January 2002, however, it organized a conference on BIG with the participation of some prominent figures of the European debate. Francophone newspapers grabbed the opportunity to make fun of the party with paragraphs entitled "Vivant is not dead."[12]

The Netherlands: The Basic Income Guarantee (Was) on the Agenda[13]

The Dutch discussion on BIG has strongly varied with the ups and downs of the unemployment rate (Groot and Van der Veen 2000: 197–200). It started in the mid-1970s, as the forewarnings of the economic crisis were emerging, and reached a summit of intensity in the mid-1980s, as 10 percent of the active population was unemployed. Between 1985 and 1993, as the unemployment rate was decreasing significantly, BIG was the subject of many scientific studies. It came back into the forefront in 1992 owing to a new report published by a governmental agency. Partly due to unfavorable unemployment figures, the discussion was again more intense between 1992 and 1995. Since the mid-1990s and the surprising "Dutch miracle" (see *supra*), BIG remains essentially confined to academic and intellectual circles; on the political scene, it became at best an internal debate within some parties. In September 1998, the Seventh BIEN Congress was held in Amsterdam. In 2002, while the unemployment rate had dropped to under three percent, the idea seemed, at first sight, far removed from the institutional agenda.

The most intense period of discussion was a direct consequence of the publication in October 1985, by the renowned and influential Scientific Council for Government Policy (WRR), of a bulky report entitled *Guarantees for Security: Perspectives for a New Social Security System* (WRR 1985). This document was part of an ongoing reflection on the future of the welfare state in the context of economic recession. The report insisted on the need to guarantee income security independently of the variations in economic circumstances: "the guarantee of minimum social benefits has to be the most important goal of social security" (WWR 1985: 7). While suggesting a profound reform of the Dutch welfare state, the suppression of the minimum wage and substantial reductions in employer's social contributions, the WRR called for the implementation of a partial BIG of approximately €200/month, "given without any work requirement" (WWR 1985: 8–9). The reactions to the report were almost unanimously negative, which is hardly ever the case for a WRR publication. The traditional proponents of BIG attacked the idea of a partial guarantee of which the amount was far below the poverty level. Unions and the Labor Party (PvdA) denounced the trend towards more flexibility on the labor market, and the government found the measures too radical, laying the report aside.

This failure had a considerable impact on the discussion. BIG was almost dropped out of the political debate until 1992. Between 1986 and 1992, it mainly became a subject for academic research in economics and sociology. In 1987, however, various groups committed to the idea launched the association "Workshop on Basic Income," aimed at facilitating coordination of the BIG proponents' activities.[14] In May 1990, the minister for social affairs and employment published a very detailed study of BIG that it had commissioned from two academics. Having proposed an account of the Dutch debate, the authors insisted that the idea of an unconditional income was less controversial than in the mid-1980s. They even asserted "if there is one European country where BIG has a chance to be on the agenda, in the short or medium term, this country should be the Netherlands" (Roebroek and Hogenboom 1990: 195).

In 1994 the formation of an unprecedented liberal–labor government coalition raised "high hopes for basic income," though only for a short period (Groot and Van der Veen 2000: 208). Firstly, BIG constituted "one of the serious alternatives to the existing social security system"[15] that was scrutinized in the summer of 1994, during the formation of a coalition under the direction of the Labor Party leader and future prime minister, Wim Kok. Representatives of the parties involved "had agreed on the principle of a BIG, but not yet on the amount."[16] Secondly, BIG was again front page news in December 1994, when two prominent ministers of the same coalition but from different parties, Hans Wijers and Gerrit Zalm, stated in interviews that a BIG or a negative income tax were alternatives to be investigated in detail. These statements triggered off harsh reactions. The Minister of Social Affairs and Employment expressed his deep disagreement with his colleagues. BIG proponents and opponents from all political parties confronted each other repeatedly through opinion columns and passionate interviews, reviving latent tensions within their own groups. In the House of Representatives, the leaders of the different groups were very negative, and decided that the idea was fit "for the dustbin."[17] Prime minister, Wim Kok, on the contrary, declared that BIG should not be dismissed in a long-term perspective, and asserted that he had been surprised by "such hasty negative reactions."[18]

Given the extreme caution that a ruling head of the executive usually manifests, this latter element is particularly instructive. It indicates that BIG was considered a worthwhile alternative by the prime minister himself. "I am not against carefully examining what we can do, on a long-term basis, with that idea," he said.[19] As one observer rightly pointed out, discussions about a BIG, which were previously "in the margins of policy-making," suddenly became an item for "the ministerial level" (Van Gelder, 1994). However, BIG quickly dropped out of the agenda onto which it had just been propelled. For it had not only proven to be at the source of internal party divisions, it also became a source of contention within the recently formed government. Furthermore, Wijers and Zalm did not receive any official support from their own political sides. Consequently, the BIG public debate faded away once again.

This episode brought to light again the crucial fact that Dutch BIG proponents are not only spread over the whole political spectrum, but also divided along ideological lines. They have always had different conceptions of the role of the welfare state and, hence, of the optimal policy package in which BIG should be integrated. In other words, it is not enough for them to unite and go beyond partisanship through groups like the Association Basic Income at the Dutch level, or the Basic Income European Network on a European scale. They still have different views on the best strategy and the desirable final outcome. This constitutes one of the possible obstacles to progress of BIG, on which I shall now focus in Section 3.

3. Four Obstacles in the Way of the Basic Income Guarantee

The Dutch debate on the basic income guarantee (BIG) was very lively and intense over the period between 1975 and 1995. The idea was discussed within all political parties of any importance, within several trade unions and social movements, and even at the governmental level. The arguments made in its favor were numerous, ranging from ethical justifications related to individual autonomy and social esteem to the call for a flexible and deregulated labor market. In Belgium, by contrast, the discussion has remained more narrowly confined to academic circles. On the political scene, the green plea for BIG made by Agalev and to a lesser extent by Ecolo has become, if anything, more timid with the passing of years. The emergence of the highly idiosyncratic party, Vivant, and its huge posters on BIG in Belgian cities, did not contribute to making it a plausible alternative in established political circles.

It is not easy to account for this considerable difference between the two countries. A crucial explanation may lie in the role played by the labor unions. Belgian unions are far more powerful than their Dutch counterparts; and they had, at least until the mid-1990s, closer links with governing political parties. More than 55 percent of the Belgian workers are affiliated to a union, a percentage that is similar to the Nordic countries, whereas less than 25 percent of the Dutch workforce is similarly affiliated.[20] For various reasons, most European trade unions have strongly opposed the idea of uncoupling work and income.[21] In welfare states where they take part in the administration of social security, they might see a BIG as a threat to their position, for in some scenarios the unconditional minimum income would replace a number of existing social insurance mechanisms. Since Belgian unions, contrary to the Dutch ones, are handling individual cases of unemployed workers within the framework of a *Ghent System*,[22] they might look even more suspiciously at the implementation of such an automatic payment system. Furthermore, a BIG would definitely make part-time and flexible work easier, a perspective that Belgian unions, again in contrast with the Dutch ones, have never really accepted. Arguably, a BIG would also tend to give individual workers more power to negotiate their working conditions. This, again, might be perceived as a threat to the traditional role of unions in collective agreements. From the very start of the discussion, Belgian unions have been very critical of BIG. Some union officials are still among the most uncompromising opponents to BIG. The preparatory report of the Christian Unions Confederation's 2002 congress on "The just income" included a section entitled "No basic income" (ACV 2002).

Several other Dutch characteristics are worth mentioning, which require further exploration. The existence of a basic pension scheme, as well as the existence of non-means-tested student grants, has certainly constituted a favorable background for the discussion of a basic cash guarantee for all. Also, the fact that a greater proportion of the Dutch unemployed are social assistance beneficiaries, hence receiving non-earnings-related benefits, may have enhanced the attractiveness of BIG. Finally, one should not forget the role played during the 1980s by independent organizations of claimants, which never really emerged in Belgium where a much larger proportion of the unemployed are affiliated with a trade union. Finally, the existence of institutions like the Scientific Council for Government Policy (WRR) and the Social and Cultural Planning Office (SCP) result in more long-term policy-relevant thinking, which may have facilitated the discussion of radical ideas like BIG.

In any case, even if the Dutch went further in public discussions on an unconditional minimum income guarantee, BIG has never been implemented so far. As in Belgium, BIG advocates always failed to get long-lasting political support. How can one explain the setbacks they had to suffer in both countries? The vast majority of the key personalities I interviewed in Belgium and the Netherlands dismissed the most common explanation, i.e., the alleged prohibitive cost of such a scheme. Rather, they focused on institutional, sociological, and, above all, ideological factors. Some of them argued that the fact that BIG had been advocated by numerous intellectuals in both countries has not enhanced its political chances. Others insisted on the scattering of BIG proponents over the whole political spectrum. Although, in this section, I will scrutinize these objections in some detail, it seems that they were neither decisive nor particular to the BIG debate. Indeed, the most important obstacle has been a moral one. Since BIG would be paid regardless of willingness to work, some believe it would contradict the reciprocity principle lying at the basis of social cooperation. Hence, according to many observers, it is highly unlikely that the Belgian and Dutch electorates will ever accept such a welfare reform.

Too Radical!

BIG has, most of the time, been presented as the core element of possible substantial reforms of the welfare state. This has contributed to giving BIG the reputation of being a very radical measure, which has obviously represented a considerable advantage for its success in stimulating academic discussions, but a damaging drawback for the sake of guiding the reform of highly resilient welfare states. Although at the end of the 1990s most proposals were structured round partial benefits, to be implemented gradually, this reputation still persists in both countries. According to Dutch green MP Kees Vendrik, who favors higher benefits targeted at the disadvantaged over a universal minimum income, BIG would be far too much of "large-scale solution, and therefore would not be suited to a well-located problem [i.e., social exclusion]."[23]

The publication of the Dutch Scientific Council for Government Policy (WRR) report in 1985 provoked many negative reactions in the same direction. An editorial writer called the WRR BIG plan "a revolution in social security." And five years later, the lesson drawn by another newspaper was still that "the break suggested was far too radical."[24] This argument was used by the government itself as a justification for the unambiguous rejection of the whole plan: "the council [WRR] has weakened his own position in suggesting, on the basis of its studies, a global project aimed at implementing a totally unprecedented system" (The Netherlands 1985: 28). *A fortiori*, similar comments were made by many observers when the Belgian public debate was launched, two months before the publication of the WRR report. The fear that such a big bang in social security would undermine the traditional welfare state's mechanisms, and thereby contribute to dismantling it, was widespread.

The fact that an overwhelming majority of actors involved in social policy consider BIG as being too radical, and therefore possibly burdened with unpredictable effects, may undermine its political chances as a medium-term alternative. At the time of the Wijers-Zalm controversy in December 1994, a Dutch BIG proponent pointed this out lucidly:

> it is absolutely justified that nobody wants the introduction of a BIG in the short term. For nobody can anticipate the social and economic consequences of such a radical change in the social security and tax system. This may be the most important disadvantage of the proposal (Polk 1995).

As BIG advocate Paul de Beer noted, BIG opponents can easily and tirelessly argue against the plan and point out that "there are other and less radical ways of reaching the same goal."[25] This observation has incited most of the Belgian and Dutch BIG proponents to modify the strategy they employed in the 1980s. Instead of calling for an unconditional right to the minimum income and claiming that redistributive mechanisms should be thoroughly transformed, they adopted a more pragmatic position. At the end of the 1990s, all main green parties were arguing for a very gradual implementation, in which BIG was seen as a long-term objective.

"It Appeals to Intellectuals"[26]

In Belgium and the Netherlands, the BIG debate has been fostered by numerous intellectuals. But in this case the academic pedigree has proven to be a double-edged sword. In fact, BIG has often been stigmatized as an alternative paradigm fabricated by intellectuals who were disconnected from social realities.

The fact that academics were stimulating the debate appeared with the utmost clarity in the Wijers-Zalm case, when two Dutch ministers suggested the implementation of a BIG. As BIG advocate Paul de Beer argues, the two decision-makers were "intellectuals, academics, economists who were freely thinking of alternatives; they thought it was possible to think in an innovative way of socially unacceptable proposals."[27] Minister of Finance Zalm, for instance, was advancing ideas that he developed when he was a professor in economics and, more importantly, a director of the Netherlands Bureau for Economic Policy Analysis. His 1994 statements in favor of a BIG formed a sharp contrast with the negative feelings of most politicians with respect to the idea, including his colleagues within the government.

The Dutch Union of Food Workers (Voedingsbond FNV) provides a good example of the negative effects of a split between the popular support for a BIG and the support for BIG by intellectuals. During the 1980s, strong union support for BIG was in some way related to the very composition of its membership. Most of the Voedingsbond FNV affiliated members were unemployed or low-paid workers, and they could therefore be seen as net beneficiaries from the possible implementation of an unconditional minimum income. However, a closer look at the history of BIG within the Voedingsbond FNV shows that the influence of well-educated staff members was decisive in the choice of the BIG strategy.[28] Neither the very didactic leaflets on BIG printed up by the union, nor the workshops that were organized in some localities, nor the training projects aimed at the members were sufficient to maintain interest in the idea. The debate ran out of steam and stopped altogether in the early 1990s. According to Van Berkel et al., who made an in-depth analysis of this episode of the Voedingsbond's history, one of the main reasons lies in the fact that it was a "top-down" debate (Van Berkel et al. 1993: 22). As the leaders themselves conceded afterwards, "it proved difficult to mobilize members on such an abstract and long-term objective as BIG." This very abstract perspective, supported mainly by the executive, was contradicting "the more concrete" interests of union members in going about their daily life" (Van Berkel et al. 1993: 22–24).[29]

In Belgium too, academics have been at the origin of the BIG debate that may not have been started without their initiative. But again the academic origin of the idea may at the same time have undermined its political chances. From the very beginning, BIG has been described by some of its critics as a dangerous utopia, disconnected from the social dimensions of politics.[30] BIG advocate Walter van Trier thinks that widespread anti-intellectual feelings within Belgian unions partly accounts for the proposal's rejection.[31] Within the green party, Ecolo, BIG was also often dismissed as an idea that was not sufficiently rooted in social movements.

Green Minister Thierry Detienne's cautious approach to BIG originates in the fact that it constitutes a proposal "which does not always take ongoing social debates and power struggles into account."[32]

The Scattering of BIG Proponents

In the Netherlands, and to a lesser extent in Belgium, BIG proponents were scattered over the whole political spectrum. They formed at best an active minority within their own formations. Hence, they were not only unable to get the proposal into their respective party's' platform, but were also unable to create a strong trend in its favor across the partisan cleavages. Coming from different political persuasions, giving different justifications of BIG, "they [had] no interest in working together."[33] According to MP Kees Vendrik, this constitutes a fundamental defect of BIG, which therefore only offers a very "weak electoral strategy." In his view, BIG is like "a washing powder that can be used in any washing machine," from the left to the right.[34] The scattering of BIG proponents has often been stressed by Dutch observers. In 1985, the left-liberal weekly magazine *Groene Amsterdammer* questioned whether a coalition in favor of BIG could ever be possible: "the basic income does not seem to be advocated by only one political side, but by many people coming from all political sides."[35]

However, one could argue that the fact that BIG advocates are spread over the political spectrum constitutes a considerable *advantage* for the proposal's feasibility. In the case of Belgium and the Netherlands, the BIG could in fact become the unifying factor of many types of coalitions. Even if the scattering was described as an obstacle by many actors in the BIG debate and by the people I interviewed, this should not be considered as decisive. The radical flavor of the idea was a more important obstacle when BIG was presented as a short-term alternative. If it is considered to be a long-term objective, to be reached through gradual reforms, this obstacle can be circumvented. It is the strategy already adopted by most Belgian and Dutch BIG proponents. The other critique, dismissing BIG as being disconnected from social realities, should not be underestimated. In both countries, it has negatively influenced the BIG debate in a significant way. But again, this does not mean that it constitutes a decisive impediment. Many social policy reforms are in one way or another related to scientific work, be it empirical or not. Academics can indirectly inspire reforms or even act as policy entrepreneurs, designing alternatives and pushing for them in governmental circles. The fact that BIG was not advocated by influential social movements or trade unions does not mean that it offers no answers to some of their specific claims, or to broader social problems such as exclusion and unemployment, which authorities have to deal with. Accordingly, the fact that BIG, as an alternative to existing patterns of social policy, was designed and advocated by academics does not make it significantly different from many other reform proposals. It should therefore not be considered an insurmountable obstacle. Hence, the major obstacle is probably of another type. It is a *moral* obstacle that clearly underlies all other minor obstacles. It consists in the rejection of an *unconditional* right to the minimum income.

The Moral Issue: "Why Pay the Lazy?"

Belgium and the Netherlands already have universal family allowances. Moreover, all Dutch citizens older than 65 have the right to a basic pension that is neither means tested nor earnings related. The existence of universal and unconditional minimum incomes at both ends of the course of life, at least in the Netherlands, could imply that a universal BIG would easily gain popular support. Dutch BIG advocates often argued that, in this sense, a BIG is already in place. However, children and retirees are not required to work, whereas the majority of possible BIG recipients would be able-bodied, and thus required to contribute to the common wealth. Consequently, the moral objection to BIG arises from a largely shared conception of justice that states that every able-bodied person should work to cover her basic needs.[36]

To take a single example, the moral objection was raised on several occasions in 1994–1995 after the statements of Dutch ministers Wijers and Zalm in favor of BIG. "Basic income is controversial, but not for financial or economic reasons," an editorial writer noted after days of heated debate; "it is an ideological debate, which relates to the fact that the link between work and income is broken: citizens have the right to an income without obligation to search for work. The majority of the Dutch population is repelled by the perspective of this 'money for nothing'" (Van Empel 1994). The work ethic is still strongly present in Dutch society. Empirical research has, for instance, demonstrated that in Europe the Dutch people are the most restrictive towards the unemployed. Friedberg and Ploug (2000) constructed an "average score of restrictiveness," including among other indicators the extent to which people insist on the duty to work when one is unemployed and endorse the obligation to accept jobs that do not match one's qualifications or experience. They concluded that in 1992 the Dutch reached the highest score of all seven European countries they analyzed in their study.[37]

Within this context, suggesting the introduction of an unconditional minimum income in an electoral platform appears to be very risky. Activation policies or reinforcement of work requirements appear much more politically profitable. For this very reason, Belgian green leader Philippe Defeyt has admitted that he would oppose any explicit reference to the radical unconditional nature of BIG in Ecolo's program.[38] In Belgium and in the Netherlands it seems that a BIG cannot be openly defended by politicians who want to bid for power. But might there not be a way of introducing a basic income without relying on such open advocacy, "through the back door" as it were? This will be the subject of my concluding remarks.

Conclusions: Two Small Back Doors for BIG

In the first section of this chapter, the strong trend towards activation in social assistance was described as a "paradigm shift" in Belgian and Dutch welfare. At first sight this transformation, which obviously represents a new political version of the work ethic just referred to in the Dutch case, offers few opportunities to proponents of a Basic Income Guarantee (BIG). As the overview of Belgian and Dutch debates shows, the radical unconditional nature of BIG with regard to work requirements constitutes the feature that most contributes to making it impossible to sell. How could BIG fit into the thick conception of reciprocity that lies at the basis of the emerging "active welfare state"? Rather than being described as a highly advanced form of de-commodification, as Esping-Andersen once did (1990: 47), it now tends to be negatively considered as the ultimate "passive benefit." It seems that if significant steps are to be undertaken in the move from targeted poverty alleviation programs to a universal and individualized minimum income scheme, they will only be indirect and incremental. Hence, a possible implementation through the back door should not be excluded.

The new emphasis on the activation of benefits and beneficiaries is ambiguous. Admittedly, the very notion of "activity" cannot be reduced to paid work in its stricter sense. Unpaid activities like caring, training or voluntary work should be included in its broad definition. For many people they also represent a way of contributing to the common wealth. In other words, "it is not hard to show that having a job and making a social contribution may or may not coincide" (Young 2000: 28). Consequently, if the purpose of the so-called "active welfare state" is to foster active participation in social life, then it should to a certain extent also value activities outside of the labor market. Belgian minister Vandenbroucke himself challenged the assumption that paid work is the only valuable social contribution. He once called for a maximization of the possibilities of active participation, while stressing that "one should not reduce this plea to participation in the labor market" (Vandenbroucke 1999: 11). In Belgium to date this view has not been translated into concrete social policies. In fact, as it appears in its preamble, the law on minimum income that takes effect in 2002 is quite restrictive: "participation in social life can take various forms; nevertheless the access to paid employment remains one of the most secure ways of achieving autonomy" (Belgium 2001b: 3). The newly created "integration income" is not yet aimed at valuing unpaid activities, and recipients are still required to enter the labor market as quickly as possible. But, as Vandenbroucke's assertion shows, there seems to be some room left for a public discussion on the very meaning of "activity." In 2000, for instance, the renowned King Baudouin Foundation published a report entitled "Work and Activity: Towards the Full Participation," which called for a relaxed conception of participation. According to the authors, the unemployment benefit should be transformed into "participation insurance," aimed at fostering unpaid activities (FRB-KBS 2000, Vanderborght and Van Parijs 2001). However, regarding the broadening of the scope of activities to be valued, the Netherlands seems to be comparatively ahead. For, despite the effective paradigm shift in welfare and the renewed emphasis on work requirements, the restructuring of the social assistance system allows for new experiments in social activation. Since 1996, municipalities have the possibility of implementing projects aimed at fostering the inclusion of the long-term unemployed through unpaid activities. Some already broadened the target group to people who refuse to enter the labor market. Recipients who take part in these noncompulsory programs can be exempted from the work requirements. In Rotterdam, one of the Netherlands' largest cities, "participation in social activation is voluntary, and the [social activation] project is not primarily aimed at re-inclusion within the labor market" (Van Berkel et al. 1999: 103). Moreover, in 1999 the Dutch government introduced an innovative scheme aimed at helping the artists on benefit. Within the framework of the Income-Security Act for Artists (Wet Inkomensvoorziening kunstenaars—WIK), some of them can be exempted from all work requirements during a maximum of four years. Although the WIK benefits are inferior to the social assistance levels, they are similar to the Belgian minimum income.[39]

Thus, some contradictory trends are at work in both countries that could offer new opportunities to BIG proponents. In fact, one common argument in favor of BIG consists in asserting that a universal minimum income would help in valuing useful and non-market activities that are not yet recognized. Following the advice of the British economist and BIG advocate Anthony Atkinson, BIG supporters could therefore compromise and promote the idea of a "participation income." Atkinson believes that "a major reason for opposition to basic income lies in its lack of conditionality"; therefore, he argues that "in order to secure political support, it may be necessary for the proponents of basic income to compromise—not on the principle of no test of means, nor on the principle of independence, but on the unconditional payment." In his view, they should support a BIG conditional on participation, in the broad sense (Atkinson 1998: 147–148). Within the framework of Belgian and Dutch "active welfare states," and given the strength of the moral objection to an unconditional income, the incremental transformation of the minimum income scheme into a modest participation income seems one of the only feasible steps towards a true BIG. The Dutch experiments in social activation show that this option should not be excluded. A participation income would be a more coherent way of giving benefits than the existing programs that imply numerous discretional exemptions. Even if this option seems less plausible in the Belgian case, it is worth mentioning that the Belgian Minister of Social Affairs (since 1999), Frank Vandenbroucke, commented quite sympathetically on Atkinson's proposal, which he called "perhaps the road of political wisdom" (Vandenbroucke 1997: 165). Consequently, in both countries the participation income could represent a significant step towards BIG. It would not contradict the reciprocity rhetoric, while simultaneously giving BIG a decisive boost. For in a further stage, "one may well realize that paying controllers to try to catch the few really work-shy would cost more, and create more resentment all over than just giving this modest floor income to all, no questions asked" (Van Parijs 2000). A form of participation income is therefore one of the most plausible ways of implementing a BIG through the back door in Belgium and the Netherlands.

However, a second type of incremental and indirect strategy could possibly lead to effective results too. The Belgian and Dutch governments are searching for new instruments to deal with the so-called "welfare traps," i.e., the fact that benefits are withdrawn at a 100 percent tax rate as the recipient enters the labor market. In both countries, refundable tax credits have already been implemented with the explicit aim of "making work pay." If, in Belgium, it remains modest and targeted at low-paid workers, the Dutch system clearly goes in the direction of a more universal benefit.[40] Before the 2001 comprehensive fiscal reform, all Dutch tax-payers benefited from a general tax exemption on part of their taxable income. The non-earning partner had to transfer this exemption to the working partner, which means that the former's financial incentive to enter the labor market was reduced. Due to the transferability mechanism, "the implicit marginal tax rate on income earned by the dependent partner [was equal] to the marginal tax rate of the breadwinner" (Groot and Van der Veen 2000: 216). Of course, this exemption scheme mainly benefited well-off households subjected to higher marginal tax rates. Since January 2001, this tax allowance has disappeared and has been replaced by a new individual "general tax credit," which is a discount on the amount to pay. Contrary to the previous scheme, the credit does not reduce the total taxable income and is therefore independent of the marginal tax rates. Consequently, it benefits all households equally. More important still for our purpose, the credit is made *refundable*. Workers' nonworking partners are entitled to the full amount of the credit (about €1,500/year), *which can be paid directly into their bank account*. They keep this entitlement as they enter the labor market, but it then takes the form of a discount on the income tax they pay, supplemented by an additional "employment rebate" of about €800. As a consequence, nonworking partners should "find it more attractive to seek paid employment" (The Netherlands 2000: 11).

In other words, since January 2001 Dutch citizens who are not doing paid work are entitled to a modest negative income tax, provided they have a working partner paying a positive income tax. If its level were gradually increased, and its payment not restricted to working families, this refundable tax credit would provide an unconditional and individual minimum income floor to all Dutch citizens. It would, in other words, provide the missing element between universal child benefits and the basic pension. Therefore, it can be said to represent a big step in the direction of a BIG. However, it is not an explicit move, since the stated objective is to launch an active tax policy that gives incentives to enter the labor market. But this has also been one of the stated objectives of BIG from the start. Again, as in the case of a hypothetical participation income, this possible implementation "through the back door" would thus be made, thanks to the "active welfare state" rhetoric.

The transformation of the general tax exemption into a tax credit has long been proposed by Dutch BIG advocates.[41] According to green Euro-MP Alexander de Roo, this has proven to be a successful strategy:

> it will quickly become clear that the amount of the credit is not high enough to have positive effects on the labor market… One will then realize that a true universal and unconditional income is a better alternative."[42]

Interestingly, the Minister of Finance, Gerrit Zalm, one of the instigators of the 2001 fiscal reform, expressly denied this. Answering the green group's questions during a parliamentary session, he asserted that "the individual and refundable tax credit *cannot* be considered to constitute a small step towards the implementation of a basic income guarantee" (Zalm and Vermeend 2000). Of course, this is a matter of interpretation. But the very fact that Minister Zalm took the trouble to make such a statement could paradoxically reveal that BIG remains a possible option. This cautious statement would then only have been a way of defusing a renewed discussion on the subject, in order to avoid splits within the ruling coalition. Actually, at the time he was a director of the Netherlands Bureau for Economic Policy Analysis (CPB), Zalm himself argued for a gradual implementation of BIG and clearly described the very first step: "one should start with the suppression of the general tax exemption's transferability mechanism"[43] Political effectiveness does not always sit easily with intellectual consistency.

Despite numerous obstacles and a strong moral objection to BIG, the idea of an unconditional minimum income is not totally out of the picture in Belgium and the Netherlands. Paradoxically, the activation rhetoric that underlies current welfare state reforms offers new opportunities for advocating a (partial) uncoupling of work and income. New incremental developments in Dutch fiscal and social policies tend to prove it. In a working paper they wrote some years ago on the BIG debate in the Netherlands, Roebroek and Berben were rightly speaking of an "incremental paradox" (Roebroek and Berben 1988). Having analyzed years of heated discussions on Dutch income security programs, they concluded that a radical reform such as BIG could not be explicitly implemented, but that no major social or political force would oppose an incremental process in the same direction.

For sure, the back door strategy lacks the grandness of the front gate. For sure, if there are good reasons to believe that the front gate will remain tightly locked, it might make some sense for BIG supporters to keep knocking—but not at the expense of the careful exploration of less pretentious accesses to the mansion, starting, perhaps, with the two I have identified.

Notes

* The author is grateful to François Blais, Lena Lavinas, and Philippe van Parijs for their detailed comments on an earlier version of this paper, as well as to Paul de Beer, Martin Rhodes, Philippe C. Schmitter, and Rik Van Berkel for useful suggestions. Interviews in the Netherlands have been made in collaboration with François Blais. This chapter is a revised version of a study that was published as a *working paper* of the European University Institute (Firenze, Italy), Department of Political and Social Sciences (SPS 2004/04).

1 http://www.basicincome.org. On September 20, 2004 BIEN turned into a worldwide network, and became the Basic Income Earth Network.

2 However, according to Organization for Economic Cooperation and Development (OECD) calculations, the outlook for the coming years is "highly uncertain and rather gloomy" (OECD 2002a: 9). Real GDP growth had fallen 0.2 percent in 2003.

3 From June 2003.

4 From January 2004.

5 Vandenbroucke has been Minister for Social Affairs (from 1999 to 2003) and, subsequently, Minister for Employment and Pensions (since mid-2003). After the 2004

regional elections, he became Minister for Work, Education and Training in the Flemish Government.

[6] For a general overview of Belgium's activation policies and a comparison with the Dutch ones, see van Berkel and De Schampeleire (2001).

[7] The compulsory integration contract for people under 25 years of age was already implemented in 1992. It involved job-seeking activity, training and counseling by social workers. However, it has not proven to be very successful, and sanctions in case of non-compliance were very few.

[8] Van Parijs is still one of the most prominent advocates of a BIG. For a discussion of his proposals in the North American context, see Van Parijs et al. (2001).

[9] "Rester 'purs' ou enfoncer un coin dans le système? Le dilemme d'Ecolo," *Le Soir*, 2 September 1985.

[10] Interview with T. Detienne, Namur (B), December 2001.

[11] For a more detailed account, see Vanderborght (2000).

[12] In French, *Vivant* actually means "alive." See "*Vivant* n'est pas mort," *La Libre Belgique*, 7 janvier 2002.

[13] For a more detailed account, see Groot and van der Veen 2000; and Van der Veen and Pels 1995.

[14] In 1991, it became the *Association Basic Income*. At the end of 2000, it had almost 250 members, mainly coming from political parties (Boerlage, Saar, and Schäfer, Emiel, interview, Amsterdam [NL], May 2000). http://www.basisinkomen.nl.

[15] "Basisinkomen was serieus alternatief tijdens formatie," *NRC Handelsblad*, 19 December 1994.

[16] Ibid.

[17] "Kamer wijst plan basisinkomen af," *De Telegraaf*, 19 December 1994.

[18] See respectively "Kamer voelt niets voor invoering basisinkomen. Zalm en Wijers krijgen ook geen steun in kabinet," *De Volkskrant*, 19 December 1994, and "Premier Kok sluit basisinkomen op lange termijn niet uit," *De Volkskrant*, 20 December 1994.

[19] "Premier Kok: basisinkomen bespreekbaar," *NRC Handelsblad*, 20 December 1994.

[20] Union density rates in 1990 (unemployed and pensioners *excluded*): 56.5 percent in Belgium and 24.1 percent in the Netherlands. Van Ruysseveldt and Visser (1996: p. 230) stress that "unemployed and retired members account for a large and growing share of Belgian and Dutch union membership; 31.7 percent of all union members in Belgium in 1989, as against 17.4 percent in the Netherlands." The union coverage rates (i.e., the percentage of workers covered under collective agreements) are much higher than the union density rates: 90 percent in Belgium and 81 percent in the Netherlands (for figures from the 1990s, see Esping-Andersen 1999).

[21] This view should probably be somewhat qualified. The case of the Dutch Voedingsbond FNV is a good counterexample, even its commitment to a BIG was related to the specific context of the "welfare without work" period, as well as to the very composition of its membership. In any case, as van Berkel (1994) has pointed out, the Voedingsbond's statement on the BIG was an "exception to the rule." In Ireland, the SIPTU (Services, Industrial, Professional and Technical Union) has also been a cautious proponent of BIG. Nevertheless, there are very few examples of European trade unions in favor of a BIG.

[22] On the *Ghent System*, see Scruggs (2002).

[23] Interview with K. Vendrik, The Hague (NL), May 2000.

[24] Respectively: "Revolutie in de sociale zekerheid," *NRC Handelsblad*, 18 June 1985, and "De zoete wraak van Douben," *De Volkskrant*, 16 June 1990.

[25] Interview with P. de Beer, Diemen (NL), May 2000.

[26] Interview with P. Besseling, The Hague (NL), May 2000.
[27] Interview with P. de Beer, Diemen (NL), May 2000.
[28] This fact was confirmed by Paul de Beer (de Beer, Paul, interview, Diemen (NL), May 2000).
[29] For an account in English, see van Berkel (1994).
[30] See for instance, CSC 1983, and "L'allocation universelle: du rêve à la réalité," *En Marche*, 20 June 1985.
[31] Interview with W. Van Trier, Leuven (B), December 2001.
[32] Interview with T. Detienne, Namur (B), December 2001.
[33] Interview with P. de Beer, Diemen (NL), May 2000.
[34] Interview with K. Vendrik, The Hague (NL), May 2000.
[35] "De triomfantelijke terugkeer van het basisinkomen," *De Groene Amsterdammer*, 19 June 1985.
[36] On this question, see for instance, McKinnon (2003).
[37] The following countries were included in the survey: Denmark, Germany, France, Ireland, Italy, the Netherlands and the United Kingdom. The average score of restrictiveness for all seven countries is 2.5, the Dutch score being 3 (Fridberg and Ploug 2000: 343). On the idea of reciprocity and the reluctance of Dutch policy makers vis-à-vis BI, see Pioch (1999).
[38] Interview with P. Defeyt, Namur (B), December 2001. In 2003, Defeyt resigned as green leader.
[39] In the official presentation of WIK, the Dutch government significantly acknowledges that work requirements can make it extremely difficult to "create works of art and to gain a reputation in artistic circles." However, WIK benefits are not totally unconditional. As in social assistance, they are means tested. Furthermore, to become entitled one must be a holder of an artistic diploma or be officially recognised as an artist by a given independent organization. One of the criteria is the revenues from artistic activity, which must be over €1,089/year. In January 2004, the monthly amount for a single person was €540.64 and €761.31 for single parents. (Ministerie van Sociale Zaken en Werkgelegenheid, http://home.szw.nl, section "uitkeringen").
[40] Regarding tax credits, the Belgian tax reform was far less ambitious. A refundable tax credit targeted at low-paid workers has been put in place, which constitutes a very modest version of the American Earned Income Tax Credit. Ecolo leader Philippe Defeyt acknowledged that the tax reform represents a wasted opportunity for Belgian BIG proponents (Interview with P. Defeyt, Namur (B), December 2001). With a true refundable tax credit of the Dutch type, it was possible to make a step in the direction of a better integration of the tax and benefit system. While designed by people who had looked closely and sympathetically at BIG proposals, the version that was eventually proposed and approved was much more watered down.
[41] For instance, the Radical Party (PPR) stated in its 1981 electoral platform that "it is technically possible to get closer from a basic income by means of the integration and individualization of the tax exemption," PPR (1981): p. 22. In 1994, as it was again thinking of BIG as a long-term alternative, the Labor Party argued for the "replacement of the tax exemption by a tax credit," which would subsequently become a "negative income tax," PvdA (1994): 42. In 1999, the green party GroenLinks also asserted that "the first step towards a basic income consists in the transformation of the existing tax exemption into a general tax credit," Van Gent et al. (1999).
[42] Interview with A. de Roo, Amsterdam (NL), May 2000.
[43] "CPB – directeur Prof. G. Zalm verwacht veel van het geleidelijk invoeren van het basisinkomen," *NRC Handelsblad*, 7 January 1993.

References

Abicht, L., ed. (1985) *Naar een scheiding van arbeid en inkomen?*, Special issue of *Komma. Werkgroep Arbeid and Milieu*, 22.

ACV (2002) *Hoe eerlijk is mijn inkomen?*, ACV-congres "het juiste inkomen," ACV-Vakbeweging, 25 January: 560.

Agalev (2001) *Een groene visie op basisinkomen*, (Brussels: Agalev).

Atkinson, A.B. (1998) *Poverty in Europe*, (Oxford: Blackwell).

Belgium (2001a) *Projet de loi concernant le droit à l'intégration sociale*, (Brussels: Ministère des Affaires sociales, de la santé publique et de l'environnement).

——— (2001b) *Projet de loi concernant le droit à l'intégration sociale: exposé des motifs*, (Brussels: Ministère des Affaires sociales, de la santé publique et de l'environnement).

Collectif Charles Fourier (1985) "L'allocation universelle," *La Revue Nouvelle*, 41 (4): 345–351.

Esping-Andersen, G. (1990) *The Three Worlds of Welfare Capitalism*, (Princeton, N.J.: Princeton University Press).

——— (1999) *Social Foundations of Postindustrial Economies*, (Oxford: Oxford University Press).

FRB-KBS (Fondation Roi Baudouin – Koning Boudewijn Stichting) (2000) *Travail et non-travail: Vers la pleine participation*, (Brussels: De Boeck and Larcier).

Fridberg, T. and Ploug, N. (2000) "Public Attitudes to Unemployment in Different European Welfare Regimes," in *Welfare Regimes and the Experience of Unemployment in Europe*, D. Gallie and S. Paugam (eds.), (Oxford: Oxford University Press), 334–348.

Groot, L. and van der Veen, R. (2000) "Clues and Leads in the Debate on Basic Income in the Netherlands" in *Basic Income on the Agenda: Policy Objectives and Political Chances*, R. van der Veen and L. Groot (eds.), (Amsterdam: Amsterdam University Press), 197–223.

Hemerijck, A. and Visser, J. (2000) "Change and Immobility: Three Decades of Policy Adjustment in the Netherlands and Belgium," in *Recasting European Welfare States*, J. Ferrera and M. Rhodes (eds.), (London: Frank Cass), 229–256.

Ireland (2002) *A Green Paper on Basic Income*, (Dublin: Department of the Taoiseach).

Knijn, T. and Van Wel, F. (2001) "Careful or Lenient: Welfare Reform for Lone Mothers in the Netherlands," *Journal of European Social Policy*, 11 (3): 235–251.

McKinnon, C. (2003) "Basic Income, Self-Respect and Reciprocity," *Journal of Applied Philosophy*, 20 (2): 143–158.

The Netherlands (1985) *Standpunt van het kabinet met betrekking tot het rapport "Waarborgen voor zekerheid,"* (The Hague: Kabinet van de Minister-President, Ministerie van Algemene Zaken).

——— (2000) *Revision of Taxation 2001, updated version*, (The Hague: Ministry of Finance).

OECD (Organisation for Economic Co-operation and Development) (2001) *OECD Economic Survey: Belgium*, (Paris: OECD).

——— (2002a) *OECD Economic Survey: The Netherlands*, (Paris: OECD).

——— (2002b) *OECD Main Economic Indicators*, (Paris: OECD).

Polk, S. (1995) "Basisinkomen roept onredelijke angsten op," *De Volkskrant*, 2 January 1995.

PPR (Politieke Partij Radikalen) (1981) *Programma 1981–1985* (Amsterdam: PPR).

PvdA (Partij van de Arbeid) (1994) *Wat mensen bindt: Verkiezingsprogramma 1994–1998*, (Amsterdam: PvdA).

Rhodes, M. (2002) "Why EMU Is – or May Be – Good for European Welfare States" in *European States and the Euro: Europeanization, Variation, and Convergence*, K. Dyson (ed.), (Oxford: Oxford University Press), 305–366.

Roebroek, J.M. and Berben, T. (1988) *The "Incrementalist" Paradox: Securing a Subsistence Minimum and the Introduction of a Basic Income in the Netherlands*, (Tilburg: Katholieke Universiteit Brabant, Studierichting Sociale Zekerheidswetenschap).

Roebroek, J.M. and Hogenboom, E. (1990) *Basisinkomen: alternatieve uitkering of nieuwe paradigma?*, (The Hague: Ministerie van Sociale Zaken en Werkgelegenheid).

Scruggs, L. (2002) "The Ghent System and Union Membership in Europe, 1970–1996," *Political Research Quarterly*, 55 (2): 275–297.

Somavia, J. (2002) "Speech by Juan Somavia, Director-General of the ILO, to BIEN Congress, 09.00 September 13" (Geneva: International Labor Organization).

Spies, H. and Van Berkel, R. (2000) "Workfare in the Netherlands – Young Unemployed People and the Jobseeker's Employment Act," in *An Offer You Can't Refuse: Workfare in International Perspective*, I. Lødemel and H. Trickey (eds.), (Bristol: Policy Press), 105–132.

Van Berkel, R. et al. (1993) *Met z'n allen zwijgen in de woestijn: Een onderzoek naar het basisinkomen binnen de Voedingsbond FNV*, (Utrecht: University of Utrecht, Vakgroep Algemene Sociale Wetenschappen).

Van Berkel, R. (1994) "Basic Income as Trade Union Policy," *Citizens Income Bulletin*, (London), 17 January: 18–21.

Van Berkel, R. and De Schampeleire, J. (2001) "The Activation Approach in Dutch and Belgian Social Policies," *Journal of European Area Studies*, 9 (1): 27–43.

Van der Veen, P. and Pels, D. (eds.) *Het basisinkomen: Sluitstuk van de verzorgingsstaat?*, (Amsterdam: Van Gennep).

Van Empel, F. (1994) "Basisinkomen in veel soorten: Invoering stuit vooral op ideologische problemen," *NRC Handelsblad*, 23 December.

Van Gelder, H. (1994) "Praten over basisinkomen is voorschot op toekomst," *De Volkskrant*, 19 December.

Van Gent, I. et al. (1999) *GroenLinks Tweede-Kamerfractie: Fisale Notitie #3*, (The Hague: Tweede Kamer).

Van Parijs, P. et al. (2001) *What's Wrong with a Free Lunch*, (Boston: Beacon Press).

Van Parijs, P. and Vanderborght, Y. (2001) "From Euro-Stipendium to Euro-Dividend," *Journal of European Social Policy*, 11 (4): 342–346.

Van Ruysseveldt, J. and Visser, J. (1996) "Weak Corporatism Going Different Ways? Industrial Relations in the Netherlands and Belgium" in *Industrial Relations in Europe: Traditions and Transitions*, J. Van Ruysseveldt and J. Visser (eds.), (London: Sage), 205–264.

Vandenbroucke, F. (1997) "A propos de l'instauration pragmatique d'une allocation universelle," *La Revue nouvelle*, 105 (5–6): 161–166.

——— (1999) "L'Etat social actif: une ambition européenne," *Exposé Den Uyl*, 13 December.

Vandenbroucke, F. and Van Puyenbroeck, T. (2000) "Activation and the Burden of Working" in *Basic Income on the Agenda: Policy Objectives and Political Chances*, R. van der Veen and L. Groot (eds.), (Amsterdam: Amsterdam University Press), 85–106.

Vanderborght, Y. (2000) "The *VIVANT* Experiment in Belgium" in *Basic Income on the*

Agenda: Policy Objectives and Political Chances, R. van der Veen and L. Groot (eds.), (Amsterdam: Amsterdam University Press), 276–284.

Vanderborght, Y. and P. Van Parijs (2001) "Assurance participation et revenu de participation: Deux manières d'infléchir l'état social actif," *Reflets et perspectives de la vie économique*, 40 (1–2): 183–196.

Vermeend, W.A. (2001) *Circulaire activering en uitstroom bijstandgerechtigden*, (The Hague: Ministerie van Sociale Zaken en Werkgelegenheid).

Vilrokx, J. and Van Leemput, J. (1998) "Belgium: The Great Transformation" in *Changing Industrial Relations in Europe*, A. Ferner and R. Hyman (eds.), (Oxford: Blackwell), 315–347.

Vranken, J. (1999) "Le minimex en mutation en Belgique" in *L'Europe face à la pauvret:. Les expériences nationales de revenu minimum*, S. Paugam (ed.), (Paris: La Documentation Française), 169–193.

WRR (Wetenschappelijke Raad voor het Regeringsbeleid) (1985) *Waarborgen voor zekerheid: een nieuwe stelsel van social zekerheid in hoofdlijnen*, (The Hague: WRR).

Young, I. (2000) "New Disciplines of Work and Welfare," *Dissent*, 47: 25–30.

Zalm, G. and Vermeend, W. (2000) *Antwoorden van minister Zalm en staatssecretaris Vermeend (Financiën) op Tweede-Kamervragen over het nieuwe belastingstelsel* (The Hague: Tweede Kamer).

Chapter 17

The Cost of Eliminating Poverty in Canada: Basic Income With an Income Test Twist

Derek Hum and Wayne Simpson

Introduction

How much would it cost to eliminate poverty in Canada? This question frequently turns polite discussion about antipoverty proposals into acrimonious disagreement about fiscal possibilities. At the same time, the cost of eliminating poverty is sensitive to the program details. Would cash transfers be universal and unconditional? Would they be limited solely to citizens? Would immigrants be eligible without a residency requirement? What adjustments would we make for people with disabilities and for people with preschool children or special family responsibilities? Most important of all, would there be a work requirement?

The idea of a Basic Income (BI) is quite simple—everyone should receive from the state an adequate income, granted unconditionally, tax-free, and as a right of citizenship, that would let them live extremely modestly. Under this formulation, there would be no work requirement, and assertions of right ignore the costs of financing the BI plan.

No modern industrial country has anything close to a BI. Further, the view that generous unconditional transfers should be given to able-bodied persons who choose not to work remains controversial. The Guaranteed Income (GI) provides a more modest alternative. It guarantees some income (G) unconditionally, but escaping poverty would depend on earnings. The GI provides less income than the BI plan since it would not eradicate poverty with one single transfer. And because the BI is unconditional, and requires no obligation to work, the BI amount would have to be set at the nation's poverty line.

This essay provides cost estimates of a BI and a GI plan for Canada. Making these cost estimates is important for several reasons. First, although Canada does not presently contemplate a BI program, estimating the costs of the GI alternative is helpful for policy discussion. Consequently, cost calculations for a BI are for academic purposes and to satisfy our curiosity. Second, Canada has considered GI proposals in the past and, some would argue, has a limited GI for some groups (e.g., the elderly), albeit with partial testing and delivered through the personal income tax system. Third, the issue of work attachment remains salient in Canadian policy debates, and the refundable tax credits used to combat poverty show Canada's commitment to income-testing delivery. Consequently, a cost estimate for eliminating poverty through a GI is instructive. One could even interpret current Canadian policy stance either in terms of an incomplete BI or as a transition towards a future GI.

Section 1 sketches various poverty measures employed in Canada. This is followed by a brief outline of how BI and GI are related to the objective of eliminating poverty. We then examine the relationship between BI and GI, demonstrating that GI is a form of BI with an added income test and equivalent to a refundable tax credit. Cost estimates for various BI and GI plans are then presented. We conclude with some remarks on administrative design and delivery issues.

1. Poverty in Canada and its Measures

Unlike the United States, Canada does not have an official poverty line, although Statistics Canada regularly publishes a set of measures called the Low Income Cut Offs (LICO). Many regard the LICO as an unofficial poverty line in Canada. It varies by the size and composition of the family as well as the population of the area of residence. Understandably, a larger family will need more income for necessities. For example, a family of four living in a community with a population less than 30,000 has a LICO of $27,197 while a family of two has a LICO of $18,017 in 2000. For a family of four living in a city with a population over 500,000 the LICO is $34,226 annually. The comparable figure for this family in a rural area is only $23,653.

Without an official poverty line, and due to the lack of transparency in calculating the LICO, Canada recently introduced an alternative poverty line called "the market basket measure" (MBM). This calculates the cost of purchasing food, shelter, clothing and other items for comfort, using actual market prices and rents in a family's area of residence. It is more intuitive than the statistical calculation of the LICO, but like LICO it recognizes regional cost of living differences. For example, the MBM for a household in a city over 500,000 people is $26,901 in British Columbia, but only $23,218 in Manitoba. Using the MBM instead of the LICO reduces Quebec's poverty rate from 21.2 percent to 10.8 percent in 1996, and Manitoba's rate from 18.8 percent to 11.1 percent. On the other hand, Newfoundland's poverty rate increases slightly (National Council of Welfare 1999).

Another popular poverty measure is the Low Income Measure (LIM). The LIM is simply one half of median income in Canada. Those whose income falls below the LIM are considered poor. The LIM is an attractive definition because of its portability across countries since, for international comparisons, all one needs is household incomes in national currency to calculate comparable LIMs.

Because we are concerned with people who cannot purchase basic necessities, as well as people who cannot earn enough to live decently, using a BI or a GI to elevate individuals above low-income (or poverty) status is usually attractive.

2. The Simple Algebra of Three Cash Transfers

We need to be precise about the different programs designed to eliminate poverty. The BI proposal is the easiest to describe. Cash transfers equal to the poverty line are granted to each citizen on an unconditional and tax-free basis (see Lerner et al. 1999). A GI typically grants some unconditional support, G, to those with zero income. If G were set at the poverty line, then the BI and GI plans would be identical in eliminating poverty. Typically, GI plans set G below the poverty line while simultaneously reducing payments by some tax rate on earnings. The tax rate is kept low so that individuals will always be financially better off working than not working. At some income threshold (B), cash payments cease.

There are many ways to combine the grant and the tax rate. One could set G so that poverty is eliminated by working a certain number of hours with earnings taxed at a negative rate. In this case, the GI assures that poverty is eliminated by combining some support and some earnings.

A third plan, the Refundable Tax Credit (RTC), has become the major technique adopted in Canada to alleviate income poverty. The positive income tax calculates tax liabilities (L) by applying a tax rate (t*) to taxable income (income Y minus allowable exemptions E). Canada also grants various tax credits (C) against tax liabilities, and the actual tax paid (R) is determined after all applicable credits. Low-income taxpayers whose credits exceed their liabilities normally receive benefits only to the extent of their taxes owed. However, refundable credits return a portion of the credit that is not exhausted by the tax liability. Characterizing these amounts as negative taxes highlights the symmetry with the positive tax system; it also emphasizes the financial aspect of proposals to eliminate poverty by connecting the generosity of the proposals with its affordability.

A summary of the payment formulas of the BI, GI and RTC proposals is given below. It demonstrates the close resemblance of these proposals if specific values are chosen. In particular, a GI is simply a BI with an income test twist, and is formally equivalent to a RTC (see Hum 1988 for formal details).

Basic Income:	$\$ = BI = PL\ (= G?)$; PL = Poverty Line
Guaranteed Income:	$\$ = G - t^*Y$; $B = G/t$ = Poverty Line
Refundable Tax Credit:	$\$ = -R = C - L$; $R = L - C = t^*(Y - E) - C$

3. Refundable Tax Credits and the Income Testing Principle

Poverty may be alleviated by various means. The government could pay all individuals an identical amount (a universal demogrant) and raise the necessary funds by an income tax. This demogrant could be paid on an unconditional basis, subject perhaps to restrictions on age, residency duration or citizenship status, but with "no requirement, no record keeping, no wondering whose shoes were under whose bed" (Lerner in Clark, et al. 2002: 34). This would constitute a *classic* BI. If the BI were set equal to the poverty line, all citizens would be assured of a cash transfer sufficient to rise above poverty. On the other hand, government might give different amounts to individuals based upon their pretax income. One method of doing this is the refundable tax credit (RTC). This is a key ingredient of Canada's present system.

RTC and GI plans can be characterized by two elements—unconditional basic support or a refundable credit, G, that is given to those with no taxable income; and some benefit reduction tax rate (t) by which the cash transfer is reduced for each dollar of taxable income. The tax credit threshold level, B, is the income threshold, or breakeven level, at which cash payments cease. For a constant reduction rate, B is simply G/t. Clearly, the higher the level of G, and/or the lower the value of t, the higher the threshold B and the greater the proportion of the population receiving payments. Individuals with income exceeding B would be taxed at a flat rate of t percent on the excess; similarly, units with incomes below B pay no taxes, but are given refundable tax credits, again taxable at a fixed rate of t.[1] If one were to set B at the poverty line, poverty would be eliminated for those individuals who work the (implicit) *social norm* hours.

What conclusions regarding poverty (and inequality reduction) can we draw concerning this type of RTC plan? Two propositions are stated without proof: (1) Given only the mild restriction that B exceeds the average income of the poor, the mean income of the poor will always be raised, and RTC/GI plans will reduce poverty; and (2) RTC/GI plans will always result in a more equal distribution of income (Kakwani 1980).

In sum, the BI eliminates poverty if it is set at the poverty line. An RTC/GI with G less than the poverty line can be viewed as a mini-BI with an income test twist. It requires some work by individuals to escape poverty. Finally, by restricting cash transfer plans to the RTC, poverty (and income inequality) will always be unambiguously reduced. It is important to emphasize just what principle is at stake when we restrict attention to the RTC. It involves accepting to scale benefits in inverse relation to income; that is, the lower the income, the higher the transfer payment.[2]

4. Estimated Cost of Eliminating Poverty in Canada

Our calculations of the cost of eliminating poverty are based on the latest data available from the Survey of Labor and Income Dynamics (SLID). SLID is a panel survey that follows each enrolled household for six years, adding a new wave of respondents every three years. Thus, each cross section of SLID consists of respondents from two waves. Respondents are contacted in January to capture information on labor market activity (wages, hours worked, etc.) and demographic details (e.g., changes in marital status or location) during the previous year. They are contacted again in May to gather information on incomes, transfers and earnings for the previous calendar (and tax) year, which is the focus for our analysis. For most respondents, the income data is obtained by accessing their tax records. Those who refuse permission to access their tax records are asked equivalent questions about income sources and tax deductions.

There are 30,212 families in SLID for the calendar year 2000 which, when appropriately weighted, represent some 12,538,249 families across Canada.[3] Statistics Canada defines an economic family as a group of two or more persons who live in the same dwelling and are related to each other by blood, marriage, common law or adoption. We adopt this definition and use the terms "family" and "household" interchangeably.

The top two rows of Table 17.1 show the state of poverty in Canada in 2000, excluding and including existing government transfer payments to families (Child Tax Benefits, Old Age Security/Guaranteed Income Supplement, Unemployment Insurance, Social Assistance, Goods and Services Tax Credits, Canada/Quebec Pension Plan, and Workers Compensation). We employ two definitions of poverty: (1) the Low Income Measure (LIM), and (2) the Market Basket Measure (MBM). The first row portrays the situation without existing government transfers. We estimate that 28.8 percent of families lived below the LIM poverty line in 2000, compared to 26.3 percent of families using the MBM poverty line. The lower MBM poverty rate reflects the lower poverty line of the MBM. The poverty gap is $40.2 billion using the LIM and $31.5 billion using the MBM. These figures establish an initial benchmark for discussion; that is, a perfectly targeted antipoverty transfer program could eliminate poverty for $40.2 billion under the LIM definition of poverty and $31.5 billion under the MBM definition if there were no adverse behavioral consequences of the transfers.[4]

The second row of Table 17.1 shows the effect of existing government transfers, which amount to $75.8 billion, on poverty. Transfer payments in 2000 leave 15.3 percent of families below the LIM poverty line and 11.9 percent of families below the MBM poverty line; and transfers reduce the poverty gap to $11.6 billion using the LIM and $7.7 billion using the MBM. Therefore, a second benchmark can be what the current transfer system accomplishes at a cost of $75.8 billion and what remains to be done in terms of poverty reduction.

We now turn to the cost of a BI program set at the Canadian poverty line that would eliminate poverty. The third row of Table 17.1 provides an estimate of the cost of a BI replacing existing government transfer payments to households. Since we are using the LIM and MBM definitions of poverty, we adopt their equivalence scales as ones that would be used in the design of a BI; that is, citizens would receive a BI that would vary according to their household size in the same fashion as the LIM or MBM measure of poverty. At the poverty line established by the LIM, the BI would cost $251.7 billion; at the MBM poverty line, the cost would be $217.1 billion. With current transfer savings of $75.8 billion, this implies that the net cost of a BI would be $175.9 using the LIM and $141.3 billion using the MBM.

This represents an additional expenditure of 16.4 percent of GDP under the LIM and 13.1 percent under the MBM,[5] both considerable sums.

BI plans transfer income to families regardless of existing income. By definition, the BI plans above would eliminate poverty as currently defined, but would not be targeted. Since the BI is universal, it provides the same benefit to all families with incomes above the poverty line as well as to all poor families regardless of the depth of their poverty. Even among poor families, circumstances differ considerably between the working poor, who may have significant earnings, and other poor families. Taking advantage of SLID's labor market profiles, we find that half of all poor families have some income from employment to augment their transfers. These families work an average of 814 hours per year using the LIM definition and earn an average of $3,719; they work 783 hours using the MBM measure and earn $3,133.[6] For a family of four, these earnings represent about 15 percent of the LIM.

Table 17.1 Estimates of the extent of poverty and the cost of basic income and guaranteed income plans for Canada

Transfer Program	**Low Income Measure of Poverty (LIM)**			**Market Basket Measure of Poverty (MBM)**		
	Cost ($b)	*Poverty Incidence*	*Poverty Gap ($b)*	*Cost ($b)*	*Poverty Incidence*	*Poverty Gap ($b)*
No Transfers	0	28.8%	40.2	0	26.3 %	31.5
Current Transfers	75.8	15.3%	11.6	75.8	11.9%	7.7
BI=PL	251.7	0.0%	0	217.1	0.0%	0
*GI: G=t*PL*						
t=30%	12.1	28.8%	28.2	9.4	26.0%	22.0
t=50%	20.1	28.8%	20.1	15.7	26.0%	15.7
t=70%	28.2	28.8%	12.1	22.0	26.0%	9.4

Source: Survey of Labor and Income Dynamics Public File 2000. Calculations by the authors, weighted to reflect the population of economic families in Canada.

Notes: [a] The Basic Income (BI) proposal gives every economic family in Canada an amount equal to the poverty line (PL=LIM or MBM) to replace existing transfers to families. [b] The Guaranteed Income (GI) proposal provides a guaranteed income equal to the negative tax rate times the poverty line (G=t*PL) and taxes earnings (only) at the negative tax rate (30, 50, or 70 percent). [c] All cost and poverty gap (poverty depth) estimates are in billions of Canadian dollars.

More modest transfers are involved in a GI, which allows the poor to retain only a portion of their earnings in determining the final transfer. GI plans consists of a guarantee (G) and a negative tax (or "claw back") rate (t), which determines the reduction in the amount transferred as income rises (G - tY). Families with incomes below the threshold, or breakeven level (defined earlier as B=G/t) receive a benefit that decreases as the family's non-transfer income approaches B. Families with incomes at or above B receive no GI benefit. From the GI perspective, a BI plan is simply a special case of the GI in which the negative tax rate is zero and the tax credit threshold or breakeven level is infinite; everyone receives an untaxed benefit. In our GI calculations we again subtract transfer payments from family income, since a GI comparable to the BI would probably be designed to replace existing transfers.

The final three rows of Table 17.1 present modest GI plans that are perfectly targeted at the poor by setting the breakeven level at the poverty line (PL); that is, B=G/t=PL or G=t*PL. For the LIM and a tax rate of 30 percent, a GI plan costs $12.1 billion; the cost rises to $20.1 billion with a tax rate of 50 percent, and to $28.2 billion with a tax rate of 70 percent. All these estimates are well below the current transfer budget of $75.8 billion because only the poor receive payments. As a result, there is no reduction in poverty below the 28.8 percent level as given by pre-transfer incomes. Note that the effect of a higher negative tax is to raise the guarantee relative to the poverty level and tax back more of all income received; it both raises and flattens the income profile for the poor. This increases transfers to the poor, and the cost of the GI plan, but reduces the poverty gap. Thus, for a tax rate of 70 percent, the poverty gap is reduced to $12.1 billion, only slightly higher than the $11.6 billion poverty gap under the existing system.[7] For the MBM, the cost of the GI plans is more modest, since there is less poverty to begin with: $9.4 billion for a tax rate of 30 percent, $15.7 billion for a tax rate of 50 percent, and $22.0 billion for a tax rate of 70 percent. Again, the 70 percent tax rate provides a poverty gap of $9.4 billion for a cost of $22.0 billion, only slightly higher than the gap of $7.7 billion under the current transfer system that costs $75.8 billion, although the incidence of poverty is 26.0 percent compared to 11.9 percent with existing transfers. Thus, these plans provide a modest level of expenditure from which to consider improvements in the circumstances of the poor.

We now look at a set of intermediate plans; BI plans that are less generous than the plan in Table 17.1 and GI plans that are more generous than those in Table 17.1 directed only at poor families. These plans might be more politically and socially acceptable both in terms of cost and poverty reduction.

Although the LIM and MBM poverty lines are both now widely used, they are not without controversy. Sarlo (1996) argues for more modest lines based on basic needs. These lines are about 70 percent of the MBM for a family of four (CCSD, 2003). Since working families who are poor generate, on average, earnings equal to 15 percent of the poverty line, we might use 85 percent of the MBM or LIM poverty line as yet another benchmark. These plans are presented in Table 17.2.

The BI plans are presented in the top two rows of Table 17.2. Reducing the transfer to 70 percent of the poverty line reduces costs to $176.2 billion using the

LIM definition of poverty and to $152.0 billion using the MBM definition. The incidence of poverty is 14.2 percent using the LIM, and 13.4 percent using the MBM, while the poverty gap is $7.1 billion and $5.9 billion, respectively.[8] Note that these results for poverty incidence are about as good as those from the existing transfer system, albeit at some additional cost. A BI set at 85 percent of the poverty line would cost $213.9 billion under the LIM and result in poverty incidence of 11.4 percent and a poverty gap of $3.1 billion; the corresponding figures using the MBM instead of LIM are $184.5 billion, 11.0 percent and $2.6 billion. This BI clearly does a better job of fighting poverty than the existing transfer program, although at considerable additional cost.

The GI plans are presented at the bottom of Table 17.2. We again use plans with guarantees of 70 percent and 85 percent of the poverty line and a negative tax rate of 50 percent, which is consistent with both the top positive tax rates in Canada and the flat tax rate that we calculate would be necessary to harmonize negative and positive taxes (Hum and Simpson 1995: Table 2). These plans are more generous than those considered earlier because they involve breakeven levels of 1.4 and 1.7 times the poverty line, respectively, thereby transferring more income to both poor and non-poor families. Setting the income guarantee at 70

Table 17.2 Additional estimates of the extent of poverty and the cost of intermediate basic income and guaranteed income plans for Canada

Transfer Program	Low Income Measure of Poverty (LIM)			Market Basket Measure of Poverty (MBM)		
	Cost ($b)	*Poverty Incidence*	*Poverty Gap ($b)*	*Cost ($b)*	*Poverty Incidence*	*Poverty Gap ($b)*
BI=0.7PL	$176.2	14.2%	$7.1	$152.0	13.4%	$5.9
BI=0.85PL	$213.9	11.4%	$3.1	$184.5	11.0%	$2.6
GI: t=50%						
G=0.7PL	$35.2	20.6%	$9.1	$27.1	18.9%	$7.3
G=0.85PL	$49.4	14.2%	$3.6	$37.8	13.4%	$2.9

Source: Survey of Labor and Income Dynamics Public File 2000. Calculations by the authors, weighted to reflect the population of economic families in Canada.

Notes: [a] The Basic Income (BI) proposal gives every economic family in Canada an amount equal to the specified proportion of the poverty line to replace existing transfers to families. [b] The Guaranteed Income (GI) proposal provides a guaranteed income equal to a specified proportion of the poverty line and taxes earnings at 50 percent. [c] All cost and poverty gap (poverty depth) estimates are in billions of Canadian dollars.

percent of the poverty line and a tax rate of 50 percent, costs are $35.2 billion, and we get a poverty rate of 20.6 percent and a poverty gap $9.1 billion using the LIM; the corresponding figures using the MBM are $27.1 billion, 18.9 percent, and $7.3 billion. This plan reduces the poverty gap compared to current transfer programs, but leaves poverty incidence higher. At a guarantee set at 85 percent of the poverty line, poverty using the LIM definition is reduced to 14.2 percent (less than the current poverty rate), the poverty gap is reduced to $3.6 billion, and the total cost of the program would be $49.4 billion. Under the MBM definition, poverty incidence is 13.4 percent (slightly above the current level), although the poverty gap is much lower ($2.9 billion) under this plan than the current poverty gap ($37.8 billion). Notice that this GI plan does better than the BI plan at 70 percent of the poverty line in the first row of Table 17.2. The GI plan generates the same poverty incidence but lower poverty gaps at less than one-third the cost.

One final plan might be considered to illustrate the cost reduction from adopting a GI plan with a claw-back rate. Consider a guarantee set at 100 percent of the poverty line and a negative tax rate of 50 percent. By definition, this will eliminate poverty in Canada. The cost of the plan would be $66.2 billion under the LIM definition of poverty and $50.3 billion under the MBM definition. These represent significant savings and a significantly improved chance of political acceptance, compared to the BI plan. At the same time, they represent a reduction in what Canadians pay (and receive) under current transfer arrangements.

5. Implementation Difficulties

Many more calculations like those above can be made, using a variety of poverty lines and assumptions. We believe that the following conclusions are robust to further simulations.

First, a pure BI, consisting of a tax-free universal transfer set at the poverty level in order to eliminate poverty completely, is too expensive and would be politically unacceptable in Canada. The drawback of the BI is its lack of selectivity. With poverty rates between 10 percent and 20 percent, universal mechanisms without claw-back provisions are target inefficient. An apple-a-day program for every child when only one of ten children cannot afford an apple is a costly way to ensure that poor children have an apple for school lunch.

Second, if the BI is set below the poverty line, then the tax and transfer system will determine the degree to which poverty is alleviated beyond the contribution of the BI. This is unavoidable, since the BI cannot exist in a vacuum; and while the BI may not be taxed, amounts above the BI will have to be taxed. The tax rate will impact the degree of poverty alleviation.

Third, we have demonstrated that the BI and GI are technically conformable; that is, a BI may be viewed as a GI with a zero tax-back rate, or a GI may be viewed as a BI coupled with a nonzero tax rate on income above the guaranteed amount. The demonstration that BI and GI are members of a larger family of income transfer mechanisms should help to clarify language, eliminate confusion about the relative merits of partially specified designs, and help us understand why cost estimates often differ so widely among proposals aimed at alleviating poverty.

Finally, our calculations and discussion ignored many important issues such as work effort responses (Hum and Simpson 1991, 1993), alterations in family living arrangement (Hum 1986), and marital instability (Hum and Choudhry 1992). Also not considered are the technical difficulties of integrating taxes and transfers (Hum 1988), problems of administrative delivery (Hum 1981), questions about adopting a flat rate tax, the degree of inequality that is optimal from the standpoint of economic efficiency (Hum and Simpson 1995), and the complications of combating poverty in a federal state (Hum 1983). Even so, our cost estimates should cause us to reflect more seriously about the best way to alleviate poverty.

Notes

[1] The reduction rate below B need not be equal to the tax rate above B, and equal tax and reduction rates will not guarantee a redistributive result (Hum 1983). Also, economic efficiency effects will accompany any redistribution, so calculating tax and subsidy rate combinations that achieve pure redistribution is a bit artificial without a full modeling of the output and incentive changes brought about in the economy.

[2] The term "income testing" is used to mean that net benefits are inversely related to pretax income. In other contexts, such as discussing the administrative design of programs, the term "income testing" is often used interchangeably with "selective." We retain the label "income testing" to avoid the cumbersome phrase "net benefits inversely related to income," believing that no confusion will arise.

[3] Ninety respondents replied "don't know" when asked about province of residence. As a result, an MBM measure of poverty could not be estimated for these families. The remainder of the sample was re-weighted to account for these 90 missing families when using the MBM measure of poverty. In practice, re-weighting makes little difference to the results because 90 missing observations is only a small percentage (0.3 percent) of the total.

[4] We ignore the behavioral effects of transfers throughout our discussion.

[5] The Canadian GDP on an expenditure basis was $1,075.6 billion in 2000 according to Statistics Canada.

[6] Earnings include paid wages and salaries and any self-employed earnings where annual hours worked are reported. Self-employed earnings are not subject to Canadian minimum wage legislation and appear to depress hourly earnings for this group.

[7] A much larger proportion of families are poor under the GI plan but the plan ensures that no one is very far below the poverty line.

[8] If the poverty line were redefined to 70 percent of the existing standard, as Sarlo suggests, the incidence of poverty and the poverty gap would be zero.

References

CCSD (2003) *The Canadian Fact Book on Poverty 2000,* (Ottawa: Canadian Council on Social Development).

Clark, C. et al. (2002) "Basic Income: The Unfinished Business of the Twentieth Century," in *Walter Gordon Series in Public Policy, Lectures*, (Toronto: Massey College).

Hum, D. (1983) *Federalism and the Poor: A Review of the Canada Assistance Plan,* (Toronto: Ontario Economic Council).

——— (1986) "UISP and the MacDonald Commission: Reform and Restraint," *Canadian Public Policy*, 12: 92–100.

——— (1988) "On Integrating Taxes and Transfers," *Canadian Tax Journal*, 36: 671–690.

Hum, D. and Choudhry, S. (1992) "Income, Work and Marital Dissolution: Canadian Experimental Evidence," *Journal of Comparative Family Studies*, 23: 249–265.

Hum, D. and Simpson, W. (1991) *Income Maintenance, Work Effort, and the Canadian Mincome Experiment,* (Ottawa: Economic Council of Canada).

——— (1993) "Economic Response to a Guaranteed Annual Income: Experience from Canada and the United States," *Journal of Labor Economics*, 11: 263–296.

——— (1995) "Reducing Spending and Increasing Equity: How Far Can Refundable Tax Credits Take Us?," *Canadian Public Administration*, 38: 598–612.

Kakwani, N. (1980) *Income Inequality and Poverty,* (Washington, D.C.: Oxford University Press).

Lerner, S., Clark, C., Needham, W. (1999) *Basic Income: Economic Security for all Canadians,* (Toronto: Between the Lines Press).

National Council of Welfare (1999) *A New Poverty Line: Yes, No or Maybe?,* (Ottawa: National Council of Welfare).

Sarlo, C. (1996) *Poverty in Canada,* 2nd ed., (Vancouver: The Fraser Institute).

Chapter 18

Can a Negative Income Tax System for the United Kingdom be Both Equitable and Affordable?

Randall Bartlett, James Davies, and Michael Hoy

Introduction

The idea of providing a universal basic income supplement to all United Kingdom citizens has a long history.[1] Although there is no agreement about how such a system would be structured, we begin our analysis with what Atkinson (1975: 227) suggests is its simplest form, paying "a social dividend to everyone, dependent only on their family status" and then raising "revenue...by a proportional tax on all income." Of course, we could adopt a graduated rate tax system (GRT) rather than a single marginal tax rate. Or, we could mix a basic income component with some means-tested benefits, rather than eliminating these benefits altogether.

This chapter investigates the distributional implications of replacing the existing income tax and benefits system for the United Kingdom with a universal basic income. Our goal is to determine how large a basic income must be in order to lead to the same degree of after-tax income inequality as the existing GRT system. The point of this exercise is not to suggest that we *should* design a new system with the same level of inequality, but rather to determine the minimum social dividend that would be required to do so. Any system with a larger social dividend will create less inequality than the existing tax system. And by determining how large the accompanying tax rate(s) must be, we also get a sense of the cost and acceptability of such a system.

One source of progressivity in the existing system is that the average income tax burden is an increasing function of before-tax income. This is the result of personal exemptions and increasing marginal tax rates. Granting means-tested and targeted benefits also tends to reduce inequality in after-tax incomes. The essential component of any Negative Income Tax (NIT) system is a universal, guaranteed (basic) income supplement, Atkinson's "social dividend", which is often referred to as a "demogrant". Most NIT systems apply a single flat tax rate to all income (including the demogrant), regardless of the source. In this way, the demogrant will be taxed back and a breakeven level of income will be determined. Below the breakeven point households will be net beneficiaries of the system, while those with income above the breakeven point will be net tax payers. Also, many NIT proposals call for replacing means-tested and targeted welfare payments with a demogrant. Although one can imagine a demogrant large enough to ensure that all low-income individuals will be net winners under an NIT, the impact on overall inequality is not a simple matter to determine.

This chapter balances these characteristics of the existing GRT system in the United Kingdom with a variety of hypothetical NIT proposals. We maintain the same tax revenue, net of benefits and credits. We begin by proposing an NIT that: (a) includes the various means-tested social security benefits and tax credits of the existing system, and (b) includes a universal income supplement based only on household status, but (c) replaces the series of increasing marginal tax rates with a single flat rate tax. Introducing a basic income supplement reduces inequality while replacing graduated tax rates with a single, revenue neutral, tax rate increases inequality.

NIT plans often call for eliminating many existing tax allowances, thereby broadening the tax base and enhancing their affordability. We construct a series of inferred "other exemptions" from our data set in order to make claimed tax payments consistent with before-tax income. We then consider NIT proposals that add to taxable income an amount equal to these exemptions; that is, we broaden the tax base by eliminating these exemptions. We also consider NIT proposals that eliminate all government transfers, while allowing their role in inequality reduction to be taken up by the NIT demogrant. This is done for both the case of no base broadening and the case with base broadening. To lead to the same level of inequality as the existing tax/benefit system in the absence of government transfers, the size of the income supplement must be larger than in our first exercise. However, eliminating existing benefits does reduce the cost, and so the direction of the change in the tax rate required to maintain revenue neutrality is not clear *a priori*. Having determined the minimal income supplement that would not worsen inequality, we can then consider how much inequality would be reduced by increasing the demogrant.

We acknowledge that all inequality measures are based on normative judgments. Atkinson (1970) argued that we should be explicit about the welfare basis of the index we use, and he introduced a family of indices based on an additive utilitarian social welfare function with iso-elastic individual utilities. Adopting this family of indices always implies more concern about inequality at the bottom of the distribution than at the top, but the degree of that bias can be varied through the choice of the elasticity parameter. While we also look at the coefficient of variation, we highlight the Atkinson indices because they allow a ready comparison of equity and efficiency considerations.[2]

The Existing Income Tax and Benefits System in the United Kingdom

The salient features of the existing United Kingdom income tax system[3] are the following: (a) the levels of personal exemption or allowance, (b) the tax brackets, with marginal tax rates increasing with income, and (c) the system of tax credits. Our sample is for the tax year 2001/2002 (April 6, 2001 to April 5, 2002). In this year each adult was entitled to a personal exemption of £4535. This increases to £5990 for those aged 65 to 74, and to £6260 for those 75 or older. These larger age-related personal allowances are gradually withdrawn from people with income above a specified limit. An individual's personal allowance, along with any other allowances, is deducted from income to determine taxable income.[4]

Once taxable income is determined, income tax is computed by using a series of increasing marginal rates. For the tax year in question, the first £1880 of taxable income is taxed at a rate of 10 percent, taxable income between £1881 and £29,400 is taxed at a rate of 22 percent, and taxable income above £29,400 is taxed at a rate of 40 percent. Offsetting the tax owed are various tax credits and other allowances.[5]

These features make the existing tax system progressive in the sense that after-tax income is more equally distributed than before-tax income, and more equally distributed than if the income tax were proportional to income and no personal exemptions allowed. Various benefits (such as the income-based jobseeker's allowance and targeted benefits for people with low incomes) also make the system more progressive.[6] The question posed in the title of our chapter (Can an NIT for the United Kingdom be equitable?), can be answered by generating a hypothetical NIT system that generates the same inequality as the existing GRT. The simple NITs that we consider have a single marginal tax rate, a property that reduces progressivity relative to the existing GRTs. However, the guaranteed income for each household can, if is large enough, make up for the progressivity lost by having a single tax rate. We find a combined minimum demogrant and tax rate that leads to this same (existing) level of inequality in after-tax incomes, which we refer to as our *critical NIT* system. Any NIT with a larger demogrant (and higher tax rate) will be even more progressive than the existing tax system. If the tax rate and demogrant required to generate the same level of inequality is not unreasonably large, then we can answer affirmatively the question posed in our chapter title—we *can* find an NIT system for the United Kingdom that is both equitable and affordable.

Before discussing methodology, one comment is in order. In many NIT proposals, including the one by Meade (1972), the size of demogrant is set to lift all individuals out of poverty. The result is often a tax rate that many would view as prohibitive, such as Meade's estimate of 53 percent. Our goal is more modest. We ask only that the NIT lead to after-tax incomes distributed at least as equitably as at present. The result will be a lower required tax rate, perhaps one in the politically acceptable range. Starting from this point, we could raise the tax rate and demogrant a little, thus reducing inequality while making our NIT more acceptable politically than more lavish schemes.

Methodology

The simplest way to compare the distributional impact of different income tax systems is to compare their tax schedules graphically.[7] Figure 18.1a illustrates the existing GRT income tax schedule for the United Kingdom tax year 2001/02 for an individual with the standard personal exemption and facing the tax brackets and rates discussed in the previous section. Figure 18.1b illustrates the relationship between before-tax and after-tax incomes.

To understand why such a tax system is progressive we need to compare it to a proportional system that taxes all income at a single marginal rate and provides no personal allowance. Such a proportional system leaves the relative levels of any two individuals' after-tax incomes the same as their before-tax incomes. Superimposing such a tax schedule (labeled PT) on the existing GRT, we see that those with incomes below the intersection point (X) pay more under the proportional tax system while all those with incomes greater than X pay less. Thus, relative to the PT, the GRT leads to higher after-tax income for those with low incomes and lower after-tax income for those with high incomes. Since the PT is neutral with respect to the relationship between after-tax and before-tax relative incomes, we can say the GRT is progressive.

Our question is whether a revenue neutral NIT will be more or less progressive than a GRT. Note that the GRT is more progressive than the PT because the GRT has an exemption and does not tax income below this level. Also, the GRT is more progressive because marginal tax rates increase with income. Thus, the GRT favors lower income households. A NIT with a single marginal tax rate has this feature of a PT noted above, which tends to make it less progressive than the existing GRT.[8] However, a positive demogrant provides a benefit of greater importance the lower one's income, and increases progressivity.[9] We can, at least hypothetically, consider the impact of increasing the demogrant to benefit a larger proportion of the population. Ignoring work incentives, one could introduce a marginal tax rate of 100 percent and a corresponding demogrant chosen to maintain tax revenue neutrality, with the result that there is perfect equality of after-tax incomes. Of course, such a tax system would not be feasible, but the mental exercise demonstrates how we can reduce the inequality of after-tax incomes by choosing higher demogrants and tax rates. Figures 18.2a and 18.2b illustrate this point by using two NIT systems, NIT_1 and NIT_2. NIT_2 has a higher demogrant and so a higher tax rate is needed to maintain tax revenue neutrality. Those with incomes below the intersection point Y end up with more after-tax income under NIT_2 while all those with incomes above Y end up with less after-tax income. Therefore, NIT_2 is more progressive than NIT_1.

One simple relationship among these graphs is worth noting here. Whenever one tax schedule intersects another one, the one that intersects from below (i.e., requires lower income individuals to pay less tax) is more progressive. This single intersection divides the population into two groups: a low-income group and a high-income group. All individuals with before-tax incomes below the intersection point end up with higher after-tax incomes, while those with higher incomes end up with lower after-tax incomes. Thus, the former schedule (i.e., the one that starts below the other) generates a distribution of after-tax incomes that is more equal. For example, in Figures 18.2a and 18.2b the schedule NIT_2 represents a more progressive tax system than NIT_1.

Comparing the distributional implications of an NIT to a GRT is more complex. If the two systems generate the same tax revenue and the same degree of inequality, then the two tax schedules must intersect each other twice.[10] Thus, those who are better off under the NIT include the lowest-income individuals (those with incomes below X as noted in Figures 18.3a and 18.3b) and the highest-income individuals (those with incomes above Y as noted in Figures 18.3a and 18.3b). The middle income group (those with incomes between the levels X and Y in Figures 18.3a and 18.3b) is worse off under the NIT. Thus, the NIT is in one sense more progressive than the GRT (since after-tax incomes are higher in the before-tax income range 0 to X) while in another sense it is less progressive (in the income range X to Y compared to incomes above Y).

Our method of finding the critical NIT system leading to the same level of inequality in after-tax incomes as the GRT begins with an NIT having a zero demogrant and a proportional tax. Such an NIT would be less progressive than the existing GRT. We then consider a series of NITs constructed by increasing the demogrant by small amounts, which also requires increasing the tax rate to maintain revenue neutrality. Each increase makes the NIT more progressive. We continue this process until we find the critical NIT system with the same level of inequality in after-tax incomes as the GRT. An NIT with a higher demogrant and tax rate will be more progressive than the existing GRT.

Household needs, of course, vary with household characteristics. One approach to this problem is to measure household income as income per adult equivalent, and consider the inequality of these adult equivalent incomes.[11] Our view is that such a correction is flawed because the theoretical and empirical basis for equivalence scales is not firm (Ebert 1997, Ebert and Moyes 2000). In addition, different scales should probably be applied in different regions of the income distribution. We investigate how a tax reform that is equitable for all family types can be achieved, from the viewpoint of a given inequality index, by applying some of the insights of Atkinson and Bourguignon (1987). By not aggregating across family types, we are able to provide a richer description of the relative merits of NIT systems with different demogrant levels and structure.

In most NIT proposals, the demogrant is intended to be universal and replace all government transfers to individuals. However, some of these payments are designed to account for the special needs of certain individuals, such as benefits for sick and disabled persons. Therefore, we consider two possibilities for implementing an NIT—an income supplement added to existing government transfers, and a system where the supplement replaces all existing payments.

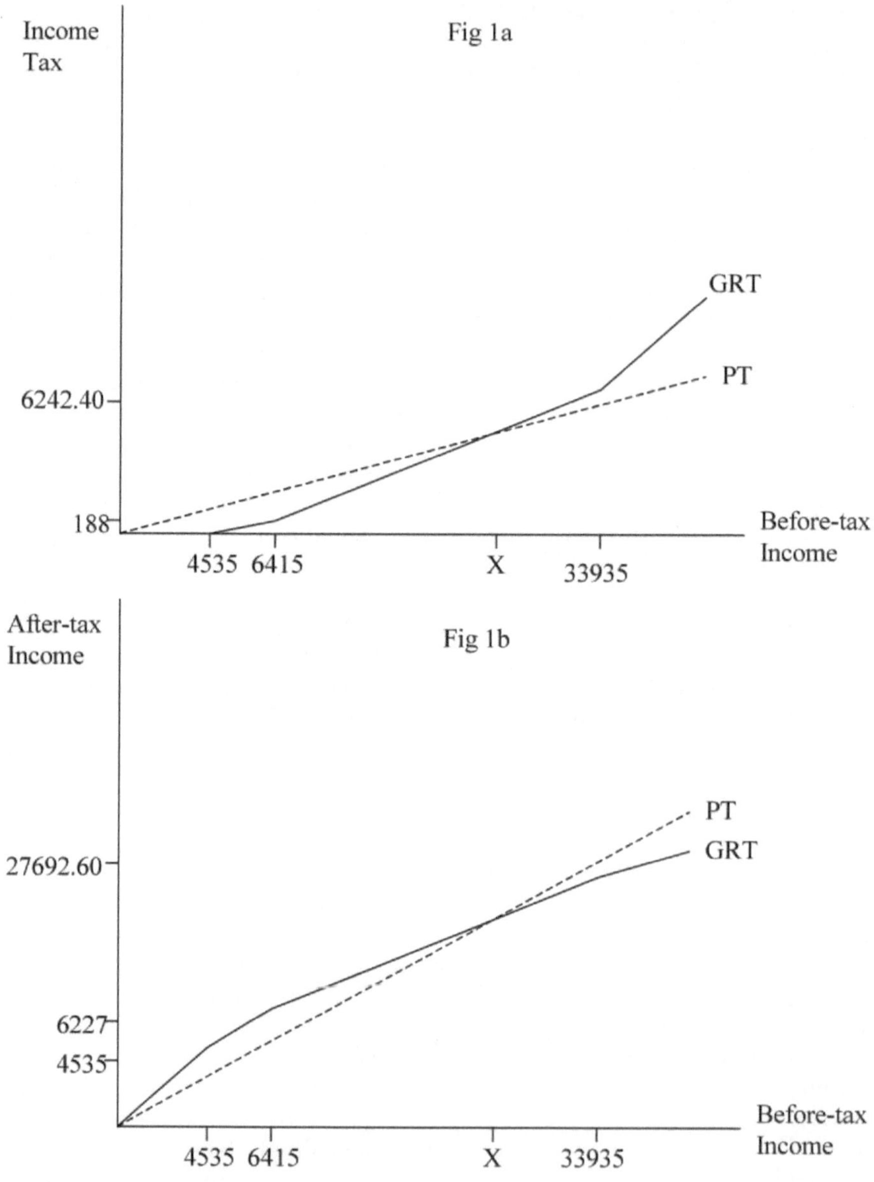

Figure 18.1 Comparing a PT (proportional tax) schedule to a GRT

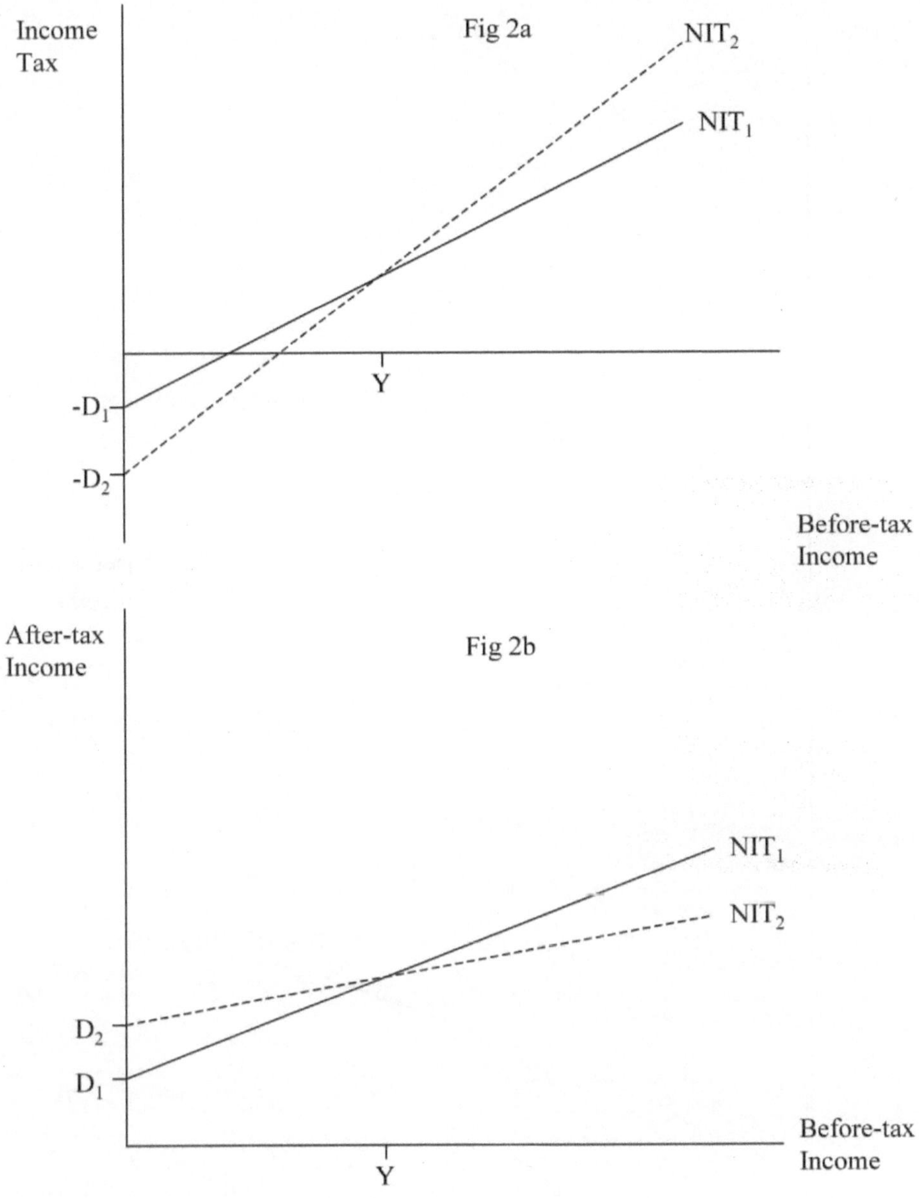

Figure 18.2 Comparing equal-yield NIT schedules

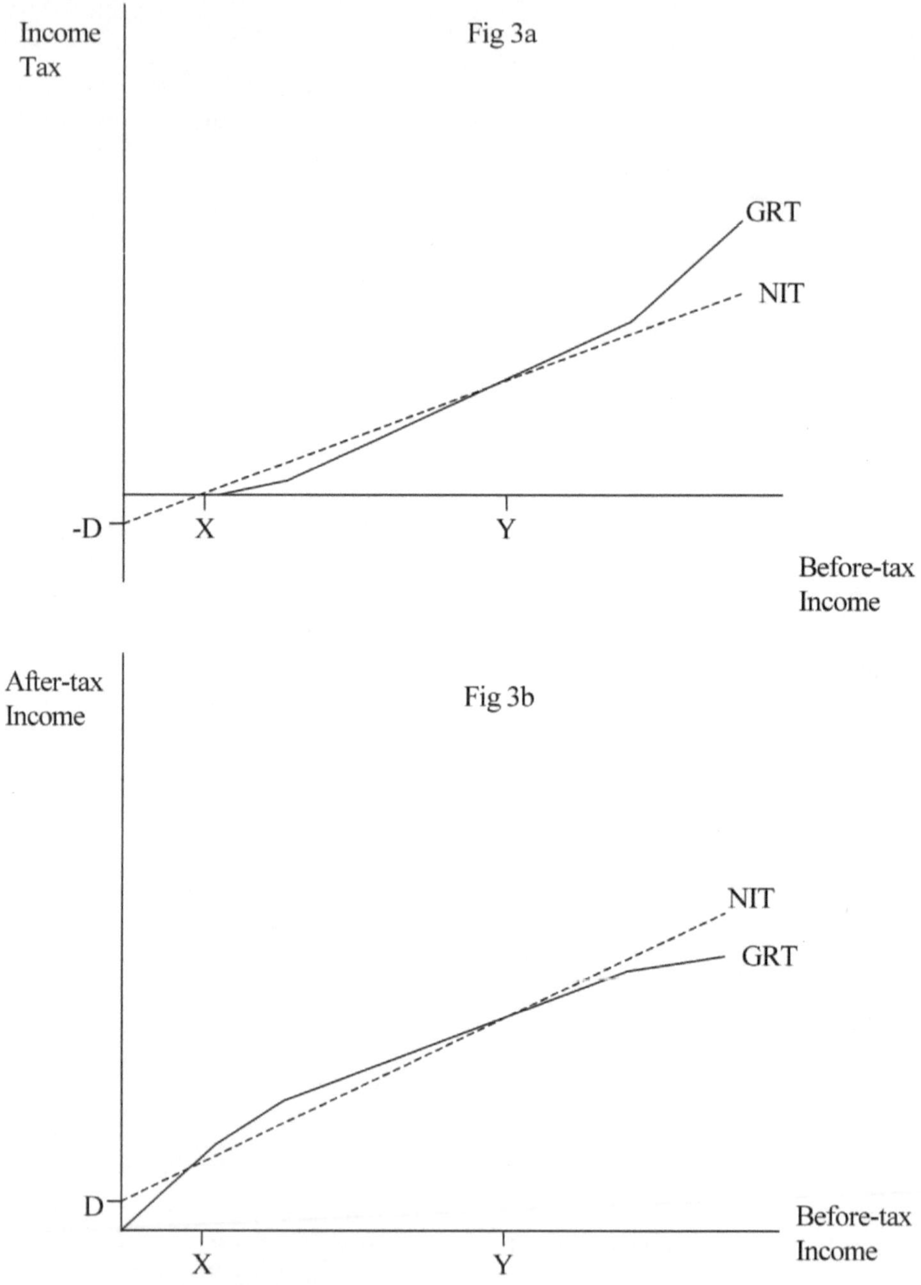

Figure 18.3 Comparing a NIT schedule to a GRT schedule

We take the United Kingdom pension system as independent of the income tax system, treating retirement pensions as if they were private income. Our rationale for doing so is that since people contribute to the system before they retire, we should treat such income in the same way as a private pension. By treating the retirement system as outside the income tax system we avoid reducing the revenue requirement for the NIT when considering the scenario in which we eliminate (noncontributory) cash benefits made to individuals.

A further contribution of the chapter is to compare the critical NIT tax rates needed for an equalizing impact, with and without base broadening. With full base broadening, taxable income under the NIT equals before-tax income as recorded in the data set and does not allow for any exemptions or allowances, including personal exemptions. We find, not surprisingly, that the critical NIT rate needed for an equalizing impact is generally lower when there is base broadening. However, the overall distribution of relative incomes differs in the two cases. This admits the possibility of either a higher or lower critical tax rate to generate the target level of inequality. In our sample, it turns out that before-tax income and other exemptions are positively correlated, with a simple correlation coefficient of 0.64 and so inequality levels are generally higher with the broad-based definition of income.[12]

Before presenting our results, a brief discussion about our inequality measures is in order. We adopt the inequality index referred to as the Mean Logarithmic Deviation (MLD) from the Atkinson family of inequality indices. Atkinson's indices are examples of a broader class, each of whose members is based on a utilitarian social welfare function, $W = W[U(Y_1), \ldots, U(Y_n)]$, where there are n individuals in society with incomes $Y_1, \ldots, Y_n$. Atkinson (1970) suggests a way of summarizing the impact of inequality changes on social welfare that depends only on the ordinal properties of W and that has strong intuition.[13] He defined the concept of "equally distributed equivalent income", Y_{ede}, which is the income that if received by all would generate the same social welfare as the actual income distribution $Y_1, \ldots, Y_n$. The gap between Y_{ede} and mean income, μ, is an appealing measure of the "cost" of inequality.

Atkinson further suggests that a natural measure of inequality would be the percent drop in mean income that could be allowed if income were distributed equally without reducing social welfare, $I = 1 - (Y_{ede}/\mu)$. This measure varies between 0 (complete equality) and 1 (complete inequality, one person with all income). It can be used to assess the impact of inequality on welfare from the viewpoint of widely varying social welfare functions. Atkinson generated the family of indices that bear his name by illustrating the general approach with the additive (Utilitarian) social welfare function with iso-elastic utility function, given by $U(y) = y^{(1-e)}/(1-e)$, $e > 0$, except for the special case of $e = 1$ where $U(y) = \ln(y)$. This latter (special) case is referred to as the mean logarithmic deviation (MLD) measure. It has a clear and straightforward interpretation—a given percentage change in income has the same impact on individual well-being and social welfare regardless of initial income. For example, an increase of £500 to a person with original income of £10,000 has the same impact as an increase of £2,000 for a person with original income of £40,000. One can see how this property reflects a concern for equality since any transfer from a richer to a poorer individual would increase overall welfare. A £2,000 transfer from a person with an income of £40,000 to a person with an income of £10,000 would increase overall welfare since the utility gain to the lower income person exceeds the utility loss to the higher income person.[14]

The MLD index places more emphasis on income transfers the lower they occur in the income distribution (Jenkins 1991). Some common inequality indices, such as the Gini coefficient, do not have this property (Davies and Hoy 1994). We also use the coefficient of variation (CV), which divides those measures that display greater concern for income transfers at lower incomes from those that do not.[15] Suppose we find a critical tax rate and demogrant that generates the same level of inequality in after-tax incomes as exists in the GRT tax system according to the CV. Then we know that, for any inequality index that places more importance on transfers to the lower part of the distribution, this critical NIT generates less after-tax inequality and is more progressive than the existing GRT. An NIT with a higher tax rate and demogrant than the critical one will be even more progressive.

Data and Results

Our study uses the *Effects of Taxes and Benefits on Household Income* data set, 2001–2002 (SN: 4773), acquired from the United Kingdom Data Archive. The original source for this data set is *The Expenditure and Food Survey*, 2001–2002 (SN: 4697).

The raw data contained 7468 households. A number of observations seemed suspect, possibly due to coding errors or incorrect income reports.[16] And because we adopted an inequality index that is undefined for zero or negative incomes, households reporting such incomes cannot be included in our analysis. We also discarded any household type containing fewer than 25 households to prevent small sub-samples from unduly affecting our overall results. Deleting these households reduced the sample to 7319 households, 1.99 percent below the original sample size.

We then deleted observations with unusual tax payments or unexplainable relationships between before-tax income and tax paid: (1) households that paid taxes less than -£500 (nine observations), (2) households that had a broad-based taxable income of greater than £65,000 while at the same time paying a negative tax (two observations), (3) households with a broad-based, before-tax income less than or equal to zero (eleven observations), and (4) households with negative after-tax income using a broad base (four observations). This reduced our sample by another 0.35 percent. Thus, our final sample size was 7293 households, which is a 2.35 percent reduction from the initial sample.

In those computations where we do not broaden the tax base, or allow the demogrant to displace existing social security programs, we treat as taxable income all sources of income except (noncontributory) government cash benefits. Most of these sources of income are, in fact, not taxable.[17]

Because we do not observe all possible tax deductions, nor can we determine the distribution of income within each household unit, it is not possible to link precisely before-tax income and tax paid by simply applying the existing tax schedule. In particular, although we can infer the maximum level of personal exemptions allowed to a family unit if each member earned enough income to make full use of his or her personal exemption, we do not know whether this is appropriate. Thus, we link taxes paid to declared before-tax income for the family unit by inverting the tax schedule and implicitly determining what would be the required *other* exemptions to make this pair consistent. Since personal exemptions are nontransferable, we may overestimate these, with the result that "other" exemptions as computed may be negative in some cases. In those cases, we set other exemptions equal to zero, since otherwise we would be adding income to those households in the no-base-broadening cases. Where "other exemptions" are positive, we treat these as legitimate deductions and reduce taxable income and after-tax income in the case of no base broadening.

For the first two exercises described below, we add nontaxed social security benefits to family income after the tax system is implemented both for the existing GRT and the NIT. Thus, the demogrant adds to government transfers.

Several exercises help to illuminate tax reform with a guaranteed basic income. Note that household types are defined by the number of adults (A) and children (C) in the household. All of our exercises, except the last one, compute critical NIT systems separately for each household type. We do this because we want to find out how household type influences the parameters required to give an NIT system the same degree of progressivity as the existing GRT system. This approach also illustrates how a coherent NIT proposal may increase inequality for some household types while reducing it for others.

Exercise 1 (Appendix Table 18.4) sets taxable income for each individual or family unit equal to gross income less nontaxed social security benefits less personal exemptions allowed less other exemptions.[18] The critical (equally progressive) NIT is created by finding that combination of demogrant and marginal tax rate that generates the same level of tax revenues and the same level of inequality as the existing GRT by household type. Required marginal tax rates are quite modest, ranging from 18.0 percent to 33.3 percent when using the MLD index.[19] Demogrants range from £319 to £3383. The required demogrant for a single-parent, three-child family is only £319 while for a two-parent, no-child family it is almost £2000. The reason for this is that government transfers remain in this exercise and the former family type pays little income tax (an average of £387) under the existing GRT while the latter, high-income family type pays much more (an average of £4299). For the latter family type, the rate flattening caused by moving from the GRT to an NIT results in a substantial loss of progressivity. This loss of progressivity must be offset by increased progressivity at the lower end of the distribution, through a substantial demogrant. For a single-parent, three-child family, very little tax is paid and so there is little loss of progressivity when moving to a flat rate tax system. Thus, with government transfers intact, only a modest boost to low incomes is required to maintain the status quo inequality in after-tax incomes for this household type.

When using the CV (coefficient of variation) to determine when the hypothetical NIT is as progressive as the existing GRT, marginal tax rates range from 16.5 percent to 41.9 percent. These tax rates (and associated demogrants) are larger than when the MLD index is our norm for equality, except in one case (A,C = 1,3). Relative to the MLD Index, the CV places less weight on the effect of raising incomes at the lower end of the distribution and greater weight on differences in higher incomes.[20] Thus, to generate the same level of inequality when using the CV, the demogrant and the marginal tax rate of the NIT must be higher. This conclusion is true in general for comparisons of "pure" tax systems when the tax schedules cross twice. However, our *real life* tax systems here include substantial deviations from the actual tax schedules in that tax paid is not entirely determined by before-tax income. This is evident from Figures 18.4 and 18.5, which illustrate the relationship between before-tax income and after-tax income under the existing system and hypothetical NIT systems. What breaks the link between theoretical and empirical results is the existence of other exemptions and nontaxable income (government transfers) that are added to after-tax income *ex-post*. These weaken the theoretical link between results with the MLD Index and the CV Index even more in the cases where we allow base broadening.

Exercise 2 (Appendix Table 18.5) is similar to Exercise 1 except that the other exemptions are not allowed and we do not reduce taxable income by these exemptions. This broadens the tax base, and so the same tax revenue as in Exercise 1 can be generated with a lower marginal tax rate and the same demogrant. All marginal tax rates are lowered by base-broadening, with rates ranging from 7.6 percent to 23.1 percent when using the MLD Index, and 5.4 percent to 31.6 percent when using the CV index. It is debatable whether these other exemptions should be excluded from the tax base since they may be legitimate deductions. However, since many NIT proposals suggest base broadening, we felt this was a useful exercise.

A few remarks on the base-broadening exercise are in order. Table 18.1 shows that when defining after-tax income using a broad-based definition we end up with greater inequality. Let the former definition of income (broad base) be denoted by Y^B (values in the second to last column on the right) and the latter definition (not broad base) be denoted by Y^{NB} (values in the last column on the right). Since for Y^B the other exemptions that are computed are viewed as part of disposable income, this means $Y^B = Y^{NB}$ + other exemptions. Since other exemptions are positively correlated with before-tax (or after-tax) incomes it is not surprising that inequality levels are higher for the broad-based definition. Thus, besides the fact that a lower marginal tax rate is required to generate the same tax revenue as with a broader definition of income, the higher target level of inequality also reduces the marginal tax rate and the demogrant required to generate the same degree of progressivity.

NIT proposals commonly propose replacing government transfers with a demogrant. In terms of affordability there are conflicting effects. Eliminating government transfers reduces the tax revenue that needs to be generated. However, to maintain after-tax incomes of low-income earners and keep inequality at the same level as the existing GRT system, which includes the government transfers, requires additional spending and tax revenue. Whether or not the demogrant is as well-targeted as government transfers in helping to maintain the existing inequality is an empirical question. Our scatter plots (especially Figure 18.4 – A,C = 1,3) show that government transfers lead to quite a bit of dispersion in after-tax incomes of families with the same before-tax income (i.e., substantial horizontal inequity). This is due to the variety of programs available to low-income families and uneven take-up rates of available benefits. In contrast, the NIT has a fixed schedule of implicit transfers over a wide range of low incomes. Figure 18.4 shows that most households with zero before-tax income end up with higher after-tax income under the existing system than with the NIT, while households with low but positive levels of before-tax income appear to be more evenly distributed above and below the NIT line.

Appendix Table 18.6 provides the results of introducing an NIT system eliminating all government transfers but not broadening the tax base. The marginal tax rates required to generate the same level of inequality as the existing tax-benefit

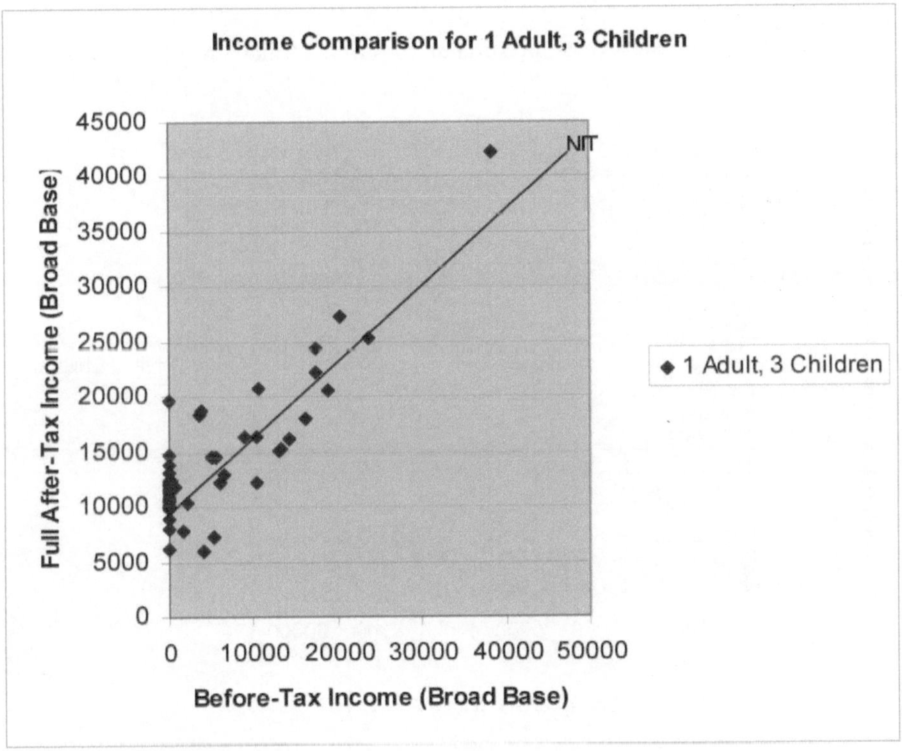

Figure 18.4 Income comparison for 1 adult, 3 children

system turn out to be higher than when government transfers are maintained (see Table 18.4) regardless of which inequality index is used. Under the MLD index the range of marginal tax rates becomes 27 percent to 79.4 percent (compared to 18.0 percent to 33.3 percent when government transfers are maintained), while under the CV index the range becomes 33.3 percent to 81.7 percent (compared to 16.5 percent to 41.9 percent when government transfers are maintained). Although a few household types require a very high NIT marginal tax rate to be as progressive as the existing tax-benefit system, these cases tend to be groups paying little tax. Eliminating both base broadening and government transfers means a very high demogrant, and so a high marginal tax rate. This aspect of an NIT system is not a concern once we generate a coherent system of demogrants and a single tax rate across all household types. Nonetheless, isolating such cases shows that we must treat certain households (particularly single-parent families) with great care when moving from a GRT system to an NIT.

Appendix Table 18.7 provides the results of eliminating government transfers in combination with base broadening. These results should be compared with

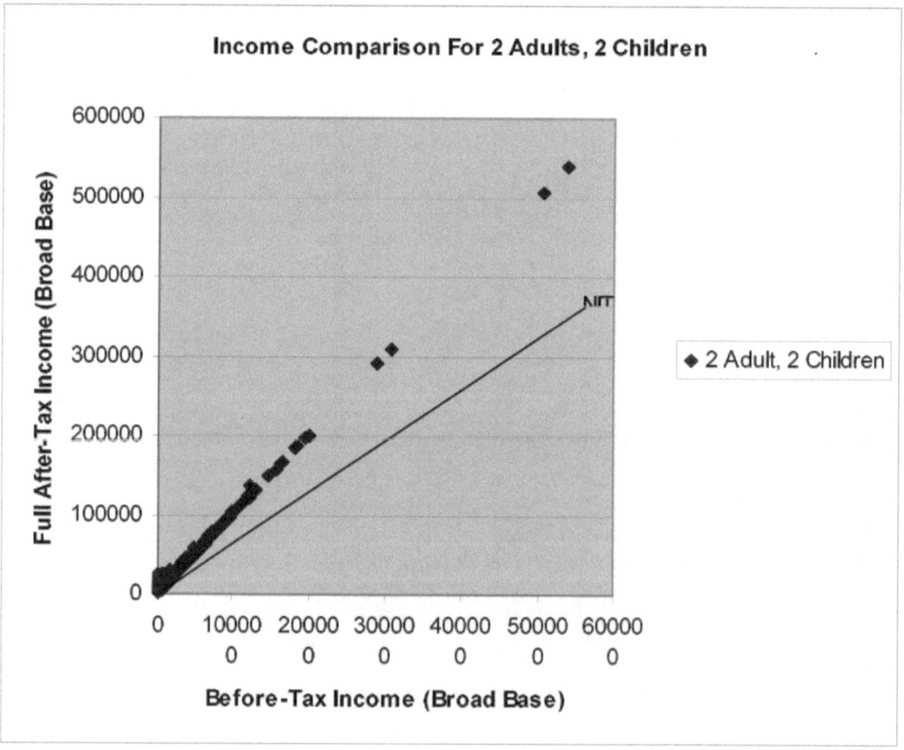

Figure 18.5 Income comparison for 2 adults, 2 children

Table 18.5 where the tax base is also broadened but government transfers are maintained. Under the MLD index, marginal tax rates range from 19.3 to 32.9 percent (compared to 7.6 percent to 23.1 percent when government transfers are maintained), while under the CV index the range becomes 19.1 percent to 37.2 percent (compared to 5.4 percent to 31.6 percent with government transfers maintained). Thus, if government transfers are eliminated as part of an NIT system, one needs a large increase in marginal tax rates if inequality in after-tax incomes is not to increase.

The above exercises allowed marginal tax rates to vary across household types and demogrants to vary in an unstructured manner. Of course, this is not politically or administratively feasible. But these exercises give us some insight into the needs of different household types when designing a suitable NIT. In any case, suggesting that tax reform leads to equivalent levels of inequality in after-tax incomes is a conservative approach that we do not support. Rather, our purpose is to find the minimal requirements of a NIT system, in particular the smallest demogrants, to make after-tax incomes at least as equal as under the existing tax system. Any increase in the demogrant (and tax rate) from this will lead to greater equality in after-tax incomes.[21]

Our final exercise uses previous results to help us select a "reasonably affordable" NIT system that is both politically and administratively feasible, and that reduces the inequality of after-tax incomes for *all* household types. Administrative feasibility requires a single marginal tax rate for all household types and a coherent system of demogrants. The size of the single marginal tax rate is dictated by the system of demogrants in conjunction with our revenue neutrality requirement. Because of economies of scale in household living, a family of size N does not require N-times as much income as a single individual to have an equivalent level of economic well-being. Equivalence scales are used to make comparisons between the amount of income families of different size need in order to be equally well off. We adopt the OECD equivalence scale based on the equation $D(N_1,N_2) = (1 + 0.7N_1 + 0.5N_2)(D_0)$; where D_0 is the demogrant for a single-person (adult) household, N_1 is the number of additional adults in the household, and N_2 the number of children in the household. $D(N_1,N_2)$ is the income required for a family of $N_1 + 1$ adults and N_2 children to have the same per capita economic well-being as a single adult who receives D_0.[22] Once we select a demogrant for a single adult, the equivalence scale for other household types $(A,C) = (N_1\text{-}1,N_2)$ is determined.

One could apply the above approach to any of the four results in Tables 18.4 to 18.7. We chose the most conservative exercise, one that does not broaden the tax base nor eliminate existing government transfers (i.e., Table 18.4), and D_0 = £2000 because it is a nice round number that ensures the demogrants for different household types are all comfortably higher than needed to maintain the same level of inequality.

The results of this "pseudo aggregate" analysis[23] are given in Appendix Table 18.8. Comparing these results with the Table 18.4 results (labeled "original" values), we find that the demogrants are higher in every case. The marginal tax rate required to generate the same overall tax revenue is 33.7 percent, which lies roughly midway between the marginal tax rates for the middle and upper existing GRT tax rates of 22 percent and 40 percent. The level of inequality, according to the MLD index, is reduced substantially for some household types and is reduced somewhat for all household types.[24] Particularly noteworthy is the impact on single-parent families. For the (A,C) = (1,2) type, the inequality index has fallen by over 40 percent (from 0.101 to 0.056). Adopting the *cost of inequality* interpretation of the MLD measure implies that the new tax system is equivalent to a gain of 4.5 percent in per capita income for this group.

By adopting a single marginal tax rate and a coherent system of demogrants, the average tax burden and mean after-tax income also change for the various household types, as Appendix Table 18.9 shows. So, relative to the existing income tax system, there is some redistribution across types with the NIT. This redistribution favors single-parent families, especially those with more than one child. Most other families with children also do better on average under the NIT, the only exceptions being types (A,C) = (3,1) and (A,C) = (4,1). Thus, for most families with children, there are two gains in moving to this proposed NIT—a reduction in inequality within the group and an increase in average after-tax income.

Conclusions

This study shows that the United Kingdom could introduce an NIT system, characterized by a single flat rate tax and a guaranteed annual income that would be more equitable than the existing GRT system and not require an excessively high marginal tax rate. Although one might argue that a guaranteed income should be high enough to lift all households above the poverty line, this may be an overly ambitious goal. Our more modest goal was to improve on measured income inequality, believing that this would be a good first step in moving towards a more ambitious basic income program.

Appendix

Table A18.1 Description of basic income data

Family Type (A, C)	No. Obs.	Mean Full Before-Tax Income (Broad Based)	Atkinson Index (Broad Based)	Mean Full After-Tax Income (Broad Based)	Atkinson Index (Broad Based)	Atkinson Index (Not Broad Based)
1,0	2015	15358	0.265	13482	0.225	0.191
1,1	244	13912	0.150	12936	0.124	0.097
1,2	187	16760	0.166	15690	0.139	0.101
1,3	52	14336	0.071	13949	0.066	0.043
2,0	2409	30112	0.225	25813	0.190	0.157
2,1	597	38415	0.215	32436	0.183	0.142
2,2	743	42731	0.200	35968	0.172	0.128
2,3	224	36952	0.174	31461	0.139	0.114
2,4	64	36287	0.230	30696	0.177	0.140
3,0	384	40237	0.176	34838	0.158	0.113
3,1	132	41733	0.148	35940	0.118	0.091
3,2	66	40718	0.160	35379	0.126	0.100
4,0	135	47361	0.126	41346	0.109	0.087
4,1	41	45221	0.104	40060	0.092	0.065

Table A18.2 Description of basic tax and transfer data

Family Type (A, C)	No. Obs.	Personal Exemptions	Mean Other Exemptions	Mean Tax Paid	Mean Government Transfers
1,0	2015	4535	2043	1878	1374
1,1	244	4535	1876	976	4894
1,2	187	4535	3256	1070	6280
1,3	52	4535	1733	387	8752
2,0	2409	9070	4010	4299	888
2,1	597	9070	5644	5980	1626
2,2	743	9070	6948	6763	2405
2,3	224	9070	4445	5491	4030
2,4	64	9070	4876	5591	6794
3,0	384	13605	5398	5399	1386
3,1	132	13605	4337	5793	2852
3,2	66	13605	4546	5339	4136
4,0	135	18140	5447	6015	1558
4,1	41	18140	5184	5162	2725

Table A18.3 Frequency of tax payers

Family Types	No. Obs.	Freq. where tax paid <= 188	Freq. where 188<tax aid<=6242.40	Freq. where 6242.40<tax paid
1,0	2015	951 (0.464)	999 (0.487)	101 (0.049)
1,1	244	156 (0.639)	84 (0.344)	4 (0.016)
1,2	187	132 (0.706)	50 (0.267)	5 (0.027)
1,3	52	43 (0.827)	9 (0.173)	0 (0)
2,0	2409	538 (0.223)	1413 (0.690)	458 (0.190)
2,1	597	61 (0.102)	384 (0.643)	152 (0.255)
2,2	743	92 (0.124)	409 (0.550)	242 (0.326)
2,3	224	37 (0.165)	131 (0.585)	56 (0.250)
2,4	64	20 (0.313)	34 (0.531)	10 (0.156)
3,0	384	43 (0.112)	224 (0.583)	117 (0.305)
3,1	132	18 (0.136)	68 (0.515)	46 (0.349)
3,2	66	12 (0.182)	38 (0.576)	16 (0.242)
4,0	135	12 (0.089)	74 (0.548)	49 (0.363)
4,1	41	2 (0.049)	23 (0.561)	16 (0.390)

Table A18.4 Critical tax rates/demogrants/break-even income without base broadening

	Atkinson Index			Coefficient of Variation Index		
Family Type (A, C)	*Critical Tax Rate*	*Demogrant*	*Break-Even Income*	*Critical Tax Rate*	*Demogrant*	*Break-Even Income*
1,0	0.236	951	4030	0.308	1814	5890
1,1	0.191	392	2052	0.208	514	2471
1,2	0.235	627	2668	0.267	859	3217
1,3	0.180	319	1772	0.165	260	1576
2,0	0.245	1890	7714	0.316	3684	11658
2,1	0.266	2280	8571	0.356	5075	15345
2,2	0.283	2678	9463	0.343	4679	13641
2,3	0.282	2573	9124	0.330	3946	11958
2,4	0.333	2858	8583	0.419	5040	12029
3,0	0.216	1854	8583	0.295	4507	15278
3,1	0.257	3143	12230	0.307	4881	15899
3,2	0.270	3383	12530	0.331	5353	16172
4,0	0.213	2598	12197	0.276	5146	18645
4,1	0.186	1810	9731	0.221	3121	14122

Table A18.5 Critical tax rates/demogrants/break-even income with base broadening

	Atkinson Index			Coefficient of Variation Index		
Family Type (A, C)	*Critical Tax Rate*	*Demogrant*	*Break-Even Income*	*Critical Tax Rate*	*Demogrant*	*Break-Even Income*
1,0	0.181	661	3653	0.173	549	3174
1,1	0.132	217	1646	0.150	380	2533
1,2	0.137	366	2669	0.157	575	3664
1,3	0.076	43	563	0.054	-82	-1511
2,0	0.191	1292	6764	0.237	2638	11133
2,1	0.200	1360	6798	0.247	3084	12487
2,2	0.200	1299	6493	0.172	170	988
2,3	0.210	1448	6895	0.261	3133	12004
2,4	0.231	1396	6044	0.316	3967	12555
3,0	0.159	798	5020	0.186	1851	9950
3,1	0.194	1794	9247	0.235	3397	14456
3,2	0.198	1957	9885	0.267	4500	16853
4,0	0.166	1602	9649	0.213	3758	17645
4,1	0.157	811	5167	0.155	1451	9363

Table A18.6 Critical tax rates/demogrants/break-even income without base broadening and without government transfers

	Atkinson Index			Coefficient of Variation Index		
Family Type (A, C)	*Critical Tax Rate*	*Demogrant*	*Break-Even Income*	*Critical Tax Rate*	*Demogrant*	*Break-Even Income*
1,0	0.381	2689	7058	0.423	3192	7546
1,1	0.654	3709	5671	0.662	3767	5690
1,2	0.683	3863	5656	0.701	3993	5696
1,3	0.794	2726	3433	0.817	2815	3446
2,0	0.316	3684	11658	0.366	4947	13516
2,1	0.364	5324	14626	0.413	6845	16574
2,2	0.403	6680	16576	0.427	7481	17520
2,3	0.474	8064	17013	0.476	8121	17061
2,4	0.555	8490	15297	0.601	9657	16068
3,0	0.309	4977	16107	0.371	7059	19027
3,1	0.404	8254	20431	0.424	8949	21106
3,2	0.439	8842	20141	0.461	9553	20722
4,0	0.270	4903	18159	0.333	7451	22375
4,1	0.344	7731	22474	0.338	7506	22207

Table A18.7 Critical tax rates/demogrants/break-even income, government transfers eliminated, with broadening

	Atkinson Index			Coefficient of Variation Index		
Family Type (A, C)	*Critical Tax Rate*	*Demogrant*	*Break-Even Income*	*Critical Tax Rate*	*Demogrant*	*Break-Even Income*
1,0	0.248	2975	11997	0.200	2302	11509
1,1	0.329	6892	20949	0.337	6965	20666
1,2	0.304	8396	27619	0.297	8323	28023
1,3	0.285	9976	35005	0.287	9988	34800
2,0	0.233	3410	14634	0.257	4112	16001
2,1	0.252	4894	19422	0.259	5151	19889
2,2	0.266	6364	23924	0.191	3341	17492
2,3	0.314	8915	28391	0.314	8915	28391
2,4	0.323	10973	33972	0.372	12455	33481
3,0	0.210	4172	19866	0.221	4601	20817
3,1	0.283	8126	28714	0.341	10394	30481
3,2	0.287	9373	32657	0.313	10331	33005
4,0	0.193	4398	22789	0.245	6784	27691
4,1	0.234	7547	32250	0.208	6437	30948

Table A18.8 "Pseudo aggregate" analysis without base broadening

					Atkinson Index		*CV Index*	
Family Type (A, C)	**Original Demogrant (Atkinson)**	**New Demogrant**	**Original Tax Rate (Atkinson)**	**New Tax Rate**	**Original**	**New**	**Original**	**New**
1,0	951	2000	0.236	0.337	0.191	0.150	0.823	0.799
1,1	392	3000	0.191	0.337	0.097	0.051	0.505	0.361
1,2	627	4000	0.235	0.337	0.101	0.056	0.554	0.411
1,3	319	5000	0.180	0.337	0.043	0.021	0.297	0.202
2,0	1890	3400	0.245	0.337	0.157	0.129	0.626	0.629
2,1	2280	4400	0.266	0.337	0.142	0.116	0.697	0.720
2,2	2678	5400	0.283	0.337	0.128	0.102	0.571	0.558
2,3	2573	6400	0.282	0.337	0.114	0.083	0.555	0.507
2,4	2858	7400	0.333	0.337	0.140	0.105	0.655	0.641
3,0	1854	4800	0.216	0.337	0.113	0.083	0.459	0.447
3,1	3143	5800	0.257	0.337	0.091	0.071	0.435	0.416
3,2	3383	6800	0.270	0.337	0.100	0.076	0.537	0.511
4,0	2598	6200	0.213	0.337	0.087	0.063	0.377	0.359
4,1	1810	7200	0.186	0.337	0.065	0.040	0.325	0.277

Table A18.9 Further "Pseudo aggregate" analysis without base broadening

Family Type (A, C)	Mean Tax (GRT)	Mean Tax (NIT)	Mean Full After-Tax Income (GRT)	Mean Full After-Tax Income (NIT)
1,0	1878	2040	11483	11321
1,1	976	-586	11082	12644
1,2	1070	-1566	12434	15069
1,3	387	-3679	12285	16351
2,0	4299	5114	21853	21038
2,1	5980	6066	26701	26616
2,2	6763	5841	29000	29921
2,3	5491	3237	27136	29390
2,4	5591	1151	26575	31016
3,0	5399	6517	29567	28450
3,1	5793	5917	31827	31703
3,2	5339	4086	31100	32353
4,0	6015	7428	35981	34568
4,1	5162	5430	35042	34773

Notes

1. As Atkinson (1975: 229) notes, such a scheme was first proposed in Britain by Lady Rhys Williams in 1942.
2. The Atkinson index measures inequality as the percentage reduction in aggregate income that would leave social welfare unchanged if incomes became equally distributed. Multiplying by aggregate income we have the cost of inequality in money units. This can be compared with measures of deadweight loss due to taxes and transfers. See also Kolm (1969).
3. For a detailed description of the existing United Kingdom system, see Leicester and Shaw (2003), from which our information is taken.
4. In our data set we can infer each individual's personal allowance from the indicated age, but we do not observe any other allowances or deductions from income. We explain later how these can be inferred from the data.
5. There is also tax relief for maintenance payments and for the blind.
6. The impact of these features of the income tax system is illustrated by comparing the inequality level of before-tax incomes with that for after-tax incomes (see Appendix Table 18.1).
7. The results in this chapter are proven formally in Hemming and Keen (1983), Dardanoni and Lambert (1998), Lambert (2001), and Davies and Hoy (2002).
8. Of course, a tax system that provides a universal guaranteed annual income supplement doesn't need to have a single marginal tax rate.
9. We have implicitly assumed the GRT is not accompanied by any (targeted) income payments (i.e., we have not yet modeled the social security system). This will be addressed later in the chapter.

10 Because the NIT tax schedule is linear and the GRT tax schedule is convex, the two must intersect either once or twice. Furthermore, if the two tax schedules generate the same tax revenue and the same level of inequality, they must intersect twice.

11 An adult equivalent scale indicates by what fraction income needs to rise when family size increases in order to keep the per person standard of living constant. See the "Methodology" section of this chapter.

12 A simple OLS regression indicates that although these two variables are correlated, a one pound rise in before-tax income is associated with a £0.29 rise in "other exemptions".

13 Kolm (1969: 186–187) first proposed this and other indices as measures of relative injustice per dollar of social income.

14 That is, provided the amount is not so large as to drive the initially richer person's income to be below the initially poorer person's original income level.

15 See Davies and Hoy (1994) for a full discussion. Intuitively, one can see that the variance of an income distribution, and hence the standard deviation, is a measure of dispersion that is symmetric about the mean of income.

16 See Cowell and Victoria-Feser (2002) and Cowell and Flachaire (2002) for a discussion of coding errors.

17 Only the job seeker's allowance and invalid care allowance are nontaxable. These represent less than 5 percent of all government transfers.

18 The mean level of these "other inferred exemptions" is reported in Appendix Table 18.2. Later we see the impact of not allowing these other exemptions (i.e., of broadening the tax base).

19 A marginal tax rate in excess of 30 percent is required for only one family type, (A,C) = (2,4), representing a small fraction of the entire sample at 64 observations.

20 See Kolm (1976), Jenkins (1991), Davies and Hoy (1994, 2002), and Chiu (2004) for discussions on this point.

21 See Davies and Hoy (2002) for a formal proof of this result.

22 This implies that, to maintain per capita well-being in a household with more than one person, each additional adult requires 0.7 times as much income as an adult living on one's own and each child requires 0.5 times as much income. See Figini (1998) for a detailed discussion.

23 We refer to this exercise as "pseudo aggregate" because we adopt a single marginal tax rate for all household types and a coherent choice of demogrants based on the usual approach to aggregating incomes using an equivalence scale. However, we maintain a disaggregated approach to the analysis of inequality impacts across different household types.

24 Adopting the CV measure gives less uniform results.

References

Atkinson, A. (1970) "On the Measurement of Inequality," *Journal of Economic Theory*, 2: 244–263.

——— (1975) *The Economics of Inequality*, (Oxford: Clarendon Press).

Atkinson, A. and Bourguignon, F. (1987) "Income Distribution and Differences in Needs" in *Arrow and the Foundations of the Theory of Economic Policy*, G.R. Feiwel (ed.), (London: Macmillan).

Chiu, W. (2004) "Intersecting Lorenz Curves and the Degree of Downside Inequality Aversion," unpublished mimeo (School of Economic Studies, University of Manchester).

Cowell, F. and Victoria-Feser, M.-P. (2002) "Welfare Rankings in the Presence of Contaminated Data," *Econometrica*, 70: 1221–1233.

Cowell, F. and Flachaire, E. (2002) "Sensitivity of Inequality Measures to Extreme Values," DARP Discussion Paper No. 60 (London: London School of Economics).

Dardanoni, V. and Lambert, P. (1988) "Welfare Rankings of Income Distributions: A Role for the Variance and Some Insights for Tax Reform," *Social Choice and Welfare*, 5: 1–17.

Davies, J. and Hoy, M. (1994) "The Normative Significance of Using Third-Degree Stochastic Dominance in Comparing Income Distributions," *Journal of Economic Theory*, 64: 520–530.

——— (2002) "Flat Rate Taxes and Inequality Measurement," *Journal of Public Economics*, 84: 33–46.

Ebert, U. (1997) "Social Welfare When Needs Differ: An Axiomatic Approach," *Economica*, 64: 233–244.

Ebert, U. and Moyes, P. (2000) "Consistent Income Tax Structures When Households Are Heterogeneous," *Journal of Economic Theory*, 90: 116–150.

Figini, P. (1998) "Inequality Measures, Equivalence Scales and Adjustment for Household Size and Composition," LIS Working Paper No. 185.

Hemming, R. and Keen, M. (1983) "Single Crossing Conditions in Comparisons of Tax Progressivity," *Journal of Public Economics*, 20: 373–380.

Hum, D. and Simpson, W. (1993) "Economic Response to a Guaranteed Annual Income: Experience From Canada and the United States," *Journal of Labor Economics*, 11: S263–S296.

Jenkins, S. (1991) "The Measurement of Income Inequality," in *Economic Inequality and Poverty: International Perspectives*, Osberg, L. (ed.), (Armonk, N.Y.: M.E. Sharpe).

Kolm, S.-C. (1969) "The Optimal Production of Social Justice," in *Public Economics*, J. Margolis, and H. Guitton (eds.), (London: Macmillan).

Lambert, P.J. (2001) *The Distribution and Redistribution of Income*, 3rd ed. (Manchester and New York: Manchester University Press).

Leicester, A. and Shaw, J. (2003) *A Survey of the UK Benefit System*, IFS Briefing Note no. 13 (London: Institute for Fiscal Studies).

Meade, J. (1972) "Poverty in the Welfare State," *Oxford Economic Papers*, 24: 289–326.

Index